Harry James on the trumpet during a June, 1979, concert in Las Vegas

Sinatra Eulogizes Harry James

Las Vegas, Nev. (UPI) — Frank Sinatra led several hundred mourners yesterday in a tribute to trumpeter Harry James, calling his former boss "one of the finest musicians I have ever known."

"I loved Harry James," said Sinatra. "I loved him for a long time." James died of cancer Tuesday at age 67.

Sinatra, his voice trembling, recounted his musical beginnings with James 42 years ago when the trumpet player stopped into a New Jersey roadhouse where Sinatra was singing for $15 a week and offered him a job with a band he was forming.

"I think I hung on to his arm so he wouldn't forget," said Sinatra.

Sinatra said James "formed what I am today . . . He was one of the finest musicians I have ever known."

"I shall miss him," said Sinatra. "He is not gone. The body is, but the spirit remains. We shall talk about him for many, many years. Goodbye, buddy, take care of yourself."

The Rev. Bill Kenny said in his final days when James knew he was dying of cancer, the bandleader wrote his own epitaph: "May it simply be said and written of me, 'He's gone on the road to do one-nighters with Gabriel.'"

A private burial followed the services.

Chicago, June 2, 1950

This, Too, Is A Hollywood Family

Hollywood—The James clan, one reason band leader Harry isn't especially interested in long road tours. In the family portrait are six-year-old Vickie, mother Betty Grable, Jessica, who is almost three, and James.

No Longer

Down Beat   Sept. 1950

Chicago — The young gentleman peering sadly at you from behind that snare no longer is noted as much of a drummer. But you may have heard him play trumpet occasionally. It's Harry James, who was 7 at the time this pic was taken and was a drummer for the Christy Brothers circus, where his dad was band conductor.

TRUMPET
BLUES

The Life of Harry James

Peter J. Levinson

OXFORD
UNIVERSITY PRESS
1999

OXFORD
UNIVERSITY PRESS

Oxford   New York
Athens Auckland Bangkok Bogotá Buenos Aires Calcutta
Cape Town Chennai Dar es Salaam Delhi Florence Hong Kong Istanbul
Karachi Kuala Lumpur Madrid Melbourne Mexico City Mumbai
Nairobi Paris São Paulo Singapore Taipei Tokyo Toronto Warsaw

and associated companies in

Berlin   Ibadan

Copyright © 1999 by Peter J. Levinson

Published by Oxford University Press, Inc.,
198 Madison Avenue, New York, New York 10016

Oxford is a registered trademark of Oxford University Press

Library of Congress Cataloging-in-Publication Data
Levinson, Peter J.
Trumpet blues : the life of Harry James / Peter J. Levinson.
p.   cm.   Includes bibliographical references and index.
ISBN 0-19-511030-7
1. James, Harry, 1916–1983.   2. Trumpet players—United States—
Biography.   3. Jazz musicians—United States—Biography.   I. Title.
ML419.J36L48   1999
781.D4'092—dc21   [B]   99-11507

1 3 5 7 9 8 6 4 2

Printed in the United States of America
on acid-free paper

To my wife, Grace Diekhaus Levinson,
and my late parents,
Gladys and Sam Levinson

∽ CONTENTS

Harry James once said to me, "Pedro, it's a shame—you were born ten years too late. That era is over. I'm fortunate. I'm one of the few who survived."

In looking back over my forty-one years in the entertainment business, I believe that James's statement was one of the most perceptive comments ever made to me. He was referring to the fact that I had missed the great era of the big bands and recognized the passion I had for his music and that of the other prominent bands.

The exhilarating, powerful, and disciplined sound of a big band that was created by anywhere from thirteen to eighteen musicians formed a dominant paradigm in the popular music of America from 1935 to 1946. The so-called Swing Era also represents the only time that jazz, a prime ingredient in this music, appealed to a mass audience. As writer Gene Lees well described the music of this period, "It was an era when a lot of popular music was good and a lot of good music was popular."

The spirited music of the big bands provided a welcome respite during a dire period in American history, a time when the country was undergoing a debilitating economic crisis and subsequently fighting a foreign war for its very survival. Harry James was one of the most celebrated personalities of this era. His melodic, sometimes syrupy-sounding trumpet during the 1940s immediately followed the two years when he was arguably the most daring and inventive trumpet soloist in any of the major big bands. This was during the years 1937 and 1938, when he was a major force with Benny Goodman's most formidable orchestra.

In 1951, when I was a third-form student at The Hill School in Pottstown, Pennsylvania, a classmate, Bob Ockene, who lived across the hall, continuously played the album of Goodman's 1938 Carnegie Hall jazz concert for months on end. It contained various blazing examples of Harry James's redoubtable talent as a jazz trumpeter. Previously, I had only been aware of James from his popular dance music, which I well remembered hearing on the radio during World War II. Listening to the Carnegie Hall album over and over had a profound effect on my life—jazz became my obsession and eventually dictated my choice of career.

I first met James in the fall of 1959 when I was a young MCA talent agent. During the next twenty-four years, or until his death in July 1983, I spent considerable time with him in New York, Las Vegas, Hollywood—on the road, at personal appearances, and during recording sessions. I also wrote several magazine articles on him over the years.

Through knowing him, I discovered the other side of stardom in the music business. Here was a musician who combined both extraordinary talent and dashing good looks, who could play a romantic ballad like no other trumpeter, which had enabled him to achieve enormous success; yet this was also a man who ruined his life through serious addictions to alcohol and gambling.

And while being married to two beautiful and caring women, the singer Louise Tobin and the film goddess Betty Grable, he was never able to satisfy his supercharged libido. As trumpeter Jimmy Maxwell observed, "Harry lived the kind of life a lot of men envied." Sometimes appearances are deceiving. His womanizing didn't really reflect his sex drive as much as it did his deeply ingrained loneliness and insecurity.

During World War II, he led the most popular big band in the country, and, with the exception of his first male singer, Frank Sinatra, was also the leading musical personality of the time. His marriage to Betty Grable, when she was nearing the peak of her career, elevated the couple to the status of Hollywood royalty.

But, perhaps because of his enormous success, James was the continuous target of the wrath of the jazz critical establishment, principally due to the wide vibrato sound of his trumpet, which they delighted in referring to as "schmaltz." They failed to recognize that jazz formed the cornerstone of his orchestras until his death. In addition, unquestionably the most accomplished bands he ever led followed in the style of Count Basie, in the years beginning in 1957 through the early 1970s.

Dan Morgenstern, the respected critic and Director of the Institute of Jazz Studies, quite accurately called the 1941 release of "You Made Me Love You" "the record that the jazz critics never forgave Harry James for recording." This is even though such highly talented jazz trumpeters as Louis Armstrong, Dizzy Gillespie, Miles Davis, Roy Eldridge, Buck Clayton, Clark Terry, Maynard Ferguson, Doc Severinsen, Kenny Dorham, Wallace Roney, and Arturo Sandoval have all been quoted at one time or another praising Harry's astounding technique and virtuosity.

Fundamentally, despite all his success and high living, Harry James led a sad and misguided life—hence the title of this biography. "Trumpet

Blues" is also the title of one of his biggest instrumental hits. Further, he was a remarkable blues player.

In researching and writing about the extraordinary life of Harry James and his band of wandering nomads, I discovered many things. Among them was the undeniable sense of family that playing with a big band instilled in its musicians. The band bus became their living room and their home.

The musicians who graduated from the bands of Benny Goodman, Tommy Dorsey, Artie Shaw, Glenn Miller, Jimmie Lunceford, Harry James, and the like received a priceless education in both music and life itself. Trying to satisfy the demands of such taskmasters also developed character. Playing with big bands never really had much financial reward for these sidemen, yet it provided a musical foundation they never forgot. It's no wonder that most of them look back on these years as among the most fulfilling of their entire lives.

In line with the way American pop culture has long enjoyed disposing of its musical heroes, sixteen years after his death, Harry James's musical greatness is almost completely forgotten. And, despite his importance as a bandleader and musician, his life story has never been fully told. Conversely, in London, the Harry James Appreciation Society has been in continuous operation for twenty-four years and is proud of its 490 members. Perhaps this helps demonstrate the validity of Dizzy Gillespie's statement: "Jazz is too good for America."

In interviewing almost 200 people who knew Harry James and in writing his story, I couldn't help feeling a profound sadness. Like so many people, because of where and how he grew up—in Harry's case as the tormented protégé of his father, Everette James, a circus bandleader—it appears that the way he lived his life was predetermined. Offstage, he never felt completely at ease; onstage, however, he was always the consummate professional. This was never better illustrated than by the tremendous stamina and strength of character he displayed during the final months of his life, determined to continue working while his body was rapidly deteriorating from the ravages of cancer.

His life and his music are deeply woven into the texture of the history of America, starting in the early 1930s and continuing for five decades. His tender ballad renditions, for example, helped allay the loneliness and anxiety Americans were undergoing during the chaotic war years.

It is my sincere hope that *Trumpet Blues* will help to reassess the musical contributions of Harry James and rightfully place him as one of the most essential trumpeters and bandleaders in the history of American music.

Malibu, California   Peter J. Levinson
January 1999

ACKNOWLEDGMENTS

When I began work on *Trumpet Blues* I knew the basic outline of Harry James's life. I soon discovered, however, a wealth of additional information that was required to tell the complete story.

As an example, it was important to relate the highlights of young Harry's formative years in the Mighty Haag Circus, the Christy Brothers Circus, and the Lee Brothers Circus. For that I owe a considerable debt to Lauren Drexler and Bill Taylor, "The Lunts of South Florida," who diligently searched out this information. Through the suggestion of Dick Allen in New Orleans, I came upon Jimmy Ille, the former circus trumpeter who was at one time the band director of the Ringling Brothers Barnum & Bailey Circus. Besides his vivid recollections of Harry's life in the circus, Jimmy described the scene in southern California that preceded Benny Goodman's historic opening at the Palomar Ballroom on August 21, 1935. Because he was there, he was able to convey the impact of that night.

I want to thank all the musicians, beginning with those who first knew Harry in Texas, such as Bill Abel, the late Alex Beller, who witnessed Harry's early development with Ben Pollack—all the way up to Louise Baranger, Ira Westley, Stephenie Caravella, and Gregg Field, who were with the last James band and were so helpful. Without the remembrances of those who rode the buses, played the dreary Monday and Tuesday one-nighters as well as the more glamorous venues such as the Hollywood Palladium, the Astor Roof, or the Driftwood Lounge of the Flamingo Hotel, there would be no *Trumpet Blues*.

I am eternally grateful to Louise Tobin, who was at first reluctant to tell the often painful story of having married Harry James when they were both inexperienced teenagers with the Art Hicks Band, who watched his rapid rise to stardom with Benny Goodman, and then stood by him during the agonizing years of 1939 to 1941, when it appeared that his young band was on a treadmill to oblivion. She witnessed the remarkable change in him when stardom beckoned and lived through its inevitable effect on their relationship.

Meeting Al Lerner and being privy to his verbatim accounts of working with Harry during the period just before the release of "You Made Me Love You" and his revealing observations of Harry during the early years of his band's success were invaluable. My thanks also go to Al's wife, Dr. Jonné Lerner, who helped provide keen insight into Harry's character.

I owe much to Ross Firestone, who is the godfather of this biography. I had admired his definitive biography of Benny Goodman, *Swing, Swing, Swing.* I hope I have at least emulated the thoroughness of his approach to biography. His suggestions concerning the manuscript proved extremely helpful.

Without the acute observations of Red Kelly and Jack Perciful, two James veterans from the Basie-influenced bands of the late 1950s through to the early 1970s, I would have been lost. They loved Harry, respected him for being the titan of a musician that he was, but also saw his serious flaws as a human being. Their stories of the days in the Nevada lounges as well as on the road were as fresh and enlightening as if they had taken place yesterday rather than decades ago.

Viola Monte was always available when I needed assistance—a telephone number, the answer to a key question, or any of a dozen other ways of being helpful. She also allowed me access to the invaluable scrapbook Everette James kept, which highlighted Harry's musical accomplishments. Unfortunately, Viola's late husband, Harry's longtime manager, "Pee Wee" Monte, died before I began work on the project. His brothers Sal and Fred Monte, who worked closely with Harry for decades, were also extremely helpful with their perfect recall of various incidents that were often amusing and sometimes poignant.

I would also like to thank Vicki Bivens and Jessica Trotter (Harry's daughters with Betty Grable) and Harry Jeffrey and Tim James (his sons with Louise Tobin) for making themselves available for interviews and allowing me to gain a sense of Harry James as a parent. Harry's last wife, Joan Boyd, and their son, Michael James, chose not to be interviewed.

Betty Grable was an integral part of Harry James's life from Christmas night 1942 when their courtship began at the Hollywood Canteen, through their divorce in 1965, and even after her tragic death in 1973. From interviewing many people about Betty, especially her good friends Betty Baez, Max Showalter, and Jim Bacon, I gained an insight into their relationship. At times I almost began to believe I knew her.

I would be terribly lax if I didn't thank Joe Cabot, who provided such vivid and painful recollections of Harry's final years. He was his Man

Friday, his father confessor, but most of all his devoted friend. As Joe said, "I was there at the final coda." He told it the way it was.

The recollections of Chris Griffin, the late Jess Stacy, and Lionel Hampton brought back the magic of the Benny Goodman Orchestra. Chris recalled the precise moment when Harry chose to turn commercial after floundering during the first two and a half years of his band's existence. Every time I called Chris, he came up with some gem.

The contribution of the late Helen Forrest added so much to this biography. She was very candid and giving at all times in sharing the story of her relationship with Harry James. She and Kitty Kallen provided the color of what it was really like when the James band performed in theaters and ballrooms during the war years. They remembered those incredible years with great affection.

Composer and arranger Johnny Mandel, who wrote arrangements for James in the late 1940s, was someone who could always be counted on for providing a unique analysis of exactly what was taking place in James's musical career. He also conveyed the essence of the music of Harry's contemporaries.

My thanks also go to the late Lew McCreary, the late Joe Riggs, Bob Edmondson, and Jackie Mills, whose observations about Harry James's personality were extremely enlightening. McCreary organized a group of fellow James sidemen for a group interview that revealed a vivid picture of the James band during the 1950s. Joe Riggs did the same thing for the 1960s and early 1970s bands. Thank you, gentlemen.

My grateful thanks also go to Frank Sinatra Jr. From working with Harry James alongside the late Phil Harris, he had much to contribute.

I also want to thank my old friends Harper Barnes, Lou Brown, the late Vince Carbone, and Frank and Mara Ceglia, as well as Army Archerd, Chuck Cecil, Richard Dondiego, Frank Driggs, Mike Eisenbath, Bill Farley, Madeline Gabriele, Tom Glenn, Bob Golden, Ron Goldstein, Arlene Hellerman, Marty Hindon, Ann King, Phil Leshin, Floyd Levin, Mark Levinson, Frank Liberman, Irv Lichtman, Pete Mikla, Tom Morgan, Dan Morgenstern, Allen Pergament, Hi Petter, Jack Rael, "Col." Jordan Ramin, Dr. Michael Reynard, Robin Roberts (the comedienne, not the Hall of Fame pitcher), Maxine Sibley, Roland Smith, Craig Stephens, Zan Stewart, Dick Sudhalter, Ed "Majesty" Sweeney, Christina Whetsel, Mary Wilmer, and John S. Wilson. Special thanks go to Martha Glaser, who enabled me to get my first job in the music business. I also want to acknowledge the help of Harry's fervent admirers, Joe Pardee, Dick Maher, Jim Cutler, and Peter K. Johnston.

Most important, I can never repay the invaluable help provided by my two assistants, Anita Coolidge and Julie Compton. Anita's tenacity, her patience, and her excellent judgment in many areas were constantly displayed during the writing of this book. Julie's nonstop good humor and intelligence while preparing the transcripts were extremely important.

My thanks also go to Digby Diehl, who contributed needed direction in the early days of this project. It was he who sent me to Rich Barber, who was very effective as my agent. The experience of working with Sheldon Meyer made me realize why he has been such a revered editor. I also want to thank Susan Day and Joellyn Ausanka at Oxford for being so helpful. My apologies to anyone I have inadvertently overlooked.

Being married to Grace Diekhaus for the last sixteen years has been the high point of my life. Her love, devotion, and sensitivity can never be measured. In addition, she was the smartest in-house editor any writer could have.

In conclusion, my thoughts extend to my mother, Gladys, a highly intelligent woman, who gave me, among many other things, an appreciation of the arts. I am also grateful to my father, Sam, whose drive and integrity instilled in me the sense of purpose to survive in an extremely difficult business.

The following are the people I interviewed for this book: Bill Abel, Berle Adams, Van Alexander, Dick Allen, Steve Allen, Ernie Andrews, Ray Anthony, Murray Arnold, Bobby Arvon, George Avakian, Jim Bacon, Betty Baez, Buddy Baker, Louise Baranger, Richy Barz, Tino Barzie, the late Alex Beller, Louis Bellson, Noni Bernardi, Vicki Bivens, Betty Bohanon, Eddie Bracken, Clyde "Stumpy" Brown, Les Brown, Dennis Budimir, Ralph Burns, Kenny Burrell, Joe Bushkin, Joe Cabot, Pete Candoli, Stephenie Caravella, Pat Chartrand, Don Cherry, Buddy Childers, Rosemary Clooney, Buddy Combine, Ray Conniff, Jay Corre, Anne Davison, Joe Delaney, Les De Merle, Tony DeNicola, Art Depew, Frank DeVol, Phyllis Diller, Buddy DiVito, Richard Dondiego, Frank Driggs, Ed Easton, Bob Edmondson, Ziggy Elmer, Nick Fatool, Maynard Ferguson, Gregg Field, Sam Firmature, Bob Florence, the late Helen Forrest, Jerry Frank, Johnny Fresco, Joe Garagiola, Hershel Gilbert, Harry Givens, Chris Griffin, Tommy Gumina, the late Bob Haggart, Connie Haines, Corky Hale, George Hamid, Jr., Lionel Hampton, Jake Hanna, Jimmy Haskell, the late Nelson Hatt, Hugh Hefner, Neil Hefti, J. Hill, E.C. Holland, Jimmy Ille, Chubby Jackson, Harry Jeffrey James, Tim James, Tom Jenkins, Jerry Jerome, Harold Jovien, Kitty Kallen, Red Kelly, Audree Kenton, Bill Kirchner, Tom Korman, Don Lamond, Jack Lawrence, Michael Leavitt, Al Lerner, Big Tiny Little, Jay Livingston, Jack Magee, Dick Maher, James T. Maher, Gilda Maiken, Johnny Mandel, John Mann, Marty Marion, Tony Martin, Jimmy Maxwell, Billy May, Lincoln Mayorga, the late Lew McCreary, Dick McQuary, Pete Mikla, Mike Millar, Ann Miller, Mitch

Miller, Jackie Mills, Ollie Mitchell, Frank Modica, Jr., Fred Monte, Sal Monte, Viola Monte, Buddy Moreno, Marion Morgan, Stan Musial, Gene Norman, the late Red Norvo, Gene Orloff, Robert Osborne, Jack Palmer, Chuck Panama, Joe Pardee, Les Paul, Jack Perciful, Tommy Porrello, the late Mel Powell, Dean Pratt, Steve Preston, Ruth Price, Bill Pruyn, Gerry Purcell, Fred Radke, Jack Rael, Dr. Arthur Rando, Uan Rasey, Bill Richmond, the late Joe Riggs, Col. Michael Ritz, Lynn Roberts, Bob Rolfe, Chick Romano, Bob Rosberg, Arnold Ross, Jerry Roy, Mort Sahl, Bill Savory, Lalo Schifrin, Loren Schoenberg, Red Schoendienst, Tony Scodwell, Mickey Scrima, Nick Sevano, Doc Severinsen, Max Showalter, Don Sickler, George T. Simon, Ray Sims, Frank Sinatra, Jr., Enos Slaughter, Maynard Sloate, Beverly Dahlke Smith, Greg Smith, Lew Soloff, the late Jess Stacy, Herb Stewart, John Stiegler, Bob Stone, Dave Stone, Elizabeth Teachout, Jeannie Thomas, Martha Tilton, Louise Tobin, Jessica Trotter, the late Bobby Troup, Rob Turk, Jerry Vale, Harry Walker, the late Helen Ward, Kenny Washington, George Wein, Dave Wells, Ira Westley, Margaret Whiting, Jimmy Wilkins, Bill Willard, the late Joe Williams, Gerald Wilson, Butch Yatkeman, and Sy Zentner.

TRUMPET BLUES

1

Everette and Maybelle

lbany, Georgia, lies 180 miles southeast of Atlanta. Today, to make the trip by car, one would drive forty miles from Cordele on Route 300 and then pick up I-75's four-to-six-lane highway for the remainder. Back in 1916, however, this highway was merely a dirt road, and Albany was home to 12,000 residents as compared to 90,000 today.[1]

It was here, on March 15, 1916, that Everette and Maybelle James welcomed a nine-pound son, Harry Haag James, at the St. Nicholas Hotel, which was located next door to the Albany jail.[2] In that year, Everette and Maybelle James were two of the principal performers in the Mighty Haag Shows—a "mud show"—a traveling circus that only played small towns touring the South and Southeast. Everette was the circus's bandmaster and Maybelle was a featured trapeze artist. The story goes that Maybelle continued performing on the trapeze until only a few weeks before the birth of their son. The Jameses and their new son remained in Albany only sixteen days before the Haag wagons moved on up the dirt road to Atlanta for another engagement.

The Haag circus poster would appear on tobacco barns and smokehouses along the dusty roads, particularly in the Appalachian South, and this would herald the coming of spring. Ernest Haag's one-ring circus was considered the favorite circus of the region. The price of admission was fifty cents—a bargain.[3]

It played many of the hill country towns in Kentucky and Tennessee.

When the show played at night, on occasion some of the citizens of the town would warn the performers that the hill folk would be coming down looking for a fight and would urge that they immediately cut the tent ropes and move on. In some places the local feuds spilled over onto the circus grounds. As a matter of fact, the Hatfields and the McCoys actually had one of their fabled shootouts on The Mighty Haag Show grounds.

In the fall, after the large circuses would close down, many of their biggest acts would come south to pick up six or eight weeks of additional work with the Haag Show. Every night, during the long, dark hours, the carved and gilded wagons traveled the back country roads in order to arrive by dawn in the next town. There were no interstate highways and no tandem semi trucks with air horns.[4]

When they arrived in each town there was a parade. The circus always had twelve cage wagons in the parade plus the huge "Pawnee Bill" band-wagon, which carried a fifteen-piece band under Everette James's capable direction.[5]

Everette Robert James was born in New Orleans in 1884. As bandmaster of the Mighty Haag Shows, he had created a formidable reputation in the circus world for his prowess both as a cornet and trumpet player and as the leader of its nine-man musical aggregation. The circus maestro sees that the acts and the music are integrated. Early New Orleans musicians Peter Bocage (composer of "I Wish I Could Shimmy Like My Sister Kate") and Charlie Love praised Everette's technical virtuosity.[6] Originally, he had joined the Mighty Haag Shows in 1906 as leader of the circus's #2 band.[7] Six years later, he joined Molly Bailey's Circus as solo cornetist, before returning to the fold with the Haag as band director a year later.[8]

Tall and thin, with a long face, a prominent nose, large ears, and a high forehead, he made an imposing appearance. He wore hearing aids in both ears as a result of too many years of being a member of bands predominantly made up of brass players and equally loud percussion instruments.

Maybelle, an attractive and athletic woman, was a trapeze artist and the prima donna of the Mighty Haag Shows. Following the entry march, she sang "Buy a Bale of Cotton" with other performers joining in the chorus. She had also become famous for her "iron jaw" act in which she was suspended from the rigging of the big top with a brace around her teeth, enabling her to perform death-defying spins as well as other acrobatic feats. It was said she could lift 300 pounds with her teeth. The *Nassau* (Long Island) *Daily Record* on August 4, 1927, referred to Maybelle as "one of the most daring and reckless circus aerialists, as dainty as a butterfly with her many whims and fancies, dressed in swagger raiment ablaze with color."

Maybelle Stewart Clark James was born in Flint, Michigan, in 1891. With her first husband, Walter Clark, she had two sons: Walter, Jr., and Lonnie, both of whom died at a young age. In addition, they had two daughters, Bessie and Fay. Fay, who was also an aerialist, traveled with her mother and stepfather in the Mighty Haag Shows.

Everette James and Maybelle Clark had met and married in the muck and glory of the circus ring, traipsing together over Texas prairies, through feud-infested Kentucky mountains, into Oregonian forests for more than twenty years. Between bottles and changing of diapers, Maybelle swung on her trapeze, played the calliope on parade, did a banjo stunt in the sideshow, rode fancy horses, and performed "sailor perch" acts on a pole.[9]

It used to be the dream of every American boy to run away and join the circus. It never occurred to Harry James. He was born into one. Young Harry first met his public at the age of eleven days when his parents introduced him to the circus audience. When he was only a year old, he was already exhibiting a musical flair by beating out simple march time on a drum.

As a toddler, he took to circus life like a poodle takes to a new toy. "Peripatetic" is the best way to describe the way he dashed from one end of the circus tent to the other. He loved watching the clowns and the freaks, learned the ways of the aerialists from his mother and his sister, and was thrilled to ride the horses, camels, and other animals. During this time he developed his lifelong respect for animals and learned to treat them in a kindly manner. But animals notwithstanding, according to Maybelle, Harry practically lived on the bandstand. The musicians regarded him as the band mascot.

Joe Cabot, the trumpeter and conductor who became extremely close to Harry James in his last years, said that, when he was a very young boy, Harry considered circus owner Ernest Haag his surrogate father. As Cabot remarked, "When Harry was very down, he would talk about his youth in the circus. He never forgot how kind 'Uncle Ernie' was to him at a time when he really needed encouragement."[10]

Everette could be a stern taskmaster and extremely exacting in his criticism of his young son, the budding musician. Years later, Harry James recalled his saying, "Someday you'll thank me for being this way."[11]

In 1919, the James family moved to the Christy Brothers Circus and Harry began playing a set of trap drums. At three, amazingly, he was given a featured number with the band, performing on a drum almost as big as he was, which proved to be a huge crowd-pleaser. Once, in the middle of his featured number, Maybelle, ever the doting mother, rushed up onto the stage to push back the cluster of curls that had fallen over his forehead and, she felt, affected his vision.

Most mothers would probably have been reluctant to see their son make the quick change from babyhood to youth, but Maybelle seemed anxious for him to grow up. She fostered his talent and encouraged him to strive for difficult goals. With the constant traveling of the circus, however, Harry's schooling necessarily suffered.

Joe Cabot pointed out that, according to Harry, Everette encouraged him to learn to play drums first so that he would learn the basics of rhythm, the foundation of all music.[12] He became more and more accomplished as he watched and imitated other circus drummers. He began to develop a style of his own, exhibiting cleverness and originality. At four, he had become a "hot music" drummer and during a three-week-long illness of the band's regular drummer was elevated to playing the trap drums with the Christy Brothers Concert Band.[13] (Coincidentally, at the same time, his future and favorite drummer, Buddy Rich, was touring the world in vaudeville with his parents, billed as "Traps, the Drum Wonder.") With incredible ease, the child prodigy of the drums was able to play two one-hour-and-forty-minute circus programs on a daily basis. A tune called "Down Home Rag" became his featured number.

The consummate child of the circus then began hanging out with the contortionists. Maybelle immediately saw that her son showed a natural talent in this field, too. She taught him various floor exercises that had helped her to develop strength and flexibility when she performed as a contortionist. By the age of five, he was billed as "The Human Eel."

When Harry was six years old, he wandered into the "pad room" (the canvas partition that is to the big tent what wings are to a regular stage) and peeked out to watch Maybelle put the trick horses through their stunts. The curly-haired youngster strayed onto the circus track just as the horses were about to come charging by. In the nick of time, Maybelle's pet horse responded to Harry's plight and leaped to the rescue by standing over him until the other horses rushed by, thereby saving him from being trampled to death.[14]

That same year, Harry was enrolled at St. Anthony's Catholic School in Beaumont, Texas, where the family had settled. Everette James was Catholic, and therefore his young son was baptized as a Catholic a year later. When he was seven, the Jameses, ever on the move, left Beaumont to join Honest Bill's Circus in Oklahoma for about a year

By the time the James family moved on to the Lee Brothers Circus, Harry did his contortionist act there as well. He joined with "Dad" Witlark, a seventy-year-old contortionist, who taught him a few of that boneless trade's simpler tricks—such as backbends, retrieving handkerchiefs in his teeth, how to tie himself into pretzel knots—and put him into the act. Dad was starting to become a bit old for this work, but he was still able to bend over backwards, put his face between his ankles, and see how his heels were wearing. Along with the young Harry, the two were billed as "The Oldest And The Youngest Contortionists In The World."[15]

In one stunt, Harry would place a lighted candle on his head and then draw a hoop over his entire body without knocking over the flame. Another trick called for young James to leap through a flaming hoop. "The World's Youngest Contortionist" also took part in "the spec," circus lingo for the spectacular, wearing a bouffant dress and curls as he sat in a giant slipper dressed as Cinderella. At one performance, the act preceding the contortionists was mostly composed of animals, and someone forgot to close the chute leading to the lions' cage. Out of the corner of his eye, Harry could see the lions emerging from the chute, but in perfect circus tradition he carried on with the show. Luckily, Captain Terrell Jacobs, the animal trainer for the Christy Brothers Circus, realized what was happening. He dashed to the chute, cracked his whip, which stunned the beasts, and, just in time, slammed the door in the lions' muzzles. Because of young Harry's handling of the situation, no one in the audience realized how close they had come to being victims of a rampaging lion.[16]

Preceding the Jazz Age of the middle and late 1920s, the circus had little if any competition as the focal point of family entertainment. Children of all ages awaited with great anticipation the coming of the circus to town. The spectacle of various daring "live" performances, the high-wire acts, the terrifying yet fascinating animals, the sideshows, the midway, the popcorn and cotton candy, and indeed the stirring march tempo of the circus band exhilarated one and all.

The most flamboyant circus performers, through years of touring, became as celebrated in their own way as today's rock stars. Master Harry Haag James was learning to become an all-around performer. Unfortunately, a mastoid condition, which led to an operation at the children's hospital, prevented him from continuing as a contortionist.

In 1927, the James family returned to the Christy Brothers Circus, by this time one of the best-known touring circuses in the country. The twenty-five-wagon, seventy-foot steel-car show toured by train all over America, Canada, and Mexico in the summer and wintered in Beaumont, clocking 19,000 miles a year. Among other attractions, it featured everything from baby African lions right up to a troupe of mammoth elephants, as well as horses, dogs, hens, goats, reindeer, even kangaroos. Along with the most elite performers of one stripe or another was Maybelle James, who was featured as "the most daring and reckless" horse rider racing around the ring straddling two horses. The almost unprecedented five-ring circus kept the eye so busy it was impossible to take it all in.

Veteran circus trumpeter Jimmy Ille contends that it was trumpeter "Skinny" Goe (pronounced "Go"), not Harry's father, who first put a cornet in eight-year-old Harry's hands. As Ille explains, "Before the show, the band sits behind the center ring. The Christy Brothers Band probably totalled about twenty-five musicians. The guys are up, and they're just barely blowing their horns because you have to save it all for the show. Skinny sits there in the trumpet section and says to little Harry, 'Blow this,' and that's how he started playing." In the years ahead, Skinny went on to have a formidable career leading various circus bands.[17]

Skinny began to secretly teach the little cornetist the rudiments of the instrument outside the flaps of the big top. One day, Everette came upon the two of them together and was amazed at the ability of his young son to play the cornet—so much so that he started teaching him to play the peck horn, an E-flat alto horn. The vowels were written down for him.[18]

By the age of nine, Harry had switched from drums to trumpet, and at eleven he was playing fourth chair in the Christy Brothers Band. He proudly wore the band's red uniform, complete with gold braid. Rapidly improving his abilities as a soloist, he soon became the first cornetist in the band.

Harry described his first experience leading a circus band: "My father went over to see his sister, who was a member of the Flying Wards, a flying trapeze act that was playing about forty miles away, and he didn't return in time for the concert. So I just went out and directed the band for the first couple of tunes. Mr. Christy was standing in the back, and my father came running in real quick—he wanted to hurry up and go out there. Mr. Christy said, 'Mr. James, Sr., we don't need you for awhile. Your boy's doing quite well.' I directed the entire concert."

In 1928, Everette gave him the opportunity to take over the leadership of the circus's #2 band. Harry was only twelve years old. This time he wore a blue uniform with gold trim. His band played opposite his father's band under the Christy Brothers big top. This also allowed him to play hot trumpet solos behind "Bessie the Beautiful High Wire Queen," among other acts. According to an article in *Billboard*, he was now the youngest circus bandleader in the world.

His father was dead-set against Harry's ever becoming a professional musician because of the constant traveling and inherent insecurities of the business. Everette instead wanted his son to become a doctor or lawyer. Yet he never insisted on Harry's completing his education. When pressed, the dignified and soft-spoken bandmaster had to admit that Harry was talented enough to make a living as a legitimate brass player.

O. A. "Red" Gilson, Jack Bell (who claims he helped Harry develop his cornet technique), Jack Carroll, and Skinny Goe were all brass players in the Christy Brothers Circus Band under Everette's direction and witnessed

Harry's rapid musical development. Gilson left the Christy Brothers Circus to become leader of the Robbins Brothers Circus Band. His admiration for Harry is shown by the fact that on the sheet music of his composition, "Robbins Brothers Triumphal March," which he wrote in 1928, is inscribed "Dedicated to Harry James." Jimmy Ille relates that this march is not dissimilar to the famous "Ringling Brothers Entry March."[19]

The two Christy Brothers bands, conducted by the two Jameses, would parade up and down the main street of each city the circus visited, doubling back on their tracks. It got to be a family joke; Harry's band would invariably start playing as Everette's band approached, often causing a comical explosion of mixed marches. Finally, they worked it out so that the #1 band would finally march by the #2 band in respectful silence.[20]

During these years with the Christy Brothers Band, Everette made use of a substantial number of band arrangements of W. C. Handy's compositions, such as "Memphis Blues" and "St. Louis Blues." And so, while developing his own trumpet style before he was even a teenager, Harry was already learning to play the blues and jazz based on the works of the revered composer known as "The Father of the Blues." It is therefore no great surprise that in later years two of his most respected trumpet solos were on these two blues classics. Everette's band also played arrangements of other contemporary jazz tunes, such as "Tiger Rag," "Milenberg Joys," and "Wolverine Blues."[21]

The repertoire of Everette James's band consisted of an abundance of marches—"Semper Fidelis," "North Wind," "Thunder and Blazes," and the inevitable "Stars and Stripes Forever." Uan Rasey, who was a trumpeter in the James band during the mid-1940s, and later recorded with the Ringling Brothers Barnum & Bailey Circus Band, remarked: "Marches are the hardest thing. There's no rest, you gotta keep playing from one number to the next. You have to be very exact. That's where Harry developed his endurance."[22]

Watching his father's every move on the bandstand obviously made a deep impression on the youngster. Jimmy Ille observed that "when Everette played the trumpet, the way he carried that horn, the way the horn stuck out in front of his body, and the way he stood in front of the band, years later you'd look and say, 'Harry James looks just like his father.'"[23]

Harry always marveled at his father's ability to play both cornet and trumpet. Merle Evans, the bandmaster of the legendary Ringling Brothers Circus ("Big Bertha," as show folks called it) from 1919 to 1969, and Everette, leading the Christy Brothers Circus Band, on occasion would lead simultaneous parades followed by band concerts. As a youngster, Harry remembered with pride when he was allowed to sit on Merle's lap. Years later, Everette dueled with Evans, who was also considered the foremost cornetist of his time. "Dad said, 'I'm going to play so high the piccolo is going to be playing the bass part.'"[24]

The constant traveling that James endured with his parents and sister in these circus bands formed the pattern for his own musical career. Also, from that time forward, anyone who heard the readily identifiable trumpet sound of Harry James couldn't help noticing that the influence the circus had on him was forever implanted in his playing.

His years in circus music, playing almost every tune at a full gallop, had developed a set of iron chops that was to hold him in good stead almost to the very end of his life, certainly well past the time when most trumpet players "lose their lip." In addition, Everette's years of stressing the basic fundamentals of trumpet playing and his strict discipline had given Harry a firm foundation that few, if any, of his peers possessed. And, as Harry himself often said, his dad was not loathe to using a switch on his butt to achieve what he wanted.

Harry James's embouchure was perfect. As several musicians remarked, "I never once saw Harry with a ring around his lip"—the telltale sign of a trumpet player who was not playing his horn "correctly." In these pre-teen and early teenage years, the young trumpeter would spend from two to six hours a day practicing and running over scales as well as passages in the Arban Book, the exercise bible for all young would-be trumpeters.

When he was only in the seventh grade at Dick Dowling Junior High School in Beaumont, Harry was asked to become a member of the Beaumont High School Band. Oddly enough, this was the first complete year he had ever been in school from the very first day to the end of the school year, for he had been traveling with the circus from April to December the preceding four years.

At Dick Dowling, he made many friends, partly due to his growing popularity as a musician. Besides that, his classmates were attracted by the colorful life he had led.

Drew Page, who was later to be a member of the saxophone section in the first James band, recalled (in his highly underrated book, *Drew's Blues: A Sideman's Life in the Big Bands*) having seen Harry play in 1929 (at the age of thirteen) at the only jazz club in Beaumont as a member of trumpeter Vic Insirilo's group. Drew was curious to encounter such a young boy playing with experienced professionals. Drew remembered, "His style of playing reminded me of [Bix] Beiderbecke's."

During these years, Harry James developed an all-consuming passion for baseball, as so many youngsters did at that time. This love of baseball would stay with him all his life. For Everette James, however, baseball always had to take second place to practicing the trumpet.

As James reminisced on a *Merv Griffin Show* that aired on November 15, 1977: "Dad would say to me, 'Here's the Arban Book ... here's two pages and a half; play that. When you get through, call me in.' I'd practice like crazy and call him in…. He'd say, 'This wasn't right, that wasn't right.' He didn't care whether it was ten minutes or two hours, but when I played those exercises correctly, then he'd say, 'Okay, go play ball' … which was a beautiful way because if a person is studying music, and they say, 'Okay, you've got two hours to practice' … and they keep looking at the clock: 'How much time do I have left?' This way I was on my own."

Invariably, Harry would cave in to his father's wishes, but the truth was he had two loves: the trumpet and baseball. Despite the hardship he felt he endured at the time, Harry always conceded, "Whatever success I may have had was due to my father sitting me down and really making me practice and practice and practice."

The Arban Book contained the composition "Carnival of Venice," which all young trumpeters learn to play at one time or another. Harry also learned the more advanced version that the brilliant cornetist Herbert L. Clark, a contemporary of Everette's, had created. Later, Harry used Clark's version of "Carnival of Venice" as the basis for one of his most successful hit records, but in his recorded version he added even further embellishments to the classic piece. Harry met Clark while Clark was touring with his own large band in the Southwest. His respect for Clark's astounding technique also had undeniable influence in the way he interpreted the "Cantabile" section of "Trumpet Blues" as well as "Flight of the Bumble Bee."

In his last years traveling with the Christy Brothers Circus, Harry James was introduced to alcohol and sex. He admitted to one musician that he started drinking when he was fourteen years old. This was not unusual for circus performers. Girls in the audience were considered easy prey. From their vantage point on the bandstand, musicians could pick out eager young girls to seduce, a ritual that would invariably begin with a few drinks after the show. It was all in a night's work. It later became an integral part of Harry's lifestyle when he began touring with dance orchestras.

By 1930, the entire nation was in the grip of The Great Depression. Conditions in the circus world were no better than in any other business. Admissions, even for circuses as important as the Christy Brothers, had sunk to twenty-five cents for children and fifty cents for adults. President Herbert Hoover assured his agonized countrymen that things would get better soon, but instead they grew steadily worse. As a result, Everette became a victim of the sliding economy and lost his job with the Christy Brothers Circus.

The James family moved back to Beaumont and began living at 2216

Railroad Avenue. Everette James's savior, and that of his family's, turned out to be the wealth of the Spindletop Oil Company, whose nearby spouting oil fields allowed the 58,000 residents of Beaumont to weather the wrath of the Depression. The city, situated on the Natches River, formed a natural turning basin, which made it an important port for transporting oil; it was also accessible to the Gulf of Mexico. This helped provide jobs throughout the area.

The Island Park Association, composed of employees from the Pennsylvania Shipyards and Petroleum Iron Works Company, whose fortunes benefited from Spindletop Oil, retained Everette as director of its newly organized twenty-four-piece band and orchestra. Fourteen-year-old Harry James came along with his father as its featured cornet soloist. Maybelle, now often referred to as "Mabel," became the leading female performer. It was noted in a Beaumont newspaper that "both Mrs. James and her daughter, Fay Stokes [her newly married name], who was also an aerialist, are receiving requests for engagements at the various fairs in this vicinity for the coming fair season. They are recognized performers."

In 1933, Maybelle's "iron jaw" act ultimately came to an end as a result of an unfortunate accident during which she was raised too quickly by the circus prop boys and every tooth in her mouth apparently jerked loose. From then on, she was reduced to sitting on an elephant singing "Bluebird" while 100 white doves fluttered about her.

Shortly thereafter, Everette turned down an offer for the family to join the newly formed Cole Brothers Circus, an amalgamation of the Christy Brothers Circus and the Clyde Beatty Circus. The Cole Brothers had bought it for $200,000—a rather exorbitant price to pay for a circus at that time. He and Mabel, however, had had their fill of the sawdust life after thirty-five and twenty-eight years, respectively. "We're not going back— ever," remarked Everette vehemently. "Wading through the mud for your breakfast three blocks away, living in a Pullman like a monkey, showing in rain, sleet, snow.... No, sir, not us!"[25]

In addition to their involvement with the Island Park Association, Harry and his father became associated with the local chapter of the American Legion Drum and Bugle Corps. This affiliation enabled Harry to play shortstop for the American Legion Team. (He couldn't play baseball on the school team because he was only in junior high.) A scout for the Detroit Tigers admired the fielding range of the lanky young shortstop as well as his left-handed line-drive hitting. For a time, it looked like Harry might become the property of the Tigers and play with its Beaumont farm team.

On May 1 and 2, 1931, Harry entered a competition in the Texas Band Teacher's Association's Annual Eastern Division contest, named for the composer Victor Herbert and held in Temple, Texas. Though still only a student at the Dick Dowling Junior High School, he was a regular member of the Beaumont High School Band, which was known as the Royal Purple Band. He won first place in the solo contest for his extraordinary rendition of Herbert L. Clark's difficult composition, "Neptune's Court." A tremendous burst of applause for his performance led to two encores.

Bill Abel played trombone in the Port Arthur High School Band that also participated in this competition. "I remember it like it was yesterday because it was so outstanding. To hear a kid that young play so excellently, so perfectly, was just earthshaking. There were a lot of good trumpet players in high school, but none of them like that—so completely above every other musician in that whole state concert. He astounded the judges so much that they wanted to give him 100 percent, but they said they never had been able to do that, so they gave him a 98. I knew Harry was really headed for big things."[26]

(The silver trumpet on which Harry played at the Temple contest is now in the possession of his #1 fan, Dick Maher. It stands in an honored place as the base of a lamp in the "Harry James Room" of Maher's Cerritos, California, home. It is a silverplated King trumpet, Liberty Model, made by H. N. White, Cleveland, Ohio.)

Although band music was never the craze in Texas that high school football has long been, winning the state trumpet championship in the Depression years was of more than passing significance, especially when one considers that the Beaumont youngster's competitors had been two or three years older. Winning this contest was the seminal event that caused the fifteen-year-old trumpeter to consider becoming a professional musician. Graduation from Dick Dowling Junior High School marked the extent of his formal education.

He began playing in dance bands around the Beaumont area and for the first time studied theory and harmony. A stint with the local Salvation Army band provided another kind of musical experience. At the same time, he reaffirmed his circus roots by appearing as a guest artist with Merle Evans's Ringling Brothers Barnum & Bailey Circus Band when the circus appeared in Beaumont.

Everette continued to be determined that Harry would never become a jazz musician. It was obvious even to Everette, however, that Harry possessed the dazzling technique and incredible stamina that could make him a successful professional trumpet player.

Years later, Tom Jenkins, the retired president of both Alvin College in Texas and Thomas Nelson College in Virginia, was a trumpet student of Everette's and recalled: "He'd sit there during the lesson holding a baton with a heavy wooden butt at the end. If you happened to miss a fingering … you'd know it 'cause he'd crack you over the knuckles with the butt end of the baton. Man, I thought my fingers would never mature." Tom defended Everette's radical teaching methods. "When I look back, I realize he was holding a standard up for me to strive for."

As Jenkins further recalled, "The older guys in Beaumont talked about how they would sneak Harry out at night to play jobs that the old man didn't like. Two of the bands Harry worked for were led by George Pegler and Pat Halpin.[27]

"What's funny is that Claude Lakey (who later became an important member of Harry's band) used to play at a club outside Beaumont called Bill Borden's," said Jenkins. "The story I heard was that Claude was the giant in those days, and Harry walked in his shadow. Claude played everything. At a jam session Claude would just work his way around the band and play every horn. He would cut the guy who he borrowed the horn from, and, of course, in the process, made everybody mad at him."[28]

Jack McGee was a bassist with various bands around Beaumont who later helped Everette out by teaching buglers at St. Anthony's. While reminiscing about Harry, he said, "Harry was such a talent he didn't stay long around here—why, he could sightread a trumpet part from 100 feet."[29]

The Depression wore on, and, despite Everette's new job with the Pennsylvania Shipyards and Petroleum Iron Works Company, he still wasn't earning the kind of money he had pulled in for years as a circus bandmaster. Finally, Harry made an important decision. "Dad," he argued, "I can make it as a musician, and it's about time I helped you and Mom out." Finally, Everette agreed.

Anson Weeks, who had a dance orchestra of some renown, toured Texas in the early 1930s. At that time, his band included Xavier Cugat on violin and Bob Crosby on vocals, who both would make their mark shortly thereafter as leaders of their own orchestras. During a one-nighter in Port Arthur, a tall, distinguished gentleman approached Weeks after each set asking, "Couldn't my son," who was sitting nearby holding his trumpet, "sit in with your band?" Weeks kept stalling Everette James until the next intermission, hoping he would forget about it and stop pressing the issue. Finally, the bandleader used the bromide that musician union regulations would not permit it. After this final rejection, Everette sternly informed Weeks: "My kid is a darn good trumpet player and you're going to be hearing a lot about him."

Shortly thereafter, young Harry attended an audition at the Baker Hotel in Dallas held by Lawrence Welk, with his seven-piece band. The gangly James, who weighed in at about 130 and was dressed in shorts, made a trip to the nearby town and approached the maestro on the stand. "You don't happen to be looking for a trumpet player, do you?" he asked. Welk looked down at the youngster and remarked dubiously, "I don't know, son. I'd have to hear you play first. Did you bring your horn?" Harry said that he had. After the band completed its rehearsal, the well-established bandleader listened to the ambitious young trumpeter. Unfortunately, Harry was a little too anxiety-ridden because the audition didn't come off too well. Reportedly, Welk's comment was: "You play too loud for my band. Sorry, I can't make room for you."

Harry's version was a little different. As he remarked, "He asked me what else I could play and I told him the drums. But that wasn't enough. He wanted guys who could play at least four or five instruments, so I didn't get the job."

Violinist Joe Gill, whose Phillips Flyers worked out of St. Louis, played a date near Beaumont and held auditions. Again, Harry arrived wearing shorts. At first he was ignored by Gill. After a while the leader reluctantly handed him some sheet music to look over, assuming he wasn't good enough to become a member of his band. The tune turned out to be "St. Louis Blues," the most difficult arrangement in the entire Gill library, but a tune James knew well from circus days.

Vernon Brown, a trombonist in the band, who was later to be Harry's close friend on the Benny Goodman Band, tried to be of assistance. "Hey, kid, look out for this phrase. It starts on a high D, double forte [very loud]. It's tricky." Ironically, the arranger for the piece was Gordon Jenkins, whose composition, "Goodbye," James was destined to play and solo on at the conclusion of every Benny Goodman performance several years later.

After he ran down "St. Louis Blues" and a few other numbers, Gill recognized the young man's obvious technique and admired his flashy trumpet style. He immediately hired him. A few days later, despite his lingering opposition to Harry's desire to play with dance bands, Everette drove him down to the location date in Galveston at the Balinese Room to join Joe Gill and his Phillips Flyers.

This engagement officially launched the career of one of the quintessential trumpet players of the twentieth century. The odyssey was about to begin.

2

Louise and Ben

On a Friday night in New York in early February 1960, I completed my work for the week as a young agent booking bands at MCA, then the foremost talent agency in the world, the CAA (Creative Artists Agency) of its time. MCA had originally been formed as a band agency by the late Dr. Jules Stein in Chicago during the 1920s.

I left the building at 598 Madison Avenue and took the subway to West 49th Street where I was supposed to meet up with the Harry James Band bus in front of the Forrest Hotel, the eternal big band hotel. James was an MCA client, and the band was headed for Lakehurst, New Jersey, to play a dance date at the Naval Air Station, renowned as the home of the dirigibles and doubtlessly best remembered as the place where the German airship Hindenberg exploded in 1936. It was my first road trip with a band, one of the few perks that a job that paid $65 a week offered. I spent the better part of the sixty-mile journey down the Garden State Parkway talking with the various sidemen in the band whom I had just begun to know. Harry was sitting in his usual third row seat on the right, and talked throughout the trip to his manager, Sal Monte.

During the gig, I listened to endless repetitions of "You Made Me Love You," "Two O'Clock Jump," "I've Heard That Song Before," "Cherry," "The Mole," and other staples of the band's vast library of hits. It was common practice for most popular dance bands of the time to repeat their tunes over and over during the course of an evening in order to please their audiences. On the other hand, it was because of this that some bandleaders began to hate playing their biggest hits. This was one of the major reasons Artie Shaw left the business. He simply despised playing endless renditions of "Begin the Beguine."

When the evening was over, we were on our way back to New York, and, although I was only twenty-five at the time, I must have been very tired and was yawning continuously, something I couldn't control and was embarrassing to me. Harry was standing in the aisle drinking his vodka and feeling very pleased with himself after another successful gig. While we were talking, he couldn't help noticing my yawning. He motioned to Sal, "Look at Pedro. We should take him across Texas for three weeks of one-nighters and see how he'd handle that." (This was the first time he'd called me Pedro.)

Harry James started working one-nighters across the highly changeable landscape of Texas in 1932 with Joe Gill's Phillips Flyers, touring as far afield as New Orleans. During his sixth month with Joe Gill, when he was making $60 a week, the band ran out of bookings and found itself stranded in Abilene, Texas.

Harry returned home to Beaumont and went back to school for a short time, but the idea of playing in another big band was too strong. He joined Hogan Hancock, one of a succession of territory bands that worked major hotel dance jobs throughout Texas, Oklahoma, and Louisiana. James next joined drummer Edward "Doc" Ross's band toward the end of 1932 for several months. The Ross Band worked engagements at the Skirvin Hotel in Oklahoma City as well as Olmo's Club and the Meadowmare Country Club in Fort Worth; the band ultimately broke up in San Angelo, Texas. He also played in bands led by the highly regarded pianist Peck Kelley (a former Joe Gill bandmate) and Marshall Van Pool, who had a popular band in Oklahoma City during the 1930s.[1] From there it was a step up to the Ligon Smith Orchestra at the Baker Hotel in downtown Dallas. Smith was a mentor to many young dance band musicians in Texas during this period.

The plethora of dance orchestras working throughout the Southwest entertaining a small segment of wealthy people was in direct contrast to the misery of economic conditions endured by the general population in this area during the Great Depression. The popularity of bands was a carryover from the 1920s, a time when dance orchestras had become nationally known following the great success of Paul Whiteman on radio.

Spud Murphy, still spry at ninety, pointed out to me, "All the major cities in Texas had hotel bands. In some cities like San Antonio, you had both the Plaza and St. Anthony hotels. In Dallas, there were both the Baker and the Adolphus."[2] Murphy left Texas before the end of the 1920s and first made his mark writing arrangements for Glen Gray's Casa Loma Orchestra and Benny Goodman. While with Goodman, among the arrangements he was most known for was a "killer-diller" version of "Darktown Strutter's Ball" that featured Harry James.

The music historian James T. Maher described the advent of radio and its effect on the dance band business both in Texas and the rest of the nation during the early 1930s. "By the early years of the Depression, everybody's sitting at home ... and by the winter of 1932, which was really the Valley Forge of the commercial history of this country, you had men who at that point were almost in total despair. So what do you do for rest and recreation at the end of the day? You turn on the radio. It's the one free thing.... In 1932 and 1933 it became commonplace to pick up your newspaper to see radio listings that would just say 'dance music.' Suddenly, radio on a local and national level gave musicians considerable work playing in dance bands."[3]

At the same time that Harry James was gaining a reputation in Texas moving from dance band to dance band, the bank robbers Bonnie Parker and Clyde Barrow, better known as Bonnie and Clyde, were becoming notorious for their exploits. The young outlaws hailed from West Dallas, a section of the city steeped in poverty and disillusionment. Bonnie and Clyde's ability to evade the authorities helped make them major figures in the folklore of the Southwest. Many people in the area identified with them, for they were robbing from the very banks that had foreclosed on their homes and businesses. Finally, on May 23, 1934, after twenty-seven months on the run, Bonnie and Clyde were killed in a police ambush outside Gibsland, Louisiana. In an example of grisly excess, which further indicated the extent of the panic, six lawmen each emptied a full twenty-shot clip from their Browning automatic rifles into the stolen 1933 Ford V-8 carrying the fugitives.[4]

Slightly over two weeks later, a photograph from the June 8, 1934, edition of the *San Antonio Evening News* shows members of the Ligon Smith Orchestra posing amid a lineup of various shiny brand-new General Motors cars in front of the St. Anthony Hotel. Harry James is resplendent in a light-colored summer suit and white shoes.

Although still in his late teens, James was already six-foot-one and weighed 150 pounds. He had a thin waist, no hips, and long skinny legs. To go along with his slinky frame, he had a large, oval-shaped head, a long nose and prominent ears, dark wavy hair, and a pencil-thin mustache. Perhaps his most provocative feature, however, was his deep-set baby-blue eyes—the bluest blue eyes this side of his future band vocalist, Frank Sinatra. He had a high-pitched voice that occasionally squeaked, and spoke with a pronounced Texan drawl. Some people noticed his resemblance to such 1930s film actors as Basil Rathbone (later to be his co-star in the film *Bathing Beauty*) and Warren Williams. Somehow it all meshed, and women found him very attractive.

His appeal also depended on his brash style of trumpet playing, especially in his soulful interpretation of the blues. Harry once explained, "I was brought up in Texas with the blues—when I was eleven or twelve years old down in what they call 'barbecue row' I used to sit in with the guys that had the broken bottlenecks on their guitars, playing the blues; that's all we knew."[5]

At the same time, he had learned the rudiments of classical trumpeting from his father, Everette, and developed an appreciation for Debussy and Sibelius. But it was shortly afterward that his whole perspective on trumpet playing changed when he heard the legendary recordings of Louis Armstrong's Hot Five and Hot Seven. From this moment on, Armstrong became Harry's prime influence on trumpet.

The ambitious young trumpeter then joined the Art Hicks Orchestra. Hicks, a violinist who hailed from Cincinnati, had been the musical director for Paul Spector's band in New York. He had married into a wealthy family that owned the Lions Stores chain in the Toledo, Ohio, area, and formed his own band. His all-American look—blond and blue-eyed—was the perfect image for fronting a 1930s dance orchestra.

In August 1934, the Hicks twelve-piece orchestra played for dancing at the Sylvan Club in Arlington, Texas, a venue frequented by wealthy oilmen. Mary Louise Tobin, a petite and pretty, baby-faced fifteen-year-old brunette singer from Denton, Texas, who had started her singing career in local Kiwanis Club minstrel shows, was the headliner of the floor show. The young singer had won an amateur contest in Dallas and was now in the middle of a statewide tour. One of twelve children from a close-knit family, Tobin looked very much like the 1970s film star Ali MacGraw.[6]

Hicks recognized her singing talent and immediately offered Tobin a job with his band. Because she was so young, he made arrangements with his new vocalist's family for Louise's sister, Dora, to accompany her on all the band's engagements to collect her salary and take care of her clothes. The Tobin sisters lived in a nearby hotel during the three-month engagement at the Sylvan Club. The only musician in the band who owned a car was the lead trumpeter, Harry James, who, because of his skinny frame, his fellow musicians referred to as "Jaybird." Hicks made arrangements for the trumpeter to drive the girls home after the gig every night at 3 A.M.

As Louise Tobin recalled, "Half the time I was asleep when we drove back to the hotel. I wasn't used to being out, I hadn't been to parties, and I wasn't allowed to date. I didn't know very much about nightlife so it was very different for me, and around 11 P.M. my eyes would begin to close."

From the beginning of the Sylvan Club engagement, however, she real-ized that she had found her calling, and it appeared that, with the financial backing of his father-in-law, the Art Hicks Orchestra was destined for suc-cess.

During the first few weeks of the rides back from the Sylvan Club, Dora sat in the front seat with Harry, and Louise sat in back. One night Dora told her younger sister, "You're gonna ride in the front seat with Harry because tonight I have a date with the piano player, and we're gonna ride in the back seat."[7]

A romance developed between Harry James and Louise Tobin within weeks of the time they met. Louise remembers Harry saying to her early on, "Do you think you could love me?" She was both surprised and flat-tered and also delighted because she, in turn, had a large crush on him. "I think what truly attracted him to me was that I was so unsophisticated and in awe of everything. He tried to educate me in the swing language. To me he seemed very sophisticated. He knew the ropes. Later, after we were mar-ried, and we were having our problems, I remember saying to him, 'You can't judge me because you brought me up.'"[8]

After three months, the Hicks aggregation left Arlington for an engage-ment at the Mayo Hotel in Tulsa, playing for luncheon, dinner, and late supper dancing. Both Harry and Louise were now getting featured billing with "America's Newest Dance Sensation," as the Art Hicks Orchestra called itself.

The romance flourished as the tour progressed and Harry asked Louise to marry him. The reality was, however, that no state would sanction the marriage of a sixteen-year-old girl. Dora was constantly watching over Louise, but, despite her hovering, Harry and Louise managed to spend time alone.

The Art Hicks Orchestra was booked to play another location date at the Commodore Perry Hotel in Toledo, no doubt due to the influence of Hicks's in-laws. Tobin remembers that during the intermission between the evening sets members of the band would flock to the lobby to listen to Hal Kemp's band, whose happy and melodic music was creating a follow-ing, on the radio. After the Toledo job, the band headed East to the Albany, New York, area. Harry excitedly told Louise, "We can get married up here." She said, "My family will never allow it." He countered with, "Your family will never know."

As Tobin candidly recalled, "At that point of my life, I believed every-thing he told me. We managed to avoid Dora and took a couple of guys from the band, and we went over to Massachusetts and found out that a three-day waiting period was required. Of course, since we were still on tour, we went back and rejoined the band."

The next day, James discovered that they could get married in New York State. They drove to a town called Millerton and were married by a justice of the peace in his office. The date was May 25, 1935. Harry James was nineteen and Louise Tobin sixteen.

On the way to the justice of the peace Harry told Louise what she should say. "Remember now, you're eighteen and you were born in 1917." As an afterthought, Louise reminded herself that having an underage bride left Harry potentially liable for serious moral consequences and herself open to possible disgrace from her own family. The young couple had so little money that they had hocked a tiny chip diamond that Louise owned. That gave Harry the cash to buy his bride a small ring. The groom was extremely nervous, so much so that when he was repeating his vows he said, "With this wing, I wee thed."[9]

After the wedding, Harry James planned how he was going to break the news to Dora, but chickened out. Instead, he called Everette and exclaimed, "Dad, I've met the girl I want to live with all my life." Everette tried to dissuade Harry, but became resigned to the fact that he was now a bridegroom and replied, "Well, son, if you really have met *the* girl, well, it's okay with us, so please bring her home so we can meet her."

Concurrent with the marriage of his two featured stars, Hicks was encountering serious booking problems. A series of dates were canceled during the orchestra's tour of the Northeast. As a result, he had to cut his payroll drastically. Harry James and Louise Tobin found their paychecks reduced to $22 a week. Harry balked and told the leader, "I'm not taking another cut. We're gonna leave."

The young couple returned to Beaumont. Everette and Mabel immediately responded to Louise and soon became close to their new daughter-in-law. After a time, Louise felt that Everette had replaced her own father, who had been killed in an automobile accident several years earlier.

Harry James left for Fort Worth to join Herman Waldman, whose band was prominent in Texas during this time, while Louise went home to Denton. She kept her marriage a secret from Dora and her family for four months. On finally learning the news, Louise's mother tried to have the marriage annulled, but Louise remained stalwart. When the Tobins finally met Harry, however, they were immediately charmed by him and accepted him as a member of the family.[10]

Waldman, also a violinist, led a "Mickey Mouse" or "sweet" band, as these bands were called in those days. There were an abundance of such bands in the early years of the Depression offering syrupy, sentimental music (as exemplified by Guy Lombardo and his Royal Canadians) that was reassuring to many people in those difficult times.

During an engagement at the Washington Hotel in Shreveport,

Louisiana, while Harry James was playing third trumpet for Waldman, he almost lost his lip. By now, he had become a powerhouse trumpet player, and Waldman's music simply was too bland and failed to provide him with a challenging musical outlet. What was most alarming, however, was that his embouchure was being severely affected.

With his new financial responsibility, Harry James had to remain with Waldman, who was paying him $55 a week, a reasonable salary for the times. Unfortunately, the only other musician in the orchestra with any ability to play hot jazz was clarinetist Bob McCracken. He and Harry were frustrated together.[11]

At this very opportune moment, enter Ben (Benny) Pollack, who had heard about the flashy young trumpeter from Beaumont, Texas. He offered James $75 a week and installed him in his jazz trumpet chair, replacing Bob Goodrich, in an extended engagement at the Lincoln Tavern in Chicago. Harry was ecstatic at the chance to play with a real jazz band.

Pollack, "The Dean of Sophisticated Swing," hailed from Chicago, the son of a furrier. He was a highly respected drummer and bandleader. He had started with the New Orleans Rhythm Kings, and watching "Baby" Dodds, the exciting drummer who had electrified Chicago as part of King Oliver's Creole Jazz Band, influenced his playing greatly. In the early 1920s, The Rhythm Kings were considered by a coterie of jazz fans and musicians to be the outstanding white jazz band. Benny Goodman, later one of his featured sidemen, said Pollack was the first drummer to consistently play four beats to the measure on the bass drum. One of his peer group, Gene Krupa, later acknowledged his musical debt to Pollack.

Pollack had seen Benny Goodman do his Ted Lewis imitation as a youngster around Chicago. His cousin, the late effervescent violinist Alex Beller, claimed he was the one who suggested to Pollack that he should hire Goodman, emphasizing that, in addition to his prowess on clarinet, he also doubled on tenor saxophone. Goodman gained his first significant professional job when Pollack hired him in August 1925 in Venice, California.

Shortly before Goodman joined the band, Ben Pollack had added alto saxophonist Gil Rodin, arranger Fud Livingston, and arranger and trombonist Glenn Miller. These four acquisitions helped shape Pollack's dream of establishing a hot dance orchestra. Returning to Chicago, Pollack achieved success with his prize possessions. The band was then well received in February 1928 in New York.

By September of that year the Pollack band had become established, and, according to bandleader Charlie Barnet, was renowned among musicians as the only white big band playing real jazz.[12] It represented the restless drive of Chicago style jazz, with its forceful and percussive sound, that differed significantly from the typical New York bands. Pollack's habit of playing with accented beats had a pronounced effect on the phrasing of his soloists.

In late 1934 in California, however, the jazz nucleus of Pollack's band—trumpeter Yank Lawson, tenor saxophonist Eddie Miller, clarinetist Matty Matlock, and alto saxophonist Gil Rodin—staged a mutiny. They rebelled at their leader's prominently featuring Doris Robbins as band singer. She was a former Ziegfield Follies showgirl who would shortly become Pollack's fiancee. Ben was convinced he could mold Robbins into a star. As a result, he lost interest in presenting jazz with his band.

The rebels then left Pollack en masse. Eventually, following the suggestion of the influential big band agent Cork O'Keefe, they formed a co-op band and joined forces with Bob Crosby in New York to assemble what soon became the popular Bob Crosby Orchestra and then the Bobcats, the group featured within the Crosby band. This was a crushing blow to Pollack, whose band never again regained its popularity.

Through Pollack's band passed cornetist Jimmy McPartland, trumpeters Charlie Spivak and Muggsy Spanier, trombonist Jack Teagarden, tenor saxophonists Bud Freeman and Babe Russin, violinist and composer Victor Young, guitarist Nappy Lamare, drummer Ray Bauduc, and later, singer Mel Tormé. (The only drummer who could in any way compare as a nurturer of jazz talent is Art Blakey, who from the 1950s to the 1980s was responsible for the development of such prominent jazz artists as Clifford Brown, Keith Jarrett, Chuck Mangione, and Branford and Wynton Marsalis, along with Wayne Shorter, Freddie Hubbard, Donald Byrd, and others.)

But it is one thing to develop talent and still another to be able to manage their often difficult personalities. This was an area in which Ben Pollack came up short. He could sometimes be abrasive to his musicians, yet at the same time had a deep-seated need to ingratiate himself with the general public as evidenced by the sycophantic tag line he adapted in closing some of his recordings: "May it please you—Ben Pollack."

Years later, Pollack was given important feature roles playing himself in both films The Glenn Miller Story and The Benny Goodman Story. The Ben Pollack story, unfortunately, remains one of the vagaries of the music business. Pollack led a band that was the model for Benny Goodman's tremendous success and had been the reluctant godfather of the Bob Crosby Orchestra. As a bandleader, he was perhaps the most important discoverer of young jazz talent, and also led a hard-swinging band. Besides that, he was a very innovative drummer, yet he never led a really successful commercial band.

I remember meeting Ben Pollack a few times at Harry James's office in Hollywood during the early 1960s. He was withdrawn and bitter, and had the look of a defeated man. Whenever he could, James would hire Pollack as the contractor for his gigs and recording sessions in Hollywood. After failed bar and restaurant ventures in Hollywood and Palm Springs, and a divorce from Doris Robbins, the tragic little drummer ended his life by hanging himself in Palm Springs on June 7, 1971, at the age of sixty-eight. Harry James never forgot what Ben Pollack had done for him and remained close to him to the end of his unfulfilled life.

When Harry joined the Pollack band in November 1935, it sounded like a combination of the Goodman and Crosby aggregations. He later referred to the experience of working for Pollack as "like being on a farm team. If you did well there you went on to the big leagues." Glenn Miller had returned to the band to play trombone and arrange; Solly La Perche and later "Shorty" Sherock and then Charlie Spivak joined with James to form the trumpet section; Harry's friend from Waco, Texas, Dave Matthews, was on tenor saxophone; Irving Fazola (né Prestopnick) was the featured clarinetist; Thurman Teague on bass; and Freddie Slack on piano. Ben Pollack felt this band was going to be the greatest of all his bands. He referred to his budding young musicians as "new world swingsters."

According to Alex Beller, who was by now a member of the Pollack band, Ben immediately recognized James's brilliant and daring trumpet style, but opposed his use of a wide vibrato on certain tunes; he dubbed it "Harry's Chinese sound."[13] Pollack featured him constantly, even having him work with Thurman Teague, steel guitarist Eddie LeRue, and himself in a trio setting. In addition, for the first time, Harry James was given the opportunity to write arrangements. Pollack also introduced two of the band's most important instrumentals, both written by Harry James.

The first, "Peckin'," was based on the phrase with which "Cootie" Williams began his trumpet solo on Duke Ellington's 1931 recording of "Rockin' in Rhythm"; it was actually instigated by the Charioteers, a trio of dancers at the Cotton Club in Culver City, California, who were appearing there with the Pollack band. The tune debuted there and soon caused a minor dance sensation with the jitterbugs, who dropped to one knee and "pecked" with their necks over the shoulders of their dancing partners. The other tune, "Deep Elm," was written in the bluesy style of black music of the time and named for the African-American ghetto in Dallas. "Peckin'" was so popular that it was featured in the RKO musical *New Faces of 1937*, starring Milton Berle, with additional lyrics by Edward Cherkose.

A typical Ben Pollack dance date at the time began with soft, melodic numbers and gradually worked into "hot" jazz tunes as the evening progressed. After midnight, the veteran bandleader and expert showman featured his young soloists, and improvisation became the byword.

While he was working with Pollack in Chicago, Harry James brought Louise to stay with him at the Carlos Hotel on the South Side. It was a hotel frequented by American League ballplayers in town to play the Chicago White Sox at nearby Cominsky Park. Being a rabid baseball fan, Harry relished the idea of being able to spend time with big league ballplayers, many of whom were his heroes.[14]

Harry James left his bride in Chicago to go on tour with Pollack. The band was booked by MCA and was constantly on the road throughout the country—from the Cotton Club in Culver City (Los Angeles) to Hamid's "Million Dollar Pier" in Atlantic City.

Unfortunately, Louise Tobin didn't have a job, and they were having a difficult time financially. To bring in a few more dollars each week, Harry drove the band's instrument truck. He drove like he played—fast and bold. His salary, however, still wasn't enough to support himself on the road and Louise in Chicago. After Louise had run up a substantial bill, the manager of the Carlos Hotel cut off her credit.

She auditioned for the famed impresario Mike Todd, who hired her as a singer in his touring revue, *Bring on the Dames.* Subsequently, Doris Robbins, who was still singing with Pollack, became ill during an engagement in St. Louis and Harry convinced Ben to hire Louise to replace her. This allowed Harry and Louise to be together for at least a few weeks.[15] After that, the newlyweds kept in touch by telephone and letter. Harry constantly told her, "As soon as I get settled down, I'll send for you."

Louise knew her husband to be shy and introverted, and believed him to be a faithful spouse. On the road with Pollack, however, he was someone very different. He easily fit in with his fellow musicians, enjoying their bawdy humor, drinking whiskey, and smoking marijuana with them.

While rooming with Shorty Sherock, Harry James also gained a reputation for playing Monopoly. This went together with playing poker for high stakes, the start of a gambling fever that continued the rest of his life. And at this point on the road, he began the pattern of womanizing that would also ensue long after.

On Harry's twentieth birthday, when the Ben Pollack band was on hiatus, he was sitting in with the band at the Gay 90's in Chicago. The emcee, Flo Whitman, asked James to play a number with the house band, which happened to include Drew Page. Harry requested that the band play "Dinah" as fast as it could. He laid his trumpet on the chair and ran out on the floor in front of the band. He astonished everyone with a hilarious tap dance routine, which broke up the house.

Drew Page remarked, "I didn't know you were a hoofer. You [sure] surprised us."

"Used to be," replied Harry, "I was a tumbler and a drummer, too, back in my circus days." At that moment, something suddenly clicked in Page's mind. "I'll be! Are you the little kid that used to come to our high school in Ada, Oklahoma, and play drum solos when you were about six or seven?"[16]

Indeed, Harry James had been enrolled at Willard Elementary School in Ada when Honest Bill's Circus wintered there. Honest Bill Newton's son, Clyde, who was president of his class, had arranged for Everette James to bring his son Harry to perform at his school.

It was also at the Gay 90's that Harry James first encountered Bernard "Buddy" Rich, who sat in with the band. After the set, he predicted, "That kid will be a great drummer someday."

Jerry Jerome, as a member of Harry Reser's twelve-piece band, the Clicquot Club Eskimos, met Harry James on Hamid's Pier during the summer of 1936 when he was with Ben Pollack. In addition to Harry's talent, Jerry Jerome admired the playing of Solly La Perche, Irving Fazola, Bruce Squires on trombone, and Dave Matthews. Even though the Pollack orchestra was playing written arrangements, Jerome admired its looseness—to him it sounded like a flexible, free-swinging small jazz band.[17]

Harry James made his recording debut with Ben Pollack on September 15 and 16, 1936. With Pollack, he was best remembered for his solos on "Song of the Islands" and "Jimtown Blues" (which duplicated the sound of a black orchestra), on Brunswick and Vocalion, respectively, and, of course, "Deep Elm" and "Peckin'," which were recorded for Varsity Records. "Deep Elm" shows just how similar the sounds of the Pollack and Goodman bands were; it also indicates the confidence James demonstrated in his playing.

Despite the popularity that "Peckin'" had already enjoyed, James didn't record the tune with Pollack until December 18, 1936. This recording was highlighted by one of Harry's daring entrances on his first of two solos; both were examples of his rambunctious brand of swing.

In his band, Pollack had incorporated a small recording group called "The Dean and His Kids." Harry James contributed an amusing comedy vocal on "Zoom, Zoom, Zoom," reminiscent of Willie Smith's subsequent vocal on Jimmie Lunceford's "Rhythm Is Our Business" and Lionel Hampton's vocal on "Vibraphone Blues" with the Benny Goodman Quartet. The exuberant playing of "The Dean and His Kids" on this tune and on "Spreadin' Knowledge Around," both on Vocalion Records, were reminiscent of Bob Crosby's Bobcats, and again James contributed a salvo of spirited solos.

George T. Simon, the editor of *Metronome* Magazine and later the author of a series of popular books on the big bands, reviewed the Ben Pollack band while listening to a radio remote from Chicago. Simon wrote of Pollack's "rip-roaring" (a most apt description) new trumpet soloist without bothering to identify him by name. Despite his anonymity, it was Harry James's first significant review.

As James recalled years later, "We were playing in Pittsburgh. We had a good, hard rockin' band, and all of a sudden we pick up a copy of *Metronome* and we see this review of the band, and it was so favorable, and I said, 'Oh, my goodness, this is so nice. We've got to find this man.'"

Simon and James met for the first time in September 1936 at a Ben Pollack recording session in New York. Simon had been invited to attend by his friends Glenn Miller and Charlie Spivak. Miller had touted Pollack to Simon as an outstanding drummer; "Now you can hear for yourself," he said.

After the session, Glenn Miller began raving about the prowess of his young friend in the brass section and introduced him to Simon. Harry finally got a chance to thank Simon for his review. The *Metronome* editor later reviewed these records with continued praise for James's playing. This marked the beginning of a long friendship between Harry James and George Simon.

As Simon recalled their first meeting, "I found him to be a very enthusiastic guy with a great deal of understanding of life in general. For a guy who was as young as he was [twenty], he was quite mature due to his upbringing, circus-band background, and traveling around the country so much and never really settling down. He had learned to fend for himself. What may have been immature was his womanizing."

Harry James's musical reputation was growing rapidly. On two separate occasions during 1936, Tommy Dorsey wired James offering him a job. Two bandleaders whose music was considerably more conservative, Henry Busse and Horace Heidt, also made him offers to join their respective bands during the same year. He turned them all down.

He made his first recordings away from Pollack doing four tunes with The Rhythm Wreckers on September 1, 1936, and the same number of tunes with Chuck Bullock and his Levee Loungers on October 2 for Mellotone Records. These recordings were made while the Pollack band was working in the New York area.

Like so many other young jazz musicians of the time, Harry James marveled at the Benny Goodman Band's ability to adapt contemporary pop songs (such as "Sometimes I'm Happy") and transform them into what in many cases became classics; at the same time these renditions delighted the dancers. It has often been said that arrangers form the imprint of a jazz orchestra. Fletcher Henderson, Jimmy Mundy, and Edgar Sampson turned out a seemingly endless supply of truly innovative charts that provided Goodman and his musicians with ample solo opportunities.

After a Saturday night gig in Ohio, Harry and Louise (who was visiting him), plus two other musicians from the Ben Pollack band, drove through the night to the Congress Hotel in Chicago to witness the Benny Goodman Band in one of the first jazz concerts on a Sunday afternoon.[18] These concerts were promoted by the Chicago Rhythm Club's Helen Oakley. It was here that James saw firsthand exactly what Goodman had created. The saxophone section, under the peerless direction of Hymie Schertzer on alto saxophone, delivered a precise unison sound over which Goodman's clarinet constantly swooped, playing incredibly conceived solos at various tempos. The brass section was driven by Gene Krupa's ferocious drumming. Jess Stacy on piano and Alan Reuss on guitar compensated for the often erratic time of Benny's brother Harry on bass, but, along with Gene Krupa, supplied a strong rhythmic foundation. Rarely, if ever, was there a big band as well rehearsed and polished. The band's sound radiated an assurance and a unanimity of conception. Louise was equally amazed by Helen Ward's singing of such tunes as "You're A Heavenly Thing," "Between the Devil and the Deep Blue Sea," and "Goody Goody."

Coincidentally, another of Benny Goodman's brothers, Irving, who had just replaced Zeke Zarchy on the Goodman Band, had read George Simon's review of Harry James's recordings with Pollack. He began listening to Harry on radio remotes of the Pollack band. He told Benny Goodman of his discovery. Irving wasn't being selfless; he merely wanted to leave the employ of his overbearing older brother as soon as he could. The talent of Harry James provided the means for an easy exit. Goodman was aware of his brother's enthusiasm, but characteristically showed little reaction.

As a result of Irving's continued prodding, however, Benny Goodman listened to a broadcast from the Cotton Club in Culver City on December 19, 1936, during which Harry James blasted out his rendition of "Deep Elm." The usually reserved clarinetist was amazed at the range and excitement inherent in James's solos and called the Cotton Club immediately to speak to him. He made Harry a generous offer to join his band at the Madhattan Room of the Hotel Pennsylvania in New York—$150 a week plus train transportation. He would replace Irving Goodman.

Benny Goodman confirmed the offer the next day by telegram. (Buck Clayton, then with Count Basie, said that when he first saw James with Pollack he thought he belonged with Benny Goodman.)[19] On receipt of Goodman's confirmation of the December 20th offer, James showed the wire to Ben Pollack. Its succinct message read: "OK advise by Western Union how soon you can come." Pollack strongly suggested to James that he accept Goodman's offer, emphasizing that joining the Benny Goodman Band meant the big time—the absolute pinnacle of the band business.

Simultaneously, Red Norvo wired James an offer to join his band at the Blackhawk in Chicago. James informed Norvo, however, that he had already committed himself to Benny Goodman. He got sixteen-year-old Jimmy Maxwell an audition with Pollack as his replacement, but Ben had already decided on hiring Muggsy Spanier.

Underneath the graciousness Pollack exhibited in advising his protégé to accept Goodman's offer was a deep and abiding anger toward Goodman. Pollack couldn't forgive Goodman for having left him after Pollack reprimanded him after a gig for appearing on the bandstand with his shoes unshined. He believed Goodman was unappreciative of the important musical development that he had achieved under his leadership. Then, to lose a gifted young musician from the band he had just honed into a fine musical organization—and one who was obviously headed for major stardom—hurt Pollack deeply.

Harry James understood and fully appreciated the opportunity that had been presented to him. Having seen the Goodman band in full cry, he recognized the true genius of Benny Goodman. He had at last reached the big leagues and was about to enter "The Kingdom of Swing."

3

The Kingdom of Swing

In 1937, Benny Goodman was quoted as saying, "I don't see why anybody wants to know about me. There's nothing to me. It's just the band." Yes, it was "the band," but this self-effacing quote is antithetical to the Benny Goodman most people experienced. He was completely self-absorbed, a perfectionist, and was known for being extremely careful with a dollar. Not only did he have trouble remembering the names of his musicians, he was also known to forget the names of his own children. To get around the problem, he referred to everyone as "Pops." Nothing in his life was ever to replace his best friend and companion, the clarinet. With it, he had achieved international stardom leading his orchestra and small groups, setting a high standard of jazz musicianship, and at the same time establishing the clarinet as an important solo instrument. Buddy Rich once remarked succinctly to me, "Without Benny Goodman, there are no clarinet players." To Goodman, music was everything, and it was completely colorblind. Twelve years before Jackie Robinson's entry into major league baseball, Goodman broke the color barrier allowing black musicians—Teddy Wilson and Lionel Hampton—to tour as part of his trio and quartet, respectively.

To truly understand the phenomenon of swing and the importance of Benny Goodman, it is necessary to examine his musically historic road trip to California in 1935 and its very real connection to the times. The significance of this tour was also to have a major effect on Harry James's musical career as evidenced by the impact of his having seen the Goodman band at the Congress Hotel in Chicago on its way back east after that historic trip to California.

Goodman led one of three bands featured on NBC's weekly Saturday night *Let's Dance* radio program sponsored by the National Biscuit Company. The others were Xavier Cugat, playing Latin dance music, and Kel Murray, playing waltzes. It premiered on December 1, 1934, and emanated from studio 8H, the same studio where, years later, the *Tonight Show* would be based during its many years in New York. Because of the positive reaction to the Goodman band on the *Let's Dance* program, Willard Alexander, a young MCA agent, decided to book a cross-country tour. He worked in close association with John Hammond, the highly opinionated record producer and jazz critic who helped assemble the band.

At 9:30 P.M. on Saturday nights, the Pacific Coast stations picked up the *Let's Dance* broadcast two hours into the three-hour program, just as the Goodman band was hitting its stride on Fletcher Henderson's arrangements of "Down South Camp Meetin'," "King Porter Stomp," and "Blue Skies." In Los Angeles, the fraternity houses at USC and groups of teenagers eagerly listened to the program and reveled in the rhythmic dance music of the Goodman orchestra. On KFWB's *The World's Largest Ballroom*, the Los Angeles disc jockey Al Jarvis heralded the upcoming Palomar engagement, constantly playing Goodman's RCA Victor records, especially "The Dixieland Band," which also explains why his records had been selling well in southern California. This provided MCA with the ammunition it needed to secure a booking at the Palomar Ballroom, the premier ballroom in the city. It had opened ten years before, calling itself "The Largest Ballroom in the West."

In May 1935, a caravan of Goodman musicians driving their own cars left New York and made long jumps between a series of unsuccessful one-nighters. The first date in Lansing, Michigan, drew eighteen people, all of them musicians from Detroit. By the time they reached Elitch's Gardens in Denver, the remainder of the tour was in serious doubt. To put it mildly, Goodman's music simply didn't register with the customers. The dance-hall operator remarked angrily, "I hired a dance band. What's the matter? Can't you boys play any waltzes?" Goodman remembered that particular night as "about the most humiliating experience of my life."

However, by the time the orchestra reached Oakland, magically a huge crowd awaited it at MacFadden's Ballroom. The exuberance of that crowd and the fact that they knew the names of the musicians proved there was an audience for Goodman's music. From there the band was routed south to Los Angeles, stopping off to play a one-nighter in Pismo Beach, where it literally played in a fish barn.

"We were waiting for Goodman," recalls Jimmy Ille, who as a teenager lived in Inglewood, California. "In that summer of '35 there were dance bands playing all along the coast around Los Angeles. In Long Beach, there was the Cinderella Ballroom; in Redondo Beach, the Mandarin Ballroom; in Hermosa Beach, the Majestic, as well as the Hut, where Vido Musso led a band; in Santa Monica, the Lamonica Ballroom; in Ocean Park, the Casino Ballroom and Lick Pier; and finally, in Venice, the Venice Ballroom."[1]

On the opening night of the Palomar engagement—August 21, 1935—there was a lackluster response to the band's first two sets. As Goodman wrote in his autobiography, "If we had to flop, at least I'd do it in my own way, playing the kind of music I wanted to. I called out some of our big Fletcher [Henderson] arrangements for the next set and the boys seemed to get the idea. From the moment I kicked them off, they dug in with some of the best playing I'd heard since we left New York. To our complete amazement, half the crowd stopped dancing and came surging around the stand."

Jimmy Ille attended that opening night with his sister. He estimates that there were about 3,000 dancers, many of them pressed up to the bandstand. (The management advertised it could accommodate 4,000 couples!) "God, what a band that was!—the trumpet section, with Nate Kazebier playing lead and Bunny Berigan and Ralph Muzillo, was amazing, especially Bunny's playing; Hymie Shertzer and the reeds. And Krupa—why, I'd never seen a drummer as explosive as he was."[2]

The two-night booking lasted seven weeks. Overnight, a new trend in popular music was born. But why this sudden acceptance in California? For decades, movements of all kinds have emanated from the Golden State. Along with the popularization of swing, the trivial pursuit of barbecuing on an outside grill, the advent of the motel, mobile homes, drive-ins, a fervent interest in Asian art, and the popularity of wine, golf, and polo were several trends that emerged from California and became national crazes during the 1930s.[3]

America now had its first pop culture hero in Benny Goodman. Not to be overlooked is that, at twenty-six, Benny was just a few years older than the college students who made up an important segment of his audience. His Palomar Ballroom triumph and its aftermath were deemed comparable in scope only to the subsequent sensations caused by Frank Sinatra in the 1940s, Elvis Presley in the 1950s, and the Beatles in the 1960s. More important, this huge outpouring of young people's emotions was directly related to the changing times, as are most trends in popular music.

The musical theme of the day changed from "Brother, Can You Spare a Dime?" to "Happy Days Are Here Again." Jazz suddenly became a paying proposition and *the* popular music of the land for the one and only time. By the summer of 1935, America was beginning to experience a feeling of hope and a sense of relief from the misery of the previous six years, which had an unemployment rate of 25 percent, a failed stock market, soup kitchens, and people riding the rails and hitchhiking along the nation's highways in search of a fresh start. In the Southwest, beleaguered by a series of devastating dust storms, people left in droves and headed for California.

Upon being inaugurated president on March 4, 1933, Franklin Delano Roosevelt offered the American people a "New Deal," emphasizing that "the only thing we have to fear is fear itself—nonetheless, unreasoning, unjustified terror which paralyzes needed effort to convert retreat into advance."

In the next 100 days, more meaningful and far-reaching social legislation was put into motion by the Congress than at any time in the history of the Republic. The nation's banks were closed, and Federal Deposit Insurance and Social Security were subsequently established. Under the direction of Harry Hopkins, Roosevelt's closest advisor, the CCC, WPA, and NRA repaired the infrastructure of the cities, roads, and public works, putting thousands of people to work. Accordingly, by 1934 the economy had begun to improve. Over the next several years there was a growing feeling of optimism that pervaded the country. This, more than anything else, provided the setting for the birth of the Swing Era.

Swing musicians soon became as celebrated as baseball players and movie stars to their young admirers. This same group of young people crowded the dance halls to dance the Lindy and hear their favorite musicians playing their now famous instrumental solos. Changes in personnel among the leading big bands were as closely observed as lineup changes with the New York Yankees.

The Lindy (Hop) actually predated the 1927 Charles Lindbergh solo hop to Paris for which it was named. It most likely started in Harlem and became de rigeur at the famous Savoy Ballroom, "The Home Of Happy Feet." Essentially, the Lindy is choreographed swing music, as Marshall and Jean Stearns described in their history of jazz dancing.

Amazingly, Louis Armstrong's big band sold over 100,000 records in 1931. In 1932, Duke Ellington wrote one of his many hit instrumentals, "It Don't Mean a Thing If It Ain't Got That Swing," but America was not about to bestow idol status on Negro bandleaders despite their obvious musical talents. What were later to be called "swing bands" were already very much in existence. In 1934, for example, the Casa Loma Orchestra under the leadership of Glen Gray registered with the college crowd.

Bands starting out were encouraged by the major agencies—MCA,

Rockwell-O'Keefe, and William Morris—to accept lower-paying jobs in hotels or ballrooms that "had a wire," that is, offered remote regional or network radio exposure. These dates often led to more and better bookings and, at the same time, served to promote a band that was on tour. Several bands achieved success by following such a plan.

After its triumph on the West Coast, Benny Goodman and his Orchestra headed east playing one-nighters en route to Chicago, where it opened on November 6, 1935, at the Congress Hotel. Here the term "swing band" was coined by none other than Gene Krupa, whose dynamic drumming and showmanship were vital components in Goodman's success. But it was not until sometime in 1936 that the press formally dubbed Benny Goodman "The King of Swing."

The Congress Hotel engagement, which had been booked for one month, instead lasted six. Meanwhile, disc jockeys in the major cities had begun to play a succession of Goodman hit records, such as "Stompin' at the Savoy," "When Buddha Smiles," "Body and Soul," "Sometimes I'm Happy," and "live" remote broadcasts provided nationwide exposure. Not only the popularity of the band but also that of the trio—Goodman, Teddy Wilson on piano, and Gene Krupa—and the quartet, with the addition of Lionel Hampton, gave the Benny Goodman organization a certain cachet.

When Harry James arrived in New York from Los Angeles by train after a three-day journey to join the Goodman band, despite the significant critical response he had received as a musician, he was lacking in self-confidence. As Harry later recalled, "I was so nervous I was shaking. I was so excited to go with Goodman." Coming east after a sleepless trip to appear in front of a New York audience as a member of the Benny Goodman Band was also incredibly intimidating.

One observer noted that when Harry James first joined Goodman, he dressed "Texas."[4] His flamboyant taste in clothes reflected his circus background. It also pointed up the fact that he had yet to absorb the sophistication of "The Big Apple." One newspaperman said, "He looked like a TB patient on a tear."

A Beaumont newspaper heralded Harry James's new association almost as if it were the birth of a child: "Mr. and Mrs. Everette James of 635 Lee Street announce that their son Harry has joined the nationally known swing orchestra of Benny Goodman."[5] A later social note in the same newspaper reported: "Harry James is a featured trumpet player with Benny Goodman's Orchestra, one of the several bands credited with advancing swing music, in the current 'March of Time' which is offered on the Jefferson [Theatre] program through Saturday."

Harry James's mate in the Goodman trumpet section, Gordon "Chris"

Griffin, recalled: "When he first got to town, Harry lived with my wife and me for about three weeks at the Whitby Apartments between Eighth and Ninth Avenues on West 45th Street. We put him up in a day bed. I remember he had an ingrown toenail, and we used to bathe it every night with Epsom salts before we went to work. Then he'd have his tuxedo on and wrap his foot in the towel, and he'd go to work looking like that." (Harry's tuxedo was so threadbare that Goodman lent him $22.50 to buy a new one at Howard Clothes.)[6]

Harry James vividly remembered his debut with Goodman on the Tuesday after Christmas 1936. "As soon as I got to the Hotel Pennsylvania, I called Benny's room to ask what time rehearsal was. Benny was in the bathroom, his brother Harry took the call and Benny told him to tell me the rehearsal was the day after tomorrow. So I had to go down and just start playing [cold].

"Benny wasn't there for the first set. He and Gene and Teddy were somewhere with the trio playing a benefit, and Lionel (Hampton) was playing drums and sort of leading the band. I remember we were playing a stock arrangement of 'A Fine Romance,' and after the first ensemble everybody would play choruses. I took one, and then Lionel called out, 'Pops, play another!' Then he called out, 'Play another' again, and the next thing you know I'm playing six choruses in a row at the dinner set! Finally, Benny came in and after the set I was standing in back, but I could hear Lionel saying excitedly to Benny, 'Hey, hey, hey, Pops, this guy can play!'"

A few nights after James joined the band, Goodman and tenor saxophonist Art Rollini (nicknamed "Shneeze" because of his prominent nose) were standing side by side in the men's room at the Hotel Pennsylvania. Rollini began telling Goodman about Harry James's remarkable playing at a jam session in Chicago a year before right after one of the Congress Hotel Sunday afternoon jazz concerts. Benny remarked angrily, "Why didn't you tell me he was so great?" Rollini replied, "I knew you would want to hire him. I just didn't want to see another man go."[7]

Jess Stacy, who played piano in the band, told me in his last interview that from the start young women eagerly responded to the young trumpeter's dashing good looks and hot trumpet choruses. "Harry was assigned as my roommate at the Pennsylvania. After a few nights he suggested to me, 'After the gig, why don't you stay down at the bar so I can use the room.' Since I liked to drink to unwind after the job, and he liked the ladies, it made a lot of sense. But after about thirty days of this same routine, I said to Harry, 'Do you have to get laid every night?'"[8]

As a member of the Goodman aggregation, Harry James was now heard on RCA Victor, then the leading label in the record business. His first recording session with Goodman took place on December 30, 1936. The material consisted of "Never Should Have Told You," "You Can Tell She Comes from Dixie," "This Year's Kisses," and "He Ain't Got Rhythm."[9] The RCA recordings, which tended to sound stiff and mechanical on occasion, unfortunately never captured the inherent excitement in the Goodman band. One reason is that many of these recording sessions took place at 9:00 A.M. following late sets the night before at the Hotel Pennsylvania or the Paramount Theater.[10] (Oh, those delicate chops!) Nevertheless, the impact that James made on the band can certainly be felt on RCA's two-volume set, *The Harry James Years*. There was now a freedom in the band that hadn't been evident heretofore.

Conversely, the Columbia albums consisted of remote broadcasts from all over the East that were recorded off the air by the engineer, Bill Savory. They capture the fire of the Goodman band on the road when the arrangements were opened up, allowing the musicians the opportunity to play longer and often more daring solos.

The best case in point is *Benny Goodman On The Air 1937-'38*. This double CD contains two of James's most exciting solos (save for "Sing, Sing, Sing") during his tenure with Goodman: "St. Louis Blues" and "Roll 'Em." The former, recorded at the Hartford Armory, begins with Goodman stating the theme of this Fletcher Henderson arrangement, followed by Ziggy Elman's broad-toned solo exhibiting his patented "Frahlich" trumpet style (which Lionel Hampton described as "kosher style"). Just as the tune is about to end, Benny signals Krupa to keep it going. With his rocking back beat, Krupa provides a foundation for Harry to play two choruses of some of the boldest swing trumpet playing ever heard before Jess Stacy's tasteful Earl "Fatha" Hines-inspired two choruses lead to the rideout with an allusion to the "One O'Clock Jump." "Roll 'Em," recorded at a Pittsburgh dance hall, a fast blues in F, written and arranged by Mary Lou Williams, the first lady of swing composing, exhibits strong elements of boogie-woogie. Following solos by Stacy and Goodman, James plays four choruses that build like a locomotive running on full throttle before Goodman returns to lead the band to its roaring climax.

A vivid example of dueling eight-bar exchanges between Goodman and James is found on the recording of "Ridin' High," also from the same CD. The band's rendition of Cole Porter's tune perfectly exemplifies the feeling the title describes. The Jimmy Mundy chart provides a setting to display Goodman's free-flowing clarinet solos working in perfect tandem with James's penchant for the spectacular. It is also a rare example of a Goodman recording of Cole Porter material.

The Goodman trumpet section of James, Ziggy Elman, and Chris Griffin became known as "The Biting Brass." It played as a unit for slightly over two years, but in that interval became the favorite of swing fans. At the same time, Count Basie had Edward Lewis, Harry "Sweets" Edison, and Buck Clayton, while Duke Ellington had Wallace Jones, "Cootie" Williams, and Rex Stewart. Bob Crosby could boast of Charlie Spivak, Yank Lawson, and Billy Butterfield. These, too, were very impressive trumpet sections. Ellington referred to Goodman's trumpet section as "the greatest trumpet section that ever was." Glenn Miller, then still struggling with his first band, called it "the marvel of the age."

The Goodman book was very difficult to play and so exacting that it required a split trumpet lead. James, Elman, and Griffin all played lead on separate numbers, although on some numbers the lead was shared by all three. Jess Stacy explained: "The trumpet section had to switch the parts. If they hadn't, the guys would have died."[11]

Jimmy Maxwell joined the Goodman brass section in August 1939 and became a mainstay of the early 1940s band. He noted, "Judging by the book, Harry played a good deal more [lead] than anybody. Ziggy was a fantastic lead trumpet player, as I found out when I joined the band. I once told him, 'You know, when you play lead, it's so easy to follow. It's like being swept along by a river.'" Ziggy said, "You should have played with Harry when he played lead…. Harry would just pull you along like you were floating down a fast-flowing river, and it was no problem at all to play with him."

Maxwell also pointed out how James's arrival changed the sound of the band. "In the 1935 band Ralph Muzzillo played lead, but he was a stiff, almost legit, first trumpet player—a fine trumpet player but not a swinging player—and, of course, Bunny Berigan, then the world's greatest white trumpet player, was in the section at that time. The second trumpet player was usually the jazz chair. That band was exciting because it was new to hear white men playing like that, but when Harry joined the band, it got looser, much looser. It just totally changed like it had been electrified. I think he brought that to the band…. Harry did something to the trumpet section and to the sound of the whole band."[12]

Buddy Childers, the veteran big band trumpeter best known for his work with Stan Kenton, said, "When I came along, you were either going to be a first trumpet player or you were going to be a jazz player. You were not going to be both. Well, Harry did both."[13]

Lionel Hampton amplified these various points: "Having a trumpet player from Texas gave us, the Goodman band, juice. Harry had something of his own to contribute and he could sure hit those high C's and F's. He had a black sound, and it was obvious he had been raised musically around black musicians. He was completely different from any other white trumpet player of his day. When Harry came he enthused the section and gave it some real style. He played 'gut bucket.' The band didn't have that fire or expression 'til he came along."[14]

Kenny Washington, the New York-based jazz drummer and host of *The Big Band Dance Party* on WBGO, New York's jazz station, "discovered" Harry's artistry through Clark Terry's saying, "You're a jazz historian— never sleep on Harry James. He was a bad dude, I'm telling you."

"I started listening to everything I could find on Harry. When I heard the studio recording of 'Sing, Sing, Sing' with Goodman—that's when I realized. When I heard what he was doing when he started that solo, the band shifted gear; he made that band shift gears. Harry must've eaten some collard greens and hung out with some African-Americans in order to get that feeling.

"And I noticed in those road broadcast records the hookup between Harry and Gene Krupa—they made that band," Washington added.[15]

In a rather technical summation of his particular style of trumpet playing, Harry James declared: "Personally, I like and play a rolling style in two- or four-bar phrases. To play this rolling style, or lots of notes style, you must have a basic knowledge of chords and progression and perfect control of your instrument." Further, concerning his technique, Harry added, "When you make a good, clean entrance and a 'planted' exit, your playing has acquired polish. It's only natural that a good beginning will enable you to create ideas more freely."

Chris Griffin was the first of the triumvirate to join the Goodman aggregation. John Hammond had suggested him to Goodman while Chris was playing in the CBS Radio Orchestra. One night Hammond encountered Griffin hanging out at the Famous Door bar on 52nd Street. When asked if he would be interested in joining Goodman, Griffin responded in this way: "It was like asking a young pitcher who is down in the Southern League (then AA) if he was ready to join the Yankees!"[16]

Ziggy Elman, born Harry Finkelman, had been a member of the Alex Bartha Band on the Steel Pier in Atlantic City in September 1936, where he played trumpet, baritone saxophone, trombone, piano, and vibraphone. Art Rollini's wife, Ena, heard him playing an afternoon show with Bartha's band on the Pier. She enthusiastically told Benny Goodman of her discovery. He instructed her to "send him up." Subsequently, at a *Camel Caravan* (the sustaining weekly radio show that featured the Goodman band) rehearsal, Elman sat in on first trumpet. Benny Goodman admired his fast runs and unique sound and hired him on the spot to replace Sterling Bose, who had only recently joined the band in California.[17]

The newly formed trumpet section blended perfectly both personally and aesthetically without any jealousy. Goodman, of course, saw the potential in Harry James from the beginning and instigated a musical rivalry between James and Elman (according to Stacy, he favored Harry) that would not only benefit the band but stimulate the public's reaction as well. Offstage, Harry and Ziggy were inseparable.

Bill Savory stressed that "the contrast between Ziggy and Harry was terrific. Ziggy used the vocalist's line; Harry didn't do that at all. Harry used his trumpet technique to express his ideas. Wake Harry up at 5:00 A.M., he'd blow a high B-flat!"[18]

All three musicians were excellent sight readers, and their work was perfected by Goodman's endless rehearsals. He thought nothing of devoting more than an hour to each new arrangement and often rehearsed the band without the rhythm section so that the band swung by itself without having to lean on the rhythm section. During these arduous rehearsals Goodman would concentrate on developing his own solos so that he could have them worked out in advance before recording or trying them in front of an audience.

As Chris Griffin observed, "I don't think he (Benny) was the natural storyteller that Harry James was. Right from the start, Harry kind of burst out on his solos, but you weren't sure where he was going." (The renowned jazz record producer George Avakian perhaps best summed up Harry's daredevil trumpet style when he said, "It's strictly like a guy racing out onto an icy pond and suddenly discovering he ain't got skates.")[19]

"Harry once said to me, 'I've never heard anything in my head that I couldn't play on the trumpet.' He wasn't bragging; he was just stating a fact. That astounded me because there were many things on the trumpet that I figured I had to sit down and work on in order to get them down right. He could do it spontaneously."[20]

One of James's fellow musicians, knowing of his circus background and aware of the standard circus repertoire, once asked him, "How about playing 'Carnival of Venice'?" "I can play it but I won't," Harry answered. "I've been playing that since I was a kid, and I'm sick of it."

The members of "the well-oiled machine," as Griffin described the trumpet section, would play an arrangement once and could play it completely by memory thereafter. Many nights they would have contests among themselves to see who would have to look at the music; the loser would have to buy the drinks.

When James T. Maher saw Harry James for the first time at an outdoor dance date in Columbus, Ohio, he immediately noticed the absolute command he had of his instrument as well as an "enormous sense of fun." Indeed, James's unquenchable spirit and enthusiasm had made him well liked as well as respected by all the members of the band. Maher continued, "I also saw that when he tried new things, it was never in an intellectual spirit. None of that stuff."[21]

George T. Simon added: "Harry had such a wonderful, fat sound. Most trumpet players, especially guys who played lead, didn't have that because they needed to use a small embouchure so they could hit high notes."[22]

Probably a dozen musicians who worked in his various bands over the years told me how they were constantly in awe of James's photographic memory. On occasion, when running down a new arrangement with his own band, he would make a musical reference to a similar phrase in one of the Goodman arrangements he had played back in the late 1930s!

It is also important to realize that Goodman's high regard for his trumpet section allowed the members a certain latitude. They took certain liberties in their section work as well as with their own solos. As a unit, they played slightly sharp so that the sound would stand out and have more brilliance. This same method had been used successfully by Tommy Dorsey. Harry James continued utilizing this technique in his own solos in the years to come.

In the trumpet section, James sat on the end to Krupa's immediate left. According to Griffin, "Harry and Gene were a duet from the beginning. They had worked out some routines together, not where they'd 'woodshed' them, but they just were natural compatibles. Harry would play, and Gene would rattle off the same thing on the snare drum. Gene would pick up on Harry, and Harry would then pick up on Gene."[23]

Without question there are more stories about Benny Goodman than there are about any other bandleader of the time. One day while the band was playing at the Earle Theatre in Philadelphia, James and Griffin found a way to handle his well-known frugality and irritating habit of never admitting to carrying money. Between shows, the musicians were to be transported by taxi to radio station WFAS to rehearse. As Harry and Chris got into a cab, Benny came running out of the stage door and jammed himself in the middle. When they reached the radio station, James and Griffin quickly jumped out and ran inside. Goodman came into the studio after having to pay the cab fare. He looked at them and yelled, "Traitors!"[24]

Jess Stacy contended that, after several months as a member of the band, Harry James came to despise Benny Goodman. Stacy claimed that Harry abhorred the way Goodman treated people without any regard for their feelings. "Harry was nice to people," said Jess. This is perhaps an overstatement on Stacy's part, who maintained a cantankerous feeling toward Benny for many years. Essentially, Harry and most of the Goodman regulars were constantly amazed at Benny's unpredictable behavior; nothing that he did really surprised them.[25]

Being a member of the Goodman band provided any musician immediate recognition. Accordingly, James's abilities as a trumpeter were quickly discovered by other musicians. On his first date away from the band, he recorded four tunes with trombonist Miff Mole's group, on February 17, 1937, which were released on Vocalian Records.

The March 3, 1937, opening at the Paramount Theater in New York found Benny Goodman making history again. The Paramount was the flagship of all the major movie theaters in the country that played bands on a regular basis as a focal point of their stage shows.

Goodman's two-week engagement, in the middle of Lent, wasn't expected to be anything remarkable. On the opening set, the band's first number, "Bugle Call Rag," featured Harry James playing one of his by now patented flamboyant solos. The teenagers screamed, whistled, and stomped, and some began jitterbugging in the aisles. The clamor continued throughout the set, which climaxed with "Sing, Sing, Sing," the ultimate "killer diller," with Harry James once again prominently featured. *Variety* described the wild melee of teenage emotion as "tradition-shattering in its spontaneity, its unanimity, its sincerity, its volume, in the child-like violence of its manifestations."

The Hotel Pennsylvania drew the Ivy League college students and adults. The Paramount, however, drew the average teenager who never had the opportunity to see the Goodman band perform but had bought the records after hearing them on the radio. The admission was twenty-five cents before 1:00 P.M.; many youngsters used that as a good excuse to cut school. Besides, wasn't freedom of expression the essence of Benny Goodman's music?

The first day brought in 21,000 admissions, hardly a barometer of the drawing power of the feature film, *Maid of Salem*, starring Claudette Colbert. Many youngsters sat through two or three shows. The theater also sold a staggering $900 worth of candy. As a result of wanting to see Teddy Wilson and Lionel Hampton, attendance of young blacks at the Paramount zoomed 500 percent, which greatly pleased John Hammond, a steadfast crusader for integration in the music business. As a result of the success of this engagement, the trend of presenting stage shows with big bands at movie palaces spread to many other cities.

As Harry James looked down at the sea of adoring faces from his perch atop the Goodman band's trumpet section, little did he realize that he and his band would be the object of their affections in this same theater six years later.

It is important to point out just how hard the Goodman musicians worked in those days. At the Paramount, the band played five shows a day (years later it became seven or eight), seven days a week. Simultaneously, it was working at the Hotel Pennsylvania from 7 P.M. to 1:30 A.M. every night but Sunday. This latter gig also included three "live" radio broadcasts. Rehearsals for the Tuesday night *Camel Caravan* broadcast took place after the gig on Thursday nights until 4 A.M. (In view of this kind of schedule, one has to conclude that contemporary jazz and rock bands appear to have a much easier time.)

Following the triumph at the Paramount, the Goodman band played a historic battle of the bands at the Savoy Ballroom (which had become known as "The Track") against Chick Webb, the little hunchback drummer whose band called the Savoy home. Buddy Rich once well described Webb as "a tiny man … and this big face, and big, stiff shoulders. He sat way up on a kind of throne and used twenty-eight-inch bass drums which had special pedals for his feet and he had those old goose-neck cymbal-holders. Every beat was like a bell."

The former publicist and entrepreneur, Helen Oakley, who was for many years the wife of the late jazz critic, Stanley Dance, was responsible for scheduling the event at the Savoy on May 11, the day after the band closed at the Paramount. Dance remembered, "The Savoy management was forced to call out the riot squad, fire department, reserves and mounted police in an attempt to hold in check the wildly enthusiastic crowds seeking admittance when the box office closed. Traffic was held up for hours in that vicinity. Some 4,000 people gained admission, and another 5,000 were turned away."

The intensity and success of the date were revealed in a photo of Gene Krupa showing him absolutely drenched in sweat, his tuxedo jacket almost entirely soaked through, while Harry James, sitting next to him, his lips worn raw, has the proverbial cat-that-swallowed-the-canary expression written all over his face. *Down Beat* reported that Webb's band won the battle by a slight margin because "in his very own field [Webb] is absolutely unbeatable."

Van Alexander, the noted arranger, composer, and bandleader, was then arranging for Chick Webb. A year later he wrote "A Tisket, A Tasket," the tune Ella Fitzgerald made famous when she recorded it with the Webb band. Van relates that, on that evening, "the dance floor was rocking so hard everyone was afraid the floor was going to collapse." He also recalls Gene Krupa admitting that Chick Webb had really "cut" (surpassed) him at that memorable performance.[26]

As Harry James later reminisced, "The stand was really small, and we didn't have room for our music stands. We had to play the parts from memory. This made a big impression on Webb's musicians, because, in those days, the only bands that did without stands were colored bands. Well, after that night, we never used the stands again. This was damn hard to do, too, because all the trumpet parts were split up and kept changing with every number. But from that time on, we really felt we were playing in the greatest band in the country."

After eight months in New York, the Goodman band headed west for four weeks of one-nighters culminating in its third engagement at the Palomar Ballroom. It was like unleashing a pack of hungry lions, eager to depart from their winter home and get out on the road.[27] On the bus, Harry was living on hamburgers, like everyone else. He was constantly involved in playing poker and other card games with Ziggy Elman and the other regulars.

This tour gave the American dancing public the first opportunity to witness the tall, lanky Texan who offered a bravura approach to the trumpet, and, while playing, puffed out his cheeks like two balloons (which predated Dizzy Gillespie). With the possible exception of Gene Krupa, Harry James had suddenly become the most celebrated member of the band, next to the leader.

En route to the West Coast, the band bus delivered the musicians to Marshalltown, Iowa, where the Los Angeles Limited was scheduled to make a special whistle-stop to pick them up. The bus arrived with only minutes to spare. Harry was the first band member to come off the bus, carrying his trumpet case with two brand new Selmer trumpets he had picked up a week before at the factory in Elkhart, Indiana. Suddenly, he remembered that he had forgotten his jacket and jumped back on the bus, leaving his trumpet case behind the bus. Just then, the railroad station agent ran up and instructed the bus driver to pull out and move the bus to the other end of the platform. The bus driver put the bus in reverse. It pulverized the trumpet case. The trumpets inside were now as flat as a piece of sheet music. Harry almost collapsed. Unfortunately, the train arrived at the junction but failed to stop. Harry and the other exhausted musicians got back on the bus for another long ride in order to catch the train at the next stop.[28]

While doubling at the Palomar, the Goodman aggregation made its second film appearance (following *The Big Broadcast of 1937*), this time in the Warner Bros. musical *Hollywood Hotel*. The era of the great bands coincided with the age of musical films. This movie is memorable for its brilliant depiction of the band about to reach its prime, playing "Sing, Sing, Sing," in addition to the quartet's rendition of "I've Got Rhythm." The musicians, bursting with vigor and youthful enthusiasm, are resplendent in white ducks, white polo shirts, ascots, and white shoes.

The most astonishing scene in the entire film takes place shortly after the opening shot when the famed movie musical director Busby Berkeley offers one of his trademark imaginatively choreographed scenes wherein the band members are shown being driven by liveried chauffeurs while sitting atop the boot of their white Austin convertibles playing their horns in section formation—Goodman in front, then the saxes, followed by the trombones, the trumpets, and then the rhythm section, playing the familiar Johnny Mercer/Richard Whiting Oscar-nominated composition, "Hooray for Hollywood." Once the musicians disengage from their respective convertibles at the airport to see their friend Dick Powell off to Hollywood, Harry James, carrying his trumpet, can be seen in close-up, singing a basso profundo "boom, boom, boom, boom" vocal break in the song.

Johnny "Scat" Davis, whose vocal version of "Hooray for Hollywood" made the tune famous, was added to the Goodman trumpet section for the film. In one sequence, Davis gets up to play what turned out to be one of Harry's James's solos. (This was an early use of lip synching, since the music was prerecorded.) Goodman protested so vehemently that the sequence was removed from the film. Leftover footage from *Hollywood Hotel* showing the band playing "I've Got a Heartful of Music" and "House Hop" was integrated into *Auld Lang Syne*, another Warner movie.

Following its engagement in Los Angeles, the band was booked into the Pan American Casino at the Dallas Exposition for eleven days, specifically to get the Exposition out of the red. This gave Everette and Mabel James the opportunity to visit with their son. They beamed with pride at his popularity. The *Dallas Morning News* reminded its readers that Harry James was still carrying a Dallas local union card in his wallet.[29]

Dallas, then as now, was a bastion of conservatism. The police force was seriously concerned about Teddy Wilson and Lionel Hampton performing onstage with their white cohorts. Before the band left by train for Dallas, Goodman was asked to make the trip without the two musicians, which he adamantly refused to consider. The immediate fear of the police was that their appearance on stage with Benny Goodman would result in a racial confrontation. Opening night, however, during the first concert, Goodman felt the pressure and refrained from featuring the quartet. That resulted in many patrons demanding a refund. During the second concert, the quartet came on stage and was a rousing success. There were no racial incidents, nor was there anything approaching that during the remainder of the engagement.[30]

Nevertheless, things could easily have become tense when Lionel Hampton drank from the "Whites Only" drinking fountain backstage. The police were called and, on their arrival, lectured Lionel about his "transgression." Fortunately, nothing happened, but as a result, James started referring to Hampton as "The Wiz." He exclaimed, "You're the wizard of all of us. Only a wizard would dare try that in Texas. If anybody gives you any trouble, I'll hit him with my trumpet!"[31]

A month after Harry James joined the Goodman band, Benny Goodman brought him up to Harlem to play in a jam session alongside a contingent of jazz heavyweights: Buck Clayton, Lester Young, Ben Webster, Charlie Shavers, Roy Eldridge, Count Basie, Jo Jones, and others. It was Harry's baptism by fire. In her controversial autobiography, *Lady Sings the Blues*, Billie Holiday related: "James was pretty hostile at first.... he came from Texas where Negroes are looked on like they're dirt. It showed. We had to break him out of that and also of the idea he was the world's greatest trumpet player. Buck Clayton was a big help. He blew him out with his horn.... Buck played a style that was sweeter than the others and closer to the thing Harry James was trying to do. It only took a few earfuls of Buck Clayton's playing and Harry wasn't so uppity. He'd had his lesson, and after that he came up to jam and loved it."[32]

Many critics as well as friends and acquaintances of the immortal jazz singer objected to this and other such observations she made in her book. She puts down Harry James as a young upstart and praises Buck Clayton, a fine jazz trumpeter. Later in the book she relates the love affair they had and calls him one of the most beautiful men she ever knew. It appears likely that her sexual relationship with Buck Clayton was the basis of her rancor toward Harry James.[33]

In one of his last interviews, Teddy Wilson told bassist Milt Hinton that he encountered none of the problems Jackie Robinson had initially faced with his Brooklyn Dodgers teammates because the members of the Goodman Band treated him like a member of the family.[34] He also emphasized that, although Harry James hailed from Texas, he exhibited no racial prejudice toward him. Harry referred affectionately to Teddy as "The Ice Man"; Teddy Wilson was one of the first jazz pianists one could truly label "cool."

Harry James served as a sideman on several of Teddy Wilson's Brunswick (later to become Columbia) Records small group dates that began on April 30, 1937. In describing these recording sessions, the sometimes acerbic English jazz critic, Albert McCarthy, said that James was enabled to "pay a little more attention to the content of his music," something McCarthy believed he so often failed to do when he was with Goodman, where he had indulged himself, instead, in a bit too much theatricality.[35]

It is also interesting to note that Wilson used Billie Holiday as the vocalist on his October 31 and November 9, 1938, recordings when Harry was the only trumpeter on the date. Billie must have been pleased with the exuberant solo Harry played behind her on "Everybody's Laughing."

Bill Willard, the former *Variety* reviewer in Las Vegas, said, "My first impression of Harry was that he wasn't really a jazz performer.... A little bit later, when he did a couple of things with Teddy Wilson, he began to get more into jazz."[36]

Benny Goodman had begun featuring Harry James playing "Peckin'" with the band. Its fast growing popularity is shown by the fact that Johnny Hodges's recording band, featuring Duke Ellington and other Ellington sidemen, including Cootie Williams, recorded the tune on May 20, 1937. This recording, with lyrics added highlighted by a vocal by Buddy Clark, became "Foolin' Myself." This was six days before Goodman recorded it. Essentially, "Peckin' " had come full circle.

Many consider "Just a Mood, I & II (Blue Mood)" Harry James's most important recording as a featured sideman and perhaps the most outstanding jazz record he ever made. The leader on the August 29, 1937, Brunswick session was Teddy Wilson. If there is any doubt about Harry James's ability to play the blues with complete restraint and introspection, this recording stops such discussion in its tracks.

To find out how this important recording session came about, I visited the late Red Norvo in his quaint New England-style home two blocks from the ocean in Santa Monica one cold January afternoon. He remembered the date as if it were yesterday instead of almost sixty years earlier. "I was booked by MCA, see … and we were to follow Benny into the Palomar. John Hammond met me and Mildred Bailey (Red's wife) that Sunday morning at 10:00 A.M. when the Superchief came into Los Angeles from Chicago. As soon as I got off the train, John told me, 'I want you to do a record date.' I told him, 'John, I've been on the train, and I haven't played for a few days. I can't even find my instrument. Gee, I don't even have a place to live yet.' John replied, 'Get yourself a hotel room and meet us at the studio at six o'clock down on Western Avenue.'

"Mildred and I decided to stay at the Garden of Allah—the place where all the New York writers and actors stayed. When I arrived, there was a xylophone in the studio. The musicians were Teddy Wilson, Harry, and a bass player (John Simmons) who John had found in San Diego. That was the first time that I had actually ever met Harry James." (Although he had wired him an offer to join his band less than a year before that.)

"John Hammond said, 'Play the blues!' So we said, 'OK.' Then John said to me, 'Do you want to start it?' And I said, 'No, I don't think so.' But then I started to play in E flat. I don't know why—it was just one of those things you do. Then Teddy said, 'That's a great key for it,' and Harry said, 'Yeah, it's good for me, too,' and that's the way it started.

"If I'm not mistaken, *Metronome* named 'Just a Mood' one of the 'Best Records of 1937' and Harry's solo was one of the 'Best of the Month' in *Down Beat* [all true!]. In fact, Glenn Miller later took Harry's choruses from 'Just a Mood,' along with a tune I wrote called 'Blues in E flat,' which he adapted for his orchestra. Glenn's version consisted of Harry's trumpet solo being played by four trumpets with Bobby Hackett playing lead. I think Bobby instigated the whole thing since he really admired Harry's playing."[37]

Jazz critic James Lincoln Collier quoted the *Down Beat* review that described "Just a Mood" as "a great record, accomplishing the purpose which its title suggests ... it is marred by no strained or sensational attempts to startle the listener. Each featured soloist takes four choruses, while the finale is a simple ensemble re-statement of the theme. In a somber vein, Harry James begins the piece, gradually his playing becomes more animated, but always in keeping with 'the mood.' Accompanied by Wilson, Simmons and Norvo, James narrates an incantory tale, a story of inner emotions. His phrasing; his tone are flawless—masterful trumpeting.... In the final summing up, we realize that here is a fanciful mood picture in music, created by a chamber group extraordinaire."

Collier observed that James's choruses on "Just a Mood" built to a climax, just as Louis Armstrong had done on his Hot Five recordings that had had a pronounced effect on James's early development as a trumpet player. Collier added, "James's solo on these records shows him to be a thoughtful player with an immaculate technique."

In his book *The Swing Era*, Gunther Schuller observed, "James contributes eloquent, superbly authoritative blues playing.... He is technically more assured and controlled than either Armstrong or Berigan but without quite their depth of feeling."

Almost a year later, Harry James played on a series of splendid records for Lionel Hampton on RCA that included "Shoe Shiner's Drag." Lionel Hampton proudly recalled how "Jess Stacy laid some wonderful chords down and made my solo what it became on 'On the Sunny Side of the Street.' Man, we had such respect for each other on those records. We always thought the other guy was just as good, if not better."[38]

The saxophone section for the recording sessions consisted of Benny Carter, Dave Matthews, Herschel Evans, and Babe Russin. While recording "I'm in the Mood for Swing," Evans, Lester Young's tenor saxophone rival in the Count Basie Band, and a poor sight reader, was having a problem in executing a difficult passage. James, who admired his playing, immediately sensed the problem he was facing. He leaned over and put the mute into his trumpet and played the passage for Evans. This quickly solved the problem—an example of a Texas trumpeter helping out a Texas tenor in distress. Benny Carter, who wrote the charts, in reminiscing about these sessions said, "Harry was really on his way to something great in those days."

Harry James was then given the opportunity by John Hammond to put together his own nine-piece band to make some records. His first of three dates for Brunswick was on December 1, 1937. Essentially, the sidemen were assembled for the most part from the Goodman band—Ziggy Elman, Vernon Brown, Dave Matthews, Adrian Rollini, and Dave Tough, Gene Krupa's eventual replacement—and the Basie band—Herschel Evans, Eddie Durham, who contributed the charts; Buck Clayton, Earl Warren, Jack Washington, Jo Jones, with Helen Humes on vocals. Harry's old sidekick from the Ben Pollack Band, Thurman Teague, played bass, and there was also the wonderful Harry Carney on baritone saxophone from the Duke Ellington Band.

One of the highlights was James's driving version of "*Life* Goes to a Party," similar to the version of the tune he co-wrote with Benny Goodman and arranged for the Goodman band. This composition originally featured Harry's solo and the trumpet section riffing briskly against the ensemble. It was written to commemorate the *Life* magazine feature story of the same name that described a night at the Madhattan Room that ran in the November 1, 1937, issue of *Life*, then the nation's leading magazine.

"Texas Chatter," another James original, was an additional vehicle for one of his more restrained solos, which contained some unexpected chord changes, along with a zesty piano solo by Jess Stacy. Other selections were such pop standards as "Out of Nowhere," "Wrap Your Troubles in Dreams," and "Little White Lies," as well as Count Basie's theme song, "One O'Clock Jump," which featured Herschel Evans on tenor. The spirited musicianship made the band sound larger than it was, and the involvement of Eddie Durham, Walter Page, and Jo Jones and the other Basieites caused the band to exhibit a pronounced Basie influence. "One O'Clock Jump" and "It's the Dreamer in Me," the enchanting Helen Humes's Billie Holiday-inspired vocal, both reached the top 10 on the *Billboard* pop chart for a total of eight weeks, thus marking the very first of Harry's hit records. Most important, the reception given these recordings also served to underscore an important decision Harry James had made—he had to have his own band.

When his Brunswick Records were released, James told *Down Beat*, "Count Basie's Orchestra is more to my liking than ever these days. The reed section, rhythm and trombone sections are as near to perfection as this human would want [but] Lester Young's tenor playing still flabbergasts me." This latter remark irritated John Hammond, who had called Young "the greatest tenor player in the country" in a *Down Beat* article. He couldn't understand why James used Herschel Evans instead of Young on his records. The pure fact is that Evans's solos were among the highpoints of James's recording sessions and have endured the passage of time. Sadly, Evans died unexpectedly of a heart attack on February 9, 1938, at the age of twenty-seven.

Harry James maintained a lifelong respect for Basie. A bootleg CD, *Count Basie Live! 1938 at the Famous Door*, was recorded from a CBS radio broadcast as part of its *America Dances* series, originating from the club on July 23, 1938, during the engagement that established the Basie Band. The recording features James playing on "King Porter Stomp," recreating his well-remembered solo. Although the Basie band plays essentially the original Goodman arrangement by Fletcher Henderson, the feeling is pure Basie.

These sessions produced some of the most inspired jazz recordings of the late 1930s. Benny Goodman fully realized that the critical acclaim of these recordings by his various star sidemen not only added to their popularity but to that of the band itself. Throughout these various recording dates, one can't help noticing the derring-do that is so much a part of Harry James's solos—the sense of going out on a limb but always methodically coming out right. They were vivid examples of a swaggering but inventive trumpet player at work.

On a Goodman one-nighter in the hinterlands, Louis Armstrong came by to see his old friend, Lionel Hampton. Hampton's vibes solo on Armstrong's seminal recording of "Shine" with Les Hite's Orchestra in 1931 had been one of the first important jazz recordings to include a vibraphone solo. Hamp waited in the wings most evenings until Goodman called for the quartet to come out to play.

Armstrong, also standing in the wings, watched Harry James intently as he soloed on several numbers. Suddenly, Louis exclaimed to Hampton, "That white boy—he plays like a jig!"[39] This compliment might be considered politically incorrect in today's parlance, but it is a perfect example of the way Armstrong used to express himself. Moreover, it certainly explains Louis Armstrong's profound respect for Harry James's playing.

The year 1937 ended on a particularly high note for Harry James, for it was announced that he had won the highly coveted *Down Beat* poll as the leading trumpet player of the year, winning over Bunny Berigan, Louis Armstrong, and Roy Eldridge in that order. This was without a doubt the most important honor he had yet achieved. The previous year he hadn't received a single vote.

To compound the honor, at the same time Harry was also the winner of the *Metronome* poll. He acknowledged this award by exclaiming, "How can they possibly vote for me when Louis is in the same contest?"

Jimmy Maxwell remembered seeing James one night after hearing a *Camel Caravan* broadcast in which he played his sizzling version of Louis Armstrong's classic "Shine" that revealed Louis's influence. "I made the most tactless remark I think I ever made to anyone when I asked Harry, 'If you can play so much like Louis, why don't you do it all the time?' He replied, 'Well, maybe you don't like the way I play. But the way I play is my way and when people hear me they say, 'Oh, that's Harry James.' They don't say, 'Oh, that's the guy that copies Louis.' He had a good point there that stuck with me."[40]

Wynn Nathanson of the Tom Fitzdale Agency was then doing public relations for the *Camel Caravan*. In an attempt to bring even greater attention to the Goodman band, Nathanson approached the renowned classical music impresario Sol Hurok, who in turn met with Willard Alexander, about presenting Benny Goodman's Orchestra, along with the trio and the quartet in a Carnegie Hall concert. It was scheduled for Sunday, January 16, 1938.

Beatrice Lillie, the beloved English comedienne, was asked to supply comedy relief from the program of swing music; however, she wisely declined the offer. A decision was made to add members of the Basie and Ellington bands to join with Goodman, Vernon Brown, Harry, and Gene Krupa in a jam session as part of the program.

The members of the Goodman band were all in a highly nervous state for several days preceding the concert. Carnegie Hall had been sold out for days and seats were put on stage on either side of the band. Pickets were out front of the hall protesting the band's playing a benefit for Spanish Loyalists.

Harry James was asked for his thoughts about the impending event. Perhaps reflecting on his own initial anxiety in joining the Goodman band thirteen months earlier, he said, "Sure I'm nervous, you know—Carnegie—after all." On the night of the concert, just before the musicians walked on stage at 8:45 P.M., Harry uttered the now famous line, "I feel like a whore in church."

The concert opened with Edgar Sampson's new arrangement of "Don't Be That Way," one of the few fresh pieces of material written specifically for the concert. Harry was later to use "Don't Be That Way" as his opener for almost all of his own band's performances.

When James got up to play his solo, the crowd applauded enthusiastically. This was followed by Gene Krupa's drum solo. The tension in the venerable hall was suddenly lifted. "One O'Clock Jump," with Harry's crackling solo, got an even greater response. Then, in the "Twenty Years of Jazz" portion of the program, James again paid homage to Louis Armstrong with "Shine," followed by "*Life* Goes to a Party." On the jam session number, "Honeysuckle Rose," he had several important moments, perhaps reflecting his happiness in having the opportunity to jam with his comrades Buck Clayton, Bill Basie, Johnny Hodges, and Harry Carney. After his solo on "Loch Lomond," it appeared as if Harry James was the hit of the night. Then, to close, Goodman brought out his showpiece, Louis Prima's "Sing, Sing, Sing," which originally had been arranged by Jimmy Mundy.

Chu Berry's composition "Christopher Columbus" had been tacked onto the piece, and over a period of time a head arrangement of the tune was developed by members of the band. Harry James's major solo, one of several on the tune, was so brilliantly conceived and executed with such boldness, showmanship, and circus flash that it is difficult to believe that he was only twenty-one years old at the time. His solos at this concert continue to rank among the most significant recorded trumpet solos of the Swing Era.

The concert ended with an encore, an exuberant version of "Big John's Special," a tune written in tribute to a Harlem bartender who was a master mixologist. It had been part of the repertoire of Fletcher Henderson's band and was written by Henderson's brother, Horace. James, Ziggy Elman, and Goodman supplied the solos. After the concert was over, the musicians fanned out to various places. Many of them headed for the Savoy to see a "battle of the bands" between Chick Webb and Count Basie, presided over by New York's leading disc jockey, Martin Block.

The response of the press to the Carnegie Hall concert was inconclusive and might even be considered negative. The New York newspapers that deigned to send critics to cover the concert sent their classical reviewers. The extremely influential music critic of the *New York Times*, Olin Downes, had little understanding, much less knowledge, of jazz. In his piece, he wrote that he had attended the concert with great curiosity, but the essence of his review was that "swing is a bore." It was his belief that he hadn't encountered "a single player ... or one original or interesting musical phrase" during the course of the concert. Deems Taylor, the eminent musicologist wrote, "A jam session is only a long cadenza and cadenzas bore me."

Down Beat headlined its review of the concert by H.E.P. (get it?) with, "Goodman came, saw and laid a Golden Egg."[41] It was only George Simon's *Metronome* review that acknowledged Harry James's important contributions: "On '*Life* Goes to a Party,' Harry, as well as Gene, led the devastating attack upon Carnegie walls, which, by the way, held nobly." He also contended that "'Honeysuckle Rose' was uninspired, uninspiring, and lagged pretty sadly until Harry James bit into a few choice figures toward its close."

Certainly, the elegance and complete spontaneity of Jess Stacy's solo near the end of "Sing, Sing, Sing" justified its considerable praise. Goodman, Krupa, and, for that matter, the entire band played superbly, but it was the release of the Columbia album of the concert (delayed until

November 1950, shortly after the acetates of the concert were discovered in the closet of Benny's New York apartment) that clearly showed the mastery of James's trumpet throughout the concert.

In 1924, after the triumphant debut of George Gershwin's "Rhapsody in Blue" in New York's Aeolian Hall with Paul Whiteman's Orchestra, one critic absurdly contended that Paul Whiteman "had made a lady out of jazz." The resultant prestige of Sol Hurok's presentation of Benny Goodman in Carnegie Hall and its ultimate success had indeed brought that "lady" into full womanhood.

This was the apex of Benny Goodman and his Orchestra and his satellite groups. It would never be quite the same again. During a March engagement at the Earle Theater in Philadelphia, Krupa and Goodman had an argument that proved to be the end of a long-simmering antagonism. Gene yelled out, "You're the 'King of Swing,' so let's hear you swing." A few days later, again on stage, Gene shouted out, "Eat some shit, Pops!" and abruptly left to start his own band. This was a devastating loss—the first of several important changes that caused the Goodman band to begin a downward slide. Harry James maintained, however, that "Benny's too great a guy to work for" and said he had no plans to leave for at least a year.

Krupa was replaced for a time by Lionel Hampton, then Dave Tough, and later Buddy Schutz. Tough relied on his incredible technique on the cymbals and offered a more understated and musical approach. But the various switches in drummers had absolutely no adverse effect on James's playing. Harry reflected, "Along comes Davy with a much simpler and just as terrific a drive. It's wonderful the way this Tough man remains unobtrusively in the background, at the bottom of everything, pushing you ahead gently but firmly, from almost underneath your chair, staying with you at all times in everything you play. He gives you an entirely different kind of boot than Gene does—so different ... that it's hard to believe that they're both drummers!"

An additional comment of Harry's at the time shed even more light on what constituted his ideal drummer: "Gene Krupa's left foot, Jo Jones' left hand, Davy Tough's right hand, and Lionel Hampton's right foot."[42] (Gene, in turn, had been quoted as saying that "Harry's hands were particularly suited to drumming.")

Jerry Jerome, who had become a Lester Young disciple after seeing the neophyte Basie Band when it debuted at the Reno Club in Kansas City, in December 1938 replaced Bud Freeman on tenor saxophone, who in turn had replaced Babe Russin. (According to Jerome, more than eighty saxophonists worked for Benny Goodman between the beginning of the historic trip west in 1935 and August 1938.) Jerome remembers Harry James as being a free spirit who was always in search of mischief to entertain his bandmates offstage, yelling out, "Wahoo!" "Harry would negotiate getting some porno films, which would be shown between the dinner and supper shows in one of the musicians' rooms at the Hotel Pennsylvania. Somebody would light up a joint and pass it around. We would laugh hysterically because they were so corny."

Another time when the band was playing at the Waldorf-Astoria, Harry James and Jerry Jerome went to the men's bar after one of the sets. As Jerry recalls, "I ordered a '7&7' (which so many young drinkers used to prefer in those days). Harry told the bartender, 'Bring him a Canadian Club. We're a Canadian Club band!'"[43]

This remark well represented the image the members of the Goodman band had of themselves. They believed they deserved the best of everything.

When it came to playing softball, Harry James was dead serious. He was the captain of the Goodman team and usually its starting pitcher, occasionally its first baseman, and always the cleanup hitter. Lionel Hampton was his battery mate. The usual lineup included Vernon Brown, first base; Chris Griffin, second base; Red Ballard, shortstop; Noni Bernardi, third base; Arthur Rollini, left field; various center fielders, and Dave Matthews, right field. The Goodman team proudly sported its own uniforms as well as its own equipment. There were frequent stops on the road to practice whenever someone spotted an empty ballfield.

In one such spontaneous intra-band game, James, playing first base, was hit in the shins by a line drive off Goodman's bat. Perhaps it was Harry's anger over what happened, but more likely it was his cunning under fire. He pulled the hidden ball trick on Benny. The clarinetist was completely chagrined at what had transpired and stormed off the field.

The Goodman team played teams from other big bands. One of the most hard-fought games was against Count Basie's band, during which Lester Young hit a long fly to left field for an inside-the-park home run, but the Goodman band finally prevailed. The team had a perfect won and lost record, which made it first in the "Big Band League."

After a successful career playing with other big bands such as Bob Crosby, Tommy Dorsey, and Charlie Barnet, Noni Bernardi segued into politics. He spent a total of "thirty-two years and one month" with the Los Angeles City Council. Noni remarked with great certainty, "I firmly believe that if a major league baseball team had ever offered Harry a contract, he would have left music immediately."[44] Since then I have often quoted Bernardi's remark; several people who knew Harry James then concur with Noni's belief.

Eventually, Louise Tobin joined Harry in New York and, for a time, they lived in a series of shabby apartment hotels before moving to the Whitby

Apartments. Louise acknowledges that she was a terrible cook but she could whip up Harry's favorite dish—red beans and rice[45]—also a favorite of Louis Armstrong's. Money was still a problem. Even then, contrary to the myth of the time, two couldn't live as cheaply as one. This was despite the fact that Harry had been raised by Benny to $200 a week and was later given even more money.

Louise Tobin sent me copies of a few scraps of grid paper dating back to this difficult period on which the couple had made meticulous I.O.U. notations. One series of figures, for instance, indicated "Harry owes me $1.57" and "Louise owes me $.91." These were telltale signs of a young couple truly struggling to make ends meet.

Louise was compelled to start singing again, and accepted a series of jobs around New York. Harry didn't want her around the band. She naively went along with his wishes, which was one reason she remained unaware of his constant womanizing.

It was during the Goodman years that Harry became friendly with Frank "Pee Wee" Monte (né Montalbano), who served as the band boy, but an unusually good one. Anybody who could repair instruments as easily as Pee Wee did and who could keep Benny Goodman supplied with an endless cache of reeds was an invaluable asset.

"Pee Wee" hailed from Belleville, New Jersey. He had been a saxophonist with Larry Funk's "Band of A Thousand Melodies," Roger Wolfe Kahn, and Johnny Watson before Chris Griffin got him the job with Goodman. He joined the band at the Palomar Ballroom in September 1937. The friendship between Harry and Pee Wee grew and was later to make an indelible imprint on both their lives.[46]

The success Harry James had enjoyed with Benny Goodman, and the distinct impression he had made on audiences, indicated that this was an ideal time for him to go out on his own. Willard Alexander, Billy Goodhart, Manie Sachs, "Sonny" Werblin, Irving Lazar (yes, "Swifty"), and the remainder of the corps of MCA Variety Department agents had already begun to show serious interest in him. (This is the same process agents have followed in the past and, no doubt, will forever undertake when they encounter a potential superstar ready to venture forth on his or her own.)

Years later, Harry James described the musical Frankenstein that was associated with his countless renditions of "Sing, Sing, Sing." "I was going through a real mental thing, and it was all built around 'Sing, Sing, Sing.' I'd been sick and they gave me some experimental pills—sulphur pills—only they weren't very refined yet. Well, they wigged me out, and it happened the first time just as I was supposed to get up and play my chorus on 'Sing, Sing, Sing.' I just couldn't make it. I fell back in my chair. Ziggy said to me, 'Get up!' but I couldn't, so when he saw what was happening, he got up and played my solo. I was completely out of my mind.

"It happened again another time, too, and so every time the band played 'Sing, Sing, Sing' I'd get bugged and scared it would start all over again. You know, that Stravinsky-type thing that the trombones and then the trumpets play just before the chorus? Well, that would really set me off. I tried to explain it to Benny, and I'd even ask him to play 'Sing, Sing, Sing' early in the evening, so I could relax the rest of the night. But, of course, that was his big number, and I couldn't blame him for wanting to hold off. Finally I just left the band. I couldn't trust myself anymore."

Starting his own band was not without certain complications. For, although Harry James was more than ready to leave, he was in the middle of an employment contract with Benny Goodman that had six months to run. Goodman was now paying him $250 a week. He was certainly well worth it since he had become the biggest star in the band.

As the time approached for James to leave, Goodman reneged on his promise to grant him an early release from his contract, claiming it was only because he couldn't find an adequate replacement. This made Harry furious. As Loren Schoenberg, the saxophonist and Goodman scholar, pointed out: "At last, Harry had had his fill of Benny. In the middle of his solo on 'Goodbye,' Harry would look at Benny and sing out 'Go to hell, go to hell.' during the closing refrain." Schoenberg also informed me that once, when Harry was so exasperated about how much Benny practiced his clarinet, he quipped, "I think he goes to bed with that thing."[47]

Finally, Benny decided to restore his brother Irving to the trumpet section. Of course, the irony was that Harry had replaced Irving a little over two years earlier. Goodman, ever the enigma, in a conversation with Arthur Rollini, referred to Harry as "a machine,"[48] yet in the ensuing years he often spoke of him with great respect.

The years under Everette's tutelage and the time he had spent on various bands including Ben Pollack's were certainly invaluable in the development of Harry's musical talent. Perhaps, more important, the two years James spent with Benny Goodman provided a musical finishing school second to none. He had matured rapidly as a musician, playing the best arrangements alongside the best musicians in the best venues. He had learned what really makes a band tick—how it functions on the road, how to pace a performance, and how to engage an audience—in addition to the myriad other elements involved in leading a big band.

Benny Goodman had come to appreciate his sense of time so much that he had Harry count off the tempos during the *Camel Caravan* radio shows. As James observed, "One thing Benny could never do was read lines and beat off tempos at the same time ... he'd finish an introduction for a band number and then there'd be dead air while he just stood there getting set to beat off the tempo, so finally they had me beat off all the tunes."

In addition, Goodman chose James to lead the band when he was otherwise engaged. This was besides having him sit in on drums when he was having his never-ending troubles with drummers in the immediate post-Krupa period.

Harry James may have been ready to start his own band, but once again money problems were a major obstacle. According to Harry, "When I started the band, I had $400—that was my bank account."

Who was going to bankroll his new band? Once again, Benny Goodman came to the forefront.

4

Ciribiribin

The year 1939 saw World War II start in Europe, when Hitler's troops invaded Poland, and Britain and France declared war on Germany. In the United States, swing was still the popular music of the land. It was a time when "everybody knew everybody," as arranger Bill Finnegan described the warm feeling he observed among musicians.[1] Some of the most enduring popular songs continued to be written. There was, however, serious apprehension on the part of many Americans who saw the oncoming specter of war.

Harry James was going through an intensive period of trying to figure out how to put a band together, one that would reflect his own musical tastes. The latter task wasn't to prove too difficult—it would be modeled after the Benny Goodman band. In fact, he tried to enlist the services of two musicians from the Goodman saxophone section: Jerry Jerome, who turned him down,[2] and the other his old Texan buddy from Ben Pollack days, Dave Matthews, who chose to join Harry in his new musical venture.

The James band would be booked by MCA, and Gerard ("Gerry") Barrett left the agency to serve as Harry's personal manager. Pee Wee Monte's brother, Al, who had worked as a band boy for Hal Kemp (he would be called a "roadie" today), assumed the same chore with the Harry James Orchestra. Actually, the association with MCA had been "arranged" two months after the Carnegie Hall jazz concert when Benny Goodman convinced Harry to commit himself to signing with MCA. However, the quid pro quo for Goodman's inducing James to sign with MCA was its agreement to kick back to Benny 5 percent of the commissions the agency would receive from booking Harry's new band.

On December 23, 1938, Harry James recorded for the last time with the Goodman band at the RCA Victor studios. Among the four sides from that session were "Louise," "Whispering," "I'll Always Be in Love with You," and the record that turned out to be the most significant, "Bach Goes to Town." After that recording, Harry did three more *Camel Caravan* broadcasts, the last of which was on January 10, 1939. Jess Stacy noted that "when Harry left, Benny would never admit it, but the guys in the band knew something was wrong.... the band was never the same."[3]

Before starting to record with his own band, however, Harry James had two other recording sessions to complete. Since he was a winner of the *Metronome* poll, he played alongside fellow poll winners Bunny Berigan, Tommy Dorsey, Jack Teagarden, Benny Goodman, Hymie Shertzer, Arthur Rollini, Bob Haggart, Ray Bauduc, and others on "The Blues" at an RCA recording session at Webster Hall beginning at 1:00 A.M. on January 11, 1939. Harry's solo on "The Blues" contained much of the quality of "Just a Mood," although it made considerably less impact with critics and record buyers.

John Hammond had another recording idea for James. He decided to record two 78 records, pairing him with Pete Johnson and Albert Ammons, the two foremost practitioners of boogie-woogie piano, then enjoying a substantial revival. They were accompanied by Johnny Williams on bass and Eddie Dougherty on drums. The results were extraordinary, as James once again illustrated that the blues were indeed his forte. "Boo-Woo," "Woo-Woo," and "Home James" were the highlights, with Harry demonstrating his complete understanding of boogie-woogie. He fit in easily, playing muted trumpet both in unison and in contrast to the eight-to-the-bar tempo laid down by the two soulful pianists.

Finally, all his recording commitments had been met, and James was ready to take the big step. As Ross Firestone documented in his definitive biography of Benny Goodman, *Swing Swing Swing*, James signed a formal agreement with Goodman that ran contrary to all his supposed "street smarts." The terms of this contract called for him to be able to borrow up to $7,000 from Goodman during the first year of his band, but the loan had to be repaid within two years. In exchange, Benny Goodman was to receive one-third of James's net earnings over the next decade. After nine-ty days, Benny could begin collecting his full share of James's net profits. This usurious deal demonstrated Benny Goodman's incredible duplicity as well as the kind of legal and financial counsel he had at his disposal, ingredients that helped make him a millionaire by the age of thirty.

Now that he had financing, although hardly an equitable arrangement, Harry James could go about selecting the personnel for his new band. With the help of Dave Matthews and Drew Page, he looked toward Texas for help in choosing as a nucleus nine musicians whose musical abilities he knew of firsthand. The only non-Texans picked were Jack Gardner from New York, Jack Palmer from Rome, New York, and Ralph Hawkins from Washington, D.C.

The complete lineup that first rehearsed as a band at Nola's in the Roseland Ballroom building in New York on January 5, 1939, consisted of: saxophonists Dave Matthews, Claude Lakey, Bill Luther, and Drew Page; trombones Russell Brown and Truett Jones; the trumpets, in addition to Harry, included Tommy Gonsulin, Claude Bowen, and Jack Palmer. The rhythm section was made up of "Jumbo" Jack Gardner on piano, Bryan "Red" Kent on guitar, Thurman Teague (Harry's old friend from Pollack days) on bass, and Ralph Hawkins on drums. Bernice Byers, an alumna of Martin Block's WNEW *Make Believe Ballroom* radio show, was the vocalist. Andy Gibson, a black arranger who had written arrangements for Harry on his earlier album and for Charlie Barnet (then referred to by patrons of Harlem's Apollo Theater as "The White Duke") began arranging jump tunes. In all, there were eighteen arrangements in the book to start along with a few "head" arrangements (band-concocted arrangements).

On that January day, Jack Palmer was about to enter the subway to go into Manhattan from Jackson Heights when he encountered Jerry Jerome. When Jerome asked where he was headed, Palmer replied, "I'm going into town to see what's happening." Jerry told him, "You know, Harry James is starting a band. He's having a rehearsal at Nola's. Why don't you go in there and say I suggested that you stop by."

As the eighty-six-year-old Palmer, who is still active as a musician ["I still got chops; it's all in the breathing," he says] remembers: "When I got to Nola's, the band was on a break. Harry asked me if I had my horn with me. I told him I did, so I sat in and played lead on a couple of things. After the next break, he called me aside and said, 'Are you interested?' I said, 'Yeah, sure.' He said, 'Well, you know you won't get much chance to play any solos, and I know you used to play jazz with Red Norvo.' Anyway, I said, 'Yeah, I understand that. That's all right. I'll love listening to you.' I was so awed to get the chance to work for him that I joined the band at $85 a week, which was what Red was paying me when I left his band. Eighty-five dollars a week was great in those days, even though I was married and had a child." In addition to playing trumpet, Jack was assigned the vocals on the scat tunes such as "Tain't What You Do" and "Well, All Right."[4]

I asked a drummer who had firsthand knowledge of the James band at the time, "Who do you think was the best musician in that band?" He replied, "I think this was about as even a band as you could find, and I think Harry did that on purpose. I believe he hired guys that were about the same caliber of musicianship, and it was the kind of band he didn't have to pay a whole lot of money for to put together. The thing about Harry was he could make a good musician out of an ordinary musician."

During the previous months, Harry had become friendly with Bernard "Buddy" Rich, the wild and cocky teenager recently acclaimed for his flashy drumming with Artie Shaw, and whom he had first admired for his playing in Chicago at the Gay 90's. When he saw him play at the Hickory House on 52nd Street with Joe Marsala's group, James had told Gene Krupa and other members of the Goodman band, "Man, this kid over at the Hickory House is going to scare you to death. Wait 'til you hear him!" Unfortunately, Buddy Rich turned down Harry James's offer and remained with Shaw; the James-Rich musical association was postponed for fourteen years, except for all-star band dates.

When the Artie Shaw Band opened an engagement at the Blue Room of the Hotel Lincoln in New York on October 26, 1938 (now the Milford Plaza), it registered with great impact, partly as a result of the huge success of its hit "Begin the Beguine." Shaw followed that up with the hit "Indian Love Call" and "Back Bay Shuffle." The Shaw band had now displaced Benny Goodman as the leading swing band in the land.

Strange as it may seem, Artie Shaw met Harry James only once, at a publicity photo call in 1941 of various bandleaders at the Hotel Lincoln. "I had seen him with Ben Pollack," remembered Shaw. "He was quite a trumpet player then, but I couldn't afford him at the time."[5]

A band's theme song was its signature and extremely important in establishing its musical image. It had to be distinctive and recognizable, especially in a band's infancy when it would be getting its first nationwide exposure on radio. For his theme song, Artie Shaw wrote a moody, ominous-sounding instrumental, which he called "Nightmare," that musically characterized his feelings toward the music business.

Harry James selected "Ciribiribin," a Neapolitan folk song, written in 1898 by Rudolph Thaler and Alberto Pestalozza. It was first brought to James's attention by the saxophonist, George Koenig, then his roommate on the road with the Goodman band. He first recorded it on April 2, 1938, while leading a band on a *Saturday Night Swing Session* radio program on CBS. As a member of the Goodman band, he recorded it again on October 13, 1938, with a Fletcher Henderson arrangement. On September 30, 1939, James guest starred with Goodman on a *Camel Caravan* broadcast playing the Henderson arrangement once again.

James's rousing, jet-propelled version, which he also arranged, was a perfect showcase for his fiery trumpet playing with its echoes of circus music. He didn't record it with his own band until April 6, 1939. "Ciribiribin" was recorded again on November 8 of the same year by the band's vocalist, Frank Sinatra, marking his next to last recording with the James band—and his only uninspiring recording with Harry James. Trumpeter Jon Faddis offered a modern version of the tune, rarely recorded today, in an album on Epic Records in 1989, and Warren Beatty was seen "playing" it on soprano saxophone in his film *Heaven Can Wait.*

Joe Pardee, Harry's longtime fan, explained that the "ripping" sound in Harry's version of "Ciribiribin" stems directly from the influence of Muggsy Spanier. "Remember, Harry knew Muggsy's work well before he replaced him with Ben Pollack's band," Joe said. "Muggsy had that open style and that fierce attack that Harry liked."[6]

Harry James told George T. Simon in a *Metronome* interview shortly before his band's debut, "I want to have a band that really swings and that's easy to dance to all the time. Too many bands, in order to be sensational, hit tempos that you just can't dance to. We're emphasizing middle tempos. They can swing as much and they're certainly more danceable." He was to maintain this same musical credo for the next forty-four years.

The uniforms that Harry selected for the band reflected his circus background. His musicians were resplendent in bright red mess jackets and white bow ties sitting atop winged collars that were combined with black dress trousers.

The leaders of the "Mickey Mouse" bands such as Guy Lombardo and Lawrence Welk established a rapport with the audience, constantly explaining their music, acknowledging the work of their sidemen, and slipping in a few jokes. On the other hand, the jazz bandleaders, as exemplified by Benny Goodman and Count Basie, let the music virtually speak for itself and felt little need for extensive verbal communication with the audience. Harry James favored the latter approach. It also veiled the withdrawn nature of his own personality. As he once told Louise Tobin, "I live in my own world. Nobody gets in there."[7] His lack of education, added to his innate shyness, influenced his difficulty in relating to the audience.

Everette James opened an account for him in a Beaumont bank to handle the band's payroll. Harry would send all the checks from the dates home for him to deposit. Everette dealt with one specific woman teller, who one day asked him, "What are you going to do with all this money you're putting in this bank account for Harry?" His father replied, "Well, he's doing all right now, but he might need it one of these days. The band might not go well."

Now that the band was formed, it was time to go on the road. A few break-in dates in the greater New York area began in early February, one at the St. George Hotel in Brooklyn in a battle of the bands with Louis Armstrong. Harry didn't realize that he was scheduled to play opposite Armstrong until he arrived at the hotel. It was an unexpected thrill to find that he was working opposite his musical idol.

James related: "I was pretty nervous anyway. It took me an hour even to decide to play—I just sat there and listened, y'know—and Louis was just great that night ... but it was quite an experience. At least there wasn't anything that would happen after that that we could get that nervous about, I'll tell you that!" Armstrong was his usual congenial self. "He was so beautiful," Harry James remembered. At the conclusion of the date, Armstrong came over to wish him good luck with his new band.

Harry James and his Orchestra's first important date was a one-week engagement that began on February 9, 1939, at the Garden Terrace of the Ben Franklin Hotel in Philadelphia. It was essential that a major hotel endorse James's music so that MCA could use the hotel music buyer as a reference for booking further location dates.

George Simon, once again, offered praise (with some qualifications) in a *Metronome* review: "Outfit gets a swell swing, thanks mostly to great arrangements by Andy Gibson, to Dave Matthews' sax, Ralph Hawkins' drumming, and Harry's horn. Hotel management insists upon unnaturally soft music. Band complies.... Some rough spots still obvious: bass intonation varies; saxes, brilliant most of the time, not yet consistent. Missed: a good hot clarinet and ditto trombone.... Personalities of Harry as leader and Bernice Byers, warbler, fine."

In the April 1939 issue, Danny Baxter of *Down Beat* magazine singled out Dave Matthews's crisp alto saxophone: "Harry lets Dave take a chorus on just about every stomp tune." The reviewer added, "The James Orchestra left Philly more polished and thrilling than many another outfit playing smarter spots than the Franklin." He concluded: "It's a safe bet that the band will return after (Red) Norvo, who followed Harry, winds up his run."

Unfortunately, Harry James's music turned out to be somewhat contrary to what the Ben Franklin management had in mind. What the hotel really wanted was a ricky-tick band that differed from James's brassy brand of swing. The Garden Terrace engagement did have one important advantage: four radio remotes per week, two of which were national. By the end of this booking, James's new band had gained some admirers, and even the staid patrons of the room began to rather like swing music.

From there the fledgling band cut its first record on February 20 in New York for Brunswick, the "Two O'Clock Jump." It was destined to become one of the biggest of all its instrumental hits; it was actually only a slight variation on Basie's "One O'Clock Jump." As James explained it, "I added triplets the last few times I played it with Goodman, so when I recorded it I decided to call it the 'Two O'Clock Jump.'"

A few weeks later, James recorded Ziggy Elman and Johnny Mercer's new tune, "And the Angels Sing," with Bernice Byers on the vocal. Harry's version didn't compare favorably with Ziggy's patented Frahlich-style trumpet solos and Martha Tilton's vocal, perhaps the most memorable of her entire career. Consequently, it wasn't the commercial success that the Goodman version was. "And the Angels Sing" became one of Benny Goodman's biggest selling records; years later Elman adapted it as the theme song of his short-lived big band. James later recorded a very compelling version of "Angels" in 1955 with Benny Goodman for Capitol that was released at the time of Universal's *The Benny Goodman Story*. On the Goodman record, Harry played in his by now familiar style, but his interpretation still revealed the influence of Ziggy's original version.

For several months, the James band failed to register on records, in some measure due to the inadequate sound quality of the Brunswick recording studio. George Simon contended that the band was much more lively and swinging in person. Harry began playing prettier jazz, featuring himself on ballads like "I Surrender Dear," "I'm in the Market for You," "Just a Gigolo," and "Black and Blue." These were tunes that had been recorded by Louis Armstrong, but James played them in a more calculated, albeit melodic style that was both romantic and danceable. These renditions were a far cry from his flamboyant sixteen-bar jazz solos with Goodman during which, as Harry described it, "I'd have to cram everything into that short space."

The competition of Shaw, Goodman, Tommy Dorsey, and, by the summer of 1939, his old friend from Ben Pollack days, Glenn Miller, caused serious problems for James's band in securing important dates. MCA couldn't come up with key hotel and theater bookings. The lack of hit records caused the failure of the one-nighters to draw the enthusiastic crowds required to establish the necessary word-of-mouth for a new band. The band began working some dates for as little as $350 a night. The jumps between dates became longer and simultaneously the guarantees began to decrease. Dance-hall operators often complained about the loudness of Harry's new outfit.

Despite this apparent nonstop series of misfortunes, James believed things would eventually turn around. Louise Tobin remembered, "He took all the blows, but he never stopped believing in his band."[8] Nevertheless, it was terribly disillusioning for Harry to fall from the heights of the Goodman years that had been filled with adulation. No less an authority than Benny Goodman himself had once remarked, "The life of a bandleader is the most confining thing in the world."

As an example of his uncertainty, Louise further recalled that Harry was sure to call his father every night during the early days and months of the band's existence, reporting to him on what went on that night at the gig. Obviously, Everette's counsel meant a great deal to him during these trying days.

Connie Haines replaced Bernice Byers in May. She was born Yvonne Marie Antoinette JaMais. At twelve, she began singing all over Florida. After winning Fred Allen's Amateur Hour at the Roxy Theater in New York and then the Major Bowes Amateur Hour, she continued to sing with bands. She came up to New York for auditions at the age of sixteen. She first auditioned for Larry Shayne, who ran Famous Music, the music publishing company for Paramount Pictures, located in the Brill Building at 49th and Broadway. The young singer was told, "There's a famous bandleader who has been listening to you from the other room. He's looking for a girl singer to join his band."

A few minutes later, James sat down in front of her while she sang, "I Cried for You" and "I Can't Give You Anything but Love." In the middle of her second song, he abruptly got up and left the room.

"I was furious. I thought he was the rudest man I'd ever met," said Haines, "but my mother reminded me I was supposed to audition for the William Morris Agency. Two hours later, Harry called to apologize."

"I'm sorry I didn't have the time to hear you finish your second song," he said, "but I had to meet my band at Penn Station to go to Philadelphia. That's where I'm calling you from. But I heard enough. You're terrific. How would you like to join my band?"

"I don't know, Mr. James," she replied. "When would you want me to start?"

"Tonight!" exclaimed Harry James. "Forty dollars a week, opening at the Ben Franklin Hotel. I'll meet the train at the 30th Street station." She was astounded, but accepted the offer.

That night, after the first set, Harry James explained to her that Yvonne Marie Antoinette JaMais would never fit on a marquee. "Think how much radio time it's going to take just saying it," he pointed out. "No, you look like a Connie to me." He stroked his ample chin. "Haines. Connie Haines. It goes with James."

Haines thought he said "Ames," which resulted in her signing her autograph as "Connie Ames." During the Mutual Broadcasting Company radio remote that night, when she was announced as "Connie Haines," she discovered her new professional name.[9]

In hopes of finding a way to jump-start the band's fortunes, Manie Sachs at MCA took a personal interest in Harry James. This was especially important since Willard Alexander had gone over to William Morris to take over its band department. Manie and Harry soon formed a close personal relationship. One of Manie's suggestions was that Harry should hire a male singer to work alongside Connie Haines, perhaps hoping to duplicate the musical rapport Bob Eberly and Helen O'Connell were then developing with Jimmy Dorsey's band.

In mid-June, Harry James and his Orchestra got its first booking at the Paramount Theater, albeit for scale, working with singer Jane Froman. Harry later referred justifiably to any Paramount engagement as "the toughest of all jobs." One night, after the last show, in their room at the Paramount Hotel, Harry was taking a nap while Louise was packing a suitcase for a late train to Boston to work with Bobby Hackett's band. She was listening to WNEW's *Dance Parade* from 11:30 P.M. to midnight on a remote broadcast, originating from the Rustic Cabin in North Jersey with Harold Arden's band. Arden featured a singer who quickly caught Louise's attention.

In recalling this extremely significant radio broadcast, Louise said, "I thought, 'There's a fair singer!' Now I didn't think he was fantastic. I just felt, 'Now that's a good singer.' I knew Harry was looking for a male singer. I decided to wake him up. I said to him, 'Honey, you might want to hear this kid on the radio. The boy singer on this show sounds pretty good.' Harry got up, and I left to catch my train."[10]

Harry James listened attentively to the singer whose name wasn't mentioned. He admired his phrasing. There was a tenderness in the way he delivered a love song. The next night, after the last show at the Paramount, Harry James, along with Gerry Barrett and Claude Bowen, journeyed to the Rustic Cabin, located on Route 9W in Englewood Cliffs, New Jersey, two miles from the entrance to the George Washington Bridge.

James asked the manager of the club about the singer he had heard on the radio. "We don't have a singer, but we do have an emcee who sings a little bit," replied the manager. The emcee and singer had also filled in as a waiter on occasion during the eighteen months he had been working at the Rustic Cabin. Earlier, he had sung at the roadhouse when trombonist Bill Henri led the band.

As James recalled, "This very thin guy with swept back hair ... climbed on the stage. He'd sung only eight bars of 'Night and Day' when I felt the hairs on the back of my neck rising. I knew he was destined to be a great vocalist."

Harry James requested "Begin the Beguine." He noticed that the singer had an unusually intimate quality. After the set, he introduced himself and asked the young vocalist if he would be interested in joining his band. "I almost broke his arm so he wouldn't get away 'cause I was dying to get out of that place," recalled the singer.

The singer was Francis Albert (Frank) Sinatra. He was not an unknown to song pluggers, radio producers, and agents—they had all heard of him. He had begun to create a name for himself around New York, having sung on other radio shows on WNEW, WOR (then in Newark), and WAAT in Jersey City. When James saw him, he had already been turned down by Glenn Miller for a job, had just auditioned for Jack Miles, who was leaving Guy Lombardo to start his own band, and was also rehearsing with Bob Chester's new band.

As the story goes, six years earlier, during the week of March 3, 1933, Sinatra had seen Bing Crosby perform at a Jersey City vaudeville house, accompanied by Crosby's friend from Paul Whiteman days, guitarist Eddie Lang. This experience instantly decided Frank Sinatra's choice of a career.

As a member of "The Hoboken Four" who won the Major Bowes Amateur Hour at the Capitol Theater in New York on September 8, 1935, he had toured cross-country by bus and train for several months with sixteen other acts, making $50 a week plus meals. This tour, his first away from his Hoboken environs, proved a valuable experience. The next few years led to all kinds of singing jobs—Italian weddings, bar mitzvahs, radio shows, and club dates. He was determined to make it. He believed that he was going to be the biggest thing around; he had no idea that his artistry would eventually revolutionize American popular music.

He had designed a plan for his career. Singing with a name band was the logical way to get exposure and build an audience. And who better to do it with than Harry James?

That night at the Rustic Cabin, Harry James discussed changing his name to "Frankie Satin," for he believed that the name Sinatra sounded too Italian. Such reasoning wasn't uncommon in those years when the names of many film stars were shortened or changed. (Sinatra, years later, quipped, "If I'd done that, I'd be working cruise ships today.")[11] Harry had already demonstrated a penchant for changing the name of his female singer. Sinatra's mother, Dolly, often considered one of the two people whose influence most shaped his personality (the other being Tommy Dorsey), was adamant about his keeping the Sinatra name.[12]

The next day Sinatra caught the band's first show at the Paramount, after which James and Sinatra met backstage in James's dressing room. Sinatra argued that he had a cousin named Ray Sinatra from Boston who was doing all right leading a band in radio and who was later to be the bandleader at the Tropicana in Las Vegas for many years. The gist of it was: "You want the voice, you take the name."

The bandleader and his new singer agreed on a one-year contract for Sinatra to be paid $75 per week. James introduced his musicians to their new male vocalist just before they got into the pit to start the second show. A week of rehearsals plus a club date at the Waldorf-Astoria followed.

Once again, Red Norvo's timing was off. He and Mildred Bailey had seen Frank Sinatra at the Rustic Cabin one night on their way to the neighboring Nyack, New York, area where Bailey's brother, Al Rinker, lived. (Rinker was one of the original Rhythm Boys, which included Bing Crosby, who had been featured with Paul Whiteman's band.) Mildred admired Frank Sinatra's singing, but at the time Terry Allen was the male vocalist; Norvo, therefore, had no need for an additional singer to work with Mildred Bailey.

A few weeks later, however, as frequently happened with bands, the situation suddenly changed. Norvo called Sinatra to see if he would be interested in joining their band, but he had already decided to go with Harry's band. "Mr. and Mrs. Swing," as they were called, had missed out on a seemingly golden opportunity. (Coincidentally, the first time I ever saw Frank Sinatra perform, in August 1960, was when he was backed by the Red Norvo Quintet at the 500 Club in Atlantic City. He introduced Frank Sinatra as "my boy singer.")

On June 30, the James band traveled with its new male singer to Baltimore for a one-week engagement at the Hippodrome Theater. Connie Haines noted: "That was the first theater we did ... and after the first show, the screaming started in the theater, and those girls came backstage. There were about 20 of them ... of course, we didn't have that many in the audience. But it happened, it was real, it was not a gimmick." The impetus for the young ladies' swooning was the ballad singing of Frank Sinatra. As an afterthought, Haines added, "Actually, it's too bad that Harry didn't have the money [to keep him] because he would've gotten in on that bandwagon.... They'd have come for Sinatra like they did later with Dorsey.

"Nobody realized how great Harry really was because he was brand new.... He had an attitude, and I guess he had that attitude because he was really frightened, being so young.... He didn't talk and, boy, he kept that control and that ego of his. Frank had the same. They were at each other, but never as much as he was later on with Buddy Rich and Tommy [Dorsey]."[13]

Jack Palmer said, "Frank was a pro right from the beginning as far as vocalizing was concerned. We knew he was talented."[14]

After that first engagement, it was back to New York and a merry-go-round of bookings that began with a stint at Roseland Ballroom's Dime-a-Dance operation on Broadway between 51st and 52nd Streets. The Roseland date was followed by a booking at the Steel Pier in Atlantic City that drew a respectable audience. After that the band returned to New York for a two-week gig at the Dancing Campus of the World's Fair in Queens. Then back to Roseland for another engagement.

Sinatra recorded the first of his ten songs with the James band for

Brunswick Records on July 13 in New York (a month later Brunswick was absorbed by Columbia Records) during the engagement at Roseland. He received an extra $25 for each side. He began his recording career with "From the Bottom of My Heart"; on the other side was "Melancholy Mood." Andy Gibson arranged both tunes.

Harry James gave Frank Sinatra ample encouragement, which the young singer desperately needed. Although he sounded tentative and more than slightly shy, he was developing a style that was as yet unfinished. Even so, he gave the impression that he truly believed the lyrics of the romantic songs he sang. He was having problems from time to time with his breathing. Harry told him to "keep the bottom filled up." Further, he advised him to exercise and suggested that he learn to jump rope.

Sinatra was well liked by his fellow band members, and showed a great sense of humor, but fundamentally he was a loner. He spent most of his time on the bus reading magazines and newspapers. As Jack Palmer remembered, "He was a regular guy. But I remember one time when we were playing the College Inn when he almost got into a fight with Ralph Hawkins who was about the same size as he was. Ralph was a little sarcastic, and I think he must have said something about singers in general. Frank wanted to take him outside, but nothing ever happened, and then they made friends."

"When Frank joined the band," Harry James later said, "he was always thinking of the lyrics. The melody was secondary. If it was a delicate or pretty word, he would try to phrase it with a prettier, softer type of voice. He still does that. The feeling he has for the words is just beautiful. He could sing the wrong melody, and it would still be pretty."

During that warm and humid summer the James band's record of "I Found a New Baby" appeared on the *Billboard* chart. Previously, James's versions of "Two O'Clock Jump" and "It's the Dreamer in Me" (with Helen Humes's vocal), produced by John Hammond when Harry was first recording on his own had been on the *Billboard* chart for a total of eight weeks in 1938. "I Found a New Baby" was the first of an astounding total of 70 *Billboard* pop chart hits by Harry James and his Orchestra that extended through 1953. If one considers that the Rolling Stones have had slightly under sixty *Billboard* pop chart hits but in a thirty-five-year period, one must conclude that Harry James was actually more of a dominating force in popular music during the years of his greatest prominence.

One night in August 1939, George Simon came into Roseland to review the band. As he was leaving, Gerry Barrett came running up to him to see what he thought of the new singer. Barrett exclaimed: "He wants a good writeup more than anybody I've ever seen. So give him a good writeup, will you, because we want to keep him happy and with the band."

Simon's *Metronome* review in the next issue praised Sinatra for his "very pleasing vocals" and mentioned that his "easy phrasing was especially commendable." Continuing his affinity for Harry's work, Simon wrote, "[James has] a band that kicks as few have ever kicked before." His review went on to praise its ability to play at the right tempo for foxtrots as well as for waltzes, tangos, and rhumbas while saluting the solos of Claude Lakey, Jack Gardner, and Dalton Rizzotto, who had recently been added to the trombone section.

Connie Haines's record of "Comes Love" got favorable airplay during the Roseland engagement, but Harry wouldn't allow her to sing it. The more people requested this tune the angrier he got. The incident reduced her to tears. In retrospect, it appears that the twenty-three-year old band-leader was trying to assert his leadership. He sometimes did the same thing to Sinatra when his records with the band were generating significant airplay.

It's unfortunate that Frank Sinatra and Connie Haines never sang duets together with the James band. Their subsequent duets backed by the Pied Pipers proved to be some of their most charming records made during their tenure together with Tommy Dorsey. Perhaps the best example of that is their rendition of Joe Bushkin's composition, "Oh! Look at Me Now."

Haines recalled a particularly memorable performance while with Harry James. "We hit a groove one night when we were doing the 'Two O'Clock Jump.' Harry kept shouting, 'One more time.' And it was such a groove that we were laughing hysterically and hopping up and down, jumping, Frank and I.... It was such a groove, hand-clapping and ... I mean, I get chills thinkin' about it. I've never had ... even with Buddy Rich and the Dorsey band, it was never that high pitch of swing that it was that night with Harry ... that was a great band—Ralph Hawkins on drums and a lot of those guys."[15]

Haines unfortunately had to leave the band in early August when the band's financial assets were attached. James had lost a lawsuit for damages involved in an earlier automobile accident, which seriously affected the band finances.

At that time, Sinatra was getting increasingly anxious about his slow ascent toward stardom. His close friend, the song plugger Hank Sanicola, encouraged him to stay with the James band, believing that success for him was only a matter of time. Harry told a *Down Beat* interviewer, "He considers himself the greatest vocalist in the business. Get that! No one ever heard of him. He's never had a hit record. He looks like a wet rag, but he says he's the greatest."

Lou Levy was a prominent music publisher running the vaunted Leeds

Music. He was very friendly with Woody Herman and had been helpful in getting Woody's "The Band That Plays the Blues" established. He seemed instinctively able to choose a hit song. One of the tunes he brought to the Andrews Sisters in 1937 was his friend Sammy Cahn and Saul Chaplin's "Bei Mir Bist Du Schon," which they had adapted from a song in a Yiddish theater musical. The song became their first big hit and later proved one of the highlights of Benny Goodman's Carnegie Hall concert and first featured the combination of Ziggy Elman and Martha Tilton. It was their precursor to "And the Angels Sing."

In the summer of 1939, Levy brought Harry James a love song called "All or Nothing at All," written by Jack Lawrence and Arthur Altman. Jack Lawrence had asked Levy for a certain amount of freedom in reworking Arthur Altman's melody in order to make it fit with his lyrics. Levy also gave the song to Jimmy Dorsey for Bob Eberly and to Freddy Martin as well.

The James band and Frank Sinatra tried out Jack Mathias's sensitive arrangement of the song at the Dancing Campus of the World's Fair and at Roseland before recording it. This was sixteen days after Hitler's blitzkrieg moved into Poland on September 1.

Drew Page remembered that Morty Palitz admonished Frank Sinatra after one of the takes to refrain from singing, "All or Nothing A-tall." "It's 'All or Nothing at All,'" he explained.[16] This was one of those rare musical instances when Frank Sinatra's diction was questioned.

The melancholy nature of the James/Sinatra pairing fit in perfectly with the changing times. From then on through the summer of 1945, romantic, often mournful ballads became the overriding theme in popular music. The song titles "I'll Never Smile Again," "Don't Sit Under the Apple Tree," "I Don't Want To Walk Without You," and so many others told the story of those difficult years.

The James band's record of "All or Nothing at All" wasn't released until the summer of 1940. It was important in first establishing on record the intimate sound Frank Sinatra had created, coupled with a new depth of feeling in his ballad singing. Although it was a dance-band record, it featured Frank's singing nearly the entire song—unlike the way band singers were typically given only one chorus. James's solo, making use of a wide vibrato, was an indication of the musical direction he would soon take.

The Jimmy Dorsey and Freddy Martin versions were unsuccessful, and, strangely enough, this classic record by Sinatra and James sold a meager 8,000 copies on its release, perhaps due to the radio ban on ASCAP songs at the time. This restriction also affected the sales of other ASCAP songs that Sinatra recorded with Harry James.

In 1943, during the heart of the A. F. of M. (American Federation of

Musicians) strike, instigated by its leader, James C. Petrillo, which meant musicians could not record new material, Lou Levy approached Manie Sachs. By then Manie was head of pop A & R (Artists & Repertoire) at Columbia Records and was desperate to release new Sinatra material. Lou reminded Manie about "All or Nothing at All": "You've got a record in there that's practically a solo by Frank." Manie played the record and called Lou back to tell him, "You're absolutely right—we're going to re-release it."

The record sold over 100,000 copies. It reached #2 on the *Billboard* pop chart. However, the billing on the label copy had been completely reversed from the original record. The label copy on the original record read "Harry James Orchestra" in bold print and, in very small print, "Vocal by Frank Sinatra." Now Sinatra's name was bigger. This change in the billing was due to Harry James's suggesting to Manie Sachs, "Frank deserves it."

"All or Nothing at All" couldn't have been released at a more opportune time. This was during the early stages when "The Voice" had begun to conquer female America. Today, "All or Nothing at All" is a song closely associated with Frank Sinatra and generally considered his only significant record with Harry James.

On the flip side of "All or Nothing at All" was Harry's composition "Flash," which might be considered a musically autobiographical attempt by James to describe his new band. Its main theme built from a piano chorus by Jack Gardner to the sax section's playing the refrain from Basie's "Jumpin' at the Woodside," while the brass plays the main theme from "Pick-a-Rib," an effective combination. Then James comes in for a solo preceding the final coda. "Flash" soon became a mainstay of the James library.

Before "All or Nothing at All," Jack Lawrence had James and Sinatra record "It's Funny to Everyone but Me" and also wrote a lyric for "Ciribiribin" for them to record. Later, Lawrence was to write lyrics for "Sleepy Lagoon" to go with the English conductor Sir Eric Coates's melody.

Jack Lawrence offered Harry James "Tenderly" in 1949, which he had written with Walter Gross, but James turned it down, only to record it later after Rosemary Clooney had finally made it into a hit. I asked Lawrence what aspect of James's trumpet playing appealed to him as a songwriter. He replied: "The wonderful attack that nobody else had and the clarity of it. The round tone that he got. You knew immediately it was special; it was like an artist's signature, like a painter who had his own [individual] style."[17]

Van Alexander saw the band in Boston that summer as his band and Harry's band were playing at the twin ballrooms, the Raymor-Playmor. He reflected: "My impression of the James band was that it was all Harry. He was wonderful and exciting. My band was a good band, but it didn't have the excitement that Harry's band had."

I asked the veteran arranger and bandleader what he thought of Sinatra at the time. Alexander said: "Oh, he was a pleasant enough band singer. He had made a couple of pretty good records, especially 'All or Nothing at All.' I did notice, however, that Frank was a quick study. He learned as he went along, and he took advantage of every opportunity."[18]

With the James band, how you played baseball was almost as important as your musical prowess. As a ballplayer, Sinatra was anything but an asset. He played right field, and his batting average was in the realm of .200. As ever, Harry was determined to field the best possible team. Almost the entire team had a background of either having played high school or semi-pro baseball. The musicians "constructed" baseball fields in cow pastures all over the East in order to be able to practice constantly. Its devotion to the sport also sometimes made the band late for gigs.

Every opponent went down to defeat against the James team except for a loss to the Steel Pier team in Atlantic City. This defeat bothered Harry. He was determined to win the rematch, so much so that, in order to comply with the league rules, a pitcher who had been recommended by Ralph Hawkins was hired for only one day as a member of the band. His fastball was so effective that the James team won the game with ease.

In a *Down Beat* byline piece, Harry James admitted that one of the problems his band was encountering involved the saxophone section. "They are just a little slower in grasping new arrangements and ideas that the arrangers and I get. Another couple of months and they'll be up to the level of the trumpets, trombones, and rhythm (section).... We have a wonderful morale, swell spirit, no cliques. The guys get along well. We know we aren't the best in the business yet. But we think we can be.... The future will reveal just how far my gang of Texans is going to go."[19]

Louise Tobin was discovered by John Hammond while she was singing at Nick's, the onetime Dixieland club located on Seventh Avenue, just north of Sheridan Square in Greenwich Village. Hammond naturally brought her to the attention of his good friend, Benny Goodman.

She joined the Goodman band immediately after Goodman had fired Martha Tilton because of her romantic involvement with Leonard Vannerson, then his manager, whom she eventually married. Benny Goodman had no idea that Louise was married to Harry James since she had never attended a performance of his band. James explained that the reason his wife was singing with the Goodman band rather than his own was because "Louise can learn more from Benny, she can make more money, and naturally she can become better known," which sounds like a rather hollow statement.[20]

"I've had a crush on her for sixty years, or since the first time I saw her with Benny Goodman on a one nighter in Washington where I grew up," related Dr. Billy Taylor, the noted jazz pianist, educator, and correspondent for CBS-TV's *Sunday Morning*. "Besides that, " offered Taylor, "she really could sing."[21] By the age of twenty, Louise Tobin had grown into a Texan beauty with decided singing talent.

Those who remember Louise Tobin when she sang with Goodman still rave over her ballad singing and her ability to sing the blues with a black sound. Jimmy Maxwell said that "Louise was a good singer, very straight, and she didn't sound like Mildred Bailey [like so many other singers did then], but she had the same approach. She sang a simple melody, which, when you have a good singer doing it, is the way it should be."[22] Benny told her, "When I get through with you, you're gonna be the greatest blues singer in the world."

"Louise Tobin's Blues," unfortunately, was never recorded by Goodman, but Harry had her perform the number with his band during a radio broadcast from the Madhattan Room. The lyrics were improvised as she sang the blues. Another blues Tobin sang was written by none other than Benny's former vocalist, Johnny Mercer, telling the story of her name, where she was from, and how she came to the Goodman band.

Louise flew out from New York on weekends to join her husband between her own singing gigs. She remarked: "Sinatra knew he was great and was not shy about expressing it. I was a little put off by his cockiness, but more than that, I was put off by the lifestyle that I knew was going on with the band at the time ... I was more concerned with my own relationship with Harry than I was listening to Frank, for which he never forgave me."[23]

After one of the November weekends she spent in Chicago with Harry, when the band was in the midst of a very successful four-week engagement at the Panther Room of the Hotel Sherman, Louise became pregnant. Shortly thereafter, while playing a date with the Goodman band at the Waldorf-Astoria, she tripped over the hem of her gown as she was walking down a flight of stairs and had a serious fall. She lost the baby. As a result, Harry insisted that she stop working. Eventually, she started singing for trombonist Will Bradley, whose orchestra worked around New York.

One night during the Panther Room engagement, a five-foot, four-inch blonde with a dynamic figure came in to join some friends. She was Betty Grable. Despite having appeared in thirty-two films, mostly musicals, she was hardly a star. She was then part of a vaudeville tour headlined by Eddie

"Rochester" Anderson, famous for being Jack Benny's foil on his weekly radio program.[24]

Betty Grable was accompanied that night by Jim Bacon, the young Chicago reporter, who later, for many years, covered the Hollywood scene for the Associated Press. "I ran into her in the Loop one day, and she said, 'Let's go to the College Inn [the new name for the Panther Room] tonight and hear Harry James's new singer.' 'Who's that?' I said. She said, 'Frank Sinatra.' I said, 'Frank who?' I'd never heard of him before. So we went to the Sherman, and, I'll never forget, the minute Sinatra started singing, every girl left her partner on the dance floor and crowded around the microphone on the bandstand. He was so skinny, the microphone almost obscured him." Years later, Jim Bacon became Frank Sinatra's best friend among the Hollywood press corps.[25]

The show at the College Inn also featured the appearance of the Boogie Woogie Trio of Meade Lux Lewis, Pete Johnson, and Albert Ammons with Big Joe Turner on vocals, long a fixture at Cafe Society in New York. With James, Johnson and Ammons performed the material that had been such a delight when they had recorded together earlier in the year. It also had great appeal to the college students who jitterbugged during their performances. The prices at the College Inn also benefited the young crowd. Drinks were 35 cents and dinner was $1.50. The usual minimum was $1 and $2 on Saturday nights.

Mickey Scrima replaced Ralph Hawkins on drums at the College Inn. Hawkins went with Artie Shaw when Buddy Rich left Artie to join Tommy Dorsey. Scrima had left Ina Rae Hutton's fine orchestra. When asked what he first thought of Harry James as a person, Mickey Scrima laughed and exclaimed: "After I figured out this was the most self-centered guy I was ever going to meet, I never had a problem with him."[26]

The band headed west for what should have been an important booking at the Palomar Ballroom. Unfortunately, it never materialized. The famous ballroom burned to the ground on October 4, only a few weeks before the band reached Los Angeles. A photograph from this period showed Charlie Barnet, whose band had been playing the Palomar at the time of the fire, holding his charred soprano saxophone in his hands.

Harry James was then being considered for the lead in the film version of Dorothy Baker's novel *Young Man with a Horn*.[27] As it turned out, the picture wasn't made until 1949, with Kirk Douglas in the lead and Harry James "ghosting" Douglas's trumpet playing.

In the wake of the devastation at the Palomar, a last-minute booking installed the band in a restaurant called Victor Hugo's on Sunset Boulevard in West Hollywood for two weeks. The engagement was anything but a success. Rather, it was a bad booking since Victor Hugo's had previously only played society bands.

The band opened with some of its loud instrumentals, despite the small size of the room, which right away angered the manager. To deter the volume, the owner had a canopy put on top of the bandstand to smother the loudness of the brass and rhythm sections. Further, the brass was forced to stuff handkerchieß into their horns, use mutes, and cover the bells of their horns with felt hats to further deaden the sound. James, however, continued to feature the band's flagwavers. Finally, as a result of the various maneuverings by the owner, Harry James quit and was simultaneously fired. This happened at the end of the first week when the band was just starting to register with the customers. Right in the middle of "All or Nothing at All," hardly a boisterous number, the owner began waving his hands and yelling, "Stop! No More! Enough!"

Mickey Scrima, the colorful Pittsburgh native who had grown up with Billy Strayhorn, later Duke Ellington's alter ego, lived in a two-bedroom apartment in Hollywood with Frank and Nancy Sinatra during the Victor Hugo debacle. He recalled this period as being a dire time. "We didn't have any money, man. We had no direction from MCA, and we weren't making any bread. It was one of those times when we had to double up." In line with that, the Sinatras prepared spaghetti dinners in their apartment for Harry James and his downtrodden musicians.

MCA was concentrating on developing the bands of Gene Krupa and Alvino Rey, in addition to Teddy Wilson's. The market for swing bands was definitely being glutted by the plethora of new bands. Besides that, the agents devoted most of their efforts booking commercial bands which made their commission reports look impressive.

Things started to look up when the band secured a week at a downtown Los Angeles movie theater and then a week at the Golden Gate Theatre in San Francisco. One-nighters across the country followed on the way to the Chicago Theatre, where they worked alongside the Andrews Sisters. There, the theater manager took one look at Sinatra wearing an ill-fitting band uniform and told James to "take that little scarecrow out of the show."

"He's my singer," said James. "He stays in."

One night, Mickey Scrima was late arriving at the Chicago Theatre, and the young singer was recruited to play the drums. After playing "Ciribiribin" and a few slow ballads, on which he "dusted" with the brushes, James wanted to have some fun. He called "Night Special," which featured an opening drum solo. Sinatra grabbed the sticks and tried to fake his way through the introduction. Harry laughed so hard at his substitute drummer's playing that he had to turn his back to the audience. Frank described the experience of playing "Night Special" as "the longest sixteen bars of music of my life."

Sinatra learned that Tommy Dorsey was in search of the right replacement for Jack Leonard, who had left to go out on his own. Jimmy Hilliard, the music supervisor at CBS in Chicago and later an executive at Warner Bros. Records, listened to Dorsey complain about his problems with Leonard over dinner.

"Have you heard the skinny kid who's singing with Harry James?" Hilliard asked Tommy. "He's nothing to look at, but he's got a sound!"

Hilliard told Dorsey about having seen Sinatra with the James band at the Panther Room a few months before. "My back was to the bandstand," he reported. "But when the kid started taking a chorus, I had to turn around. I couldn't resist going back the next night to hear him again. He's got something besides problems with acne. Harry can't be paying him much. Maybe you can take him away."

Various dance bands were playing in Chicago that week at the annual Christmas benefit party given by Chicago's Mayor Ed Kelly, endorsed by the musician union leader James C. Petrillo. After the James band's performance at the benefit, Sinatra was slipped a note by Tommy Dorsey's manager, Bobby Burns, asking him to meet Tommy the next afternoon at his suite in the Palmer House. "I couldn't believe it when Frank showed it to me. The note was written on a torn off piece of a paper bag," said Nick Sevano, Frank's friend from Hoboken, who was then working for him as his valet.[28]

The thought of meeting Tommy Dorsey made the young singer extremely nervous. He knew that "The Sentimental Gentleman of Swing" could be brusque and a tough taskmaster. Dorsey had heard Sinatra on a remote broadcast with the James band and on records. He had even met him once briefly when Sinatra auditioned for Bob Chester's band. Nevertheless, the trombonist insisted that Sinatra audition. He sang "Marie," the song Jack Leonard had made into a hit and that had first brought the Tommy Dorsey Band to fame back in the winter of 1937.

Tommy Dorsey liked what he heard. He made Sinatra an offer of $125 a week, one that was difficult to refuse. Nancy was pregnant, and, despite his warm feelings toward Harry and the musicians, the band's future seemed bleak. Frank Sinatra needed money desperately.

In speaking about being given the opportunity to join the Tommy Dorsey Band and what it meant to him, Sinatra later referred to it as "the General Motors of the band business." More specifically, this was the band that, in addition to its leader's melodic trombone, was also built around its singer and its vocal group, the Pied Pipers. It was the band every young singer dreamed of joining. Dorsey even had formidable songwriters like Matt Dennis writing solely for his band.

Frank Sinatra went backstage at the Chicago Theatre to discuss with Harry James the offer he had received from Dorsey. When he entered his dressing room, he discovered James busy reading a magazine. Not wanting to disturb him but needing to get his attention, he walked in and out of the room. Finally, James put down his magazine.

"What's bothering you?" James asked him.

Sinatra told him that he would be happier opening a vein, but that Tommy Dorsey had made him an offer to join his band and could pay him $50 a week more. Harry James generously told him he would not stand in his way. They dissolved their business relationship with a handshake.

In an interview with Fred Hall in 1976, Harry James recalled the moment vividly. "I said, 'Well, if we don't do any better in the next few months or so, try to get me on, too.'"[29] In an analytical look at Sinatra's ultimate decision to leave Dorsey to go out on his own slightly more than two-and-a-half years later, Harry told Martin Block, "I think it cost Frank and the management people he signed with [MCA] upwards of $65,000 to get out of the contract. It really wasn't at all a strong or even a legal contract because at the time he signed with the Dorsey band he was still under contract to me! But they didn't think about that."

Mickey Scrima, whom Harry referred to as "Pinocchio," recalls that Sinatra's last gig with the James band was a week long engagement at Shea's Theatre in Buffalo. The film was *Balalaika*, starring Nelson Eddy and Ilona Massey. Appearing on the same bill were the comic and pantomimist, Red Skelton, and the trampoline team of Burt Lancaster and Nick Cravat.

At one particular show, Sinatra was on stage singing way out in front of the band with no lighting except a pin spot. The audience couldn't see that Skelton was directly behind him telling him jokes. Sinatra began laughing so hard he had to stop singing. Skelton proceeded to come up to the microphone and imitated the way Frank sang a ballad while Frank stood by, laughing and playfully punching him. The audience howled at the repartee between the singer and the comedian.

Sinatra had relished the camaraderie of the James band. Yet, Mickey Scrima surprised me by saying, "I don't care what you've read or what you've heard, as far as the band was concerned, the only guy who thought this guy had a real future was Harry James."[30]

Frank Sinatra left the James band in Buffalo on January 26, 1940. He never forgot that night: "The bus pulled out with the rest of the guys after midnight. I'd said goodbye to them all, and it was snowing. I remember there was nobody around, and I stood alone with my suitcase in the snow and watched the taillights of the bus disappear. Then the tears started, and I tried to run after the bus. There was such spirit and enthusiasm in that band [that] I hated leaving it." (This was one of the few accurately portrayed scenes from Sinatra's period with Harry James in the CBS-TV miniseries, *Sinatra*.)

As Louise Tobin emphasized to Sinatra scholar Will Friedwald, "In seven months with Harry, Frank learned more about music than he'd ever known in his life to that point. He learned about phrasing and about conducting." Friedwald contended: "Harry provided a working model of how to pack an emotional wallop.... From James, too, Sinatra could have learned how to intermingle pop song tenderness with blueslike invective, how to swing ... how to personalize a melody."[31]

The best recorded representation of the 1939 Harry James Band is the box set put out by Hindsight Records entitled *Bandstand Memories 1938–1948*. It consists of broadcast recordings from Roseland and other locations. It also contains several songs Sinatra never recorded commercially with James and serves to chronicle his early musical development. As an afterthought, it's also rather amazing how Sinatra dealt with a notoriously out-of-tune piano at Roseland.

Harry James and Frank Sinatra remained friendly for the next forty-three years and performed on several engagements and television shows together. Frank was a frequent visitor to the Driftwood Lounge at the Flamingo Hotel in Las Vegas during the nine-year period when James and his band reigned supreme. James first told me during a magazine interview—and it soon became a show business legend—that he had recently reminded Sinatra that he still owed him five months on their original contract at $75 a week. Frank had remarked, "Any time you want me, boss. I'll be there."

In December 1939, the readers of *Down Beat* chose Harry James and his Orchestra as the winner of its "Best Sweet Band" category. In a bylined article in *Hit Parader* magazine, James tried to explain the transition in his music: "My own feeling, and I'm sure many readers will agree with me, is that it's not necessary to make any definite distinction between sweet and swing, or between swing songs and ballads. Music, and particularly popular music, has made enormous advances in the last seven or eight years, since the beginning of the Swing Era, so that a new musical blend has emerged—something which combines the best features of both sweet and hot. There have always been both forms and always will be. There's no reason why sweet should ever replace swing or vice versa.... As long as we concentrate on making good music, the sweet-swing problem will take care of itself."

Harry James, who had originally won both the *Down Beat* and *Metronome* polls on trumpet in 1937, heralding a blazing new jazz talent, was now leading a band that was definitely heading in a totally different direction. Indeed, the times they were a changin'.

5

You Made Me Love You

In 1940, New York was undisputedly the greatest city in the world. Although it had been untouched by war, much of the city was still struggling from economic hardship. Midtown New York, however, was fast, brash, and confident. It was swing music, Joe Louis, Joe DiMaggio, and the World's Fair. Its population was about seven and a half million, one-third of whom were immigrants.[1]

One of those immigrants was Dick Haymes, born in Buenos Aires, Argentina, on September 13, 1918, the son of Benjamin Haymes, a Scottish mining engineer turned Argentine cattleman. Marguerite, his Irish-born mother, was a top voice teacher who had previously toured in Broadway musical comedies. Haymes had been educated in Europe and had attended Loyola College in Montreal for a year. Both he and his half brother, Bob (they had the same mother), were musically inclined. Bob later became a New York radio personality and also wrote the pop standard, "That's All."

One day in the winter of 1940, Harry James and his Orchestra were rehearsing at the World Transcription Studio at 711 Fifth Avenue. Larry Shayne had arranged for Haymes, then a budding songwriter, to audition his songs for James. Early in the rehearsal, Harry looked up and saw an attractive young man walking into the studio carrying a folio of songs under his arm. He introduced himself, whereupon Harry asked him to run down the tunes for him. Haymes sat down at the piano to accompany himself while singing his songs.

At the completion of his presentation, James remarked, "Well, your songs are nice, but we can't use any original music. [At the time, new songs were being assigned to the various bands by the record companies.] But I would like to offer you a job as a vocalist." Haymes replied, "That sounds great to me." Louise Tobin believes that Larry Shayne wasn't that crazy about Dick's songs either, but recognized the fact that Haymes was a legitimate singing talent and wanted to allow Harry to "discover" him.[2]

Dick Haymes had already sung with bands in the New York area, among them Bunny Berigan's. This was before he left for Hollywood, where he worked as an extra and a stuntman. Reportedly, he doubled for one of the seamen who were shot and fell into the sea in the original MGM film of *Mutiny on the Bounty*. That part of his career was cut short after a fall from a horse while working in a film, and he returned to the East.

Haymes replaced Fran Hines, whom Harry had given a short-term contract but whose singing didn't thrill him. In fact, Hines recorded only one number with the band, "Palms of Paradise." He resigned and returned to his native Buffalo to sing on radio station WGR-WKBW.[3]

Dick Haymes was very self-conscious when he got up to sing, constantly clearing his throat and then taking a handkerchief out of his breast pocket and putting it to his mouth. This became his routine before he approached the microphone, taking long strides, looking awkwardly around him, and finally inhaling deeply before starting to sing.

Strange as it may seem, his singing wasn't really influenced by having worked with jazz trumpeters like Harry James or Bunny Berigan. He readily admitted, however, how much the romantic aspect of Harry's playing helped develop his singing style. As Haymes explained it, "Sometime after I joined Harry, he started showcasing my work. I think the singers were probably responsible for that. Later on he learned dynamics because when I first joined the band everything was at level and everything was loud, loud, loud. It was a revelation to hear myself."

On his initial dates with the band, Dick Haymes had to endure girls coming up to him exclaiming, "Can we have your autograph, Mr. Sinatra?" Even at this early juncture, Frank Sinatra was a hard act to follow.

Conversely, in the fall of 1939, the pop music department at Columbia Records didn't respond positively to Sinatra's singing. Harry James, however, had insisted that Frank Sinatra was his vocalist and said he would continue to record with the band. James's belief in Sinatra, coupled with the fact of the band's poor record sales, contributed to its being dropped by Columbia and to its subsequent move to Varsity Records, a smaller label with limited distribution. By that time, Sinatra had left James.

Eli Oberstein had left RCA Victor for Varsity and agreed to sign Harry James on the understanding that MCA would provide him the opportunity to sign some of its newly emerging orchestras. Dick Haymes recorded such tunes as "How High the Moon," "Fools Rush In," "The Nearness of You," and "Maybe" with James on Varsity Records. Unfortunately, none of them became hits; some of these sides were later released on Hit and Elite Records.

In the first half of 1940, James had two hits with "Ciribiribin" (that peaked at #10) and "Flight of the Bumblebee" (that hit a high of #20), which Eli Oberstein had suggested he record. The nation's most powerful columnist, Walter Winchell, referred to him as "the torrid trumpeter whose swing crew via CBS rates Big-Time attention."[4]

Harry James then optimistically billed himself as "The Nation's #1 Trumpeter." In reality, his band had yet to create a significant impact, and its leader was still very much in debt.

Harry owed $5,000 to the Greyhound Bus Company. Therefore, "re-po" representatives of the company constantly badgered him at venues where the band was playing and later even lay in wait for the band bus at crossroads outside of town. As a result, Lenny Hessinger, the band's resourceful and devoted bus driver, learned to maneuver the band out of town by driving through back streets, alleys, and backyards. Once, while Hessinger was driving into Old Orchard Beach, Maine, the brakes went out on the bus, and it careened downhill on a road leading to the beach. The bus didn't stop until its front wheels reached the Atlantic Ocean. Putting a good face on a bad fact, some of the musicians stripped off their clothes and dove into the water.

Despite the bad times, the freewheeling musicians kept things lively. Al Lerner, the band's pianist, and Dick Haymes often picked up dogs and other pets. Once, some monkeys that had escaped from a pet store came aboard the bus and left an indelible impression.

Don Reid became the road manager. He packed a licensed .45 pistol since he carried the band's payroll. A voracious drinker, he relished shooting out streetlights and even the lights on the bus. Occasionally, when he was in his hotel room and it was time to turn out the lights, he would grab his .45 and shoot them out![5]

Some nights there wasn't enough money for everyone to have rooms, so Harry would get a suite, specially designed for traveling salesmen to display their goods, which had a couple of bathrooms. The musicians would come in and clean up before the gig and sleep on the bus en route to the next job.

The band played some awful joints. Out-of-tune pianos, ramshackle dressing rooms, and faulty microphones were the norm. Bands who weren't in demand and couldn't get the important dates had to endure these conditions. Harry James still spent whatever extra money he had on new suits and shoes and sported a new Chrysler Saratoga convertible with wood on the sides and plaid upholstery. He believed a bandleader had to keep up a necessary front.

While on tour, the James band and the Goodman band sometimes found themselves in the same city. Invariably, Harry James would come over to see Benny Goodman, unless their hours conflicted. One night in Cleveland, the James band had the night off. James came up on the Goodman bandstand, grabbed a chair, and sat down behind Jimmy Maxwell in the trumpet section to watch the festivities. Maxwell recalled, "Naturally, it made me nervous. I didn't play well. Benny didn't like what was taking place and called me down to the band room at intermission.

"I don't know. It's just one of those nights," I told him. I didn't want to tell him that Harry was making me nervous, but he knew.

"Is Harry making you nervous?" asked Benny. "I don't know why that should bother you." As Maxwell explained, Benny then proceeded to deliver him the compliment of his life: "You play much better than he does."

"I could see the wheels going around in Benny's head," the trumpeter remembers as Benny added, with a glimmer in his eye, "potentially."[6]

From the beginning of his career, Harry James had always developed strong friendships with important people. Manie Sachs was one of them. In September 1940, Sachs became head of the pop music department at Columbia, a position from which he could be of decisive help to James. Because Sachs already had a great personal regard for him and was convinced that the James band was going to make it, he brought the band back to Columbia.

One of its first Columbia records was a remake of "Flight of the Bumble Bee," the familiar theme from Rimsky-Korsakov's opera, *The Tale of Tsar Sultan*. This classic James record featured Harry's solo, followed by an abrupt change of mood to a swing arrangement. (Rimsky-Korsakov's operas were attractive to big bands at the time; another one was the source of Tommy Dorsey's "Song of India.") Just as "Ciribiribin" had been recorded by Harry twice within the space of a year, "Flight of the Bumble Bee" was recorded again a year later with the addition of a string section, which provided an even more dramatic setting.

Now that Harry James was once again signed to Columbia, this time with the promise of considerably more record promotion, Sachs assigned Morty Palitz, a talented and concerned producer, to work with the band. Mickey Scrima recalled: "Morty loved the band, and he loved all the guys in the band. He knew we were just about ready to burst, and he did everything he could possibly do to make it happen.

"With Varsity the guys in the booth just set the band up. Morty had padding put on my bass drum to get the sound right. When we played the recordings back, you could tell the difference in the band and how much better it sounded." [No doubt this was due in large part to the high ceiling of its spacious Liederkranz Studio, an old German social club then located at 58th Street between Lexington and Third Avenues, which had a natural echo.] Mickey added, "Morty would never say, 'That's perfect, let's do another one.' He would say, 'That's good, let's try one more.' Morty was the kind of guy who told you the truth. He'd say, 'Hey, the brass is a little too loud.' He had a great ear, man."[7]

It is therefore perhaps easier to understand why Dick Haymes (or "Strongheart" as Larry Shayne called him) subsequently had such hits as "I'll Get By" (which, when it was re-released in 1944, became the #1 record in the country for six weeks), "Ol' Man River," "You've Changed" (which he sang in a low F after Lynn Richards, then the band's female singer, couldn't handle it), and "A Sinner Kissed an Angel." The latter tune was not the huge success it was expected to be on its own, but was nonetheless a hit because it appeared on the flip side of "You Made Me Love You."

Haymes could and perhaps should have been the biggest male singing star of the 1940s. He was stunningly handsome and masculine, blond and blue-eyed, and had an air of sophistication. More important, he had one of the richest and most distinctive baritone voices extant. Rumor had it that Haymes turned down the lead role of Joey Evans in Rodgers and Hart's *Pal Joey* on Broadway in 1940 to remain with Harry James. Instead, the role went to Gene Kelly, which made him a star.

Although cynics contended that Frank Sinatra hardly had the best voice and his looks were not thought to be of movie-star caliber, he still sang with an intimacy that connected with the vulnerability of female America during wartime. Perhaps just as significant, he worked diligently on improving every aspect of his craft. Dick Haymes, however, like Vic Damone and Jack Jones later on, blamed others for their own shortcomings and possessed neither the will nor the serious dedication required to become a major star.

The ever reliable Nick Buono, or "Count," as Harry referred to him, joined the trumpet section. He settled into that position for the next thirty-nine years (longer than any musician in the band's history), except for two years in the air force during the latter part of the war. One of the kindest and most jovial musicians I've ever known, the gravel-voiced trumpeter was beloved by every member of the band and was a special favorite because of the home-cooked Italian recipes he prepared in his hotel room while on the road. By the 1960s, however, for no discernible reason, Harry began speaking to him only when necessary. Oddly enough, according to Joe Cabot, every year on Nick's birthday, Harry took him to dinner and gave him $1,000.[8]

As described earlier, Harry James enjoyed tagging people with nicknames. He referred to Haymes as "Zombie," and for good reason. One day, while playing the first set at the Paramount Theater, he noticed Haymes wasn't waiting in the wings as the band played the introduction to one of his featured numbers. He signaled Al Monte to call the singer, who was staying at the Astor Hotel, just around the corner from the Paramount's stage door. Haymes had overslept, and upon hearing that he was supposed to be on stage he leaped out of bed and into his clothes. Harry was forced to vamp and play an unusually long introduction. Minutes later, Zombie arrived on stage—out of breath, unshaven, his clothes disheveled, his hair uncombed—to sing his number.[9]

While working for James, Haymes perpetually borrowed money and suits from him as well as from the other musicians and rarely, if ever, paid them back. Nick Sevano, who later managed Haymes and was constantly running after him to collect his commission, remarked, "Dick invented ways to spend money!"[10]

Mickey Scrima described the way Dick Haymes looked down on people. "He always had to be the big shot. In reality, he was a sophisticated jerk." Nevertheless, he agrees that "Dick could have been up there in the Bing Crosby class."[11]

Dick Haymes had met Joanne Dru, later a film star, when the chorus line from the Copacabana (which Joanne was a part of) worked onstage with the James band in an engagement at the Paramount. He stole Joanne away from Al Jolson and married her on September 1, 1941. Harry James served as his best man.

At the end of that year, Dick Haymes joined Benny Goodman and eventually replaced Frank Sinatra with Tommy Dorsey when Sinatra left to start his solo career on September 3, 1942. Haymes went from there to star on radio and then films.

Harry James began to enjoy some success on records with such semi-classical pieces as his own composition, "Concerto for Trumpet" as well as "Flight of the Bumble Bee," "Carnival of Venice," and "Trumpet Rhapsody," which was one of his favorite recordings. He acknowledged that "I've never played it at concerts or in theaters or anyplace in person. It's so difficult to play—just about impossible—so I'll let the record speak for itself." Besides illustrating Harry's dazzling triple tonguing trumpet technique, however, these classical pieces were played and arranged with a decided swing flavor.

The late Mel Powell, the eminent Goodman pianist and arranger who later became a classical composer and won the Pulitzer Prize in 1990 for his "Concerto for Two Pianos and Large Orchestra," believed that "Harry made a significant career mistake in not venturing further into the classical field. Look what it did for Benny Goodman and Artie Shaw. They commissioned composers like Aaron Copland, the young Leonard Bernstein, and Norman Dello Joio to write music for them to perform in concerts and record.

"Woody Herman had Igor Stravinsky compose 'Ebony Concerto' for his 1946 Carnegie Hall concert, which was recorded. This lent prestige to all of them and showed exactly what brilliant musicians they were. Harry was equally accomplished. At that point, he was both a prodigy and a virtuoso. He certainly could have created an equally impressive reputation as a classical trumpet player. It wouldn't have made him a lot of money, but it would have given him an even greater reputation. Unfortunately, I don't think Harry even thought about that."[12]

Elizabeth Teachout, a prominent opera coach in New York, saw James play on a Kansas City date in 1980. After watching him perform, she compared the sound of his trumpet to the voice of Beniamino Gigli, one of the most important tenors following the death of Caruso. Teachout believes: "Their sound was sort of similar. They both made use of a vast vibrato. The thing I think of with Gigli that I often associate with Harry was that they both had a dramatic sound. People thought of Gigli, for better or for worse, as having one of the most sensuous voices in opera, which a lot of highbrow people thought was vulgar. He was sentimental and a little bit excessive." By the very nature of her musical descriptions, one can readily understand the comparison between the two artists.[13]

James became friends with Alec Wilder, the composer and arranger, who was adept in the pop, jazz, and classical worlds. They had first met when Wilder wrote an original clarinet piece for Benny Goodman while Harry was a member of the Goodman band. Harry recorded Alec's tune, "It's So Peaceful in the Country," with Dick Haymes. He continued to admire the delicacy of Debussy's compositions, as had Bix Beiderbecke, and asked Wilder to arrange and orchestrate "Golliwog's Cakewalk" for the band. Because it had a jazz feel to it, James was pleased at Wilder's results; he played it a few times, but never recorded it.[14] Nor did he record arrangements of "Clair de Lune" and "Afternoon of a Faun" that Jack Mathias supplied. These were still more examples of potential classical crossover opportunities that remained unrealized.

Al Lerner joined the James band on June 30, 1940. He was hired to replace Jack Gardner on piano, but the process was most unusual. Harry had neglected to give Gardner his two-weeks' notice. As a result, on Lerner's arrival for his first gig with the James band, the bandstand was set up with a piano at either end with Jack Gardner seated at one of them.

"Jack was very perturbed about the whole thing," Lerner recalled. "I told him, 'I want you to know this has nothing to do with me. I had no part of this whatsoever.' I said to Harry, 'I don't understand what's going on.' Harry said, 'Well, we're gonna use two pianos here and at the Paramount.'" Lerner thought to himself that few if any big bands used two pianos.

At the Paramount, the stage was again set up for the two pianos just as Harry planned. When the stage show began, Gardner had the book of arrangements in front of him, while Lerner had to fake his part. Suddenly, Gardner, totally wasted, passed out just as Bea Wein, guest-starring on the bill, was starting to sing her signature tune, "My Reverie."

"There was no arpeggio," said Al Lerner, "so Harry quickly pointed to me. Fortunately, I knew what key the song was in. During the show, the musicians kept passing the various charts across the band from Jack on the left to me all the way over on the right. The lighting man darkened the side of the stage where Jack was out cold, his face resting on the keys. It was almost like a Laurel and Hardy routine.

"I played the rest of the show, and afterwards the pit recessed down below the stage and the movie went on. Claude Lakey and a couple of the guys got Jack on their shoulders like you would going through the jungle in Africa after felling an animal. You gotta realize Jack weighed 400 lbs.! They had to get around the organ, the one Don Baker played for years and years there. Finally, they got Jack out of the door and up to the band room. Harry didn't fire him, but in those days Harry never fired anybody. He would make it rough for you, though."[15]

This was the beginning of an often contentious relationship between Al Lerner and Harry James. The pianist claimed that Harry neither gave him the credit nor compensated him for writing arrangements for some of the band's film appearances or for contributing the bridge of the arrangement of "Music Makers." (The record of the tune became so popular that for a few years James changed the band's billing from "Orchestra" to "Music Makers.") Continuing his diatribe, Lerner pointed out, "Nobody got close to Harry. The guys respected him only as a great musician. The respect ended there. You couldn't sit down and have a conversation with him. He didn't know what to talk about except music and baseball. He wasn't educated nor was he an avid reader. He never read books. Nothing."[16]

Shortly after joining Harry James, Lerner married. Six weeks later, the band played the Steel Pier in Atlantic City. Lerner remembered, "There were two broads standing in front of the bandstand. Harry came over to me and said, "I got the blonde, and you've got the…" I said, "Harry, I don't do that stuff." He says, "I want to tell you one thing: it will always be there. It's there when you want it, it's there when you don't want it." That was his philosophy. Most times Harry took advantage of it "when it was there."[17]

Nevertheless, Harry James continued to have a warm personal feeling for Al Lerner as well as a great regard for his musicianship. He popularized the nickname "Pillowhead" that guitarist Ben Heller gave Lerner because of his mass of curly hair. Al Lerner enjoyed playing Harry James's music, and because of the closeness he had developed with his fellow musicians, he remained with the band for slightly over four years.

Every band had a spokesman, the musician who served as the intermediary between the leader and the band. On the Tommy Dorsey Band it was Ziggy Elman, whom Dorsey respected greatly. On the James band, Claude Bowen, the lead trumpeter and Harry James's old friend from Texas, filled the role. In addition, Claude also helped Harry out financially when crises arose, such as meeting the payroll or dealing with the Greyhound Bus Company. According to Lerner, Harry James never really appreciated Claude Bowen's unselfish devotion.

Lerner further recalled: "I'll never forget one day when we were working in a theater in Washington, Pennsylvania (near Pittsburgh). It was right after 'Music Makers' became a big hit. We were downstairs below the stage rehearsing a new arrangement. After the rehearsal, Claude approached Harry. He asked, 'Can I talk to you a second? The guys all got together, and we would like a little raise.' Harry replied—and this is verbatim, 'Anybody who doesn't like what they're getting—he can get lost,' and walked away."[18]

Obviously, the morale of the band was at a low ebb. This resulted from the meager salaries, the constant long jumps between often terrible dates (with the resulting lack of sleep), and the seemingly never-ending lack of public acceptance. The average salary for the musicians on the road was about $75 a week. The musicians didn't realize, however, that James was losing money at the rate of about $1,500 a week. The record royalties coming from Columbia were just enough to stave off his considering filing for bankruptcy.

Still, the band had some important admirers. George Simon was, without question, Harry's most enthusiastic booster in the jazz press, since he had first stated in *Metronome*, "Harry James has the greatest white band in the country, and, for that matter, so far as this reviewer is concerned, the greatest dance band one has ever known, and that's leaving out nobody!" (Benny Goodman then incredulously stomped into the *Metronome* office and demanded of Simon, "Do you really think so?")[19] Frank Driggs, the jazz historian and photo archivist, agrees. He firmly believes the 1939–40 James band was the greatest white swing band ever.

Gerald Wilson, who later started his own band, which has continued to the present, featuring his dynamic arrangements and compositions, was then a member of the trumpet section of the Jimmie Lunceford Orchestra. He declared: "I can remember one night we were playing at the Paramount

Theater. I left from the stage door and walked around to Eighth Avenue on my way to the subway. I knew there was a door into the Hotel Lincoln that led up to the ballroom. Several nights I went up there and stood in the back to watch this really beautiful musician. I always knew Harry was going to make it because he had a good band and he was such a strong force as a leader. I think he became one of the greatest white bandleaders we've ever had," Wilson concluded.

Five years after Wilson first saw him lead his band at the Lincoln, James began playing "Spruce Juice," a jazz instrumental Wilson originally had written for drummer Lee Young, Lester's brother. It had been featured by the bands of Les Hite, Benny Carter, and Woody Herman. Willie Smith, who had been Wilson's close friend on the Lunceford band, brought the tune to Harry James's attention.

During one of the many quiet nights at the Blue Room of the Hotel Lincoln, James would take George Simon aside and excitedly said, "I've got a great idea. I'm going to add strings." "You're absolutely out of your head!" Simon retorted. He warned James of the dire impact of such a move on his standing with critics as well as his fans. The bandleader claimed, however, that adding strings would mean "we can play any spot with that combination." After more than a little soul searching, however, he refrained from making such a radical move.

MCA kept the band working in ballrooms interspersed with some theater engagements. Harry's shyness and nervousness in front of a theater audience was perhaps best illustrated by a *Variety* review of a booking at the Orpheum Theatre in Minneapolis on November 23, 1940: "Miss Jean (actress Gloria Jean) was interviewed by James, who, at the opening show, appeared to be ill at ease in his radio reportorial role, and had to refer to a paper for his questions. At times he was almost inaudible, even over the mic."

As often happened with a band that had an indefinite future, several personnel changes took place. Raids had taken their toll on the band; now it was James's turn to make his own changes. He described the reason for the switches in personnel in a curious manner when he told *Metronome*: "A swing band's got to feel like playing all the time. And to feel like playing swing, you must have inspiration. Unfortunately, white men can't seem to get that inspiration anytime they feel like it from within, the way the colored fellows can, so you've got to give them some sort of an outside stimulus."

At the Brunswick Hotel in Boston, where the band was scheduled to open in September 1940, James announced, "Some of you will find notices in your mail slot in the morning." Mickey Scrima, Dick Haymes, and Al Lerner were all convinced they would be fired for different reasons.

Instead, almost the entire Texan contingent left over from the original band departed.[20]

The most significant changes saw Ben (Benny) Heller strengthening the rhythm section by replacing Red Kent on guitar; Claude Lakey, originally on tenor saxophone and recently a member of the trumpet section, took over the band's co-founder Dave Matthews's alto saxophone chair; Dave opted to remain in New York as a freelance arranger. The rambunctious Vido Musso, Harry's pal from Goodman days, joined on tenor saxophone, and deservedly got featured billing. John Mezey replaced Sam Donahue, who left to join Benny Goodman. (Throughout his career, Donahue was unfortunately never given the acclaim he deserved for both his saxophone playing and years later for his leadership of the Billy May and Tommy Dorsey "ghost" bands.) Hoyt Bohanon, one of the most accomplished trombonists to work in a big band, and who had been a member of Vido Musso's short-lived band, also joined the James band, replacing Truett Jones.

Another acquisition in October 1940 could have been fifteen-year-old Mel Tormé.[21] He had been brought by Henry Kalcheim of the William Morris Agency to meet Harry James backstage one night at the State-Lake Theater in Chicago after the band ended its performance. Tormé remembered: "He treated me like an adult, an equal.... I played and sang several of my songs. One particular tune really interested James—'Lament to Love,' my minor-keyed torch song, which he had me play and sing three times."[22]

When Tormé's uncle Art, who had accompanied him to the theater, brought out a photograph of Mel playing drums, James's eyes "widened a bit." He said, "What I really want to do is hear Mel play drums." Two hours later in front of Harry James, Mickey Scrima, Dick Haymes, and several members of the band, Tormé played a drum solo. They all applauded, and Harry James shouted out, "Neat!" Don Reid remarked to Tormé's uncle, "We'd like to add Mel to the band. He could sing the rhythm things that Dick doesn't do, and we'd like to feature him on drums.... We would have Mel play a specialty number with the band and Harry. Let him finish his current semester and we can plan for February."[23]

Mel Tormé returned to Hyde Park High School in anticipation of a job with the James band. Don Reid wrote a letter confirming James's continued interest, even mentioning the possibility of Dick Haymes being his roommate on the road. In December, Reid wrote Tormé again, this time raising the possible problem of child labor laws, which he said he was working to combat. February 1941 came and went. Reid finally wrote again expressing his deep regret that "in order to hire Mel, we would be forced, by several states, to also hire a full-time tutor, which frankly we cannot afford."[24]

This proved to be just another unfulfilled show business promise that many young people are forced to endure. The story, however, did have a partially happy ending, for in June 1941 Harry recorded Tormé's composition, "Lament to Love," with Dick Haymes on the vocal. It hit #10 on the *Billboard* chart during the week of August 30. The tune was also recorded by several other prominent bands and singers.[25]

The newly invigorated James band suddenly started to show a sense of strength and élan. It did sensational business in its repeat engagement at the College Inn at Chicago's Hotel Sherman during the fall of 1940.

Betty Grable had stopped off in Chicago with her good friend, Victor Mature, who was en route to Broadway to star in a play. Mature had recently starred in *One Million B.C.* and was in Chicago publicizing the film. Grable, in turn, made personal appearances for two weeks with the comedian, Ken Murray, at the Chicago Theater. *Down Argentine Way*, which she had just finished shooting, was playing at another theater.

For the second time in slightly over a year, Betty Grable came into the College Inn, this time with Mature, during the James band's appearance.[26] Again, she was primarily interested in James's male singer, who, in this case, was, of course, Dick Haymes. She had met Haymes while she was working on Broadway earlier in the year and looked forward to seeing him perform. After one of the sets, Dick introduced Harry James to Victor Mature, and Betty Grable met Harry James for the second time.

Grable exclaimed: "I was fascinated by his light blue eyes. He was so quiet that I found I was doing all the talking. He looked so thin, I felt I just wanted to feed him huge nourishing meals! As for instant romance? Nothing doing! I was still legally married to Jackie (Coogan)."[27]

The year 1941 proved to be a watershed year for America. Young men were being drafted into the armed forces as the country prepared for the inevitable war. On December 9, two days after Japan's brazen attack on Hawaii's Pearl Harbor naval base, America declared war on Germany and Japan. It was also in December 1941 that Harry James finally became a star.

As the year began, Harry James played another Paramount Theater engagement. He then made the vitally important decision to add strings to his orchestra, specifically for the Paramount date. George Simon, as well as several other important jazz critics, were appalled. He defended his move by claiming that "Morty Palitz suggested I add a woodwind section and a string quartet. I settled for the strings."

To further diffuse the issue, he told Simon in a subsequent *Metronome* interview, "It's only an experiment. If it works, fine. If it doesn't work, we won't use it." The much-maligned quartet of string players consisted of

Sam Rosenblum, Stan Stanchfield, and William Schumann on violins and George Koch on viola.

During those two weeks at the Paramount, the band played five sixty-five-minute shows daily, beginning at 11:36 A.M. and concluding with an 8:56 P.M. show; these shows consisted of both the band's set and its playing behind four acts. This was in addition to being featured on the Fitch Bandwagon show from 7:30 to 8:00 P.M. on the NBC-Red Network and then again from 10:30 to 11:00 P.M. for the West Coast. *Variety*, in a more favorable review, wrote: "James exercises showmanly discretion. The band can give with a brassy violence as ear-blasting as the next swing aggregation, but its confabulations of this description are deftly counter-balanced with some fine arrangements of a softer and more melodic idiom." The accompanying film was an apt choice, the Fred Astaire swing musical, *Second Chorus*, which also featured Burgess Meredith and Paulette Goddard, as well as Artie Shaw and his Band.

Harry James participated in the *Metronome* All Stars recording on the night of January 15, his opening day at the Paramount. Although he had been up since 6 A.M. and had done five shows and would be doing five more the next day, he never complained. He enjoyed seeing Ziggy Elman again and having the chance to again play in the same trumpet section. His most noteworthy contributions to this session were his characteristically swaggering solos on "Bugle Call Rag," splitting the lead with Ziggy, and, more particularly, on "One O'Clock Jump." Despite the ambivalence of the musical journey he was embarking on with his own orchestra, his playing on this session, just as on the All Star band session back in January 1939, proved he could still maintain his standing as an innovative jazz trumpeter alongside the best of his peers.[28]

In his continuing quest to bring original material to Harry James, Morty Palitz found the Yiddish folk song, "Eli, Eli," written in 1898 by Jacob K. Sandler. It dealt with the centuries-old persecution of the Jews and sounded very much like old Orthodox chants. Among others, Al Jolson had recorded a vocal version of the song, and the renowned violinists Jascha Heifitz and Mischa Elman had made transcriptions of it. During the Paramount gig, James wrote an instrumental arrangement of the song based on these transcriptions. He wanted to present a serious and dignified treatment of the melody without a trace of swing. His recording on January 22, 1941, marked his first use of strings on records. In addition, his emotional solo was praised for its pathos. In an attempt to establish the proper mood to play the warm and dignified, yet mournful song, Harry James wore a yarmulke during the recording session, thus becoming perhaps the first method trumpet player.

He first played "Eli, Eli" at a Flatbush Theater booking in Brooklyn nine days after having recorded it. As a publicity stunt, Harry James was photographed with Rabbi Jacob Altman, who was "invited by Harry to approve the mood and treatment of the James version of the song."[29]

In Dallas on March 3, 1941, Louise Tobin gave birth to their first son, Harry Jeffrey. Shortly afterward, Maybelle and Everette James were visiting their new grandson and daughter-in-law in her small apartment in Dallas. After their visit, when they left the apartment, Maybelle James abruptly collapsed and died.[30] She was only forty-nine years old. James had just finished playing "Eli, Eli" when Louise called him in New York at the Paramount, informing him of his mother's death.

Harry flew to Dallas to see his new son. Louise was confined to her bed with complications following the birth. Louise Tobin's sister, Virginia, Everette James, and Harry James drove to Beaumont for Maybelle James's funeral. Harry James then drove back with Virginia to Dallas before returning to Florida to rejoin the band.[31] He never played "Eli, Eli" again.

Three months later, James changed the entire string section with the exception of Sam Rosenblum on violin and added Al Friede on cello. This was the lineup of string players that provided the dramatic backdrop when Harry James recorded "You Made Me Love You" on May 20, 1941. It was destined to be the most successful and familiar instrumental record of his entire career. The sheet music alone sold an astounding one million copies.

It was also the recording that Dan Morgenstern, the well-respected jazz critic and head of the Institute of Jazz Studies, rightfully described as "the record that the jazz critics never forgave Harry for recording. This was despite the fact that he continued to play some formidable jazz solos and good music as well."[32]

George Avakian contends: "I always thought that 'You Made Me Love You' came straight out of Louis Armstrong. Harry didn't imitate Louis, but he had that quality, that power, that Louis had on ballads, especially when he reached the end of a phrase. The schmaltzy, sobbing-like phrases, of course, didn't come out of Louis at all. Harry borrowed that from Ziggy Elman's sentimental playing."[33]

Ah, the schmaltz! That German word, which means "sentimental or florid music or art," was used to describe Harry James's solos for the remainder of his career. In delivering the schmaltz, the sound of his trumpet now exhibited a much fuller vibrato, something he had demonstrated on occasion while with Ben Pollack and Benny Goodman and had used to advantage on his record of "All or Nothing at All." Harry preferred to describe his newly adopted trumpet style as an attempt to play with inner conviction. "I think the biggest thing with music is being sincere. I play it as I feel it. I believe in everything we play."

As mentioned earlier, "A Sinner Kissed an Angel" (by James's close friend, Larry Shayne), with Dick Haymes's vocal, was expected to be a big hit. The standard "You Made Me Love You," with a splendid commercial arrangement by Gray Raines that made full use of the strings for a romantic effect, was considered a suitable instrumental tune for the "B" side.

For some reason, Columbia didn't release the record until the latter part of the summer. This was possibly because of its fear of a backlash from the jazz critics. In line with that, in *Metronome* George Simon said facetiously that Harry James played the song "with an inordinate amount of feeling, though many may object and with just cause to a vibrato that could easily span the distance from left field to first base."

The "singing" on "You Made Me Love You" was supplied by Harry James's trumpet. As James pointed out, "I play as if I'm singing," making light of his concerted effort to interpret the lyrics of romantic songs in his playing. He also acknowledged that on the night he recorded "You Made Me Love You," he suddenly remembered Maybelle's suggestion, when he was a young circus cornetist, that he should play the way she sang, in a pretty and lyrical fashion. This quality then became a trademark of his many hit ballad renditions.

Coincidentally, Sidney Bechet, one of the classic New Orleans jazz musicians and the man who set the standard for the soprano saxophone, was also the victim of brickbats for his wide vibrato on the soprano at exactly the same time (the summer of 1941) Harry James was. In his biography, *Sidney Bechet, the Wizard of Jazz*, John Chilton wrote: "No listener could doubt Bechet's musical abilities, but for some people his wide vibrato was anathema, an aural hardship that prevented them from enjoying any of his work." Bechet was asked by the late jazz critic, Leonard Feather, about the criticism of his vibrato on the soprano. His answer echoed James's sentiments: "I play every number the way I feel it…. I look at the lyrics and try to get the same effect through my instrument that the words of the song express."

Harry James had been well aware that "You Made Me Love You" had been an important record back in 1914 for Al Jolson. It had been revived by Judy Garland in the MGM film *Broadway Melody* of *1938*, with a special arrangement written by Roger Eden, adding the famous verse, "Dear Mr. Gable." This followed her initial performance of the song at a studio birthday party for "The King" (Gable). Subsequently, Garland recorded "Dear Mr. Gable: You Made Me Love You" for Decca Records, which proved to be the turning point in the career of the sixteen-year-old actress and singer.

A few years later, it was to have the same effect on the career of the twenty-five-year-old trumpeter. Harry James had heard Judy Garland's record constantly being played on request shows on WNEW in New York and had been greatly moved. Following that, he had heard Bing Crosby's version with the Merry Macs, released in the fall of 1940. He convinced Morty Palitz that he should record it. Harry's trumpet successfully achieved the yearning quality Judy Garland had expressed in her vocal rendition.

Even with the abrupt change in the musical tastes of America, fifty years later, Harry's record of "You Made Me Love You" was prominently featured on the soundtrack of Woody Allen's *Hannah and Her Sisters*, one of his most highly praised films. Allen has used several of Harry James's records to enhance a romantic mood in other films as well.

In late January 1939, on the day Harry James left the Goodman band, Chris Griffin vividly remembered James remarking to him and Ziggy Elman, "I'm going to be doing some things with my band you guys are going to censor me for." "We looked at each other in amazement. We weren't sure what he meant," Griffin remembered.[34]

In May 1941, while on a two-hour break from his job playing four or five shows a day with the CBS Radio Orchestra, Chris Griffin walked across Eighth Avenue to see Harry James and his band at the Blue Room of the Hotel Lincoln. After the set, Griffin reminded James about his puzzling remark from a few years earlier. "When you said you'd be doing things Ziggy and I wouldn't like, did you mean things like that version of 'You Made Me Love You' you just played?" he asked. Harry smiled and replied, "That's right, Chris, and there's going to be a lot more like that."

Griffin added, "I think it was in the back of his mind even before he left Goodman that he could play commercial music as a last resort if everything else failed. And, of course, his tone was sure a great one for commercialism, plus the fact that it could project."[35]

Jess Stacy summed up his feelings: "I think people were waiting for it. Harry put his heart and soul into it."[36] Stacy's widow, Pat, wonders whether the frustration Bix Beiderbecke and Bunny Berigan felt in their failure to be accepted by the public for playing hot jazz weighed heavily on Harry James, and if he thought a more emotional way of playing would create success for him.[37] Certainly he had tried valiantly to make it with a swing band, but the public obviously didn't want that or wasn't ready for it, and he was heavily in debt. Was it the feeling that war was imminent that caused the trend toward more romantic music and was that the real reason for Harry James's steady drift toward commercialism? In retrospect, there is probably credence to all of these arguments in explaining the change in James's musical direction.

Comedian Mort Sahl, an astute observer of the big band phenomenon, summed up Harry's new musical approach. "Harry realized that strings are neutral, and they will help amplify anything you want people to feel.

He made commercial use of them to convey romanticism. The band looked good on stage and played well. Let's face it, the way Harry played ballads—he was the home office. Look how good the music was. It had a logic; it was so simple and yet it was stretched out. These renditions were like what Frank Sinatra did; they both made them into mini-dramas. Standing up there playing with the trumpet section and then coming out in front to play his solos gave his performance both drama and power. Sure, he was playing commercial music, but he had chops, and he was committed when he was playing a ballad. He wasn't a businessman waving a wand.

"You know, those bandleaders, coming out of the Depression, when people should be hopeless, I think they got to a point where they dared to dream. They were poets.

"The dignity of an orchestra taking the stage, whether they came out of the pit at the Paramount or they came out on a revolving stage at the Flamingo, it made you step up to that level, too. The musicians asked you to participate. You had to be somewhat hip."[38]

In the liner notes of the Columbia Legacy CD *Harry James and His Great Vocalists*, Will Friedwald insists that both Harry James and Louis Armstrong were "extroverted, exhibitionistically emotional players who were oft times willing to push the envelope of conventional taste to make every performance more exciting, which explains why a trumpeter-leader like James would become a superstar while more reserved players like Charlie Spivak never attained that status. The difference between James and Spivak is the difference between pure technique and technique put to emotional use; the difference between James and Clyde McCoy is the difference between the best kind of schmaltz and the worst kind of corn."

Harry never lost his all-consuming interest in baseball, which he now decided to adapt to music. He wrote "Flatbush Flanagan" (and gave the name to his new terrier), "Dodger's Fan Dance" (adapted from the ballet, "Dance of the Hours," in Ponchielli's opera "La Gioconda"), which was on the other side of Mel Tormé's "Lament to Love," and then "Take Me Out to the Dodgers, Rogers" in tribute to his favorite team, the Brooklyn Dodgers. James became close friends with Dodger manager Leo Durocher and several of the team's regulars. He spent many afternoons at Ebbets Field, often in the company of fellow rabid Dodger fan, George Simon. This provided the color and inspiration for writing these tunes. His enthusiasm for baseball became so well known that Dorothy Kilgallen commented in her July 1, 1941, column in the *New York Journal-American*, "On days when the Dodgers win, [Harry] leads his men like an inspired Toscanini."

In Everette James's living room was a table lamp made from a gold-plated Selmer trumpet given to Harry by the Brooklyn Dodgers. The team's autographs were engraved from the bell on down to the first crook, which therefore rendered it useless as an instrument. The first valve became the switch that turned the lamp on and off.

While the Dodgers were on the road, Harry's team played teams from various other bands in hotly contested afternoon baseball games in Central Park. By adding string players, the band now had enough men to field two teams, and they often paired off against each other in warm-up games. In one game, Bunny Berigan was the umpire behind home plate, complete with Dixie cups and a bottle of gin. He got so drunk during the course of the game that he couldn't continue and had to be replaced.[39]

Heavy drinking was endemic among big band musicians then. Violinist Glenn Herzer, who spent the summer of 1941 as part of the string section, was no exception. Al Lerner recalls how his fellow "mice" (as both Harry James and Tommy Dorsey referred to string players) would form a wedge around Herzer when the section stood up to play a solo. They were constantly afraid he was so drunk that he would fall down.[40]

That summer, one of the legendary stories about Harry James and his Orchestra took place, one that had some credence. The jovial Dutch-born tenor saxophonist, Johnny Fresco, a Jew who had left Europe fleeing from the Nazis, joined the band to replace Vido Musso. James had heard Fresco playing with Ben Pollack on a radio broadcast from the Casa Manana in Culver City and called to offer him a job. Fresco was reluctant to leave, since Ben Pollack had been like a father to him, but Pollack told him to accept James's offer. History was repeating itself.

Right after the saxophonist arrived in New York, he checked in at the Piccadilly Hotel, just around the corner from the Lincoln. The next morning he introduced himself to Harry James at the rehearsal. Harry said to him, "What do you play?" Fresco answered, "What do I play? I play tenor saxophone and double on clarinet." James said, "No, what position in baseball?" (Every musician Harry James hired for years afterward was asked that question.) I replied, "What? I never heard about baseball, and I'm not a sports nut; fights, soccer, maybe, but in Europe these days you don't think about baseball."[41]

James had to settle for Fresco's occasionally filling in by playing right field. Johnny Fresco admitted that he, as well as some of the string players, hated playing baseball because of the fear of breaking their fingers. One observer believes that one of Harry's problems with the band was that he seemed more interested in hiring men for their ability to play baseball than for their musical talent.

Al Lerner stopped playing baseball because of an incident that occurred while Harry was at bat. "I was playing third base. He hit a ground ball that I scooped up, and I threw to first. He was out. He went past the bag and then came back and put his foot on the bag. I yelled, 'You're out!' He said, 'I'm safe!' He asked Al Friede, who was playing first base, 'What was I?' Al said, 'I think he's safe.' I threw down my glove and shouted to Harry, 'If you're the leader on the field, too, I quit,' and I walked off."[42] (Twenty years later, Harry walked off the field in the ninth inning in a game with Ray Anthony's team in Las Vegas after an umpire's call went against him while he was pitching.)[43]

One afternoon, the bus pulled off the highway so that the musicians could play a game. The bus got stuck in a ditch. It cost Harry $300 to get towed and the band missed its gig that night.

It took sixteen years, but Johnny Fresco finally had the last laugh on Harry James. One night in July 1957, he came in to see Harry at the Flamingo in Las Vegas. He spotted a bright new talent in the person of Johnny Audino in the trumpet section. By this time, Fresco was the contractor for the ABC Network Orchestra. He offered Audino a job with the orchestra in Hollywood. When Audino gave Harry James his notice, James was furious. He called Fresco in Los Angeles and started yelling at him. "Now, wait a minute," Fresco said, "I don't give a damn about his trumpet playing, but he's a hell of a shortstop!"[44]

In 1971, when Harry was appearing on the *Hollywood Palace* television show and was backed by the ABC Orchestra, he encountered Fresco once again. Johnny remarked to him, "Harry, it's about time you talked to me." James opened a fresh bottle of vodka, his beverage of choice for many years, and offered him a drink. "Johnny," he said, "you wanna know something? That answer you gave me years ago when I was so angry at you about hiring Johnny Audino was the funniest line I've ever heard!"[45]

The fall of 1941 began the most significant period in the ongoing saga of the Harry James Orchestra. First, on September 9, along came five-foot, six-inch-tall Frank Pee Wee Monte, who had recently departed as manager of Benny Goodman's band. Monte had spent his time well with Goodman by learning all the intricacies of the band business.

It was Al Monte who told James that his brother was available. Harry immediately contacted Pee Wee Monte at the Forest Hotel and asked him to take over the management of the band. Pee Wee had originally encouraged Harry James to form his own band; now his job was to transform the James band into a solvent musical organization. They sealed the deal with a handshake. Thus began a close yet often troubled association that was nevertheless mutually successful for many years.

The band had been in debt for almost the entire three years of its existence. When Pee Wee Monte assumed control, James was approximately $42,000 in debt. Monte, ten years James's senior, felt he could conceive of a way to rescue the band.[46] One of Monte's first moves was to alert MCA that there would be no more 400- to 500-mile one-nighter jumps that the musicians had been enduring for much too long. He explained, "I quickly set up a rule that 200 miles would be the maximum travel distance between dates, even if it meant turning down an occasional engagement. Nor would I allow the band to travel at night after the completion of dates that had already been booked." (Before Pee Wee took over, the musicians often didn't know where they would sleep; they often drove through the night, and rest on the bus was hard to come by.) "It all worked out well— no accidents and no exhausted musicians."

Right after Pee Wee took over, the band played a series of nine one-nighters and showed a slight profit. Henceforth, every transaction was supervised and recorded. A budget was imposed, and the musicians were now paid on time.[47]

Actually, two years before, when Harry James started his band, he had forecast, "Of course, I can't expect to make much in dollars and cents right off … I think in the long run, though, I'll be making out much better financially."[48] It appeared as if this was finally about to happen.

Also, that September, Helen Forrest (née Helen Fogel), from Atlantic City, asked James for the chance to audition with his band. A highly respected band singer who had sung with Artie Shaw and Benny Goodman, Forrest had lost her job with Shaw when the clarinetist quit the band business the first time and abruptly departed for Mexico. She was with Goodman for twenty months, having replaced Louise Tobin, but she left after a succession of problems with his often peculiar personality.

Helen Forrest recalled, "I had met Harry casually a few times, but as soon as I heard the record of 'You Made Me Love You,' I decided I just had to sing with his band." James told her, "I'll be happy to hear you, but we have a ballad singer in Dick Haymes. I need a jump singer. I also can't afford you." When Forrest approached Haymes at the rehearsal, he said, "Don't be afraid of anything. Don't worry about me. There's room for both of us."[49]

Before she auditioned, Harry and Pee Wee decided that if the musicians voted for her, she was in. She sang the Gershwin classic, "But Not for Me," which she later recorded successfully with the band. When she sang the song, the band spontaneously applauded. Helen was hired at $85 a week (and $100 per recording), even though she was making $125 a week with Goodman and $185 a week back in 1939 with Artie Shaw.

As Forrest explained it, "I told Harry, 'I don't care what you pay. There's only one thing that I want. I want to start a chorus and I want to finish it

Don't put me in the middle and then have me sit down.' Harry's answer was, 'Okay, Babe.' And that's what he did—he let me do it my way, and that's why those songs became so famous."[50]

Helen Forrest was a great admirer of the work of another band singer, Ella Fitzgerald. They had a long friendship, and Fitzgerald was equally a fan of Forrest's singing.

Forrest's decision to join the James band was of tremendous importance both to herself and to Harry James. She became the most important female vocalist ever to work with his band, was featured on some of its greatest hit records, and eventually began a love affair with Harry that, by her own admission, she has never recovered from.

At the very beginning of their working together, Dick Haymes and Helen Forrest formed a close platonic relationship based primarily on a mutual admiration for each other's singing talent. Later, it resulted in their working together on the Autolite radio show from 1944 to '47 backed by Gordon Jenkins and his Orchestra. Haymes later named one of his daughters after her. Helen enjoyed Dick's spontaneous sense of humor. She recalled how they started out by making faces at each other while seated next to each other on the James bandstand.

Forrest believed that Haymes "could outsing Frank Sinatra while blowing bubbles. There's no contest for me. He had a better sound and a sweeter voice than Frank. Besides, Frank didn't have the range that Dick had."[51]

At first, Harry James couldn't understand why Helen couldn't memorize a song after singing it for the first time. He failed to realize that very few people had his photographic memory. She was compelled to write the lyrics on a card, which she held in the palm of her hand, while in the process of learning a new song.[52] Almost immediately, however, James and Forrest established an undeniable musical groove. "Along with Harry's Jewish phrasing we began to sound like a couple of rabbis chanting together," was how she described it. "There was a cry in our music."[53]

Her devoted admirer, Mel Tormé, had a slightly different take on it. Mel contended, "She 'kvetched' a lot with Harry"; he preferred instead her singing with Artie Shaw.[54]

In October, Eugene "Corky" Corcoran, a sixteen-year-old tenor saxophonist from Tacoma, Washington, left Sonny Dunham's band to replace Dave Matthews, who had departed to assist Hal McIntyre with his new band. James had originally learned about Corcoran from Joe Thomas, the featured tenor saxophonist with the Jimmie Lunceford band. Pee Wee Monte had also been very aware of his playing. As part of the agreement to join the James band, James was compelled to reimburse Dunham, who had only recently paid $500 for Corcoran's appendectomy.[55]

Besides being a formidable saxophone player with a full, raw sound influenced by Ben Webster and Coleman Hawkins, Corcoran was also a terrific third baseman, something that had obvious appeal to James. He adopted Corcoran and became his legal guardian, apparently circumventing the child labor laws that prevented Mel Tormé from joining the band a year earlier. For a time Corcoran addressed James as "Pop." Corcoran was to become one of the principal soloists in the band during several tenures over a thirty-five-year period.

Martin Block, on WNEW, had begun playing "You Made Me Love You" steadily during its first two weeks in release on his *Make Believe Ballroom* program. But, in the parlance of present-day record promoters, it was a record that "had to be worked" (constantly promoted), since many program directors and disc jockeys around the country weren't immediately that enthusiastic about it.

Glenn Miller's record of "Chattanooga Choo-Choo" was giving it formidable competition among big band recordings. It took three months before "You Made Me Love You" reached a peak of #5 and wound up spending eighteen weeks on the chart. "A Sinner Kissed an Angel" charted briefly a month later. These two records had a profound impact on the future popularity of the band.

In October, the Music Makers returned to Maria Kramer's Blue Room of the Hotel Lincoln for another extended stay, this time for seventeen weeks. This booking included several nationwide remote broadcasts on CBS with Mel Allen, who later did remotes as announcer with the band from the Astor Roof. Through this association, Allen became very friendly with James and Mickey Scrima. Later, he became famous as the radio voice of the New York Yankees.

The *Billboard* review of the Blue Room opening noted: "The eighteen-man band has improved tremendously and is playing dance music that's really exciting.... It's a full solid instrumentation capable of bringing to sharp life the colorful arrangements of Dave Matthews."

While at the Lincoln, James attended the Brooklyn Dodgers-New York Giants pro football game at the Polo Grounds. When he was asked by a newspaperman if he was Harry James, the bandleader, "No," he answered, "the football fan. When I'm on the bandstand, I'm Harry James, the bandleader. But when I'm at a football game, I'm Harry James the football fan." He impressed the writer with his knowledge of college football, emphasizing that he had a .900-average in predicting winners.[56] It appeared as if his growing passion for gambling had found a new outlet.

With Harry James seemingly on the cusp of stardom, Robbins Music finally published the book, *Harry James Trumpet Method*, co-authored by Harry and Everette, who was then teaching eight- to twelve-year-olds trumpet, trombone, saxophone, and clarinet at the two St. Anthony Schools in Beaumont. Selling for $2, the book combined academic training and modern studies along with ten of Harry's most renowned solos, including "Ciribiribin," "Flight of the Bumble Bee," and "The Two O'Clock Jump." Advertised as being "ahead of the times, it stands above all other methods. Technical studies cover the hand trill, half valve glissandos, alternate fingering for high notes, chords, triple tonguing, transposition, lip slurs, breath control, rhythms, etc." For several years, the book was established as an important trumpet manual in schools across the country.

E. C. Holland, who has been head of the Houston Local 65-99 for more than twenty years, was a student of Everette's for three years when he was a boy. On the publication of *Harry James Trumpet Method*, he eagerly read Harry and Everette's trumpet treatise. Holland observed, "Some of the solos he played, like 'Carnival of Venice'—certain little trills when he would be ad-libbing—things like that were all in his book." In summing up what he felt separated Harry from other trumpeters, he said, "The fire in Harry's solos and his melodic lines were entirely different [from anyone else's], and he did it with a good sound."[57]

Late that fall, the James band arrived at the Brooklyn Paramount at 8 A.M. after having driven all night from a date in Pittsburgh. Fans were lined up around the block waiting for the first show. As James remembered, when he got off the bus, "I thought there had been an accident or a fire or something because we hadn't seen a big crowd since we had started the band. So I walked up and asked somebody, 'What's wrong? What's everybody doing?' and the guy said, 'We're waiting to see Harry James.' I said, 'You're kidding. We're a hit?!' I didn't have any idea. All of a sudden 'You Made Me Love You' had caught on."

Following that triumph and several other successful dance dates, the band returned to Pittsburgh for an engagement starting New Year's Day 1942 at the Stanley Theatre. The day was bitter cold, the kind most people would prefer to spend indoors, especially since it was usually a day of recovery after perhaps an overly indulgent New Year's Eve. Instead, it was the beginning of a very successful week with both the audience and the press. Further, it was the first totally successful theater engagement in the band's almost three-year existence.

Herbie Mann, the musician who more than any other made the flute commercially acceptable in jazz, once described the motivation of every performer when he said, "Everyone who goes into show business is a perennial optimist. It's like the lottery—you always think your number is going to come up. You work like hell hoping for that day when it will finally happen."[58]

All the grueling years of hard work and dedication had at last paid off. MCA's band department was suddenly deluged with offers for Harry's band. "The Octopus," as the agency came to be called—its tentacles were everywhere—knew exactly what to do. At last, Harry James and his Orchestra had become a bona fide attraction.

6

Trees, The Legs, and The Lip

Lew Wasserman and the other members of the MCA hierarchy decided in early 1942 that its handsome trumpet-playing bandleader should be in the movies. As a result, after submitting proposals to various studios, two offers for "B" films were accepted. George Chasen, one of the most astute agents in the industry, who was also representing Betty Grable and guiding her to stardom at 20th Century Fox, became one of the team of MCA agents working on the James account.

The first film appearance for Harry James was a two-day shoot in New York for RKO in a picture called *Syncopation*. In it, he was part of a "Swing Fan's Dream Band" as selected by the *Saturday Evening Post* poll.[1] The remainder of the band consisted of fellow bandleaders and noteworthy sidemen such as Benny Goodman, trombonist Jack Jenny, Charlie Barnet, violinist Joe Venuti, guitarist Alvino Rey, pianist Howard Smith, bassist Bob Haggart, and Gene Krupa, who were seen playing in a jam session at the climax of the movie. Director William Dieterle attempted to trace the story of jazz and how it grew, starting in 1906. Unfortunately, the emphasis on its history got in the way of the film's plot. Jackie Cooper was the male co-lead playing a trumpet player (ghosted by Bunny Berigan) along with Adolph Menjou, and the female lead was Bonita Granville, who attempted to portray a New Orleans-bred piano player (ghosted by Stan Wrightsman.)[2]

Following *Syncopation*, James played the lead in a Universal musical quickie (sixty-nine minutes), *Private Buckaroo*, in which the band and Helen Forrest were joined by the popular Andrews Sisters, Dick Foran, Donald O'Connor, Huntz Hall, Moe Howard (later one of the "Three Stooges"), and Joe E. Lewis, the veteran nightclub comic, who had been the frontman at the Lincoln Tavern in Chicago when James first joined Ben Pollack. *Buckaroo* was a standard program musical that started production on April Fool's Day, 1942.

The premise of the plot is that Harry James is drafted into the army and his band goes with him. In one of the musical numbers, while he is still a civilian leading his band, he wears a more than slightly draped tuxedo complete with a long, drooping gold chain, a sign that the zoot suit was coming into fashion. In contrast, Harry James parading with his musicians in close formation wearing a dark brown army uniform replete with rifle, cartridge belt, and spats, was a sight that did little to establish him as a dashing leading man.

There is another telling observation in *Private Buckaroo* of perhaps more than trifling significance. When he is not soloing, James is seen conducting the band while cradling his trumpet in the crook of his other arm. This is a habit he doubtlessly acquired from watching Benny Goodman, who carried his clarinet in much the same way, like a king would a sceptre. This particular way of holding his trumpet at the same time indicated his respect for the instrument.

Among the twelve musical numbers in *Buckaroo* were renditions of "You Made Me Love You" with Helen Forrest's vocal, "Flight of the Bumble Bee," and "Don't Sit Under the Apple Tree," the latter with the Andrews Sisters, backed by James and the band. Despite the film's meager budget, director Edward F. Cline showed a flair for staging lively musical numbers.

The *Los Angeles Times* dismissed *Private Buckaroo*, however, as "like an endless series of tests of show headliners ... sometime they ought to get together and make a picture."[3] Universal's advertising copy for the movie broadcasted "Hot 'n' Sweet—Right on the Beat! Yeh, man!—Even the Jeeps are Jivin' ... in this wacky khaki caravan of zoot-tunes and zesty US Oh! Honeys!" Perhaps partly because of this 1940s hipster pitch, *Private Buckaroo* grossed over $1,000,000, a very respectable figure in those days for a "B" film.

The army even found something it liked. In one scene, Harry James awakens the troops playing "Reveille." A recording of his version was soon played at army posts throughout the war.

While filming *Buckaroo* at Universal, Harry James, Helen Forrest, and the band shot a fifteen-minute featurette, *Trumpet Serenade*, with the Jivin' Jacks and the Jills dancers, who had appeared in *Buckaroo*. To save money, it was even filmed on the same set. Forrest sang the very timely "He's 1-A in the Army and He's A-1 in My Heart." This short subject was one of many Harry starred in over the next two decades, which, although lacking any real production values, were fundamentally the predecessors of today's music videos.

In order to reach Southern California to appear in films for their film appearances, Harry James and the band traveled across America by bus doing one-nighters and theater engagements. Only this time, James was doing business—substantial business—setting attendance records at places he had played several times before along with new venues such as Maria Kramer's Victory Room of the Hotel Roosevelt in Washington and Frank Daily's Meadowbrook on the Pompton Turnpike in Cedar Grove, New Jersey. It was at the Meadowbrook that the James band appeared on the first *Spotlight Bands* radio program, sponsored by Coca-Cola.

Before the shooting of *Private Buckaroo* began, the band was booked at the Golden Gate Theatre in San Francisco for the second time. This time the gross was $41,000, topping Sammy Kaye's previous record of $35,000.[4]

Harry James was now drawing enthusiastic crowds of young swing addicts who had begun to elevate him to idol status. They often traveled from great distances, even in the wake of the early days of gas and tire rationing.

Now that James was emerging as a star and beginning to make money, Pee Wee Monte figured it was the opportune time to buy back Benny Goodman's financial interest in the band. Monte loaned Harry part of the money to complete the transaction. James paid Goodman something close to $20,000—not bad for an investment of $4,500 three years previously.

As a postscript, Mel Powell had a drink one day with Harry. He confided to him that Goodman had offered him financial backing if he wanted to start his own band. Harry immediately blurted out, "Don't!"[5]

Columbia released James's records, the keynote of any band's success, in timely fashion. Once one record had run its course, another was ready for release. The song pluggers now approached Harry first before other more prominent bandleaders, promising to put money behind any song of theirs he would record. It was obvious to the top executives of the major music publishing companies that Harry James led the hot band of the day, and the best and most melodic songs were initially offered to him first.

Shortly after the recording of the hit novelty song "The Devil Sat Down and Cried," by the singing triumvirate of Haymes, Forrest, and James, Dick Haymes left the band and was replaced by Jimmy Saunders, formerly "Sonny" Saunders, from Philadelphia. Years later, on a *Merv Griffin Show*, while Harry James and Dick Haymes were bantering with each other, Dick reminded Harry that he had fired him. Harry countered with, "I did not fire you. I merely said, 'You may go.'"

Helen Forrest had her first of several smash recordings with James when Frank Loesser and Jule Styne brought "I Don't Want to Walk Without You" to James, a tune that would forever be associated with the trumpeter and his band singer. When Jule Styne first played the song for him, Harry thought the tempo was too fast and insisted on doing it as a ballad despite Styne's protests. Fortunately, James's judgment was absolutely correct.

If there ever was a song that expressed the yearning and uncertainty of young American women in the early months of World War II, it was this record. Yet, seeing this and other ballads performed in personal appearances by Helen Forrest, with Harry James playing his rich, authoritative solos behind her, provided a feeling of reassurance at a time when there was little good news on the war front.

At a grandiose all-Gershwin concert at the Shrine Auditorium in Los Angeles on June 18, 1942, with the Los Angeles Philharmonic under the direction of Paul Whiteman, Harry James showed just how much the Loesser-Styne composition meant to him. He insisted on unexpectedly inserting it into his performance before playing a "Porgy and Bess" medley.[6]

Helen Forrest described their musical chemistry: "We had the same feeling for a song. Harry had a sense of what would work that was unsurpassed by anyone I ever worked with. He also underlined the melody like nobody else. For me as a singer, he was the best person to play behind a singer there ever was."[7] At the same time, Forrest was also well on her way to becoming known as "the best girl singer with a band, bar nobody," as Mickey Scrima aptly described her. The drummer added, "When you listen to some of the dumb things that she recorded, you realize that she made them all sound good. On 'I Had the Craziest Dream,' her intonation was absolutely perfect."[8]

Released in late February 1942, "I Don't Want to Walk Without You" was the most popular record in the country for two weeks and remained on the *Billboard* chart for almost four months. An underlying fact was that there were 500,000 jukeboxes in operation by 1941 compared to 25,000 when the Goodman band was launched. They were fed by salvos of nickels from exuberant teenagers who fueled the popularity of this and subsequent James records.

As a result of his selection as the country's favorite bandleader, due to the popularity of "I Don't Want to Walk Without You," Harry James soon received a gold record for making an unprecedented six more appearances on *Spotlight Bands* within a two-month period. This was one more than Tommy Dorsey, who was selected a total of five times on the basis of the popularity of his record of "This Love of Mine," featuring Frank Sinatra.

With the country at war, along with the resultant changes in popular music, Harry James decided there was no reason for him to compete with Goodman, Basie, Ellington, Lunceford, et al. Instead, he had chosen a far more commercially lucrative formula, figuring rightly that audiences wanted their heartstrings twanged. In his definitive book, *The Swing Era*, no less an astute musical authority than Gunther Schuller, the eminent composer, musician, and musicologist, described this formula as "irresistible: a star instrumentalist, technically invincible, romantic ballad singers ... and heady arrangements using strings, all superimposed on the vestiges of a jazz orchestra.... It was to turn into an incredible bonanza when James acquired Helen Forrest.... The point about Helen Forrest's success with James was not so much how she sang—she had always done that—but how effectively the James Orchestra and its arrangers supported her singing, enhancing it, and drawing from her many truly magical performances."

Schuller continued, "James saw that a singer of Helen Forrest's potential could in fact be a dominant force in the popular success of an orchestra, in effect a co-leader ... Other bands, especially Dorsey (with Sinatra) copied the formula. Singers took over the popular music field, jazz as swing was more or less driven out certainly as a leading force."

Harry James, however, refrained from totally betraying his jazz heritage, for he continued to mix ballads with swing tunes. "The Mole," the theme song of Chuck Cecil's nationally syndicated big band radio show, is a good example. Dave Matthews, who had become a disciple of Duke Ellington, continued to write charts and original tunes such as "Duke's Mixture" for James, while LeRoy Holmes (probably best known for his hit record of the theme from the John Wayne film, *The High and the Mighty*) contributed jazz instrumentals such as "Trumpet Blues" and jazz voicings to some of the band's ballad arrangements.

By December, Harry James and Helen Forrest were seeing more of each other off the bandstand than on. He affectionately dubbed her "Trees." Harry and Louise Tobin had been drifting apart from one another for months. James had little interest in the responsibilities involved in being a father. Simultaneously, Louise Tobin at last realized the extent of his womanizing. She discovered that his association with Maria Kramer was something more than a working relationship. She also found out that, while he was in Florida with the band and unable or unwilling to come home after Harry Jeffrey's birth, he was involved with Eleanor Holms's stand-in from her then-renowned aquatic show.

Tobin now not only had the responsibility of her infant son, but also the care of Everette James, who continued grieving over his wife's passing.[9] Harry James decided that his wife and father, accompanied by Tobin's sister Virginia, should drive to New York and move into the sumptuous apartment he had rented at 72nd Street and Riverside Drive. He and his father had already started their trumpet instructional book and needed to work closely together to finish it.

Despite the strain in their relationship, Louise agreed to the move. The long drive, however, became too much with a tiny baby. Finally, in Missouri, she and her young son boarded a train to complete the trip, with Everette and Virginia continuing by car.

The atmosphere in the apartment was extremely trying for Harry James, what with a constantly crying baby, Everette's ongoing grief, and the pressure of the deadline to finish his trumpet book. He began staying overnight at the Lincoln, explaining to his wife that all the confusion kept him from getting his rest. In reality, he was living there with Helen Forrest.

When Tobin realized what was happening, she confronted her husband. The situation was further complicated because she again found herself pregnant. She demanded that he get rid of Helen Forrest and come home. As she remembered this extremely stressful period, "He was reluctant to do that, and I never understood if it was to keep her with the band or what. Harry defended his actions by saying, 'I've got to keep this band going. You'll just have to do the best you can.'" All this tension upset Everette, and he decided to return to Beaumont.[10]

What followed was a period of total despair for Louise Tobin, or as, she described it, "the disintegration of my life as I had known it. I soon experienced the dark side of this man to whom I had been married all these years—his inhuman side, that cold, icy stare like you're not there ... his absolute indifference to his own children. This was especially hard for me since it was his idea to start a family. This other side of his personality seemed to prevail as time went on, and he became more, shall I say, in love with himself. He shut the world out and just did as he pleased, when he pleased, and how he pleased."[11]

She became suicidal and wrote her sister, Lucille, in California to take care of Harry Jeffrey if anything happened to her and to be sure that his father wasn't in any way involved with his upbringing. A few days later, three of her sisters came up from Texas and intervened. They brought her and her young son back to Denton. After a time, she moved to Los Angeles to live in a tiny apartment next to a building Lucille managed in order to await the birth of her second child.

Originally, James had wanted to name his second son Jascha after Jascha Heifitz; Tobin had wanted to call him Joshua. They settled on Jerin Timothy Ray, who arrived on March 21, 1942, at Good Samaritan Hospital in Los Angeles. The bandleader was not in attendance for this birth either.

At first, after Harry and Louise's separation, the band's publicist, Ade

Kahn, decided, as part of his campaign to bring attention to Harry in the gossip columns, which then had more importance to the public than feature stories, to link him and Helen as "an item." This was a distinct improvement and a departure from such tasteless column morsels as "Harry James suggests that Joe Stalin should warble to the Nazi army, 'I've Got My Ice on You,' " and "'Harry James suggests that all knitting clubs adopt the following slogan, 'Remember Purl Harder.' "

By the winter of 1942, Harry James and Helen Forrest were very much a couple. Walter Winchell wrote, "Hottest twosome in town, Harry James and his chirp Helen Forrest are making real-life love songs."[12] Louella Parsons soon reported in her popular Hearst newspaper column, "Harry James, the jitterbug maestro and his wife, Louise Tobin, have decided they can 'walk without each other, baby' [a play on the lyrics of "I Don't Want to Walk Without You"]. She will file for divorce any day now."[13] However, there was more infighting between the Jameses yet to come.

While his home life was coming apart, Harry James's public success continued to soar. To indicate exactly how hot James was with record buyers, Paul Southard, the sales manager at Columbia, announced that during the week of March 13, 1942, for the first time in the history of Columbia Records, two records by the same artist would be released.[14] They were his million-seller "Easter Parade" (which reached #2), backed with "Crazy Rhythm," as well as the even more popular record, "Sleepy Lagoon," backed with "Trumpet Blues."

Manie Sachs brought "Sleepy Lagoon" to Harry's attention. Harry readily acknowledged this fact in an NBC special, *Some of Manie's Friends*, in February 1959, following the premature death of Sachs, one of the most loyal and selfless friends of talented performers in the history of the entertainment business.

With "Sleepy Lagoon," Jack Mathias crafted an incredibly romantic setting, borrowed from Debussy's "L'Apres-midi d'un Faune," which featured Al Lerner's fluttering introductory piano solo backed with the strings. (When the chart was about to be recorded, the musicians noted that Jack had facetiously written on it, "Beat Me, Daddy, 28 to the Bar!")[15] In addition to Harry's warm solo, Hoyt Bohanon contributed one of the most well-remembered trombone solos of the entire Swing Era.

Harry James respected Hoyt Bohanon's musicianship immensely. On the recording of "Caprice Viennois," he experienced extreme difficulty in reaching a particular high note—a big octave jump at the beginning of the arrangement. He noticed that Hoyt could make the note on every take. He asked him, "Do you wanna play the solo?" The modest trombonist replied, "Gee, Harry, thanks."[16] When Hoyt eventually left the band, he was the first-call trombonist for years at Warner Bros; his haunting solos were prominently featured on Alex North's memorable score for *A Streetcar Named Desire.*

"Sleepy Lagoon" was #1 for four weeks and proved to have more staying power than any James record released thus far. It remained on the *Billboard* chart over four months.

Speaking of *Billboard*, its 1942 poll showed that the James Band had moved from 32nd to #3 among college students. It had also won Martin Block's *Make Believe Ballroom* poll. Bob Weitman, the good friend of many bandleaders as managing director of the Paramount Theater and later a Hollywood producer, predicted that in six months to a year Harry James would overtake Glenn Miller, who had finished first in the *Billboard* poll three years in a row. "He has had [talent] all the time. But he realized that while he played a great trumpet, probably the best in the business, he needed something else. So he added a cello, and a couple of fiddles, made some fine records, and began to climb fast."[17]

To keep the streak going, "Trumpet Blues" turned out to be one of the most requested jump (read jazz) records for Harry. LeRoy Holmes's arrangement owed much to the feeling inherent in the Fletcher Henderson-Jimmy Mundy charts for Benny Goodman, featuring call and response devices and a series of riffs by the trumpet section. The record of "Trumpet Blues" also served to display the precision and brilliance of the James trumpet section, features that would continue to be the trademark of all of James's bands.

Harry James and Helen Forrest were living the romantic dream their music was bringing to America. They became engaged, although, as Louise Tobin later snapped, "How could they be engaged when he was still married to me?"[18] To the end of her life, Helen Forrest wore the diamond ring that James gave her, although it was cut down to fit on her little finger.

Everette James became reconciled to the fact that his son wasn't going to get back together with Louise. On seeing Helen Forrest perform with him, he remarked of their association, "Musically, wow!" For a time, Harry seriously considered marrying Helen and discussed the matter with his father; reportedly Everette, although he liked Helen, objected to his marrying a Jewish girl.[19]

In her candid and informative autobiography, Helen Forrest made perhaps the most telling observations ever published about James's sexual appetite. "He could have had almost any woman he wanted. And did. Beautiful, ugly, tall, short, thin, fat. Harry had all he could handle, and he handled all he could. They rolled in and out of his room at an alarming rate, some of them so homely you couldn't believe he'd bother. The boys in the band used to say Harry would go to bed with anything in a skirt even if he had to put a bag over her face.

"Harry would laugh. It flattered the hell out of him to be told he was a sex symbol. He loved it.... he was attractive and charming. He could sweet-talk his way out of any situation.... There was a lot of the little boy in him. You laughed about him and loved him, no matter what."

As for her own sexual awakening, the singer admitted: "Harry was my teacher, and he was a great teacher. Very gentle, kind, caring about your pleasure as much as his. Harry loved ladies. He not only liked to make love to them, he loved them and cared about them. I cared about Harry. As the song goes, I was wild about Harry. He was the one I wanted. Harry was the most faithless son of a gun who ever lived.... Marriage didn't stop Harry from running. He was the world's champion long-distance lady chaser."

Ralph Burns, renowned for his work with Woody Herman and the only composer to win an Oscar and an Emmy in the same year (1974), explained Harry James's insatiable sexual appetite as symptomatic of "bandleaderitis." As Burns noted, "Bandleaders then were like the rock stars of today— great sex objects."

It was Forrest's belief that some of Harry's womanizing was attributable to the extreme loneliness that surrounded him during his entire career. My feeling is that his loneliness dates back to the isolation of growing up in a circus atmosphere. Helen added that she never found him able to be alone at any time while she was on the band.

After a performance, she would wait to go out with him, but she was never certain about whether it would actually happen. "I would wonder," she said, "is it me tonight or is it that broad from the audience. Sometimes he would just not show up." She would often hear female voices coming from James's dressing room, and would return to her room alone.

Before he came into her life, Helen Forrest realized that she had singing talent, but she thought of herself as homely. She had experienced a difficult home life growing up in a poor family in Atlantic City and Brooklyn and was left with an inferiority complex. It's therefore not surprising that she put up with his constant cheating. She really believed she wasn't good enough for him and that the other girls were more attractive. Forrest contended that, "Harry was happiest when he was playing a beautiful ballad. He was at peace, and he knew he was loved when he was playing the trumpet. He was a different person when he played. He knew nobody could hurt him. I think I provided him with some of that warmth during our affair."[20]

In May, columnists started heralding the news that Harry James and Helen Forrest would marry "when their respective decrees arrive." The truth of the matter was that neither Louise Tobin nor Helen's estranged husband, the Baltimore-based drummer Al Spieldock, were in any hurry to get a divorce from their respective mates. Therefore, their loosely defined romantic arrangement simply continued the way it was.

The eight-week booking that commenced on April 28, 1942, marked the James band's debut at the Hollywood Palladium and coincided with the end of filming *Private Buckaroo.* Opening night drew an audience of 8,000. The engagement saw 160,000 people attend what had become the most important ballroom on the West Coast and earned a net profit of $88,000, beating Tommy Dorsey's previous attendance record by $20,000. Winchell informed his readers of the difference between the success Harry enjoyed at the Hollywood Palladium and the debacle at Victor Hugo's during the band's last appearance in Hollywood two years earlier.[21]

Helen Forrest told me, "Unlike Artie Shaw, Harry enjoyed being a star, a celebrity. He loved hearing the cheers and having the fans reach for him and swoon over him." With his newfound stardom, suits became his one extravagance. He switched from loud sports jackets to tailor-made pin- and chalk-striped suits. These suits hung so easily on his lean and athletic frame that one writer compared to that of a college football end.

On occasion, he could even display a wry sense of humor. Once, while Forrest was singing "But Not for Me" onstage, as James was leading the band with his back to the audience, he pulled a delicatessen ham on rye from his pocket and took a large bite, and then offered it to her as she was finishing the last chorus. She said she could barely finish the song. "I just screamed with laughter and ran from the stage as the audience roared."[22]

Eddie Bracken, the comedian who starred in several Paramount films during the 1940s and has endured as both a character actor and a producer, once appeared at the Paramount Theatre for two weeks backed by the James band. The occasion was the premiere of Bracken's film, *Reach for the Stars.*

"I just remembered, ya know, when you're #1 in something you develop an air about you and a surety about you that's absolutely unknockable," recalled Eddie. "Harry was the boss of that band and the president of the United States when it came to blowing that trumpet. He also had a marvelous sense of humor, and whenever I would go out of my act and add things, he would be on the floor. He loved pantomime. [No doubt due to his own circus performing days.] I used to do crazy things like Red Skelton, and I know that he loved Red."[23]

Louella Parsons reported in her syndicated May 23 column: "Hollywood is getting hep. The 'hep cats,' 'the rug cutters' and the 'swing bings' are getting all their favorite swing bandleaders in the movies.... Harry James, who is coming into his own in a big way, received nearly 3,000 letters a week when he played at the Palladium in Hollywood. That's more than the average star receives." Not wanting to sound unhip (or unhep), Parsons added, "It is characteristic of the 'hep cat' set that they are disgusted with 20th Century Fox for calling the swing leader's next movie, *Springtime in the Rockies*. It should be *Swingtime in the Rockies* [one of Harry's featured solo numbers in the Benny Goodman/Carnegie Hall jazz concert], according to the rootin' tootin' rug cutters."

The radio announcer and former big band musician, Jerry Roy, believes Harry's style of playing during the Goodman years owed something to Bunny Berigan. "When you get to the low notes, a low C and D, you're hearing the way Bunny played with Benny in the '35 and '36 days," he contends.[24] No wonder then that in the midst of filming *Springtime in the Rockies*, Harry felt a great indebtedness to Bunny, who had died suddenly of pneumonia brought on by alcoholism. He arranged a benefit dance date at the Palladium on June 20 and the proceeds went to Berigan's widow, Donna.[25]

Harry James's appearance with the band and Helen Forrest in the splashy 20th Century Fox musical, *Springtime in the Rockies*, was also significant as the first technicolor musical ever to feature a name band. Directed by Irving Cummings, the film started production in late June 1942. Starring in this extravaganza, which was very representative of movie musicals of this period, were Betty Grable, John Payne, Carmen Miranda, Caesar Romero, Charlotte Greenwood, Edward Everett Horton, and Jackie Gleason.

Because he had so much work in Hollywood during the summer of 1942, James rented a home in the Hollywood Hills, while Helen Forrest leased an apartment close by. The fact that they were still married to others "and you didn't move in with someone as easily in those days as you do today" was the reason for their separate residences, according to Helen.[26] One night James called Forrest to say he would see her shortly after completing a business meeting with Pee Wee Monte. After waiting a long time, she called him impatiently to find out what was going on and heard female voices in the background. Harry explained that some of the musicians were having a party at the house, but that he was not involved in it and would soon be over to see her. His recently hired road manager, Sid Beller, ex-Ben Pollack sideman Alex's brother, got on the telephone and corroborated Harry's claim of complete innocence. Forrest decided to investigate for herself, only to discover an orgy taking place. She broke into his bedroom and found the trumpeter wearing only trousers, which he quickly zipped up. Yelling and screaming at him, she wound up delivering a swift and determined kick to his rear end, which almost sent him flying off a balcony.

Sid Beller called as soon as she got back to her apartment. He began breaking up with laughter. He and the musicians simply couldn't get over the fact that she had hauled off and kicked their leader with such gusto. When she asked why Harry hadn't called, Beller explained that Harry wasn't mad and that he had laughed as hard as any of them.

James didn't call nor did he come over to apologize. Soon, he began avoiding her away from the bandstand and she realized that he was seeing other women on a regular basis.[27] However, because of her job as band singer, she was compelled to keep her sometimes formidable temper in check.

At the Hollywood Canteen, the counterpart of the Stage Door Canteen in New York, which had been originally conceived by John Garfield and Bette Davis and located in what is today dingy downtown Hollywood on Cahuenga Boulevard, there was a sign posted: "Through these portals pass the most beautiful uniforms in the world." The late Maxine Andrews, one of the Andrews Sisters, said: "The Canteen brought out the best in the people as well as in the entertainers. Those who gave so many hours to sit and talk and dance with the GIs, and those behind the scenes in the kitchen and elsewhere, deserve medals of their own."[28] It was reported that Betty Grable set a record for having 300 GIs cut in to dance with her during an hour's time.

On the recommendation of Darryl F. Zanuck, the head of production at 20th Century-Fox, Harry James first brought his band to the Canteen to play on Monday nights from 9 P.M. to midnight during the early days of filming *Springtime in the Rockies*. In their initial days on the movie, Harry James remarked to Helen Forrest how "stuckup" he found Betty Grable. Gradually, however, a mutual respect developed, and James and Grable had lunch together several times at the Fox commissary. He learned that she had been at the Palladium one night to see the band during the first days of shooting. There was still no semblance of a romance, however.

On its release, Carmen Miranda's Portuguese version (!) of Glenn Miller's hit, "Chattanooga Choo Choo," nearly stole the picture. *Springtime*'s most enduring musical contribution, however, was "I Had the Craziest Dream," for which the studio expanded the James band to sixty pieces and, for some reason, dressed Helen Forrest in Native-American garb.

James and the band played one chorus of the tune before Helen Forrest's voice was heard and before she appeared on screen. A crowd of couples surrounding the bandstand suddenly parted and revealed Helen singing. Betty Grable was very disappointed that she wasn't asked to sing the plaintive Mark Gordon and Harry Warren ballad. Ironically, "Craziest Dream" eventually became Harry James and Betty Grable's "song."

Betty Grable looked radiant in her various outfits designed specifically to showcase her chorus-girl figure. The *Time* reviewer wrote, "Miss Grable has a body like an electric eel and she uses it with frenetic incisiveness." Theodore Strauss of the *New York Times* saw the film on its November 6, 1942, debut at the Roxy Theater and wrote: "For the record it should be mentioned that each appearance of bandleader Harry James on the screen was the signal for frenzied applause."

In the entire film Harry actually had only one line of dialogue: "How was it?" Betty Grable's response was, "As usual, Harry, too terrific."

Springtime in the Rockies combined all the right ingredients and broke the attendance records for a Fox musical at the Roxy. Further, it turned out to be one of the biggest grossing films of the year, garnering Grable a hefty raise from Zanuck. In Glasgow, Scotland, the film was so popular that it played continuously at the Picture House for an astounding total of seventeen years![29]

Now that *Springtime* was behind him, Harry James went back on the road, and he and Helen Forrest resumed their romance. That spring, a series of hit records kept James even more in demand. In order, they were: "Skylark" (even though Forrest was firmly against recording the song and had a problem with the bridge); "I Remember You" (a #1 record); "One Dozen Roses" (Jimmy Saunders' only hit); "Strictly Instrumental" (one of maestro Leopold Stokowski's favorite jazz records); and "But Not for Me" (another #1 record for Helen Forrest). The first quarter of 1942 saw Harry James selling between one million three and one million four records as compared to 325,000 during the first quarter of 1941.[30]

On August 19, 1942, the band began its first of several important engagements at the Astor Roof in New York. In the first week, it drew 8,500 cover charges, again beating (by 600) a record previously set by Tommy Dorsey.[31] This booking was also important to Harry personally, for in the audience one night were Enos Slaughter, Terry Moore, and Ray Sanders, respectively the right fielder, center fielder, and first baseman of the pennant-bound St. Louis Cardinals. These ballplayers then brought in various other teammates. Their enthusiasm for his music caused him to switch his allegiance permanently from the Dodgers to the Cardinals.[32]

Corky Corcoran, Harry's only close friend in the band, became as rabid a Cardinal fan as James. He often wore a Cardinal uniform on recording dates. (The James softball team also later wore Cardinal uniforms.) On one such occasion, James changed the structure of an arrangement, thus taking a solo away from Corcoran. The saxophonist responded, "If you ain't gonna use me, why'd you suit me up?" in true baseball parlance.

With Harry's incredible success on records, in ballrooms, hotels, theaters, on radio, and now in films, his own weekly radio show was the next logical step. Glenn Miller, who hosted his own radio show on CBS, was negotiating with the War Department to obtain a commission for himself, and there was speculation on which band would replace him. Gambling on receiving an offer to succeed Glenn Miller, Pee Wee Monte turned down several offers from various other radio shows.

In the summer of 1942, CBS brass approached Harry James about taking over Miller's fifteen-minute show at 7:15 P.M. on the network Tuesday, Wednesday, and Thursday nights. At first, there was opposition from Ligget and Meyers, which owned Chesterfield, largely because its executives believed that James was Jewish—whether it was his prominent nose, his recording of "Eli, Eli," his sentimental approach to love songs, or any of several other reasons. Because of this apparent anti-Semitism, James turned down the offer from the cigarette company.[33]

Finally, the two parties resolved their differences, and on September 24, 1942, Glenn Miller had two surprises for his nationwide radio audience. The first involved his band's version of "Juke Box Saturday Night," which contained several takeoffs on various easily recognized musical styles, including an imitation of James's trumpet playing. At the conclusion of the number, Miller announced, "That lad that imitated Harry James really did a job. The reason: because it was Harry James himself. Harry, come out here and say something." James uttered little more than a cursory, "Thank you."

Then Glenn Miller produced his second surprise: "Harry, naturally, we're very reluctant to give up our 'Moonlight Serenade' program after such a pleasant association with Chesterfield for such a long time, but, since I've got a date with Uncle Sam coming up, I can sincerely say I'd rather have you take over our regular Tuesday, Wednesday, and Thursday spots than anyone I know. You've got a swell sponsor and a great product, and with you and Helen Forrest and that band of yours, I know you're going to do a wonderful job. Sounds like the right combination to me. So, next Tuesday, get to work, Mister!" What followed was the slowest and saddest rendition of his famous "Moonlight Serenade" theme song that Glenn's band ever played, and indeed the show ended before it was completed.

Interestingly enough, Glenn Miller could have recommended the bands of Charlie Spivak, Claude Thornhill, or Hal McIntyre, in all of whom he had a financial interest. Although Miller and James were complete opposites in behavior and temperament, they had a respect for one another that dated back to the time they spent on Ben Pollack's band together. Harry was forever grateful to Glenn for suggesting him as his replacement.

Glenn Miller officially left the dance band business that night, but his Army Air Force Band—composed of such fine musicians as trumpeters Zeke Zarchy (from his original band) and Bernie Privin, clarinetist "Peanuts" Hucko, tenor saxophonist Vince Carbone, Mel Powell, guitarist

Carmen Mastren, bassist Trigger Alpert (from his original band), drummer Ray McKinley, arranger Jerry Gray (from his original band), and "The Creamer," singer Johnny Desmond—was without question even more outstanding than his earlier band. It was really more of a concert band than a dance band, although it served both functions in Great Britain and subsequently in France after Miller's tragic death in a flight over the English Channel on December 15, 1944.

The Miller legend was created by the lingering popularity of his many hit records, and the film biography with James Stewart only served to further it. The Glenn Miller Orchestra that began in June 1956 with Ray McKinley as leader and currently led by trombonist Larry O'Brien, has been the most consistent "ghost" band for more than four decades, touring for more than forty weeks a year. Over the years, the American musical critical establishment still has not given the Miller legacy much approbation. Artie Shaw echoed the thoughts of some of his contemporaries when he said, "It would have been nicer if Glenn had lived and his music had died."[34]

The popularity of the Chesterfield shows caused Armed Forces Radio Service to rebroadcast these programs throughout the world for the men in uniform. They were issued on transcription as *The Harry James Show.* During the war years, Harry and the band did many other shows that were heard on the Armed Forces Radio Service.

During the latter part of 1942, after replacing Glenn Miller, Harry James and the band broadcast all the shows from New York while the band played successive jobs at the Astor Roof, the Paramount Theater (where Harry was paid $12,500 a week), and the Lincoln Hotel. All were situated within a one-block radius. The band also appeared on the *Jack Benny Radio Show* (#1 in the nation at the time) and made subsequent appearances on the show the following year when it was in Los Angeles working on films.

Barry Ulanov in *Metronome* provided an accurate evaluation of the Harry James Band circa 1942 when he wrote: "Rarely has the public's faith in a band been so generously rewarded as it has in the organization headed by Harry James. Of the #1 favorites of recent years, Harry's gives its fans the most for its money.... His taste is the public's taste, and his pulse runs wonderfully right along with that of the man in the street and the woman on the dance floor....

"Whether or not you agree with or accept Harry James' taste doesn't matter in appraising this band. It's not the band of tomorrow. It's not an experimental outfit. It's not even the brilliant jazz crew that Harry fronted a couple of years ago. It's just a fine all around outfit that reflects dance music of today perfectly."

*   *   *

Harry James and Betty Grable renewed their friendship when they both entertained at a huge Christmas Eve party at the Hollywood Canteen. Betty casually mentioned that she needed a ride home, whereupon they left together at midnight when the Canteen closed. They stopped for hamburgers at a drive-in restaurant close by at the corner of Cahuenga and Sunset Boulevard where clusters of fans approached them, giggled, and asked for autographs.[35]

Their first date was dinner at Romanoff's, the highly celebrated Hollywood restaurant of the 1940s. The romance started from there, and with it an intense sexual relationship. On December 28, Grable threw a big party at the Palladium for James's December 28 opening. They were able to spend New Year's Eve together since, in January, James and the band were about to start shooting their first film for MGM: the technicolor musical, *Best Foot Forward*.

For Harry James, the year 1943 promised to be even better than 1942. He could look back on having grossed about $750,000 from film appearances, one-nighters, and record royalties in 1942. In that same year, he had won forty-two national popularity polls, including the *Down Beat* poll, as the #1 band in the country.

On January 16, 1943, another Jule Styne song with lyrics by Sammy Cahn, "I've Heard That Song Before," reached the *Billboard* pop chart for its first of twenty-five weeks; it was the most popular record in the country for an astounding thirteen weeks and proved to be the biggest James-Forrest record of them all. Before recording it, James decided to speed up the tempo from the version Styne had played for him. Once again, he showed what a total musician he was in making such a key decision.

At one point, the record sold so rapidly that Columbia announced that the wartime shortage of shellac prevented more copies from being pressed. It sold 1,250,000 records and was the biggest hit the company ever released. Its broad acceptance proved the veracity of composer Kurt Weill's statement, "Music is not bad just because it's popular."

As a result of the success of *Springtime in the Rockies*, along with his continuing popularity on records and on personal appearances, MCA sold Harry James to MGM as a contract player. Regarding the studio, which boasted that it had "more stars than there are in the heavens," the novelist John Updike observed, "The grandest of the major studios, MGM, was also perhaps the stupidest; certainly its products—bouncy musicals and family comedies and bloated costume dramas—didn't ask much intelligence from the American moviegoer."[36]

Best Foot Forward perhaps best illustrated Updike's sentiments. Adapted from George Abbott's Broadway production, which starred June Allyson and Nancy Walker, the film version found them reprising their roles. Besides the two young actresses, the film starred Lucille Ball, William Gaxton, Tommy Dix, and Gloria De Haven. The setting was a military school where the march tune "Buckle Down, Winsocki" was played. It soon became one of the first important rallying songs of World War II. Without question, the film's highlight was Harry's jitterbug sequence with Nancy Walker that was both sensual and comic. His agility, which he had developed under the circus tent and later served him so well on the baseball diamond, was very apparent on the dance floor. Such James favorites as the "Two O'Clock Jump" and "Flight of the Bumble Bee," which *Time* said "[made] an old-fashioned trumpet solo sound like a first lesson in occupational therapy" were also included in a prom sequence.[37] *Variety* contended, "Scholastic zest and pep, and the musical interlude, successfully carry the extremely fragile story premise."[38]

James's next MGM musical, *Two Girls and a Sailor* (originally called *A Tale of Two Sisters*), began shooting immediately following *Best Foot Forward*. This musical again starred June Allyson and Gloria De Haven, along with Van Johnson and Tom Drake. In addition to Harry James and his Orchestra, the film featured such musical guest stars as Lena Horne, Jimmy Durante, Jose Iturbi, Xavier Cugat and his Orchestra, and Virginia O'Brien. The *New York Times* wrote, "The film was a joy and a delight … it spins melody, humor, whimsy, and romance with a cast of engaging performers." The plot was a rather predictable wartime musical set against the backdrop of a "private canteen" à la the Stage Door and Hollywood Canteens. Besides Harry's numbers, the popular "Estrellita" and "Flash," June Allyson sang "Young Man with a Horn" with the band, which also backed the great Durante on "Inka Dinka Doo." James admired Durante and thoroughly enjoyed working with him.

Away from MGM, however, there were complications in the newfound James-Grable affair. For some time, Betty had been involved with the actor George Raft, who, at forty-seven, was twenty-one years her senior.[39] They had been originally brought together by Jack Benny's wife, Mary Livingston. Their liaison was referred to as "the Love Affair of the '40s" by the Hollywood press, although, in fact, they had first dated briefly in the early 1930s when she was merely a teenager. They appeared everywhere together, and Raft lavished her with gifts. Along with this largesse, however, came a stifling control. According to Betty Baez, for many years Betty Grable's closest friend, Raft was constantly telling her what to wear and when, and generally monitoring her appearance.[40] To further complicate things, he was legally married, although he had been separated from his wife, Grayce Mulrooney, for over twenty years.

George Raft was a product of New York's "Hell's Kitchen," and a former dancer-turned-movie-tough-guy who, in retrospect, might be considered a second-rate Humphrey Bogart. He was very friendly with the notorious Benjamin "Bugsy" Siegel, fresh out of "Murder Incorporated," who had migrated to Los Angeles to look after the interests of Meyer Lansky and his associates. On occasion, Raft had beaten her, so Grable knew how potentially dangerous he could be. She also knew he was a sore loser and would not give her up without a fight. Raft had Harry and Betty put under surveillance. One night the couple's lovemaking in Betty's bedroom was interrupted by a loud thud followed by a stream of groans and profanities. Looking out the window, they saw one of George's flunkies, Ben Platt, limping away. He had fallen from a neighboring tree while attempting to spy on them.[41]

Despite the implied threats, Betty Grable and Harry James started going out together in public. One night they went to see Benny Goodman at the Palladium. A few evenings later, they were dining in a Sunset Boulevard restaurant when Raft approached their table and began shouting obscenities at Grable. Harry James leaped up and hit Raft with a right cross. He continued with a flurry of punches that floored Raft before the fight was stopped. Flashbulbs went off, and the next day newspapers headlined "Actor and Bandleader in Brawl over Betty Grable."

Darryl Zanuck was furious at the news. He called Grable off the set of *Coney Island* to report to his office immediately. The diminutive mogul sternly reminded her that being involved in such an altercation had a serious effect on the wholesome image the studio's publicity office had crafted for her. Her first reaction was to tell him off, but she held her temper. She realized that even superstars can be put under suspension, as she later would be when she turned down various scripts.

Betty Grable definitely enjoyed the spotlight, and being the focus of a nightclub fight only served to feed her ego. She was also flattered by James's chivalrous behavior in this crisis. The incident served to sever her relationship with Raft, and despite his constant barrage of apologetic letters and flowers, jewelry, and finally a fur coat, she absolutely refused to see him.[42]

"I would have married George a week after I met him," Betty Grable revealed to Louella Parsons, whose column served as Grable's forum to disclose the exclusive news, "but when you wait two-and-a-half years, there doesn't seem to be any future with a married man." In her appraisal of the situation, Grable seemed to have conveniently left out the fact that Harry James, too, was still married.

In 1942, Betty Grable had suddenly emerged as an important movie actress and was about to become the biggest female star of her time. Her starring role in *Song of the Islands* had resulted in a sudden avalanche of

1,000 fan letters a week, and, more important, boosted her to eighth position among the top 10 box office stars. The next year she became the #1 box office star in the industry. She was to remain in the top 10 for eight more years, longer than any star in the history of the motion picture business.

The climb to the top had been anything but easy for Elizabeth Ruth (Betty) Grable, born December 18, 1916, in St. Louis, the daughter of Lillian and Conn Grable.[43] She had a sister, Marjorie, and a brother, John Carl, who died from pneumonia before his second birthday.

Betty Grable started out as a dancer and singer, following the direction of Lillian, her determined stage mother. Lillian needed a hip operation at the time of her pregnancy with Betty and chose not to have it. This later caused her to rely on crutches, a cane, or a wheelchair to get around.

In 1929, at the age of thirteen, Betty Grable headed for Hollywood with her mother, hoping to star in movies. For the next several years, she appeared in chorus roles and bit parts, and frequently posed for "cheesecake" photos. Within a year, she became one of the first "Goldwyn Girls," along with Paulette Goddard and Lucille Ball, the striking group of singer-dancers who subsequently appeared in three film musicals produced by Samuel Goldwyn.

In 1933, she spent most of the year singing with Ted FioRito's Orchestra while the band toured California. Then short stints with the bands of Jay Whidden and Hal Grayson followed. Lillian chaperoned her on these tours. While working for FioRito, she met the wives of various dance band musicians. She heard firsthand about the isolated and lonely life they led waiting for their husbands to come home from their one-nighter tours. Unfortunately, the young bandsinger didn't fully grasp the problems inherent in such a life, nor could she realize how they would later have serious repercussions in her own married life.[44]

During this time she fell in love with Charlie Price, the drummer in FioRito's orchestra. The two young lovers discussed getting married, but when Price asked Lillian Grable's permission, he was stunned by her declaration: "Betty will never marry a musician; she's going to be a star!"[45]

Returning to film musicals in 1934, Betty Grable performed in her first featured dance number on film (with Edward Everett Horton) in one of the first epic Fred Astaire–Ginger Rogers musicals, *The Gay Divorcee*, which resulted in an RKO contract. She next appeared in *Follow the Fleet* with the terrific twosome. During these films, she witnessed the crass behavior of Ginger Rogers toward chorus dancers. Grable never forgot this, and, years later, when she became the bigger star, always showed respect for the chorus dancers, while treating Rogers in a decidedly icy manner.

During the period she sang with Ted FioRito, Grable met Jackie Coogan, the one-time child superstar from *The Kid* with Charlie Chaplin. Coogan's fortune had been stolen away by his greedy parents, which ultimately resulted in the "Coogan Law" being passed to protect the wages of child performers. He was attempting to rebuild his shattered career. Betty's interest in his welfare turned into a love affair that caused a rift in her relationship with Lillian. Jackie Coogan and Betty Grable were married on December 20, 1937, two days after Betty's twenty-first birthday.

After graduating to co-starring roles with Coogan in the Paramount musicals, *College Swing* and *Million Dollar Legs*, and making radio appearances with him, Grable saw her own career suddenly cool off. Her marriage became troubled because of Coogan's constant infidelities and heavy drinking. As a result, Grable divorced Coogan on October 11, 1939, arriving in Santa Monica Court with her new lover, Artie Shaw.[46]

After being shown some provocative publicity photos of Betty Grable performing at the Golden Gate Exposition in San Francisco, Darryl F. Zanuck was so intrigued that he wanted to know who she was. This led to his immediately signing her to a Fox contract. Composer and producer Buddy DeSylva had seen Betty perform at the Golden Gate Exposition, and, since Zanuck had no immediate film ideas for her, she accepted De Sylva's offer of the role of Alice Barton in Cole Porter's *Du Barry Was a Lady*. The musical opened on December 6, 1939, on Broadway and starred Ethel Merman and Bert Lahr.[47]

Although she had a somewhat less important starring role, she was a sensation in the show. *Time* called her "a lovely little trick who knows her stuff in both songs and dances," although it cautioned that she was "not so blonde as pictures."[48] The critics adored her, and she became the toast of Broadway. Cole Porter remarked, "If the show accomplished nothing else, it once and for all made it unnecessary to identify Miss Grable as 'Jackie Coogan's ex.'" Following that, she appeared on the cover of *Life* magazine.

While in New York, she renewed her relationship with Artie Shaw, who, many decades later, still remembered her as "a gorgeous girl. She probably had the best body of any girl I ever knew."[49] Their romance had an abrupt end, however, when Shaw eloped with Lana Turner on February 12, 1940.

Zanuck, of course, was well aware of Betty's success on Broadway and brought her back to Hollywood to star opposite Don Ameche in *Down Argentine Way*, replacing Alice Faye, who had taken ill. It began shooting on June 21, 1940.[50] This was Betty's breakthrough film, the first of a grand total of twenty-six movie musicals Grable made for Fox. Most of them followed a formula: a lively musical score performed in a backstage setting, a tall, dark, and handsome leading man, male and female sidekicks, and Betty Grable playing the part of a spirited, provocative young woman who worked hard to attain success and marriage. Naturally, it was wrapped up in garish technicolor that showcased her freshness and blonde beauty.

These 1940s Grable musical vehicles could in no way be compared to the more meaningful and artistic musicals turned out by the Arthur Freed unit at Metro-Goldwyn-Mayer at the same time, such as *Meet Me in St. Louis, 'Til the Clouds Roll By, Ziegfield Follies, On the Town, The Pirate,* and *The Barkleys of Broadway.* The American moviegoing public however, adored Grable to the tune of well over $100,000,000 in box office receipts for Fox in an era when movie admissions were less than a dollar and marketing campaigns hadn't even been thought of.

And how they worshipped *the* photograph! The picture of Betty Grable looking over her shoulder, dressed in a white backless one-piece bathing suit, wearing an ankle bracelet (given to her by George Raft), became the most celebrated cheesecake photograph of the war years,[51] even exceeding the popularity of the famous pose of Rita Hayworth kneeling on her bed adorned in a negligee. Begining early in 1943, it was tacked over the bunks of GIs from the Aleutian Islands to Algeria. From then until the end of the war, according to Fox, over 3,000,000 prints were made and distributed, mostly to the armed forces. Captured German and Japanese soldiers were found carrying it in their backpacks. It even had its honored place above my cot when I was a ten-year-old camper at Camp Kewanee in East Jewett, New York, during the summer of 1944.

Given this photograph, it seems difficult to comprehend the fact that Betty Grable didn't relish posing and would only permit a few shots for each pose. Frank Powolney, the photographer, believed the term "pinup" was born with the release of this photo.[52] It also established Betty as representing a new kind of sexuality—fresh, natural, with a hint of flirtation—a departure from the smoldering, rather exaggerated image projected by Jean Harlow during the 1930s. For the rest of her life, she was approached by war veterans telling her how much the photograph meant to them, how it reminded them of the girls back home, and how it helped them to withstand the aftermath of combat.

On February 16, 1943, Betty Grable, carried aloft by three servicemen, one from each of the armed forces, added the impressions of her right leg and both feet to the celebrated cement courtyard at Grauman's (now Mann's) Chinese Theatre on Hollywood Boulevard.[53] The next step for Fox was to have her legs insured by Lloyds of London for $1,000,000. She patted one leg and said, "This is half a mil," and then the other, "and this is half a mil—you little money makers." Through the valiant efforts of its publicity department and her own talent, 20th Century Fox had given birth to a megastar.

Betty Grable and Harry James spent time relaxing with the Zanucks at their home on the beach in Santa Monica. They both enjoyed the informality and generosity of Virginia Zanuck, who arranged for them to have adjoining bedrooms during their visits. Zanuck liked James, but had certain misgivings that, if and when he married Betty, her appeal to the public and servicemen might suddenly be diminished.[54]

Now that *Best Foot Forward* and *Two Girls and a Sailor* were completed, Harry James and the band headed for Chicago on a train for a week of Chesterfield shows and then on to New York for four weeks at the Paramount. Other bands that could afford it, like Benny Goodman and Duke Ellington, had traveled by train in the past. Because of gas rationing, it had become almost a necessity. With Ellington it was a must because of the constant Jim Crow conditions throughout the South and Southwest that his band constantly faced while on tour.

By 1943, the Music Makers totaled twenty-seven musicians. The string section was now composed of four violins, two violas, a cello, and a bass, plus the addition of two French horns. With these expanded sections, the romantic sound of the band on ballads was heightened even further. On the jump tunes, the strings merely played chords, which was very dull for the musicians, but Harry figured rightly that they just couldn't sit there and play nothing.

Violinist Gene Orloff, who for years has been a successful contractor for record dates in New York, was a member of the string section for several months in 1942. Orloff contends: "The strings were only used in an average way. It's my feeling there could have been even better arrangements written because that string section was really pretty good."

Now retired in Boca Raton, Florida, after a long and lucrative career in the recording studio and years spent with Sid Caesar's *Show of Shows* and *The Perry Como Show*, Arnold Eidus, the concertmaster of the string section, admired Harry's musicianship and also liked him personally. "He wasn't that emotional a person. I think he was shy—and I never heard him lose his temper. After I left James, I worked one week with Tommy Dorsey before I quit. I wouldn't work for that man for all the money in the world. He wasn't my kind of person."[55]

Although Orloff thought violinist Sam Caplan was a mediocre player, Sam was a particular favorite of Harry James. Like James, he relentlessly pursued women. Not only did he get them for himself, but he often approached women at dance dates saying, "Would you like to have a drink with Mr. James?" During that time, Sam also provided marijuana for Harry and the rest of the band.

Trombonist Bill Abel, who had participated in the Temple, Texas, high school competition as a member of the Port Arthur High School Band back in 1931, joined the band at this juncture, replacing Dalton Rizzoto. He was a friend of alto saxophonist and singer Johnny McAfee, who brought him to Harry's attention. He remembers: "Harry was probably the best leader as far as treatment of the band that I'd ever worked with. Anytime he ever corrected you or corrected the section, he did it with precise instructions, and he'd say, 'That's the way I want it played.' That's all you'd hear; he wouldn't rant and rave."

In those days, when the band played the Paramount, the first of the five shows began at 10:30 A.M. They also did two Chesterfield radio shows, one for each coast, three days a week, that had a national audience of 35,000,000 listeners. During the last week of the Paramount engagement, the band doubled at the Astor Roof for two sets a night that ended at 1 A.M. Their musical workday during that week lasted almost fifteen hours.

With the country starved for "live" entertainment, and the James band continuing to record hit after hit, it had become the most popular dance band in the nation. James's fan base was from ten to seventeen years old, and there were now 167 Harry James fan clubs in operation. With the possible exception of Bing Crosby and Frank Sinatra, Harry James had become the biggest musical star of the time.

The money kept rolling in for James as well as for his musicians. The band was usually grossing between $20,000 and $30,000 a week on the road and as much as $40,000 at certain times later that year and in 1944. It had a weekly payroll of between $5,000 and $6,000. With record and publishing royalties, film appearances, one-nighters, theater and ballroom engagements, radio appearances, and so on, the Band grossed over one million dollars in 1943. Broadway columnist Earl Wilson speculated James was netting half of that.[56]

Pete Candoli, the revered lead trumpeter who played with several major big bands—most prominently featured with Woody Herman and Stan Kenton—has enjoyed a long career as a studio musician. He got to know Harry James during this period and believes that James was carefully packaged—perhaps more than he was actually aware of. "If you ever saw his picture on posters or on a new hit coming out on a piece of sheet music, they portrayed him like a WASP Caesar Romero. He was always dressed in a sports jacket with the horn next to him. The publicity people and the studio people decided what Harry James represented. They had the tailors make his suits, and the way he looked in them added to his popularity. If you were a producer at any one of the studios, all you had to do was write a part for the band and put the main man, whether it was Harry James or Xavier Cugat, in the picture."[57]

Because James was so shy and retiring, I asked Candoli whether Harry went along with the image that had been created for him. "He didn't care after a point. He thought, 'I'm Harry James. They know who I am. They like me.' The success, the hits, and the photographs, first class everywhere, all the way. It got to be where it didn't bother him. He always was what he was.

"He would have loved to still be a jazz musician. It had nothing to do with the music or his blowing or his desire to play. I guess what he endured early on had an effect on what he became. If you look another way—how he played was also a factor—the playing was marvelous. He played beautiful, sweet ballads. He had a tremendous facility."

Candoli made the keen observation that, although Harry James was very masculine, the sound of his trumpet playing was actually quite feminine. "Bobby Hackett played pretty ballads. [James admired Hackett's playing.] They weren't feminine enough, however. In those days Harry was in the midst of the romantic aspect of his playing. All the tunes that the publishers gave him, they were all tailored to him."

The Paramount engagement, that began on April 21, 1943, was referred to as "James's 30-Day Riot." The *New York Times*, which was located around the corner on West 43rd Street, had its doors blocked by the influx of teens and pre-teens who began standing in line at 4 A.M. on opening day, some of them wrapped in blankets and a few even carrying lanterns. By 9 A.M., the line was thought to total 7,500 fans.

Outside, the kids broke a large plate-glass window and a policeman's rib as well. Inside, the young fans jitterbugged in the aisles and up on the tiny bandstand. Ushers were posted in front of the stage to push them back. It was absolute pandemonium. Harry had sandwiches brought in rather than risk going out to a restaurant and getting mobbed.

The noted journalist, Max Lerner, wrote in the newspaper *PM* that here was a modern version of the old Greek processions in honor of Dionysus, who was the Greeks' excuse for cutting loose in the spring. "Only instead of the radiant young god, you get a tallish young man with a horn," he added.[58] Another *PM* feature writer, Albert Deutsch, found an analogy between the James jitterbugs and the Children's Crusade in the year 1212.[59] Seeing the band during the first week of the Astor Roof, *Harper's Bazaar* referred to Harry as "a mundane Gabriel, a slender young man with oil-slicked curls, enthralling adolescents.... He looks cold but blows hot."[60]

Al Lerner remembered that Dave Barry, the Broadway comic on the bill, got a good many laughs during the first show. "But the kids stayed all day. They had sandwiches with them. By the time of the third show, they knew every joke; they'd throw out the punch line before he could get to it, which was very depressing for a comic."[61]

To alleviate some of the boredom from playing show after show at the Paramount, Al Lerner injected his own brand of humor by purchasing a water pistol. Several other musicians followed suit. Squirting contests erupted between Al and other musicians from one end of the band to the other. Finally, Mickey Scrima started griping about the water damage done to his drum heads. At first, Harry didn't catch on to what was happening since his back was to the band. Finally, Bob Weitman had had enough. He was standing in the wings and yelled out during the midst of a show, "Okay, kids, stop with the squirt guns!" Of course, the young fans in the audience thoroughly enjoyed watching the war games taking place on stage.[62]

Since the area around the *New York Times* building had been inundated by the frenzied youngsters and their destructive behavior, its editorial page writer was compelled to remind adults that these kids represented only one-one-thousandth of New York's young, with the rest safely at home helping mom and dad. The *Times*'s august music critic, Olin Downes, who had haughtily dismissed the Goodman Carnegie Hall jazz concert five years earlier, found James, "a very good player who can summon a heart-throb of a vibrato, do stunts of triple-tonguing and virtuoso figuration." He sniffed, however, that he heard little to distinguish him from "a round dozen of his highly publicized colleagues of the same calling."

The famous partygiver Elsa Maxwell, in her May 20, 1943, *New York Post* column, waspishly expressed the thought that James was serving "emotional gin" to minors. "Instead of ushers," Maxwell wrote, "the Paramount should have psychiatrists to show patrons to their seats."

Not all of his fans were minors, however. A gray-haired seventy-year-old woman swooned, "I just have to see him. He sends me!"

Abel Green, the venerable editor of *Variety*, perhaps best characterized the James phenomenon when he wrote, "There's something healthier about this manifestation of juvenile spirit than what we now look upon as Prohibition's Jazz Age."[63]

Attendance for the first week was estimated at 163,000 and the gross receipts $105,000, an all-time record for a nonholiday week. James could revel in the fact that the attendance was about 2,000 more than Benny Goodman had attracted during his first week at the Paramount back in 1937. The theater, which had 3,664 seats, was forced to schedule six and later seven shows a day beginning at 7:30 A.M.

Understandably, as a result of the murderous schedule, James's phenomenal stamina exhausted itself and he suffered a minor nervous breakdown. Bob Weitman hired an expensive psychiatrist to consult with James over the period of a week, and after several hours of therapy, he surprised everyone by his seemingly bizarre prescription. He advised James that he should get back to work as quickly as he could or suffer permanent damage to his career.

Singer Buddy Moreno had joined the band at the Hollywood Canteen after leaving Dick Jurgens's popular band in the Midwest. When Moreno arrived at the Paramount the morning after Harry's illness, standing in the wings he heard a trumpeter playing James's solos. He knew it wasn't Harry; instead it was Jimmy Campbell, a member of the trumpet section. Bob Weitman told Moreno what had happened and quickly pressed him into service. He told him to go out in front of the band and inform the audience of James's illness.

"I was met by a sea of groans. I leaned over to the saxophone section and asked Claude Lakey what the next tune was. Claude informed me it was 'The Mole.' He suggested, 'Just take your hands, bring 'em up, bring 'em down, give us a down beat. We'll take it from there.'" As Moreno remembered it, "It was quite an experience, kind of like being thrown to the wolves."[64]

Frank Sinatra filled in with the band for a few days during James's illness. When "The Voice" came out on stage in front of the band, it caused almost the same reaction from the audience as James had. This was Frank's first appearance at the Paramount since his history-making eight-week appearance with Benny Goodman's band on December 30, 1942.

Following Sinatra, Henny Youngman fronted the band for a few days. Herschel Gilbert joined the band at the Paramount as a violist, fresh out of Juilliard School of Music. He went on to become a three-time Oscar-nominated composer, but is perhaps best remembered for writing the theme of the popular television series *The Rifleman*, starring Chuck Connors. Gilbert was quickly introduced to show business on stage by Youngman's slapping his cheek and admonishing him, "Didn't I tell you to practice?"

In a May 16, 1943, article in the *New York Times* magazine by S. J. Woolf, Harry James was referred to as "The Pied Piper of Gotham." Harry analyzed his appeal, particularly to young people, when he remarked: "Rhythm comes natural to everyone. And when kids hear it they respond to it. But they haven't got all their feelings under control. They are not ashamed of showing that they are happy or sad. Most of them are full of emotions that are ready to burst out. They have to get rid of these overflowing feelings, and listening to music gives them a good healthy outlet."

In the first six months of 1943, Harry James's staggering record sales of $3,500,000 were far more than any other record company's previous sales figure for a six-month period. These figures were second only to Bing Crosby's.

Away from his succession of musical triumphs, Harry's marital situation remained unresolved. Louise Tobin was still living in Los Angeles. Shortly after her second son's birth, she had gone back to work singing with Lud Gluskin's band on a CBS radio show.[65]

Louise was then friendly with the Newman family. There were seven brothers, five of them in show business: Alfred Newman was then the most powerful music man in Hollywood as the head of the music department at 20th Century Fox. Emil was a conductor in films; Lionel was then a rehearsal pianist at Fox; Marc was an agent; and Robert was a studio executive. Lionel Newman had previously conducted the music for Tobin in an Earl Carroll revue and recognized her beauty together with her singing talent. With his brother Alfred's help, Marc Newman arranged a Fox screen test. Louise tested well, which led to Marc's starting to negotiate a contract for her. She, however, asked him not to proceed further—she really wanted to sing more than she wanted to act.

Louise Tobin and Harry James finally worked out an agreement for child support totaling $1,100 a month for her two sons. James still never discussed getting a divorce. An important factor for him was maintaining his 3A draft status (married and sole support of a family). This was certainly preferable to being reclassified 1A, which would make him eligible for the draft.

During James's trip back east, Betty Grable had missed him terribly. Her close friends Martha Raye and Dorothy Lamour tried to boost her morale, but with little success. Lucille Ball remarked, "I remember I'd go to see her, and she'd lie on the floor with her radio right next to her ear when Harry was appearing in Chicago or some place. Everything else would stop when he was playing. It would be blaring, and she'd be listening to that horn." To quote the vernacular of show business gossip columnists of the time, Harry kept "the long distance phone wires ablaze" with calls.

Not surprisingly, after finishing production in May on *Sweet Rosie O'Grady*, Betty asked Zanuck if she could go to New York to visit some friends.[66] He asked her if her proposed trip was merely an excuse to see Harry James. Betty admitted that she loved him; Zanuck gave her some time off, but asked Betty to keep any more news of her romance with Harry out of the press until Harry was at least divorced. Then, if all went well, they would be free to marry with the studio's blessing.

Lillian Grable counseled Betty that perhaps she would be better off single for a while. Grable replied, "I'm twenty-six and single and that's practically middle aged. If Harry wants me, we're going to get married."[67] Although Lillian wasn't that keen on Harry, she recognized his newly found status as a highly popular musician. Of course, she didn't want Betty close to anyone who might wrest control of her daughter from her.

Betty Grable left by train for New York with her sister, Marjorie. After a passionate reunion with Harry at the Astor Hotel, he proposed and Betty accepted. He then asked her point-blank if she could handle the adulation of his fans after they were married. Betty Grable laughed and said, "That will be the least of our problems. I'll just get Wells Fargo to escort you home from the theater every night."

One afternoon she and her friend, Paula Stone, who had been under contract to RKO with Betty Grable in the early 1930s and then was a Broadway producer, were walking in Times Square. Suddenly, a roar went up from the crowd. Someone shouted, "BETTY GRABLE!" Throngs of people rushed toward them, which terrified Betty. Paula Stone immediately grasped the potential seriousness of the situation and began speaking gibberish to her, with Betty reciprocating. A young man standing behind them overheard them and yelled out, "That ain't Betty Grable." With that definitive pronouncement, the crowd subsided.[68]

Stan Musial, following up on the rave reviews from his St. Louis Cardinal teammates, started listening to Harry James's records and first saw him perform at the Astor Roof. The two grew to be close friends, and Musial became James's favorite ballplayer. "Stan the Man" remarked, "You know, one thing I noticed right away. Harry's eyes were really different. There were only two other people I've ever met who had crystal clear eyes like him—Bishop Sheen and the Duke of Windsor."

One evening at the Astor Roof, Helen Forrest spotted Betty Grable sitting alone intently watching Harry James and the band. By the look in her eyes, Forrest realized that Grable represented a serious rival. Until then, she had been completely unaware of Betty and Harry's romance. Grable's eyes suddenly met hers, and Betty silently mouthed, "Sorry."

Grable was at ringside several more nights. The intensity of their relationship caused James to sometimes arrive on the bandstand during the middle of the first set and then leave early. Within a few days, Harry broke the news to Helen Forrest about his plans to marry Betty. Forrest was devastated and heartbroken.

One night shortly thereafter, Sid Beller and Sam Caplan talked Helen Forrest out of jumping from a ledge outside her third-floor apartment. She was then pulled inside to safety by a few of the musicians. She was never sure whether Harry knew about her suicide attempt, but assumed he must have learned about it. He never made any mention of the incident, however. Immediately afterward, Mickey Scrima and some of the other musicians formed a protective cocoon around her, which helped alleviate the hurt.[69]

By way of contrast, now that her personal happiness was assured, Betty Grable returned to Los Angeles. She began making hospital tours to visit wounded soldiers back from the war in the Pacific. The experience of facing the terrible repercussions of war had an immediate and pronounced effect on her outlook. Instead of being constantly fawned over as she was at the studio, she now saw the real world for the first time in years. The challenge of facing soldiers in the wards, many of whom had been maimed in combat, also enabled her to overcome her shyness in meeting new people.

She was more than willing to endure all kinds of adverse conditions when she entertained for the troops, and, as a result, the GIs sensed a strong sense of dedication in her performances. One such occasion was at Fort Bragg, North Carolina, where she performed before 5,000 soldiers for two hours on a cold, rainy afternoon dressed in a white satin sequined gown. She made many such appearances all over the country at USO camp shows throughout the war, as did Harry James and the band.

Almost all the people interviewed for this biography stressed how unaffected and natural Betty Grable was and emphasized how she rarely took her stardom too seriously. Perhaps this was because she had served a long apprenticeship in Hollywood before becoming a star. As an example of her sometimes self-deprecating wit, she once described her appeal to Jim Bacon by referring to herself as "the truckdriver's delight."[70]

Betty once told Paula Stone, "You know Lana Turner and Joan Crawford deserve to be stars. I don't ... They know how to act the part. When they go out, they're all dressed up, and I hate to dress up. I just feel uncomfortable. I don't like all the attention, and I don't deserve it."

To illustrate just how important Betty had become, German radio propaganda broadcasts referred to her as "a creation designed to take the enemy's mind off what they are fighting for ... there is more to life than Pepsi-Cola and Betty Grable." On the Pacific front, the notorious Tokyo Rose also attacked her, referring to her as "poison."

At this point, however, there was a serious complication that would have a major impact on the future of Harry James and Betty Grable: Betty was five weeks pregnant. Harry quickly approached Louise for a divorce. She demanded that a trust fund be set up for their two sons and that Harry assume responsibility for the resultant taxes. In addition, she requested money to lease a house she had found on Olympic Boulevard in Los Angeles so that she could properly raise the children.

James's lawyer discussed the seriousness of the situation with Louise. He pointed out that, if she failed to divorce him right away, she would never receive any money to support her children. When she questioned his hard line, he dropped the bombshell. He informed her of Betty's pregnancy and emphasized that unless James married Grable right away, Grable's career was over and so was James's. She would then receive nothing.

Louise had little choice. She went to Juarez, Mexico, where she obtained a mutual consent decree from Judge Xavier Caballas on July 2, 1943. This left Harry James and Betty Grable free to marry. Years later, as Louise observed with great irony, "Harry never let me wear makeup—no lipstick.

Then he turned around and married a gorgeous showgirl. I also couldn't reconcile the fact that a man who played with such sweetness could treat me the way he did."[71]

Betty Grable was rehearsing for the aptly titled musical *Pin Up Girl* and was given a few days off over the July 4 weekend. She and Harry decided that he would come out from the East where he was working and marry her in Las Vegas; they had long since been against having a big church wedding in Hollywood that the studio wanted to stage.

Harry James and Manie Sachs, who would be his best man, left Newark by train after a gig, en route to Las Vegas via Chicago. Getting there, however, was not that easy. As happened so often during wartime, due to heavy military traffic, transcontinental trains were often late. They changed trains in Chicago to Union Pacific and were almost two hours late in reaching Las Vegas.

Grable, accompanied by her bridesmaids Edie Wasserman, wife of Lew Wasserman, and Betty Furness, then Grable's stand-in, who later became an important television personality, endured a non-air-conditioned train ride that took almost twelve hours to cover the 285 miles between Los Angeles and Las Vegas. With her entourage, a wilted Grable, wearing a canary-yellow suit, proceeded to the Frontier Hotel to unpack. The wedding was to take place there at its Church of the West. They then climbed back into their limousine to meet James and his best man's train. Betty Grable was tense, tired from the trip, perspiring, and kept chain-smoking cigarettes that made her even more nervous. Overzealous fans and hungry photographers surrounded their car. Foolishly, she had believed their wedding could be kept a secret.

When the train pulled in, Harry was the first one off and Betty rushed into his arms. They raced for the limousine as photographers' flashbulbs popped, and drove to the Church of the West, where the Baptist minister, C. S. Sloan, was to marry them.

A large throng of fans surrounded the church, even though it was 4 A.M. Grable and James pushed through the crowd to get inside the church, thus also managing to elude the press eager for interviews. Only Fox photographers, one of whom was Frank Powolney, were allowed to photograph the newlyweds at the wedding reception.

Harry James wore one of his dark blue pin-striped suits. Betty Grable wore a form-fitting dress, both new and blue. To complete her traditional bride's ensemble, she wore old high-heeled shoes and carried a handkerchief she had borrowed from Alice Faye. After the five-minute, double-ring ceremony, which took place at 4:15 A.M., Betty called her mother excitedly to announce, "This is Mrs. Harry James speaking." Lillian's first question to Betty was, "Were there many photographers there?"[72]

Following the small reception, they spent their wedding night at the Frontier Hotel. The next morning they headed for Hollywood by train. Betty returned to the set of *Pin Up Girl* and Harry began rehearsing for the Chesterfield show.

The media trumpeted the news of their wedding everywhere. Bob Hope, on his popular radio show, naturally couldn't resist a few quips about their marriage. He characteristically dubbed them "The Legs and The Lip."

Pee Wee Cooks

Hollywood—"If all the guys who ate my meals from coast to coast," says Harry James' personal manager, Pee Wee Monte, "become paying customers, I'm in." James himself is the first patron of Monte's new Sunset Strip restaurant, and is shown with Pee Wee above. Monte has put his three brothers, Al, Sal, and Fred into aprons, so the kitchen is straight family style. Pee Wee and Fred, who is the band's road manager, will still hit the road with James, going back to the hot stove when they get a chance. *1950 D.B.*

7

Hollywood Royalty

Shortly after Harry James and Betty Grable's wedding, the GI's coined a phrase that was transposed into song to the tune of "I Want a Girl Just Like the Girl that Married Dear Old Dad." It was, "I want a girl just like the girl that married Harry James."[1] Grable's marriage didn't hurt her appeal in the least and only increased James's popularity. Subsequently dubbed "The Queen of the Movie Musical" and "The King of the Bobbysoxers," they became the toast of the Hollywood fan magazines at a time when such magazines were an important media outlet.

The Jameses began married life at Betty's home on Stone Canyon Drive in Bel Air.[2] "The Girl Next Door" was turned into "America's Perfect Wife." Each day, after coming home from Fox, Grable traded her leotards and spangled costumes for an apron and a vacuum cleaner—following the domestic routine of a 1940s housewife. However, since she was no great cook ("My mother wasn't much of a cook simply because she herself never learned"), they often dined out; ultimately, they hired a live-in cook.

Harry James, of course, was signed to MGM. He was also classified 1-A in the draft. Within a week of their marriage, the studio requested that his Beaumont draft board defer him until he had finished his next picture, *Bathing Beauty*, pleading that, since he had already pre-recorded his music for the film, it would be extremely costly to replace him. The draft board sent back word that it would seriously consider the case.[3]

The leads in *Bathing Beauty* were Esther Williams and Red Skelton. This film established Williams as a "pinup favorite." "Wet she's a star, dry she ain't," was the way comedienne Fannie Brice pegged her. Williams conceded, "All they ever did for me at MGM was to change my leading men and the water in the pool."

While in production, the lighthearted film was originally titled *Mr. Co-Ed* because of its inane premise that had Skelton attending a girls school in order to regain the affections of Williams, who was a teacher there. The studio changed the title, however, to *Bathing Beauty*, since the story was essentially weak and the film merely a showcase for Williams's superb figure and aquatic abilities.

The film provided a joyous reunion for both Harry James and Helen Forrest with Red Skelton. James and Skelton reminisced about their engagement at the Shea Theatre in Buffalo back in early 1940, during which Red had consistently broken up Frank Sinatra's performance. Forrest and Skelton recalled the days in the early 1930s when Skelton was the emcee at dance marathon contests in Atlantic City and Forrest literally sang for small change.[4]

Helen Forrest's rendition of "I Cried for You" had been shot for *Best Foot Forward*, but ended up being cut from the picture. To everyone's delight, it was restaged and included in *Bathing Beauty*. In the fall of 1942, the song, with an arrangement by LeRoy Holmes, had been yet another sentimental ballad hit for the James-Forrest combination, remaining on the Billboard chart for nineteen weeks and peaking at #2. Its popularity caused *Time* to refer to James as a "modern Gabriel" and Forrest as "the throb-voiced torcheuse."[5]

"I Cried for You" also gave Helen Forrest her most glamorous moment on film. She was radiant in a form-fitting red gown. She also unveiled her new nose. While filming the number, one of the musicians was so taken by Helen's stunning new look that he remarked, "We have our own 'Bathing Beauty.'"[6]

Actually, while working on *Springtime in the Rockies* with Betty Grable, the band singer had first considered having her nose fixed. She felt completely intimidated by Betty's looks, although this was actually months before Harry and Betty's romance even began. She discounted her own voluptuous body.

For the film, director George Sidney conceived an unusual presentation of the "Hora Staccato." Harry James's brilliant trumpet performance of this violin masterpiece (reminiscent of "Flight of the Bumble Bee") had previously been recorded by both Fritz Kreisler and Jascha Heifitz. James's solo, though, was almost upstaged by the band's string section, upon which the camera remained focused from several unusual angles. The five numbers he performed in *Bathing Beauty* represented perhaps his most outstanding trumpet playing ever recorded on film.

The *New York Times* movie critic, Bosley Crowther, rightfully called *Bathing Beauty* "a colorful shower of music, comedy, and dance."[7] Unfortunately, this film was James's last MGM movie musical appearance for over a decade.

Producer Jack Cummings, who produced *Bathing Beauty*, had great faith in Harry James's ability to carry a film as a leading man. He tried to get MGM interested in producing a biographical film about James, starting with his life in the circus, called *Trumpet Man*.[8] It was anticipated that Betty Grable could co-star in the film on a loan-out from Fox. This was just another film property announced with some fanfare that never went into production.

Several months after finishing *Bathing Beauty*, James's Beaumont draft board notified him of his impending physical examination. Due to the ongoing mastoid condition that had first affected him in his "Human Eel" days in the circus and resulted in a punctured eardrum, he was classified 4F, or unfit for military service. This also explains his long-standing aversion to flying—because of the nonpressurized cabins in those days, flying would often cause a severe and painful flareup of his condition.

Meanwhile, back in New York, in August 1943, the eighteen-year-old Viola Paulich left the Equitable Life Insurance Company and was hired as the secretary at the band's office at 1440 Broadway. She had first met the bandleader in 1939, saw the band at the World's Fair, became his biggest fan in the New York area, and went on to establish his most important fan club.

Fred Monte, the third Monte brother to work for Harry James, who set up the other fan clubs, was drafted. Paulich replaced him and took over the job of answering the huge amount of fan mail when the office moved to 170 South Beverly Drive in Beverly Hills in early 1944. From there she became Pee Wee Monte's assistant. He once said, "Viola knows more about the band than we do." Over a period of close to forty years, she was an important part of the business half of the James band.

Harry James came into the office one day and proudly addressed Paulich as his "amanuensis," loosely meaning a secretary or assistant. She was duly impressed. He was ever conscious of his lack of education and consequently kept a dictionary with him on the road, anxious to expand his vocabulary.[9]

Pee Wee Monte was also drafted. He wound up in a cushy job in Special Services during his May 1943–May 1944 stint in the army, booking bands at various army bases in the greater New York area. During this period, working mostly from the Astor Hotel, he booked several important dates at military bases for the James band. Dave Hylton, the band's well-liked accountant, served as its interim manager.

Once Harry James and Betty Grable began married life together, Harry became increasingly inaccessible to his musicians and others working with him. "There's no question about it, Harry changed drastically," observed Fred Monte.[10] Charlie Barnet referred to Harry as "the Mystery Man." Quite simply, he became emotionally unavailable.

Everette James's combination of shyness and stoicism had undoubtedly left its mark on Harry James, but the magnitude of his huge success in the early 1940s also had a pronounced effect on his psyche. He had gone through his own kind of hell getting to where he was. He began drinking more, adding to his obvious detachment. Marrying Betty Grable and suddenly becoming part of Hollywood royalty and its attendant social whirl challenged his innate shyness. Now, not only was Harry aloof from his working colleagues, but he and Betty also kept away from the Hollywood social scene, which they disliked intensely. They found their own fun going to ballgames, horseback riding, playing golf, and even bowling.

There is a very meaningful photo I came across showing Betty Grable displaying her dazzling smile to her co-workers at a 20th Century Fox cocktail reception while Harry James is smiling weakly and staring into space above the crowd surrounding Betty. Fundamentally, neither of them relished spending much time with actors or studio people. Grable, however, knew how to play the game.

Harry James took over Lillian's role in advising her daughter on her career. Betty often mentioned to her friends how low key and gentle Harry was in dispensing constructive criticism. From the beginning of their romance, she had gained more than a wifely respect for his prodigious musical talent and the patience he had developed during his years as a performer. This latter trait, she admitted, gave her insight into dealing with some of her own difficulties that came with superstardom.

Betty Grable introduced Harry James to the thrill of horse racing, which she had first learned to enjoy with George Raft. They became regulars at Hollywood Park. Soon, they began driving to Del Mar, north of San Diego, for the four- to six-week meeting every summer, where they socialized with Bing Crosby, Jimmy Durante, Pat O'Brien, Betty and Harry Ritz, and Joe Frisco, the famous stuttering gambler.[11]

Betty and Harry Ritz became the best friends of Betty and Harry James. Betty (Grable) had known Harry Ritz since they were both in films in the mid-1930s when he was part of the famous Ritz Brothers comedy team, renowned for their spinning eyeballs. Harry (Ritz) had first become friendly with Harry James from personal appearances they made together in theaters and became a devoted swing fan. (The comedian referred to the bandleader as "Hesh," the Yiddish version of Harry, a nickname many others picked up on over the years.)[12] In the fall of 1942, Harry had a major hit with "Mister Five by Five," the novelty song that had been introduced in the Ritz Brothers' film, *Behind the Eight Ball.*

The meeting of the two couples at Del Mar cemented their friendship.[13] The two Bettys became close almost immediately since they had similar tastes and shared an offbeat and boisterous sense of humor. As an example, one day Betty (Ritz) visited Grable on her movie set dressed in an elegantly embroidered silk Chinese *cheongsam*. Grable looked her over carefully and remarked, "Well, look who's here—the one and only Chiang Kai Schmuck."[14]

While Harry James was on tour, Betty Grable spent considerable time with the Ritzes. One person who knew the foursome well contends that Betty's often colorful language stemmed directly from Harry Ritz's use of profanity.[15] Years later, the two Bettys quarreled and, for a time, their relationship cooled while Betty Ritz was carrying on a romance with Rafael Baez, a Mexican bullfighter, whom she subsequently married. Once the Jameses moved to Las Vegas, the Bettys resumed their friendship again and remained close friends to the end of Grable's life.

At various tracks, the Jameses became increasingly friendly with the jockeys, trainers, grooms, and all the other racing people. For James, these individuals were not dissimilar to the circus or carny people he had grown up with. Fred Monte noted, "I think they had more friends in that world than in the business they were in."[16]

Their common interest in gambling on horses inevitably compelled them to buy horses of their own. James purchased a half-interest in a horse named "Devil Egg," which paid $114 to win the first time they raced him. Shortly after that they decided to become serious breeders and purchase more racehorses, with plans of developing their own racing stable, just as Fred Astaire, Robert Taylor, Louis B. Mayer, Erroll Flynn, Spencer Tracy, and other Hollywood personalities had done.[17]

Joe Hernandez, the renowned track announcer at Santa Anita, arranged for them to buy seven thoroughbreds from C. H. Jones and Sons in 1946.[18] Later, James and Grable sued to recover $105,000, allegedly the price they paid for the horses. Their suit charged that the horses were represented as being in "perfect running condition," whereas none of them were in the proper condition for racing. The fact that five of the seven horses did race, and that two subsequently won and were deemed desirable by other parties, ultimately argued against the plaintiffs. The lawsuit was dropped in July 1948.

At one time, their stable totaled twenty-eight horses that were managed by Betty's father, Conn, at their sixty-two-acre ranch in Calabasas, the "Baby J." "Big Noise" and "James Session" were their two significant moneymakers. When "Big Noise" won the Del Mar Futurity, the $26,000 winner's share of the purse was enough to make Harry and Betty the leading owners at the 1951 meeting at the seaside track. Overall, their horses earned a total of $30,750. In 1954, "James Session" ran in the Kentucky Derby. The horse went off at 71-1. He ran better than his odds, but not good enough to win, finishing eighth.[19]

Some of their horses were "claiming horses"—horses entered in a race by an owner but claimed by other owners after the particular horse failed to finish in the money. When they lost, these horses were immediately put up for sale or "claiming."[20]

The Jameses' interest in horses inevitably led to a love of western gear. Harry began buying riding jackets, spurs, and boots for Betty while he was on the road. She reciprocated by purchasing silver inlaid saddles for him.[21]

Despite her love for horses and the track, Betty Grable's work at the studio still came first. After finishing Sweet Rosie O'Grady opposite Robert ("Marcus Welby") Young, she began shooting Pin Up Girl, which became one of the biggest hits of 1944, and made a cameo appearance in Four Jills and a Jeep. Harry James remained hopeful that he could develop a more substantial film career, which would keep him off the road.

Betty's pregnancy soon became obvious, and she took maternity leave from the studio. On his own, James put on almost twenty pounds in their first year of marriage. In October they moved to a home formerly owned by Bert Lahr at 2301 Beaumont Drive on three acres off Coldwater Canyon in Beverly Hills. There they awaited the birth of their first child.[22]

Harry James, however, still had dates that had been booked before their marriage and went back on tour. He wasn't ready to stay home and bathe in the luxury of the Hollywood good life—he had worked far too hard to attain his own newfound superstar status. Certainly the public had shown no inclination that it had grown tired of his romantic music.

The remainder of 1943 continued to be remarkably successful for Harry James. Years later he acknowledged, as proof of his success, that he had paid only $25 in federal income tax in 1941 but the staggering total of $620,000 in 1943.

Besides constant radio airplay for his records, his continuing string of hits was enhanced by playing them "live" for national audiences on remote broadcasts. In addition, the band appeared three times a week on the Chesterfield show and Friday nights on Coca Cola's Spotlight Bands. In a photograph taken in August 1944 at a Spotlight Bands show, Harry James is seen sitting on a stool with his fractured foot encased in a plaster cast. The injury resulted from his attempting to slide into third base trying to stretch a double into a triple at a ballgame.[23] (Spotlight Bands ultimately concluded its broadcasts in 1945 with Harry appearing on its last show.)

Above: Harry makes his debut in a family portrait in 1916. This includes his sister, Fay; his mother, Maybelle; and Harry, on his father, Everette's, knee. The James family was then featured with The Mighty Haag Shows. (Viola Monte Collection)

Below: Harry James, the fledgling drummer, is shown with a bevy of clowns, each carrying a different instrument, during his days with the Christy Brothers Circus, circa 1920. (Viola Monte Collection)

Harry as a teenager, carrying a baseball glove, standing with his father, Everette. The elder James was almost single-handedly responsible for nurturing his son's enormous talent, but in the process Harry paid a heavy emotional price. (Viola Monte Collection)

Above: Art Hicks and his Biltmore Aristocrats are shown in this July 1934 photo at the Sylvan Club in Arlington, Texas. During this engagement Harry James (back row, left) met Louise Tobin, Hicks's band singer, who within a year became his wife. (Frank Driggs Collection)

Below: Benny Goodman is shown on the afternoon of January 16, 1938, rehearsing his peerless band preceding the concert in Carnegie Hall that evening. James, playing trumpet on left, arguably gave the finest musical performance of his career that night. (George T. Simon Collection)

With Harry James in white dinner jacket taking center stage, his orchestra plays at the Panther Room in the Hotel Sherman in Chicago, 1939. Band singer Frank Sinatra (center front) awaits his cue. (Frank Driggs Collection)

Harry James and Frank Sinatra, Caesar's Palace, Las Vegas, November 1968. In twenty-nine years, the roles had been reversed. The singer was now the star and the bandleader was in the background. (Courtesy Caesar's Palace)

Above: The James band at the Commander Hotel in Rome, New York, in the fall of 1939. Frank Sinatra is seen holding a coffee cup on James's left. (Nancy Sinatra Collection)

Below: Harry James holds his son, Harry Jeffrey, while his manager, Pee Wee Monte, holds his brother, Jerin Timothy, as Louise Tobin looks on. Photo was taken in the mid 1940s during Harry's only visit to see his sons while Louise lived in Los Angeles. (Louise Tobin Collection)

Harry James doing what he loved best, pitching and playing baseball, with a bevy of adoring female fans watching. Photo is from the early 1940s. (Frank Driggs Collection)

Above, left: Helen Forrest and Harry James are shown in the MGM film musical *Two Girls and a Sailor*. Forrest never looked more radiant. (Richard Dondiego Collection)

Above, right: Dick Haymes and Helen Forrest are shown with their boss, Harry James, in a 1941 photograph. After the two singers left the James Band, they had hits singing duets on Decca Records, appeared for a few years together on the Autolite radio show, and remained lifelong friends. (Richard Dondiego Collection)

Below: Harry and Kitty Kallen ride around in a jeep after a performance at a naval base during World War II. (Kitty Kallen Collection)

Above: Betty Grable, shown in the most important pin-up picture of World War II. (Movie Star News)

Below: Harry James and his band tear up the Paramount Theater while enthusiastic teenagers dance on stage during the famous "James Riot" in the spring of 1943. Pianist Al Lerner is on the left. (Ken Whitten Collection)

Carmen Miranda, the celebrated Brazilian bombshell, and Harry in director's chairs off the set of the 20th Century Fox musical *If I'm Lucky*. They collaborated on the production number "Jam Session in Brazil." Note Miranda's trademark platform shoes. (20th Century Fox Film Collection)

Harry James and his Orchestra cook, with the leader playing a conga drum on a Wisconsin one-nighter in the late 1940s. Buddy Combine is on drums, Bob Rolfe on trumpet, and the redoubtable Willie Smith on alto saxophone. (Buddy Combine Collection)

Above: Harry James and Betty Grable are shown dining out in Hollywood with their best friends, Betty Ritz and Harry Ritz of The Ritz Brothers. (Betty Baez Collection)

Below: Harry James shows Kirk Douglas a thing or two about playing trumpet off the set of *Young Man With a Horn*, the 1950 Warner Brothers film. Harry ghosted for Kirk in the title role as a trumpet player and helped him assume the bearing of a jazz musician. (Frank Driggs Collection)

Above: Doris Robbins and Ben Pollack, along with an unidentified chef, serve Betty Grable and Harry James at Pollack's restaurant, Pick-A-Rib, during a Christmas party. James never lost sight of the valuable contribution Pollack made to his career and helped him whenever possible. (Viola Monte Collection)

Below: Harry James and Betty Grable are shown at New York's Stork Club in 1943 with a pack of Chesterfield cigarettes (Harry's radio sponsor) and a bottle of Sortilege perfume, in which company Stork Club owner Sherman Billingsley had an interest. (Ken Whitten Collection)

Above: A good day at Del Mar, during the mid 1950s. Harry is shown with, from left, daughters Jessica and Vicki, the beloved comedian Jimmy Durante, Betty Grable, and jockey Bill Skuse. (Mac McBride at Del Mar Thoroughbred Club Collection)

Below: Four leading bandleaders helped to form the D.O.L.A. (Dance Orchestra Leaders of America) in 1955 to try to infuse new life into the band business. From left, Harry, Les Brown, Lawrence Welk, and Freddy Martin. Unfortunately, it was too little, too late. (Viola Monte Collection)

Above: Elvis Presley and Harry James are shown in a photo during a rehearsal preceding the April 3, 1956, Milton Berle NBC special, shot aboard the USS *Hancock* at the San Diego naval base. The show was one of the first color TV specials produced. Shortly after the show, James told his daughter Vicki that Presley had no future in the music business. (Viola Monte Collection)

Below: Viola Monte and her husband, Pee Wee Monte, the longtime secretary and manager, respectively, of Harry James and his Orchestra, are shown in the office in front of a collage of James photographs. (Viola Monte Collection)

Above, left: The author shown with James at a theater in Dayton, Ohio, in March 1961 while writing a magazine article on the trumpeter. (Peter Levinson Collection)

Above, right: Buddy Rich, the drummer Harry James admired more than any other, is shown with the trumpeter, with Nick "Count" Buono in the background, in a photograph taken at Disneyland in the early 1960s. Buono played almost forty years with the James band, longer than any other sideman. (Viola Monte Collection)

Below: "Gentlemen Songsters Off On a Spree." From left, Harry James, Red Kelly, Jack Perciful, and Corky Corcoran, in a 1964 photograph. (Red Kelly Collection)

The love and respect that Harry James and Louis Armstrong had for each other is apparent in a late 1960s photograph taken at Harold's Club in Reno. Armstrong was Harry's inspiration when he started playing trumpet, and the two were close friends for many years. (Viola Monte Collection)

Above: Phil Harris (the real Dean Martin) and Harry James photographed on Harry's birthday during the 1970s. Harris was James's closest friend. Phil, along with Frank Sinatra, gave the eulogy at Harry's funeral. (Viola Monte Collection)

Below: Harry, showing the ravages of cancer, in an April 1983 photograph taken at a recording session in Hollywood with Nelson Riddle. Sal Monte looks on. It was James's last recording session. (Sal Monte Collection)

Following the gigantic success of "I've Heard That Song Before," came "Moonlight Becomes You" (with Johnny McAfee on the vocal), the instrumentals "Velvet Moon" and "Prince Charming," the re-releases of "All or Nothing at All," "Two O'Clock Jump," and "Flash," "I Heard You Cried Last Night" (vocal by Helen Forrest), and the instrumental, "Jump Town." These re-releases were caused by the ban on musicians recording new material that was inexplicably ordered by James C. Petrillo in August 1942. The others had been recorded before the ban and, as a way of getting around the ruling, were held for systematic release by Columbia Records.

Petrillo had ordered the end of all recording by musicians on August 1, 1942. The ban lasted until November 1944. Singers, however, were not affected by Petrillo's decision, and the major labels began recording singers with choral accompaniment, especially as exemplified by the many recordings Frank Sinatra made at the time. It is also important to note that these recordings only served to further the popularity of singers in competition with the bands.

A fervent teenage fan of Harry's named Hugh Hefner was then attending Steinmetz High School on the west side of Chicago. As Hefner recalled, "My perceptions of love really came from the movies and the music of the 1940s, which was an intensely romantic period. There was also something very romantic about the band business, and Harry James was certainly a romantic icon," he added. "It's hard for kids today to realize that. For us, it was comparable to rock music now—to be part of any of that.

"Harry was my all-time favorite. I collected everything that he did on 78. I still have them. His horn was almost like a vocalist. It had a very romantic connection, and Helen Forrest was, for me, the best of the band singers. Those songs really spoke to the heart. We still play that music here at the Mansion. On Wednesday nights, when we play cards with my friends from the old days in Chicago, we play all the big band stuff as background."[24]

I asked the founder of *Playboy* if he liked Harry's recorded work in the 1960s when it had more of a jazz flavor. "No," he replied. "The stuff that really had meaning for me—part of it is musical appreciation, but part of it clearly is nostalgia which was directly related to an emotional connection to where you were at the time."

In the chronicling of Harry James's greatness as a trumpet player, the importance of the Parduba mouthpiece that he favored has been overlooked. The Parduba contains a double cup inside and is basically a shallow, softer mouthpiece that a trumpet player can't easily press his lips into. Over the years, it has rarely been used by big band or symphonic trumpet players who have a piercing or powerful sound, which was always a key ingredient in his playing.

James believed that the Parduba model #28 throat, when he first adopted it in the Goodman days (and which was quickly picked up by Ziggy Elman and Chris Griffin), changed his entire career. It was later used by several members of the James brass section and also by Louis Armstrong and Ray Anthony. Harry never departed from playing a Parduba mouthpiece.

Dean Pratt, who runs the Jazz Composers Service and leads his own band in the New York area, was at one time a member of Buddy Rich's trumpet section. He has long been a fervent admirer of James's trumpet technique and attributes a great deal of his success to the Parduba. "I think it gave him more endurance and range. Endurance is what every trumpet player wishes he had, and that's something Harry was always known for having. It also made hitting high notes easier. And, you know, in the late '40s and early '50s, when the band would be off for a few months, Harry could just pick up the horn and start playing without even having to warm up. The design of the Parduba had a lot to do with his ability to do that since almost no trumpet players I've ever known have ever been able to lay off for a matter of months without practicing for days before they went back to work." (James once explained why he never needed to warm up: "If you breathe correctly, then you can blow correctly.")

I asked Pratt if James's prowess was partially due to his ability to execute triple-tonguing, circular breathing, and other tricks of the brass trade. "No," contended Pratt. "I don't necessarily think he circular breathed. I do think he had extremely good breath control despite the fact that he was a heavy smoker. He built up an amazing breath control over the years and learned to deal with the effect smoking had on him. I also think that's the reason he puffed his cheeks out when he was with Benny Goodman.

"It's also important to realize that with the Parduba, if you press your lips to it, chances are no sound will come from it. You have to use only so much pressure on it; otherwise the sound will stop."

This led to my asking Pratt why it wasn't adopted by a great many trumpet players. The trumpet authority replied: "Because they're simply not capable of using it. It's not easy to play a shallow mouthpiece, and most people that use them can't get a big or even a good sound with it.

"Guys like Harry, of course—you could probably give 'em any mouthpiece, and they're gonna somehow figure out how to get the sound that they get because a lot of it, for my money, comes from the heart. A trumpeter's sound is like [his] character; it's also how they talk, what they do. It's something inside them. Great sounds come from great musicians like Harry James or Dizzy Gillespie. It's certainly not all mechanical, and it's not at all related to the instrument or the mouthpiece."

The Parduba mouthpiece also contributed to Harry's method of playing with a wide vibrato. Those who admired his sound from the 1940s onward knew how soulfully he played on ballads. "The people who put down Harry's playing were really anti-vibrato. By that I mean too much vibrato. That's what really bothered them," Pratt added.[25]

Harry James's trumpets, with the Parduba mouthpiece, were custom-made by Selmer and later by King. The valves were set forward from their usual position to accommodate Harry's long arms, which made the fingering easier for him. His horn was the largest of the four standard trumpet sizes and was a variation on the Louis Armstrong model.

Billboard voted Helen Forrest "the Most Popular Female Band Vocalist" of 1943, after she had been an also-ran in this poll during the four previous years. It was not surprising, therefore, that on December 2, 1943, after being besieged by interested agents and managers, Helen Forrest signed with manager Billy Burton and made her last appearance with the James band on the Chesterfield show. Her departure took place almost six months later than it should have. Because of the recording ban, she was unable to make any more records with James. The fact remained that they had collaborated on no fewer than nine hits, including two gold records—each one indicating one million in sales.

Night after night she was forced to endure the reality that she and James were no longer romantically involved. And she had to endure it while standing only a few feet away from him, singing the romantic ballads that musically had defined their relationship—"I Had the Craziest Dream," "I Don't Want to Walk Without You," "I Cried for You," and so on. Given the romantic nature of the latter song in particular, with its meaningful lyrics, she found she couldn't look at James while she sang it. The last straw came one night after Harry played the verse too plaintively—even tauntingly, she thought. She complained to him, "Don't do that." Although she may have possibly misconstrued James's motives, she contended that "there's a streak of cruelty in every lover. They have to get that jab in when the affair is over."[26]

One night in early 1944, Helen Forrest came to see the band at the Palladium. After the gig, Harry approached her and asked, "Do you want to meet me?" Helen smiled and said, "I don't think so." She remarked, "Here he was married to the biggest pinup girl in the world, and this was only months after they had been married."[27]

Shortly after that, Betty Grable encountered Helen at Mike Romanoff's elegant Beverly Hills restaurant. She came over to Helen's table and, for the first time, the two women carried on a conversation. Betty concluded it by saying (once again), "I'm sorry it had to be you."[28]

Richard Dondiego, a Sherman Oaks sales and marketing consultant, who was also Helen's close friend, believes "Harry and Helen's love for each other was very incongruous. Harry loved her as much as he could love anyone for a period of time, but I also think he was also very much in love with her talent, which was considerable."[29]

Unlike some other bandleaders, who might have been afraid of the high caliber of Forrest's talent, James wasn't the least bit daunted. Following his first band, he always surrounded himself with highly accomplished musicians and singers. He saw how Benny Goodman pushed talented musicians into the limelight and how it benefited the band. The audience loved it. Simply speaking, if you had talent, Harry James wanted you as part of his orchestra. As he described it in baseball terms to me once in an interview years later, "It's the .210 hitters you have to worry about."

Billy Burton, who was then representing Dick Haymes and Jimmy Dorsey and his Orchestra, among others, started Helen Forrest's solo career off with a booking at the Orpheum, then an important theater in downtown Los Angeles. He then booked her into the Roxy in New York. Decca Records signed her, and, after some moderately successful solo records, she recorded some memorable duets with Haymes, who was also recording for the label. Over a period of slightly over two years, the duo had ten top 20 records on the *Billboard* chart.

The success of these records boosted the popularity of their collaboration on NBC's Autolite radio show, where they were backed by Gordon Jenkins and his Orchestra. Unfortunately, Forrest's solo career never really flourished as it should have. She suffered from the lethal combination of bad management and her own inability to re-invent herself as a prominent singer on her own. Reflecting on her career with the bands, and more particularly her days working for Harry James, she remarked wistfully to me, "Why did that era ever have to end?"[30]

(Frank Sinatra Jr. said that in the early 1960s, when his father first saw him sing along with Helen Forrest at the Americana [now the New York Sheraton] with the Tommy Dorsey "ghost" band under the direction of Sam Donahue, he pointed out to Frank, Jr., "If you really want to become a good singer, you can't do any better than to listen to that lady who's sitting next to you.")

Although Harry James could never really replace Helen Forrest, he did come close when he hired Helen Ward. While with Benny Goodman in 1935, Ward had been the first female singer to make a significant impact with a major dance band. She had left Goodman before James joined the band, although as a special guest star she sang "You Turned the Tables on Me" on a *Make Believe Ballroom* radio show backed by the Goodman band (that included James) on April 29, 1937. In addition, she had recorded "Daddy" with James's band on May 20, 1941, during the same session when "You Made Me Love You" was recorded.

In late 1943, Helen Ward returned to New York after spending six weeks in Reno divorcing record producer Albert Marx, who years before had taped the Carnegie Hall jazz concert for Goodman. Ward remembered exactly why she joined James: "I went to see Benny at the New Yorker, but he was going out on the road, and I had had one-nighters up to here! Harry, on the other hand, was going to stay at the Palladium for a good while and also had the Chesterfield show. Of course, when I joined Harry, the recording ban was still on. The only records available of my singing with Harry are a few remote broadcast recordings that are now available on Hindsight Records."

Unfortunately, the combination of Helen Ward and Harry James was not a perfect match. I asked her what was the source of their disagreement. "Mostly musical," Ward answered. "He saw it this way, and I saw it that way. Nobody realized what it was like to step into Helen Forrest's shoes. I've always admired her singing. We did so little rehearsing [could this be the aftermath of the many arduous rehearsals Harry James had endured while with Benny Goodman?], and it was difficult to learn every one of her tunes as well as the arrangements. It's really a shame because I had looked forward to working with strings. Harry had to change the keys of all of Helen's tunes for me because I sang lower than she did. That maybe started it all. We just didn't get along. I wound up calling Harry 'Mr. Betty Grable.'" Ward left the band after only a matter of months.

They finally literally kissed and made up at the Riverboat in New York one night in 1968 when she came in to see Harry and the band perform. She never saw him again. "Despite our differences," Ward concluded, "I always thought of him as a fabulous musician. I knew that he was absolutely tops—on a par with Benny Goodman. They didn't come any better."[31]

Due to the lengthy Palladium engagement, Harry was at home in Beverly Hills when seven-pound, twelve-ounce Victoria (named for Betty's character in *Springtime in the Rockies*) arrived almost a month early at 4:45 A.M. on March 3, 1944, at Cedars of Lebanon Hospital. (Coincidentally, this was exactly three years to the date after her half brother, Harry Jeffrey, had been born.) It was a difficult birth for Betty Grable, who was in labor seventeen hours before finally having a Caesarean section. Everette and his new wife, Alma (a widow whom he had known in the Christy Brothers Circus when she was a costume seamstress), and Conn and Lillian Grable were all at the hospital when their granddaughter was born.

Under the auspices of James's publicist, the venerable Henry Rogers, Betty Grable told the press: "I was feeling pretty uncomfortable, but I honestly think it was much tougher on Harry. Once it was all over and the nurses took Victoria away to clean her up, Harry excused himself from the room. I was puzzled. I had seen him going several shades of gray, but I thought he was stronger than to run away from it all! He returned several minutes later with a book of crossword puzzles. I didn't know whether to laugh or cry. If he had brought me just one puzzle, that would have been understandable—but a whole book full! I remember wondering, 'Just how long does he think I'll be here?' … Knowing that I loved crossword puzzles, he felt that they would please me more than flowers or perfume."[32] That evening Harry left the hospital twice to do his two nightly Chesterfield shows.

As Vicki laughingly reminded me during the course of an interview, "Because of the publicity that I got when I was born, there's no way I can lie about my age."[33] That September, *Life* magazine ran a full page pinup nude photograph of Vicki lying on her stomach, legs kicking behind her, flashing a million-dollar smile. She was referred to as "The Littlest Pinup." Today, Vicki still bears a strong resemblance to her father.

Following Vicki's birth, Betty Grable recuperated at home. She quickly became used to her new routine and for a time seriously considered giving up her career. Being a wife and mother provided a sudden sense of fulfillment that superstardom hadn't. James felt otherwise. He angrily told her, "If you quit the movies, you can say goodbye to all this. I don't make nearly enough money to keep us in this style." Betty was taken aback by her husband's outburst, since living in style wasn't really that important to her.[34]

While at home, Betty continued to smoke heavily, eventually going through two to three packs a day. Harry relaxed before dinner with a very dry Beefeaters martini, and Betty joined him. After dinner, they would each have two vodkas on the rocks. Life was easy—they seemingly had it all.

The Jameses' interest in gambling, which had started at the racetrack, became increasingly important. For example, on New Year's Eve 1946, they joined producers Irene Selznick and Edward Golding as well as director Sam Wood and others at a gambling den. Six armed bandits crashed the party and absconded with between $20,000 and $40,000. Betty Grable told a reporter, "I was so excited I just didn't know what happened. It was all over quickly. The holdup men didn't bother any of the guests present."[35]

Zanuck ended her ten-month respite at home by assigning her to star in *Diamond Horseshoe*, named after Billy Rose's celebrated New York night-club. With James's prodding, she was in excellent physical shape on her return to work and wore some of her most revealing costumes in the film. Her co-star was none other than Dick Haymes. Harry Warren contributed two tunes for Dick to sing that became standards, "I Wish I Knew" and "The More I See You."[36]

Ann Miller had starred as a singer and dancer in some of the best remembered MGM musicals. She and Betty Grable had been friends since they danced in musical revues at the Los Angeles Theater. Miller said of Grable: "She was so cute—why, she was a walking cheesecake! She wasn't a great singer, she wasn't a great dancer, but she was so gorgeous that you were mesmerized. She photographed like a million bucks, and what incredible coloring she had."[37] Once Betty registered as a full-fledged star, she had a clause in her contract with Fox that obligated her to star only in Technicolor films.

A year and a half later, when she again co-starred with Dick Haymes in *The Shocking Miss Pilgrim*, Harry James and the band were playing an engagement at the Lick Pier in Ocean Park, now Santa Monica. During the making of the film, Grable and Haymes started an affair. The singer later admitted to Helen Forrest that Harry came after him at a restaurant brandishing a gun. In the end, cooler heads prevailed, and the public never learned of the incident.[38]

When he was on the road, Harry James called Betty at home every night. He cared for her deeply, but he was also checking up on her. In effect, he was projecting his own behavior onto her. His infidelities weren't only taking place on the road, but in his dressing room at the Hollywood Palladium and in cars in the parking lot. Reports of Harry's constant womanizing had little effect on Betty, however. She had such an overpowering love for Harry that, like Louise Tobin, she at first refused to believe them.

MGM decided not to pick up the option on James's five-year contract. George Chasen at MCA immediately began negotiating a new contract for him at 20th Century Fox. In the meantime, Harry and the band appeared in the film short, *All Star Band Rally* backing Frank Sinatra on "Saturday Night Is the Loneliest of the Week" and Bing Crosby on "Buy, Buy, Buy a Bond."

Pretty, petite, and vivacious Kitty Kallen joined the band at the Astor Roof on May 22, 1944. During 1943, Kallen had spent an unhappy year singing with Jimmy Dorsey, whom she claimed was anti-Semitic. She had replaced Helen O'Connell. Her association with Dorsey resulted in such hits as "They're Either Too Young or Too Old," "When They Ask about You," and "Besame Mucho," the latter a duet with Bob Eberly. After that unfortunate experience, she said she had no interest in going on the road with another band.

The young Philadelphian had started in show business as a little girl by appearing on the Horn and Hardart *Children's Hour*. As a teenager from 1939 to 1941, she was featured with the orchestra led by the beloved trombone player Jack Teagarden who she still credits as her foremost teacher.

Kallen recalled his important directive, "Little Pud" (as he called her), "sing the melody, read the lyric, but tell the story."[39]

Despite Kitty Kallen's insistence to Pee Wee Monte that she didn't want to travel any longer, Harry James telephoned her and made her an offer she couldn't possibly turn down. He told her: "I've been listening to you. I like what you're doing."

On November 11, 1944, the recording ban was at last lifted, and the James band began recording once again for Columbia, with whom he had signed a new contract. Kitty Kallen proudly recalled the two-year period she spent singing with the James band, during which they collaborated on two top 20 hits, six top 10 hits, and two #1 hits. "Working with Harry wasn't work. I couldn't wait to get on the bandstand. He was the most professional man I'd ever worked with. [This was reflected in] his whole approach to the band. You knew you were on that bandstand because he liked what you were doing. You never had to be stroked or patted on the back, and there was never any kind of pressure."

I asked Kitty Kallen how Harry James tried out new material. "At home, we would rehearse once a week, but never on the road. The new scores were submitted, and Harry would decide which tunes he liked. Then I would be handed a lead sheet to learn from. That night, we would be on a location, and we'd play the song. The next day we would record it. Harry would have the score in front of him that first night, and from then on never looked at it—in addition to which I never ever heard him warm up. He never asked me to sing a song any other way except the way I wanted to do it in the first place.

"On the last set, on one nighters, we would really improvise. Every once in a while Harry would play the drums. He was incredible, and he could also dance like no one else. The whole experience was unbelievable, and it was fun."

James hoped Kallen would develop a close friendship with Betty Grable, but Kitty kept her distance. She made it a practice not to get close to the wives of musicians in the band, partly because she saw too much of what was going on during road trips. Over time, she developed a great personal respect for Betty. Kallen recalled: "Betty was touring with us on the train for about two weeks in Pennsylvania. One night the train was so full of soot, Betty's blonde hair turned black. There was no beauty salon to go to. We laughed and laughed as we washed the soot out of our hair."[40]

The vivacious singer confirmed something that had been told me by several veterans of James's band: "When we did a record date, Harry would deliberately play a 'boo boo'. (On the original record of 'You Made Me Love You,' there is an obvious clam in the second chorus.) His reasoning was that only God could make it perfect. If the feeling was there, that was what was important to him. I remember on one record date he stood on a table to create a particular sound on a certain number. He always knew what he wanted."

Kitty Kallen recorded the first of two resounding hits with the James band on her very first session on November 21, 1944. "I'm Beginning to See the Light" was initially a Duke Ellington instrumental, written by Duke and by his alto-saxophone star, Johnny Hodges; James and Don George wrote the lyrics. (Jimmy Maxwell always believed that Harry was inspired by Johnny Hodges, "especially in his beautiful and sentimental approach to a ballad.")[41] George had previously offered the song to several bandleaders with no success, but Harry James saw its magic immediately.

Legend has it that "I'm Beginning to See the Light" was played on various landing craft when the Americans landed in Normandy on D-Day. The James band was heard on a CBS remote from the Astor Roof that historic night. The broadcast was interrupted by the unconfirmed news from German radio that the landings had begun.

Some of Kitty Kallen's other hits with the James band were "I'll Buy That Dream," "Waitin' for the Train to Come in," "11:60 P.M.," and "Guess I'll Hang My Tears out to Dry." Her most popular record, "It's Been a Long, Long Time," could be compared in both lyric content and feeling to the Helen Forrest hits from the early, grim days of the war. By July 1945, however, when "It's Been a Long, Long Time" was recorded, there was a feeling of exultation in the lyrics Kallen sang; they underscored the fact that the troops were now about to begin coming home. She remembers the song was so popular that she sometimes sang it as many as eight times a night.

She also quickly learned of Harry's devotion to the St. Louis Cardinals and his friendship with the team's brother battery of Mort and Walker Cooper. "One of them [probably Mort] gave him a baseball glove. He clutched that glove on the bus all the time and wouldn't let it out of his sight. God, did he treasure that glove! We didn't always eat together, but we'd be in the same dining room, and he would bring it with him. One day, someone got hold of his glove and handed it to me. He was upset that it had disappeared, even momentarily, and acted like a little boy until he got it back."[42]

Band musicians and singers love telling stories about their experiences on the road. Kitty had one she especially relished sharing: "We were playing in San Diego at the big naval base, and it was just jammed. The people were literally crowded in like sardines. I had a little problem. When I laugh very hard, I wet my pants, and I laugh easily. We were about to go on the radio on a remote broadcast. I was wearing an evening dress that was light colored on the bottom, with a black velvet top. There's a woman standing there about three rows out. She's tall, and she's waving her hand trying to get Harry's attention. She had been cheering so enthusiastically that she had dropped her teeth, and because it was so crowded, it was impossible to find them. On the opening bars of 'I'm Beginning to See the Light,' all you can hear is the rhythm section. I'm doubled up laughing. Harry can't play, he's laughing so hard. The guys in the band could see that I had wet my pants. Nothing but laughter—the whole band broke up. They couldn't even play their horns, either!"

In August of that year, Kallen was feeling blue after the end of a love affair. On August 20, the band convened in Hollywood to record "I Can't Begin to Tell You," the Oscar-nominated tune Betty Grable had sung in *The Dolly Sisters*, in which she co-starred with her arch rival, June Haver. Kitty explained to James that she just couldn't record that day. Fortunately, Grable was visiting at the recording session. James asked her to replace Kallen; coincidentally, they both sang in the same key.[43]

The result was hardly a sterling performance of the song, but not surprisingly the record stayed on the *Billboard* pop chart for twelve weeks and peaked at #5. Betty was billed as "Ruth Haag," an amalgamation of her real first name and James's middle name. Presumably, she couldn't use her stage name because of her relationship with 20th Century Fox.

By now, Harry James fully realized that the focus had shifted away from bands to singers. Of course, he was one of the first bandleaders who really showcased his singers. He was at the peak of his career, but it was the vocal hits that were really making the most impact. On dance dates, the audience came to see and hear the singer sing his or her hits. Sometimes people couldn't dance because the dance floor was so crowded. If they were dancing, they would quickly stop when the singer walked to the microphone and listen intently to the rendition of the song.

Harry James saw that Kitty Kallen had all the necessary ingredients to make it on her own. He magnanimously told her, "You're ready," pointing out if she didn't leave then (the end of 1945) she would regret it.[44] Over the next two decades, Kitty Kallen enjoyed a successful career as a pop singer and had major hit records of such songs as "But Beautiful," "Little Things Mean a Lot," "It Could Happen to You," "If I Give My Heart to You," "In the Chapel in the Moonlight," and "My Coloring Book."

The vocalist who spent more time with the Harry James Orchestra than any other, however, was Buddy DiVito. Buddy was singing with Eddie Oliver's band at the Edgewater Beach Hotel in Chicago, where his featured number was "The Music Stopped." Eight days after beginning work with Oliver, who led a successful society band, DiVito came home one night in early December 1943 and found a message for him to call Harry James at the Palladium in Hollywood. At first, he thought it was a joke played on him by his brother, who was then training horses in southern California.

He returned the call. The voice on the other end said, "Hi, this is Harry James. Would you like to join my band?" Buddy replied, "C'mon, Pete, what is it? You're short of money again? I'll send you a few bucks."[45]

James interrupted, "Look, this is Harry." He had heard him sing "The Music Stopped" on a remote broadcast with Oliver's band from Camp Grant, the army base near Chicago. He instructed DiVito to go over to the MCA office in Chicago the next day to pick up his train ticket to Los Angeles. The band singer gave Oliver a week's notice and joined the James band at the Palladium, replacing Buddy Moreno, who was going into the service. DiVito recalled, "I was very proud that Harry was the #1 band in the country, and I got to go with him. This was a big honor for me. I was making $150 a week, but I thought I was suddenly a millionaire."

Opening night at the Palladium, Harry James announced to the audience, "This is our new vocalist who's joining us tomorrow." DiVito had had no rehearsal, but there was an arrangement of "The Music Stopped" in the James book. The leader called the tune, and Buddy DiVito made his debut. After the applause subsided, Harry informed the audience, "You'll be hearing Buddy tomorrow on the Chesterfield show." The next day he repeated the song on the radio program. During his four years as vocalist, he also sang with the James band when it was featured on the Danny Kaye radio show.

Harry once referred to Buddy DiVito as "a real good little singer who used to move the [band] truck for us with one hand."[46] He contended that he wasn't quite that strong, yet Buddy admitted, "I was very mechanically inclined. I was also the character in the band."[47]

Although he was referred to as "Two-Beer DiVito" because of his low tolerance for alcohol, Buddy recalled wonderful parties with Harry and Betty and his fellow musicians. "Every Christmas Harry gave the band a big party, and we'd give Harry a gift. One Christmas, when he still had the ranch, we gave him two sixguns and a surrey.

"When he and Betty had that big house up on Doheny Drive, Harry gave a big party and I was the bartender. I got everybody drunk. Betty threw me out of the house. 'Get out of here, dago,' she yelled. 'I don't want you around.' I ruined the party, but I loved it."

The still robust DiVito who, at seventy-nine, says, "I just hope to go to 108," remains an avid James fan. "As a trumpet player he was the ace. As a musician—his intonation, hearing—he'd have sixteen strings and thirty-five musicians all told, but he could pick out one fiddle player playing the wrong note."

Buddy DeVito mentioned how generous Harry was to his men, emphasizing that everything was paid for on the road but meals. When I first interviewed him, he was wearing a black belt with a solid gold buckle. On the reverse side of the buckle, along with the first bar of "Ciribiribin," was inscribed "Buddy—March 1945—Harry James." He proceeded to pull out a similarly inscribed gold cigarette lighter. When he eventually left the band in 1947 to start his own band in Chicago, Harry James sent him a supply of red jackets, the kind his band members often wore as part of their uniforms.[48]

Sometimes Harry James, alto saxophonist Willie Smith, and clarinetist Eddie Rosa would travel between dates with DiVito in his Oldsmobile, the first of many Oldsmobiles that Buddy has owned over a period of fifty years. DiVito's penchant for driving fast caused the car to be dubbed "The Oldsmoplane."

One night after a dance date in rural Iowa, DiVito, ever the character, attempted to even a score with bass trombonist Charlie Preble. He got drunk and grabbed a baby lamb from a nearby pasture and brought it back to the hotel hidden under his overcoat. He was intent on putting it in Preble's bed. Unfortunately, the lamb wasn't happy in its new surroundings. When the desk clerk asked the singer what he was carrying, the lamb bellowed, "Baaahhh," flew out of DiVito's arms, and ran out of the hotel.

During this same period DiVito was singing the James band's version of "Linda," which was then a hit for Doris Day and Buddy Clark. As a result of the incident with the lamb, Harry started introducing DiVito by saying, "Here's our featured vocalist, 'Baaahhhddy' DiVito singing 'Linda.'" When DiVito got to the phrase, "When I go to sleep I never count sheep," the entire band would stop playing, stand up, and bellow "Baaahhh." This routine continued at most performances for months to come.[49]

DiVito's one regret was that, despite the many songs he recorded with Harry, too many of them were on the "B" side of the record and therefore weren't promoted. Although he lost out on "The Love I Long For" and "All of My Life" (the "B" sides of Kitty Kallen's popular "I'm Beginning to See the Light" and "11:60 P.M."), Buddy scored with his own hit records of "The More I See You," "If I Loved You," "I'm Always Chasing Rainbows," "And Then It's Heaven," "Laura," and "This Is Always."

Although the focus was beginning to center on the band's vocalists, four instrumentalists joined the band and significantly improved the quality of its performances. They were alto saxophonist Willie Smith, guitarist Allan Reuss, valve trombonist Juan Tizol, and pianist Arnold Ross.

At the same time, the band's two veteran mainstays departed. Al Lerner left in May to join Charlie Barnet, whose personality and more jazz-oriented band was more to his liking. Then Mickey Scrima had a row with Harry in the midst of a recording session onstage at the Huntington Hartford Theater in Hollywood, which was also the former home of the well-remembered Lux Radio Theater.

Harry James complained about how loudly Scrima was playing. "You play louder than Gene Krupa and Buddy Rich combined! Just play what's written," he ordered. Scrima muttered something, which led James to suggest, "Maybe you should start your own band." The drummer replied, "Maybe I will." Harry James countered with, "Well, start it now! Pack up your drums and get the hell out of here!" Carl Maus was brought in immediately from across the street at the NBC studios to play for the recording session and the Chesterfield show that night.[50] Mickey departed and joined his friend from the 1939 band, Frank Sinatra, on the CBS radio show, *Songs by Sinatra*.[51]

I once asked Red Kelly, without question the hardest swinging bassist James ever hired, how important Willie Smith was to the band and what his main contribution was. Kelly answered: "He was the heart and soul of the band for almost twenty years. Everything revolved around him on any band he was ever on. He would grab a band all by himself on alto saxophone and swing it."[52]

Trombonist Lew McCreary added, "Willie played so solid he made everybody feel good. I used to sit there and just yell. He gave the band a lift like a great violin concert master would do for a violin section."[53]

A former star with the Jimmie Lunceford Orchestra, Willie Smith joined the James band at Frank Dailey's Meadowbrook after a stint in the navy. Smith had been recommended to Harry James by Juan Tizol, who became his roommate and close friend. His distinctive and lyrical sound is heard on his solos on "Cherry," "It's Been a Long, Long Time," "Young Man with a Horn," and "Deep Purple," among various James hits. In the summer of 1946, he also had a hit record of his own with the band on "Who's Sorry Now?" It was a *Billboard* pop chart hit for eighteen weeks that peaked at #2. The record featured his vibrant alto solo and his rhythmic vocal. He repeated the piece almost nightly for many years.

When a ballroom operator would tell James that he wouldn't allow Willie Smith to appear as part of the band because he was black, Harry absolutely refused to give in and told Pee Wee Monte to give him his money back. Almost always, the buyer would suddenly change his mind— Harry James was too big an attraction. Of course, in those days mixed bands weren't even permitted on bandstands anywhere in the South. As a precaution, while traveling across Dixie, Willie never registered under his own name but under the name of "Joe Rossi" or "Joe La Porta." In some cities the local black professor, doctor, or other professional men got to know Willie Smith and often arranged for him to stay at their homes. When he couldn't find a place to stay, he was often forced to sleep on the bus.[54]

Jackie Mills, who spent four different periods playing drums for James, remembers an incident one night in Alabama when some fans invited Willie Smith and him to dinner. "We were sitting next to these three people, two women and a man. I had to go to the bathroom and as I got up to leave the table, I picked up the woman's purse that was in front of me. I remarked how heavy it was and gave it back to her. I said to her, 'What have you got in there—a gun?' She replied, 'Yes, I shoot niggers.' Willie turned four shades whiter!

"Once, we got chased out of some town—the sheriff and the Ku Klux Klan were both after us. We got on the bus and got out of there just in time. They found out that there were two black guys on the band." (The other was Juan Tizol.)[55]

When questioned about Willie Smith's race, Harry James dared anyone to point out precisely which musician in the band was black. His sallow skin and slicked back dark hair usually enabled Willie Smith "to pass." Some even thought he was Asian.

Jackie Mills recalled walking with Smith through the casino at the Flamingo Hotel in Las Vegas one night en route to the band room behind the bandstand. Willie was wearing the porkpie hat that he favored. All of a sudden, a gambler reached out and grabbed Willie's hat, saying, "Maybe this Chinaman's hat will give me good luck."

Willie Smith was almost as well known for his superstitions and compulsive behavior as he was for his playing. When he took his hat off or opened his instrument case, he would have to say "Rootie-Tootie," which occasionally led Harry to introduce him to the audience as, "Our altoman, Mr. R. T. McVooty."[56]

If a musician happened to say "thirteen," Willie would say "fourteen" fourteen times. At the end of the night, before he left the bandstand, he would have to touch every arrangement in his book of arrangements and finger every single page; when he first joined Harry James, the book contained somewhere between 200 and 300 arrangements. At the end of the date, when it came time for him to put his horn into its case, he would put it in, take it out, put it in, take it out, and then put it in many times until it felt absolutely right. He would also put his thumb in his belt and over the watch fob pocket of his trousers and say, "fourteen, fourteen, fourteen, fourteen...." And whenever he would use the bathroom for washing or shaving, he would have to turn the water off and on a certain number of times before he would use it and then he would leave it running.[57]

Red Kelly added, "Willie had been there for so many years he knew every part, but he had to take every part out and open it up—that was one of his idiosyncrasies. It didn't matter if it was a new or an old arrangement ... he had to read it."[58]

Guitarist Allan Reuss, one of the unsung heros of the Goodman band when Harry was a member, worked for James for about a year. Harry knew full well what Allan's value was to the rhythm section. He was part of Harry's Quintet recording of "I'm Confessin'." More significant, Allan's simple yet effective short solos opened and closed the arrangement of "I'm Beginning to See the Light." For years afterwards, James hired Reuss for specific recording dates.

Harry James was fortunate in hiring Juan Tizol, the Puerto Rican–born valve trombonist. Tizol played in the band from 1944 to 1951, and then sporadically during the latter 1950s and early 1960s. He had been an essential part of the ensemble sound of Duke Ellington's band in the 1930s and 1940s and wrote jazz standards like "Caravan" and "Perdido" while working with Ellington.

With James, Juan Tizol had more solo opportunities. A nonsmoker and nondrinker, he wore his dark hair slicked back and usually sported rimless, square-shaped glasses. His shy yet strong and dignified composure, as well as his sense of humor, gained him immediate respect from his fellow musicians. Whenever James was in a musical quandary, he invariably turned to Tizol for assistance; Juan conducted the band whenever James wasn't on the bandstand. The bass trombonist never had to practice. He spent much of his time on the road taking care of his good friend, Willie Smith.

Arnold Ross (né Rosenberg) proved a valuable asset to the James band as an accompanist to the singers; he was also an accomplished soloist. From his vantage point at the piano, he could easily spot attractive and eager young women on the dance floor. Like Sam Caplan, Arnold Ross would approach likely candidates on Harry's behalf.[59] Of course, the romantic nature of Harry James's music, plus the fact that Betty Grable was his wife, created an irrestistible combination. James and Ross often pursued women together; when Betty discovered this fact, her attitude toward Ross cooled.

The small, bespectacled pianist played the composition "Kitten on the Keys," which was used as the background theme of the 20th Century Fox musical *Do You Love Me?* (The film was originally entitled *Kitten on the Keys.*) In the film, he also ghosted the piano playing for Maureen O'Hara, the female lead opposite Harry James and Dick Haymes, and was featured in a jam session on a train involving Harry and various musicians from the band.

James often took Arnold with him when he went to the racetrack. At that time, the bandleader had the opportunity to buy a small share of the Cleveland Indians. Under the terms of major league baseball rules, James would have had to divest himself of all of his racehorses, and he wasn't prepared to do that.[60]

Starting in 1944, the James band was often restricted to playing only weekend engagements in Los Angeles. This gave James more time at the racetrack and Ross the opportunity to take other gigs. Arnold participated in several of the first "Jazz at the Philharmonic" concerts put on by Norman Granz that featured Charlie Parker, Lester Young, and Willie Smith.

Bebop was becoming increasingly important in jazz, and Ross felt its influence. As he observed, "Here I was playing Johnny Thompson's arrangement of 'I've Heard that Song Before,' and then I was playing 'Lady Be Good' with all the key changes."[61]

Arnold Ross left Harry James to become Lena Horne's pianist and conductor. One night while with Horne in New York, ex-Woody Herman bassist "Chubby" Jackson introduced Ross to Dizzy Gillespie while Dizzy was playing with his big band on 52nd Street. Sometime later, while in Paris with Horne, Arnold recorded a small group album as a sideman with Dizzy featuring Don Byas and the rhythm section from Horne's group.[62]

Because Ross had been musically involved with both Harry James and Dizzy Gillespie, I asked him how he would compare the two as trumpet players. "They had very different styles, but I really think Harry was a better player. He had more of a command of the horn, he had better range, and, of course, he could play anything. Obviously, Dizzy had more modern ideas, and he was more of a stylist."

Arnold's opinion differs greatly from that of Al Lerner, his predecessor on Harry's band. Lerner explains, "When I was first with Harry, I heard Dizzy's solo on 'Jersey Bounce' with Les Hite's Orchestra [recorded on the Hit label in early 1942]. It absolutely floored me. Harry had all the technique in the world, he had good ears and all that, and he could really play the blues, but what he didn't have was an innate chordal structure. He was too basic. Harry also didn't have the tonal sense that Dizzy had."[63]

On Ross's return to Los Angeles, he became a heroin addict. Suddenly, his budding reputation as a bebop pianist whiz went awry. He eventually spent six years in Synanon and was ultimately cured of his habit. He later became the pianist for Jane Russell, Edie Adams, and accompanied Frank Sinatra on several recordings and concerts with the Nelson Riddle Orchestra. That's Arnold's memorable piano solo on Nelson's hit record of "Lisbon Antigua."

There is a wonderful postscript to the association of Buddy DiVito and Arnold Ross who worked together in the James band for three years. One day in the mid-1980s at the Penmar Golf Course in Venice, California, a husky, middle-aged man approached Ross, took off his sunglasses, and said, "You don't remember me." Ross replied, "Of course, I remember you. You're ... you're Buddy Greco." "No," said the singer-turned-businessman, "I'm Buddy DiVito."[64] Since then, DiVito has helped Ross financially.

Arnold and Buddy speak on the telephone twice a week, and Buddy brings him down to Sun City, Arizona, for regular visits. The pianist still plays occasional solo piano gigs.

During her last years, Helen Forrest suffered greatly from arthritis and various heart problems. Kitty Kallen and her late husband, Bud Granoff, helped defray Helen's sizable medical bills as well as getting S.O.S. (Society of Singers) to help her out. Buddy DiVito and Kitty Kallen are two caring and compassionate members of an industry that has never shown sufficient interest in helping its needy veteran performers.

Another musician, trombonist Ray Conniff, started writing arrangements for Harry James while he was being mustered out of the army in 1946. He wrote frequently for him until 1953. During this period his diverse compositions and charts included "September Song," "East Coast Blues," "Vine St. Blues," "Tango Blues," "Romanian Rhapsody," "Rudolph, the Red-Nosed Reindeer," as well as "Redigal Jump" and "Beaumont Ride" (named for two of Harry and Betty's racehorses), and a 1952 version of "Hora Staccato."

Conniff is arguably the most successful commercial arranger in the history of the record business, having recorded for Columbia Records for forty years. He recalled how he began writing for Harry James: "I was living in a rooming house in Hollywood and saw the Palladium marquee that said 'Harry James.' I wrote 'I'll be Easy' and brought it to Harry there. I don't think he requisitioned me to do it. Of course, I had been with Artie Shaw before I went in the army, and he knew who I was. He played it at a rehearsal and liked it. He probably paid me $50 or $100 for it.[65]

"Harry was a little bit different than Artie in that he wanted the arrangements to be really musician-type arrangements," Conniff pointed out. "He also wanted them to be a little more complicated than Artie did. Artie was more interested in commercialism and selling records; Harry was interested in having a ball with the music, and for the boys in the band to love the chart. He didn't care if the people out front really understood that much, but amazingly he was very successful by doing it that way. He used to bug me a bit because he wouldn't play the charts in the tempos that I had written them.

"When I worked for years and years with all those different bands, I never really had a smash record of any of my arrangements. The closest was probably Artie's ''S Wonderful' and Harry's 'September Song.'

"You wrote what you thought was right for the arrangement, but then you thought, well, he's the leader. I've got to keep him happy. You wouldn't write the trumpet solos you'd normally write if you were bringing in an arrangement for Harry. When I'd write solos on the jazz things, I always wrote them with a Louis Armstrong approach. He never commented adversely, and he would play them."

It was then that Conniff, after listening to the records of swing hits like "Begin the Beguine" and "In the Mood," saw that such arrangements contained repetitious phrases that gave them a special appeal to the public. He told Mitch Miller, then head of pop A & R at Columbia, of the new approach in his writing. Mitch said, "Why don't you try that on those next four tunes for Harry's upcoming record date?" Conniff did just that, but the net result was that Harry hated his new style. He had them all rewritten right in the middle of the recording session.

Ray Conniff and Harry James finally parted during a rehearsal at the Palladium after Ray brought in a dance arrangement of "Ruby," the popular theme from the Jennifer Jones film. Harry asked, "Why don't you write more in the bop style?" Ray replied, "I just don't feel bop; it has kind of a floating beat, and I like to hear a driving beat. It isn't something I do well, and I think you should get some guy like Neal Hefti who writes that way. He'd do a better job. Let's shake hands. It's been a great relationship.

"I started thinking, 'Maybe I should start writing for the people that are buying the records—the ones that are going to the ballrooms.' That's when I started doing my own thing. I became successful when I used my same writing approach, but I wrote things that people could always understand, could dance to, or listen to. The singers kind of replaced strings. I used the singers two ways: I used them doubling in with instruments at times, and then other times I would use them as kind of a background pad, the way Harry used the string section a lot."

Conniff, like so many others who worked for James in one capacity or another, remarked: "I never got close to him as a person. I felt there was always a kind of a barrier there that I was never to cross. He made me feel that way."[66]

Another brilliant arranger is Billy May, now retired in San Clemente, California, and highly regarded as leader of his own band in the 1950s and for his vibrant and often wistfully humorous arrangements for Frank Sinatra. He saw Harry James in a different light: "Harry always had the attitude of a movie star rather than a jazz trumpet player. He also made sure he got his money's worth from you. I think this stems from the taskmaster ways of his father. That's where he developed those iron chops. I would say, though, that he was a much nicer person to work with than Glenn Miller. There was also a looseness about Harry in running a band, something that Charlie Barnet had.

"I can remember Christmas 1944, when I first worked for him. He gave a check for $200 to all the musicians in the band. When Pee Wee Monte came out of the army, everyone got a bottle of Scotch. At that Christmas party, I remember we were all listening to the radio and heard the news that Glenn Miller was missing in action over the English Channel. I remember not being surprised at hearing this terrible news. I remarked that Glenn had said to me, 'Bill, I plan to come out of this war as some kind of a hero.' Of course, Harry was very shocked at the news as he and Glenn had been good friends."[67]

As a staff arranger for Harry James, Billy May believes the most accomplished arrangements he created for him were on "Autumn Serenade" and "Carnival." He also wrote James's arrangements for the *Do You Love Me?* film and for all his radio show appearances as well.[68]

Harry James's Chesterfield show went off the air on March 23, 1944. The band then appeared on the *Danny Kaye Radio Show* from January 6 to June 1, 1945. At that point Danny Kaye had become a major Hollywood film star. Predictably, Harry James, with his natural penchant for performing, became a perfect stooge for Kaye and developed into a better than average comedian on the show.

In the summer of 1945, as part of an eastern tour, the band played the Astor Roof and also did the Pabst Blue Ribbon show. By this time, Harry had taken over from Kaye as the program's host. Betty Grable and their daughter Vicki joined Harry in New York, and the family took an apartment at the Beresford at 81st Street and Central Park West.

As part of this New York trip, singer Bea Wain remembers joining Betty on the deck of a tugboat as the *Queen Mary* arrived with thousands of troops returning from the recently concluded war in Europe. "The men were hanging out all the portholes and were jammed on the decks cheering Betty. There was the din of all the boat horns honking in the background, while a group of fireboats sprayed great cascades of water in welcome. What a homecoming for those guys—Betty Grable heralding their return!"[69]

In February 1946, after almost two years of radio shows, film roles, layoffs, and merely wanting to stay home, Harry James began doing one-nighters again. That spring and summer saw the release of two of his 20th Century Fox pictures, *Do You Love Me?* and *If I'm Lucky.*

These two films represented ill-fated attempts to make a leading man out of Harry James. The first was hampered by a foolish script, which, to his consternation, Betty Grable had previously turned down. Maureen O'Hara was cast as the love interest for Harry and Dick Haymes. Harry exhibited a decided natural flair as a leading man, playing the part of Barry Clayton, a bandleader (what else!). In the finale, Haymes gets the girl. Harry James walks away despondently, only to have the camera zoom in on a taxi door opening to reveal the shapely legs of Betty Grable. Betty smiles "Hello," and then James jumps in the cab and away they go.

Bosley Crowther wrote in the *New York Times*: "With and without his trumpet, James acquits himself very creditably. In fact, James proves quite an actor. His poise can't go unnoticed, and in closeup he's particularly at ease." Yet *Time* observed, in its unfavorable review of the film, "Harry James makes hardly any pretense of acting but blurts his trumpet often enough and loud enough to please even his most insatiable fans."[70]

If I'm Lucky might be subtitled *Como for Governor* (although its original title was *You're for Me*). This black-and-white musical cast Harry James as singer Perry Como's sidekick and followed the premise that a crooner (Como) runs for governor in order to provide exposure for his musical cohorts so that they might become radio stars. James had several scenes in which he proved his worth as an actor. In addition, his strong physical presence gave him added credibility.

Crowther wrote a dismal review of the film: "The plot would require the kindest tolerance, even if it were played by a couple of dozen Marx Brothers in the broadest style of burlesque."[71] The cast included Vivian Blaine, Phil Silvers, and Carmen Miranda. Only the title song, which Blaine sang twice, was close to being a hit. James and Miranda dueted on "Jam Session in Brazil" and joined the ensemble in the closing number, "Follow the Band." *If I'm Lucky* ended Harry James's career as a movie actor.

Even more devastating was the steadily decreasing demand for big bands that began in the early summer of 1946. Attendance at ballrooms, night clubs, and one-nighters declined sharply. Wartime prosperity had ended. Veterans, as well as young people, were saving their money to buy houses and appliances instead of spending it going out to dance. Numerous other factors caused the decline of the band business, but, fundamentally, as noted earlier, it was the rise of the singers and their seizure of the public's interest that was of paramount importance.

In early December, Harry James announced that he was disbanding at the end of the year. So did Benny Goodman, Tommy Dorsey, Les Brown, Woody Herman, Jack Teagarden, Benny Carter, and Ina Ray Hutton.[72] It was exactly ten years, almost to the week, since he had joined Benny Goodman at the Hotel Pennsylvania. Harry observed, "Today's younger generation doesn't dig the dance jive. Until a big, fat majority of young people get the urge to dance again, instead of standing in a trance watching a singer, there won't be any appreciable upswing in the dance business."

Was this truly the end of an era? For many it was—but not for Harry James.

8

The In-Between Years

Harry James's retirement was short-lived. Beginning February 10, 1947, he recorded nine tunes in three sessions for Columbia with a handpicked recording studio band. He started using a ringer, Frank Beach, the lead trumpeter in the 20th Century Fox Orchestra, as his lead man. Beach, who could provide the section with the particular piercing sound James favored, played on several subsequent albums.

By that spring, James had put a new band together. It was minus Corky Corcoran, who left to work for Tommy Dorsey for a year before returning. On April 4, the band began the first of three national tours that year. James and Pee Wee Monte reasoned that, if they were to survive in the postwar music business, certain changes had to be made. But they were determined to maintain the band's high standards so that it could continue to deliver its many hits with precision and excellence.

Bands had always made most of their money from one-nighters, playing ballrooms where they worked on a guarantee against a percentage basis. Therefore, they could thus potentially gross the most money on ballroom dates. Harry James realized that the ballroom promoters had to be dealt with first. He agreed to lower the guarantee in exchange for a percentage of the box office receipts based on a lower breakeven point. That way, if the band drew well, everybody won. As a result of their suggestions, admission prices, which had reached $4 for the likes of Harry, were cut to $2.

Salaries for traveling musicians had skyrocketed during the war years when there had been a great demand for bands. Despite high operating expenses, business had been generally so good that everyone made money. Now, there was suddenly a desperate need for bandleaders to reduce their payroll if they were to show a profit. Bands were disbanding for longer and longer periods of time as the number of dates and guarantees diminished. Veteran sidemen would return to their original bands, but often at reduced salaries and frequently as part of a smaller aggregation.

Harry James and Pee Wee Monte's innovations couldn't singlehandedly reverse the inevitable trend. Other bandleaders wouldn't or couldn't go along with their way of thinking and refused to allow any changes in their contracts. Additionally, in the next two years, people stayed at home to watch television. This was the same intriguing contraption James had first seen on display at the World's Fair in 1939. Ultimately, television became the final nail in the big band coffin.

Eames Bishop, the retired MCA agent who booked bands for the agency from 1937 to 1960, emphasized that the Pacific Coast and the far western states remained good sources of revenue for big bands even after the war, a fact that has been often overlooked. "There were still ballrooms where we booked Harry for $1,500 against 60 percent of the gate. He would often walk out with at least $3,000 to $4,000 even in smaller places. I must say, though, that back in 1940 and 1941 there had been thirty to thirty-five one-nighters in that general area."[1]

Unlike Larry Barnett, who ran MCA's variety department and had dismissed Pee Wee Monte as "just a band manager,"[2] Bishop remarked: "Pee Wee was a friendly little fellow who took good care of Harry. He knew what he was doing."

Despite what was happening to the band business, the grossing power of Betty Grable and Harry James as a show business couple remained undiminished. In 1946, the Treasury Department announced that the Jameses led all married couples in gross income in the nation that year. The following year it was revealed that Betty Grable at $299,300 (more than even Darryl F. Zanuck) was the top moneymaker among U.S. women. This same announcement also noted that Harry James had earned $100,036 alone from 20th Century Fox for his movie appearances in *Do You Love Me?* and *If I'm Lucky*. They used some of this income to buy an additional ranch with sixty-nine acres in Woodland Hills.

On May 20, 1947, Jessica, like her sister, was born five weeks premature at Cedars of Lebanon Hospital. It was a difficult delivery, causing unforeseen hemorrhaging.

In September, as the tight 1947 National League pennant race wound down, Harry's beloved St. Louis Cardinals were nosed out by the Brooklyn Dodgers. As a dedicated Cardinal fan, Harry spent time either in New

York, Brooklyn, or St. Louis attending games. Often he would work out with the team.

As Joe Garagiola, then catcher for the Cardinals, remembered: "When a guy from another field, who was a Hall-of-Famer, just to use an analogy, like a Harry James … hey, when he came on the field, I was in awe…. Butch Yatkeman (the clubhouse boy) always seemed to have a uniform available that would fit Harry. Harry would often take infield practice. Naturally, I would get the ball thrown to me by the first baseman after Harry, playing shortstop, scooped up a grounder and threw to first during these drills. I often wondered, if he sticks his thumb or one of his fingers in front of a ground ball, he wouldn't be able to play for six months, and then I figured if he got a bad hop and it hit him on the lips…. It didn't seem to bother him, and I'll tell ya'—he was a pretty good looking athlete."3

Harry's favorite Cardinal player next to Stan Musial was second baseman Red Schoendienst, who said, "All of us just loved Harry's trumpet playing. He was a hero to us, and it turned out we were heroes of his."4 For many years, after their playing careers were over, the two players would often see Harry either on the road or in Las Vegas.

Late that fall, the band played The Click, a popular Philadelphia nightclub that the band had previously played several times, including an engagement that summer. Frank Palumbo, the reputed mafioso who owned The Click, was able to get Harry a new white Cadillac sedan when such deluxe cars were at an absolute premium. In return, Palumbo needed a favor—he wanted Harry to hire his protégé, a young Frank Sinatra wannabe named Vinni De Compo. That meant the end of Buddy DiVito's four years with the James band.

Di Vito took the firing philosophically, "It was just one of those things that had to happen." He returned to Chicago, where for five years he led his own band, with his musicians often wearing the red jackets James had offered him as a severance gift.5

Vinni De Compo recorded "You Can Do No Wrong" as a duet with Marion Morgan and the band; it showed his promise as a ballad singer. But he didn't fit in. The sullen attitude he constantly displayed didn't mix well with the musicians or the leader. "Harry put up with more from Vinni than I'd ever seen him tolerate from anyone else," drummer Buddy Combine recalled. "On the bandstand, Vinni would comb his hair constantly with an oversized comb; he would be late getting on the stand, and he'd practically say, without actually saying it, 'Go to hell, Harry.' De Compo lasted only a few months before Harry let him go."6

A year earlier, James had been looking for a female singer. He heard the Jimmy Joy Band on the CBS affiliate from La Martinique in Chicago and admired the band's vocalist. The singer and her manager, Jack Rael, who played saxophone and managed Joy's band, met with Harry at his suite in the Sherman House. Rael decided he didn't want his client to sing with another band, despite James's obvious status. "That took guts on my part," remembers Rael. "I had about $20 in my checking account at the time." He later signed her to Mercury Records, and she became the biggest selling female vocalist of that era. The singer was Patti Page.[7]

Instead, Harry James hired Marion Morgan. She joined the band in June 1946 after singing with the orchestra of Caesar Petrillo (James Petrillo's brother) on WBBM in Chicago. Originally, she had auditioned for Ben Pollack, who had recommended her to James.

Two weeks later, Marion flew to Los Angeles and began a three-and-a-half-year stay with the band. From the girl singer's chair on the James bandstand, she was in a position to view the changing band business. "I was there when the band was going downhill, although I didn't really realize it. Harry was still coasting on his stardom. We played the same songs, usually in the same order, night after night. I think that may have been one reason he started drinking more than he had—the monotony of it all."[8]

Buddy Combine, the drummer, who, because he didn't drink, was referred to by Harry as "Jack Armstrong," felt that Harry's personality differed when he was on the road from when he was performing at the Palladium. "When we were on tour he'd turn into a nice guy. He was one of us. Then we would get back to L.A., and he'd assume this Hollywood star bit, and he would change.... I can't tell you how many nights when we were playing the Palladium that Harry would have a chick in the back room. Betty would come through the side door. We'd say, 'Betty's here, Betty's here.' Word would get back to him, and he'd get rid of the girl. Some nights I know he never even went home."[9]

The bus used by big bands on the road had a cylindrical shape and was not dissimilar in layout from a submarine. It was confining—the band members spent all their days there. It was boring, malodorous, funny, lonely, yet it was the most economical way to get to the next job.

On the bus, Harry James sat in the third row. ("That's his row, and don't sit in it!" remembered Buddy Combine.) Pee Wee Monte sat in the front seat and Marion Morgan in the second row. The baseball equipment and team uniforms were put on the bus first for games against college teams and even penitentiary teams. That was followed by cases of liquor. (During a tour of Connecticut, the bus made a special trip to the Smirnoff factory to buy several cases of vodka direct from the manufacturer.)[10]

Perhaps due to the excessive drinking that took place on and off the bus, the language among the musicians was often raunchy. As Marion Morgan recalled, "The musicians were terrible with girls on the bus—filthy mouthed. I said, 'Look, I can't stand any more of these four-letter words, it's killing me!' Harry never spoke up and said anything; if he'd opened his mouth and said, 'Enough!' it would have stopped."[11]

Often, a cold would start on the bus, and one musician would pass it to another. It would spread down one side of the bus and then up the other. By the time it returned to where it originated, the cycle would start anew. If it wasn't for Dexamil, a speed derivative, supposedly half the bands on the road wouldn't have made it; musicians took half a Dexamil on a daily basis as a way of combating fatigue and colds, but it also provided the energy for them to perform. Some overdid it by combining the drug with alcohol. Harry, however, had such a strong constitution that he rarely got sick.[12]

Buddy Combine noted: "I saw Harry get on the bus at nine o'clock in the morning with his little [baseball] cap on carrying two jugs and watched him drink all the way to the next town. The rest of the band— we're all dead tired. Harry would come on the job that night just like he stepped out of a steambath—happy, healthy, and ready to play."

"He was always first off the bus and would go directly to his room," added Marion Morgan. (In habits apparently left over from his circus days, on the way to his hotel room, Harry would search out the nearest fire exit before his bags were brought up. He always insisted on staying in a room on the lowest floor, partly because he suffered from vertigo.) "After the job, you would never see him again until the next day on the bus."[13]

Combine added, "But, if we got into a town, say at four in the afternoon, we'd sign into a hotel. The bus driver would find where we could play baseball. If Harry's team won, life was beautiful; if his team lost, there was no end to the way he would pick on you. Those light blue eyes would look right through you."[14]

Marion Morgan also revealed, "I don't think I exchanged more than a thousand words with Harry during all the time I worked for him. Onstage, he had a beautiful presence with a nice body type, and he had those magnificent blue eyes that sparkled. However, he wasn't too personable with the audience. While he was pleasant, he wasn't the kind of guy to be overly friendly. He gave all his warmth and love through his trumpet. There just wasn't much left. I have to say, though, that there wasn't a night on the bandstand that I didn't get goose bumps listening to his trumpet.

"He never said, 'How are you?' He never asked if I liked the songs. He just handed me the songs, and I sang them.... I had nothing to say about anything I did. I never sang any of Helen Forrest's hits. They were never, never played."

For the most part, Morgan was assigned "cover" versions of various hits of the day. Her 1947 rendition of "As Long as I'm Dreaming" is a perfect example of the warmth and sincerity with which she sang a ballad. This recording is included in the Columbia Legacy CD *Harry James and His Great Vocalists*.

Marion Morgan often had a problem when returning to her hotel room ("and we stayed in the best hotels") after a gig. The girl who was with Harry that night would often say that she was the girl singer, which would therefore provide her with access to Harry's room. The house detective would then approach Marion: "The girl singer's already checked in. Who are you?" She would explain, "Well, there's a group of us who sing with the band"—a white lie that protected both Harry and herself.

With it all, Marion found Harry could be sympathetic when unforeseen problems occurred. One night, Bruce McDonald, the band's pianist, played an arpeggio as the introduction to "Embraceable You." She absolutely froze and couldn't remember any of the words of the Gershwin classic. "I looked around at Harry and told him that I didn't know what to do. He played the introductory chords of the melody, but it didn't matter. After the set, I was sure I would be fired. Instead, Harry said to me, 'Marion, let me tell you what happened to me once in New York at the Paramount Theater. I forgot the song we were playing. I had to learn it all over again.'"[15]

When I asked Marion whether she had ever seen Harry and his father Everette together, she smiled and said, "Oh, yes, Everette was a doll. Harry didn't have Everette's personality or his sweetness. Everette talked to you anytime, anyplace."

She went on to further underscore how Harry still depended on Everette for advice. "I can remember one time at the Palladium when Harry and Everette were having a pretty deep conversation. Harry was holding his trumpet and was listening intently to Everette tell him about how to change his embouchure since apparently Harry was having trouble with his front teeth."

Marion Morgan left the band after complaining to Ben Pollack (she was then recording for his Jewel Records) that Harry James didn't feature her, even though she had sung with the band for four years. She also had never received a raise from her initial salary of $125 a week, while Buddy DiVito was being paid $160 a week. (Many years later, she learned why Harry wouldn't give her any more money—he needed it for betting on horses.)

She overheard Ben Pollack discussing her problems with Harry James one night at the Palladium. He told Pollack, "Look, the singers have ruined the band business. I don't give a damn." "That broke my heart, and I quit that weekend."[16]

Sid Beller had finally decided to leave his job as the band's road manager just before Marion Morgan left. They had fallen in love. Beller became her personal manager and later her husband. Morgan was featured on the highly popular 1950s television program *Stop the Music* and had a promising recording career.

A few years later, she and Sid Beller went to see the band when it was in New York. "I had already noticed that, once a musician left the band, he never came back to see Harry. We went backstage," Marion continued. "When he saw us he barely said hello."[17]

There were no longer any starring parts for Harry James in Hollywood films. He did have a cameo playing himself, but not performing, in a United Artists movie starring Jimmy Stewart, Paulette Goddard, and Burgess Meredith called *On Our Merry Way* in 1947. Another UA picture in the same year was *Carnegie Hall*, in which he was featured playing "57th Street Rhapsody" backed by a symphony orchestra.[18]

On radio, the band moved from one show to another. Beginning on February 13, 1948, James and the band appeared for twenty-six weeks on *Call for Music* on CBS with Dinah Shore and Johnny Mercer. In recalling *Call for Music*, Buddy Combine said, "It was amazing. Harry would read from his script since he had a running part in the show. Then he would conduct the band with one hand, and he would never miss a beat while playing the trumpet with the other hand.

"Another reason I can't forget *Call for Music* is the fact that at the end of the show's run, the band's kitty [fines levied for lateness and other minor infractions] amounted to quite a bit of money. Instead of having a party for the musicians as most bands did, Harry took what was in the kitty and bet it on one of his horses. Naturally, he lost. After it happened, he laughed and sloughed it off by saying, 'What's the difference? The atom bomb's going to get all of us anyway.' "[19]

The atomic bomb didn't destroy the band business; instead, among other things, it was the rise of bebop that affected it. Through the acceptance given Dizzy Gillespie, Charlie Parker and their disciples, bebop grabbed the attention of young people. Ironically, when he first started playing with name bands, Dizzy Gillespie was a trumpeter very much in the Harry James mold. Suddenly, Woody Herman and Stan Kenton became the major innovators among the big bands.

Herman had returned to the band business in the fall of 1947 with his incredible Second Herd (the "Four Brothers" Band) composed of a cluster of talented young musicians—Ralph Burns, Stan Getz, Zoot Sims, Neal Hefti, Al Cohn, Don Lamond, Shorty Rogers, and Serge Chaloff—who proved that bebop could both be successfully adapted to a big band setting and still be commercial.[20] At about the same time, Stan Kenton's band became prominent. Kenton referred to his often ponderous music as "progressive jazz." He disliked playing for dancing; instead the concert hall became his milieu.

By 1947, Benny Goodman had also recognized bebop. He first consulted with the talented arranger, composer, and pianist Mary Lou Williams, who had written "Roll 'Em" for his band a decade earlier. Under her guidance, Goodman put a new band together, with Williams contributing compositions written in the new idiom, including "In the Land of Oo-Bla-Dee" and "Lonely Moments." He also brought in Chico O'Farrell, who became an innovative arranger in the new style and wrote "Shiska Bop," "Bop Hop," and "Undercurrent Blues."

Benny Goodman sounded considerably less at ease playing bop than Harry James later did. He really didn't make much of an attempt to depart from his patented swing clarinet style. Playing his Swing Era arrangements of "Stealin' Apples" or "Blue Lou" with bebop saxophone voicings were superficial attempts to play bebop. He did have in his band, however, Wardell Gray, one of the most respected bop saxophone players of the period.

Following in the path of Herman and Goodman, Harry James made two significant changes. He gave up his string section entirely after first cutting it down to four violins. Strings were now both costly and musically out of step with the times. Next, he hired arranger Neal Hefti, who left Woody Herman and joined James's trumpet section. Over the next eighteen months, Hefti contributed a library of bebop compositions and arrangements that were in vivid contrast to the James band's standard repertoire.

With his incredible ear and mastery of the trumpet, Harry James didn't find it difficult playing bebop. On the Fresh Sound recording from this period, which features many of Hefti's compositions, James sounds like a trumpeter reborn playing with an intensity reminiscent of the vigor he displayed during the Goodman years. Moreover, his entire band reflected this same spirit. Its sound was suddenly transformed into that of a vibrant jazz orchestra. Ziggy Elmer (not to be confused with Ziggy Elman), teaming with Juan Tizol, gave Harry two thrilling trombone soloists to go along with his veteran saxophone stars, Corky Corcoran and Willie Smith, who changed their styles not a whit yet sounded comfortable with the new charts, despite the misgivings Neal Hefti had about their playing. The rhythm section was comprised of Bruce McDonald on piano, Tiny Timbrell on guitar, along with Joe Mondragon on bass and Don Lamond on drums, both of whom also came over from the Herman Second Herd.

Don Lamond became so important to Harry James that he was paid weekly whether the band was working or not. The drummer, known for his subtle use of dynamics, was doubly valuable to James because he was a good center fielder as well. Lamond still relishes the period he worked for

Harry. "I got a thrill when he'd stand next to the trumpet section to my left and he'd play over the whole band. He was a marvelous lead player."[21]

Lamond also admired the unpretentious behavior of Betty Grable. "One Sunday, Harry invited Neal, Joe and me out to his ranch. Betty waited on us all day. I remember her father told us he couldn't understand why she was a movie actress, but, of course, everybody else could. Years later, I was with Mitch Ayres' band on the Perry Como show when Betty was the guest star. I remember she named every guy who had been in the band when I was there. I couldn't believe it."

Regarding the impact of Don Lamond and the others, Harry James said: "The most important thing that makes me want to play is this new band of mine. They're up on the stand wanting to play all the time, so how could I possibly not feel like blowing? I haven't had a bunch like this since my first band."[22] It was arranger Johnny Mandel's feeling that "when Harry stopped trying to be the big commercial guy, I think his good bands really began."[23]

I asked Neal Hefti if Harry James had then felt that the parade was passing him by. "Yes, he did. When he saw that one of his rivals, Woody Herman, was cashing in on bebop, he realized that his new music belonged to Charlie Parker, but it sure as hell didn't belong to Woody Herman. He had listened to the same records that everybody else did—Dizzy Gillespie, Charlie Parker, etc."[24]

Many of the tracks in the Fresh Sound collection were culled from *The Harry James Show*, a navy recruiting radio show emceed by Don Wilson, Jack Benny's famous announcer. Several of the Hefti tunes that Harry James titled were either gamblers' phrases ("Six, Two, and Even") or racetrack expressions. "There They Go" referred to the starting gate at Del Mar. "Proclamation" was the name of a horse. "Bells" recalled the bells ringing at the starting gate when the race began. The influence of the racetrack on Harry was everywhere.[25]

Louise Baranger, a mainstay of Harry James's last trumpet section, was enthusiastic about his recorded excursion into bebop. "He's playing high G's or F's on that CD, which, in the late '40s was unheard of. When Maynard Ferguson started doing that everyone thought it was incredible. And they're big notes—he's not squeaking it out, he's playing up there. You hear him playing jazz and it's easy for him. At the end of a solo he blows a high G as big as a house. He could have capitalized on that—his chops and his technical ability—but the public wanted him to play 'You Made Me Love You,' 'I Don't Want to Walk Without You,' and 'Sleepy Lagoon.' I guess when you become a personality sometimes it detracts from your art."[26]

Another musician, drummer Kenny Washington, commented on James's playing during this period: "When the bebop sounds started in the early '40s, most people turned their noses up at it, but Coleman Hawkins said, 'Hmm, I think there's something interesting here.' He got with all those young cats like Dizzy to check out what they were doing. He took a little bit of that and added to what he already had, which made him a better musician. Harry was the same way. Most of the Swing Era trumpet players stayed there except for Roy Eldridge and a few others. But Harry was very open to it rhythmically and harmonically. He was able to adapt to bebop and handling those changes. He wasn't just playing half notes and whole notes, he's playing lines."[27]

Despite the musical explorations he was undertaking, the days of his youth were also still with him. In an incident that could be described as "you can take the boy out of the circus, but you can't take the circus out of the boy," Harry appeared at an important Hollywood benefit at the Pan Pacific Auditorium in 1948. Merle Evans was still leading his famed Ringling Brothers Barnum & Bailey Circus Band. Jimmy Ille was then a member of Evans's highly regarded band. "God, it was wonderful to see Harry back in his element again. When he came in, he asked Merle if he had the arrangement of 'North Wind' with the clarinet part. Merle let him put on the bandmaster's cap and suggested he lead the band on this number." From then on, whenever Jimmy Ille would see Harry James coming through New Orleans with his band, they would talk about that afternoon.[28]

By the end of the 1940s, several important ballrooms continued to feature name dance bands. One was the Steel Pier in Atlantic City, which George Hamid, Jr., who ran the Pier with his father, referred to as "The Valhalla of the Big Bands." Since the early 1930s, musicians had relished working in its Marine Ballroom ("half a mile at sea"), which drew highly enthusiastic audiences. In addition, there was the festive atmosphere that pervaded the Atlantic City season, with its famed boardwalk, wide sandy beaches, surf, and salt air.[29]

In 1949, the entertainment business was changing in other ways. Hamid vividly remembers that the James band was booked to open the season at the Pier on Easter Sunday. "Harry's trumpet playing was crystal clear, and you couldn't believe it—the people poured onto the Pier. We did 27,000 people—the biggest day we had had since the war was over. In those days, the girls wore beautiful pastel hats on Easter Sunday, and they all had high-heeled shoes on. They'd go to the Ballroom to dance and they would come out with their shoes in their hands."

The James band still was drawing well in most locations through the end of the decade, but ballrooms continued to close, so there were fewer places for big bands to work the jumps between dates became longer. From the fall of 1946 until August 1950—when Harry James had the original (instrumental) hit on Livingston and Evans's "Mona Lisa"[30]—none of his hit records could compare in sales with those released during the war years. Strangely enough, the business the band was doing on personal appearances wasn't that affected by his decreasing record sales—at least for a time. Columbia continued advancing monies to James because his earlier recordings continued to sell.

When Don Lamond decided to leave the road in 1949, James hired Louis Bellson—like Don Lamond, a very musical drummer, but also someone who played on top of the beat, the way James liked it. When Bellson moved to Los Angeles, he shared an apartment with Juan Tizol, who brought him to Harry's attention. Bellson had left Tommy Dorsey ostensibly to live in Los Angeles and study with the composer Buddy Baker. Even today, he continues as a student of Baker (now at USC) in film composition.[31]

Buddy Baker at eighty-two is as robust as a twenty-five-year-old but with the musical knowledge of the compleat musician. In Baker's fifteen arrangements for the James band, he utilized his unique harmony system which intrigued James. This system was based on the theory that every type of chord has its own scale. They got together over a more than a thirty-year period to discuss and practice this system. Baker believes: "Without mentioning any names, some of the people they're raving about today … I don't think they're in the same league as Harry as far as being trumpet players. I always thought he was the most exciting trumpet player that ever lived. I looked at him sort of like being a Heifitz—he would come out and play something without saying anything. He was so confident in what he did. I never heard him play a solo that didn't have a real spark to it.

"There had to be two things in Harry's bands—strong, strong trumpets, and a strong drummer. Harry, Tommy Dorsey, Artie Shaw, Benny Goodman, Basie, and Duke, they all had one thing in common: they could play good jazz and you always knew what tune they were playing. It didn't get so complicated."[32]

Reflecting on the excitement of this period, Louis Bellson commented: "You can imagine the excitement that Elvis Presley and Michael Jackson created. That's the reaction that big bands had in those days. When Harry James played the 'Two O'Clock Jump,' 'You Made Me Love You' or 'Bugle Call Rag,' people just freaked out. They just stopped while they were dancing to listen. We would play before 3,000 people at the Palladium, but I remember some of those navy and air force bases where we played before fourteen or fifteen thousand people. It was just a sea of faces. The excitement came from the music and the reaction of the people. They hung onto every note. They were up on the records, and they were up on what Harry was about."

Bellson also appreciated that Harry James gave him several solos and that he also was able to play his own compositions like "Skin Deep" and "The Hawk Talks." Most people think the latter concerned Coleman Hawkins. In reality, Harry James was "the Hawk," an allusion to his prominent nose, which increased in size and width in proportion to his alcohol consumption over the years.

Since Louis Bellson has worked with just about every major jazz trumpeter during his long career, I asked him what they thought about Harry James. "Clark Terry said, 'What can you say? The man was complete. He could do it all'—they were good buddies for years. Charlie Shavers loved him. Roy [Eldridge] used to talk about him all the time. Everybody said, 'There's no question about it, that cat can play.' And when they said it, they meant it. I bet if Bix was living and had the chance to see Harry, he'd be one of the guys he'd mention right off the bat."[33]

Speaking of Bix Beiderbecke, Lalo Schifrin, the distinguished film and television composer and former Dizzy Gillespie pianist, who composed a suite entitled "Rhapsody for Bix," also saw Bix's influence on James's playing. On hearing "The Truth," a tune co-written by Harry James and Matty Matlock for James's *Double Dixie Album*, Schifrin noted: "When Harry plays in this style, he shows Bix's influence. I can feel it." He made the same observation after listening to James's playing on other albums as well. "He's trying to play Armstrong, but it comes from Bix. What I'm saying is that maybe he listened to Armstrong directly without having gone through Bix, but the reaction—how he projected his perception of Armstrong—is very similar to the one Bix had.... Of course, James had more technique than Bix had," he pointed out.[34]

Finally, after years of waiting, Warner Bros. prepared *Young Man with a Horn*, loosely based on Dorothy Baker's novel that concerned the career of Rick Martin, a thinly disguised Bix Beiderbecke. In the midst of a November 22 through Christmas night 1949 engagement at the Palladium, Harry James spent his days as musical advisor on Michael (*Casablanca*) Curtiz's film. Kirk Douglas played Rick, and James supplied his trumpet solos. Working on the picture provided an opportunity for him to illustrate once again his mastery of all kinds of music ranging from "Silent Night" to "Can't We Be Friends?" Band members such as Juan Tizol, Corky Corcoran, Willie Smith, Hoyt Bohanon, and Nick Fatool, as well as guest musicians Babe Russin and Jimmy Zito, either were seen on camera or heard on the soundtrack.[35]

In *Young Man with a Horn*, Hoagy Carmichael delivered one of his customary understated and totally believable portrayals as Douglas's piano-playing sidekick, "Smoke" Willoughby. Harry James supplied not only the musical backing, but also helped Kirk Douglas assume the bearing of a jazz musician. Doris Day was cast as his devoted admirer, and Lauren Bacall played Kirk's patron-of-the-arts wife in a confusing, ill-defined role.

In the *New York Times*, Tom Pryor wrote, "Although *Young Man with a Horn* has more in the way of dramatic faults than is good for it, somehow it all adds up to a rather agreeable movie. That soundtrack is wonderful, after all, and, for which, thank you so much, Mr. Harry James."[36] *Time*, however, believed, "Most of the trumpet work ... is badly out of character. It has all of James' technical finesse but is often nearly as commercial as the kind of music that trumpeter Douglas rails against."[37] Most of the jazz fraternity heartily agreed with *Time*'s comments about the commercial treatment of the music heard in the film.

Just before Harry James's work on the film began, he called Doris Day's former boss, Les Brown, to ask whether he thought he could "nail" Doris.[38] History never recorded what happened between them on a personal level, but they later enjoyed a hit record together—"Would I Love You (Love You, Love You)" in 1951.

A year later, Harry James and the band were seen on camera playing the title song in the Fox musical *I'll Get By*, the tune that had been originally a hit for James with Dick Haymes. The film starred Bill Lundigan, Dennis Day, June Haver, Gloria De Haven, and Steve Allen. James also helped produce the music heard on the soundtrack. That same year (1950) he did an unbilled cameo in a Jimmy Stewart movie, *Jackpot*, in which only his voice was heard.

During the postwar period, Harry James had become the best known trumpet player in the public's mind. As Johnny Mandel expressed it, "What Harry did was to make everybody aware of what a trumpet sounded like. The musicians knew how important Louis Armstrong was, but the public thought of him as an entertainer because of the way he mugged and sang. Up to then it had all been clarinet players—Benny, Artie—and then Tommy Dorsey on trombone. There had to be a trumpet player of this magnitude, and Harry was so flashy. He was really the first real mass-media trumpet star. He was also the guy who made kids want to play the trumpet."[39]

As a mass-media trumpet star and the husband of Betty Grable, Harry James had problems when the band was traveling on tour. At this juncture, Sal Monte, the fourth Monte brother, had been discharged from the army and joined the band, specifically to take care of James on the road and serve as a "beard" (a man employed by a male star to accompany him when he appears in a public with a woman not his wife).

As Sal Monte described it, "I just hung out with him. Harry took care of himself as far as his valet needs were concerned. I saw that the bags got into his room right away. I set up the bar. I went out to dinner with him every night. I called the bellboy to get the bags out. Not once, wherever we were, did I ever have to pick up a tab for anything.... He just wanted somebody with him at all times. He didn't want to be seen running around."

From the time he went on the road after marrying Betty Grable, Harry James was constantly besieged by fans approaching him asking either "Where's Betty?" or "How's Betty?" The profusion of such inquiries eventually affected his ego, and it was often difficult for him to handle. In those days, among his often surly replies, fueled often by several drinks, were, "She's at home washing my socks" and "How's your ma?"[40]

James's two sons, living with Louise Tobin in Texas, were also affected by the fame of Betty Grable and Harry James. Harry Jeffrey, in his first day at school, was asked his name. He said, "My name is Harry James." The teacher countered, "When you're ready to tell the class your real name, you may stand up and tell us." She added, "So I guess Betty Grable is your mother."[41]

Tim James asked Louise one day, "Mommy, do you have any pictures of you when you were younger?" Louise said, "Yes, I do." She asked why. Tim replied, "I told the teacher that you were my mother, and I wanted to show her that your legs are better than Betty Grable's."[42]

Louise Tobin kept her two sons informed about their father and his career, although Harry showed little interest in the boys. He visited them once when both he and Louise were living in Los Angeles, but, after they moved to Texas, he never went to see them again. Several years later, James called and asked Louise to put them on a plane to Los Angeles for a visit. On their return, Louise asked if they had had a good time. The reply was, "Daddy didn't seem to have much time for us, but Betty Grable certainly is a nice lady."[43]

Their grandfather was brought to Los Angeles in 1953 to live at the Baby J Ranch to run the place after the death of Conn Grable. Everette and Alma James reluctantly made the move to southern California. In Beaumont, Everette had enjoyed his status as a highly respected music teacher and the father of Harry James, the hometown boy who made good. However, in speaking of being relegated to living in the San Fernando Valley, Everette remarked, "They put us out on the ranch and buried us."[44]

He and Alma saw Betty, Harry, and their other grandchildren, but they spent considerable time with Pee Wee Monte and Viola Paulich, who had married on April 21, 1951, after more than a decade of working together. The two couples spent many evenings together playing canasta, which had become the rage during the early 1950s.[45]

*   *   *

Harry James couldn't ignore the fact that Betty Grable was the bigger star, but their huge combined incomes could still stretch only so far. By the 1950s, they both had acquired substantial gambling habits, although Betty was never a match for Harry. As Sal Monte is fond of saying, "No matter what, he'd bet you on the weather." James now began using Grable's money as a backup.

As a bachelor, Nick Sevano lived in a three-bedroom Hollywood apartment. His clients, Vic Damone and Al Martino, often stayed overnight. Since the apartment was located close to the Hollywood Palladium, Harry James would often drop by, and he decided to leave a supply of vodka there. Shortly thereafter, Sevano told James that he and Mickey Rooney planned to spend a day at Hollywood Park. James gave Sevano $5,000 to bet on a "special" horse at one of the races. Rooney, who for many years had been— and still is—a rabid horseplayer, said to Sevano, "I gotta find out who he's talking to. There's a God up there who must be giving him tips." Naturally, he followed his lead and bet on the same horse. According to Nick, Harry's horse finished dead last by perhaps ten lengths. In total shock, Rooney remarked, "Where the hell is the horse? I can't even find him." Sevano told James, who merely laughed it off as just a bad day at the track.[46]

Nat Dyches was the assistant to Harry Brand at 20th Century Fox with the responsibility of running the day-to-day operation of the publicity department. In that capacity he dealt with Betty Grable on a regular basis. Dyches was also an inveterate horseplayer, whom Grable came to respect for his knowledge of horses. Betty, in turn, was called "the Queen of the Handicappers."[47]

One day, Dyches was approached by Grable to place $100 with his bookie across the board on one of the James's horses. During the course of a busy afternoon, Nat completely forgot to place the bet. When the horse won, Betty asked Nat to collect on her bets. He was, therefore, forced to come up with the money on his own. (It's unknown whether he eventually charged the payoff to his studio expense account.)

In 1951, the Internal Revenue Service hit the Jameses hard, disallowing significant expenses charged as deductions on their federal and state taxes for the training, feeding, and upkeep of their horses and racing stable. What's more, the Baby J Ranch was attached as well. For not the first time, nor the last, Harry James was bailed out by Pee Wee Monte.

Pee Wee had originally bought ten shares of Hollywood Park at $60 a share. Over the next several years, the stock split several times. He reportedly later wound up with about 500 shares of the famed racetrack.[48]

Fred Monte had come back to work for Harry James after two and a half years in the army. He replaced his brother, Al, who had retired as band boy, and had been promoted to road manager after taking courses in accounting and bookkeeping through the GI Bill. He replaced Sid Beller when he departed from the band. As Fred Monte is quick to admit, "Harry James pulled me out of the ghetto. In Belleville [New Jersey] in those days young Italians either were bookies or loan sharks. Do you know what it meant to me to go to work for Harry? It saved my life!"

This same devotion came to the fore when the five-foot, seven-inch Fred Monte had it out with a gang of hoodlums who taunted Corky Corcoran and other James musicians at the conclusion of a date at the Edgewater Beach Ballroom in San Francisco. "They were ready to take Corky apart. They called the guys 'Hollywood queers.' I jumped off the bandstand and attacked this big guy who was after Corky. (Corky Corcoran's drinking had become a major problem.) I was beating the shit out of him when the police came. I was at an advantage. The dance floor was slippery, and I had rubber-heeled shoes on. Harry missed all the action since he had already left by cab. The gang members vowed to kill us the next night in Oakland, so we had a police escort to, during, and from the gig. We got out of town, but it was pretty hairy."[49]

An important James alumnus had his own problems at the same time. As the *New York Daily News* intoned, "Anybody know of a bigger bore just now than Frank Sinatra?" At Columbia Records, Sinatra and Mitch Miller couldn't agree on much of anything regarding what was suitable material for Frank to record. Harry James began having similar difficulties with the record company.

On July 19, 1951, the James band recorded three numbers with its original male vocalist. One must assume that someone at Columbia had believed that pairing Sinatra and James would produce renewed interest in both their careers, as neither had come up with a hit record in some time. Columbia achieved its goal with "Castle Rock." This onetime Louis Jordan hit had lyrics added by Ervin Drake and the arrangement was written by Ray Conniff. Harry James later referred to this record as "the worst thing that either of us ever recorded." Before the last chorus, Sinatra shouts out, "Go get 'em Harry—for old time's sake." "Castle Rock" was Frank Sinatra's last hit with Columbia and is significant in revealing a newly honed swagger in his delivery. It spent eight weeks on the *Billboard* pop chart, peaking at #8.

Almost fifty years after he last worked with Harry James, Mitch Miller, at a spry eighty-seven, remembered: "The first time I saw him with Benny Goodman, the hairs on my neck rose up every time he soloed. You heard six notes, you knew it was Harry James. He had his own identity ... so he's halfway home. Then, he's a fine musician, which he was, and he had the temperament to lead musicians and surround himself with fine people.

Success was guaranteed. That's why Harry rode so high, and he never took it seriously."

In explaining the recording business of the early 1950s, the still musically active Miller said, "Albums didn't mean anything until the LP came in. If you had hit singles, then you'd sell the album. You didn't set out to make a jazz record as a single. If jazz was right for the arrangement, you did jazz. Look at 'Perdido' with Sarah Vaughan. That had jazz. My recording James was more a labor of love."[50]

A collaboration between Rosemary Clooney and the James band with strings added was recorded in May of 1952. The album consisted of Academy Award-winning songs. "You'll Never Know," originally introduced by Alice Faye in the Fox musical, *Hello, Frisco, Hello*, was released as a single by Columbia and became a #18 *Billboard* pop chart hit. This recording illustrates Clooney's ability, even then, of singing lyrics with total conviction.

The warm and gracious Clooney recalls this session: "It was so long ago, but I do remember that Harry played the introduction to 'You'll Never Know' before breaking into 'Happy Birthday,' since it was recorded on my birthday, May 23. He was a delight to work with, but I always felt his deep blue eyes looking at me. I sensed that there was more than music on his mind. Fortunately, either my manager, Joe Shribman, or my husband Joe (Jose) Ferrer was at the studio doing the recording sessions.

"Years later, I developed a close friendship with Buddy Rich, when he was working for Harry, and I was playing the main room at the Flamingo. I noticed that Harry would never come over to join us while I was talking to Buddy. He became distant. I always thought there were many layers to Harry's personality."[51]

"The Great James Robbery" of April 1951 was a major story in big band annals. It transpired when Duke Ellington induced Willie Smith to leave Harry's band to replace Johnny Hodges, who was making one of his sporadic unsuccessful attempts to establish his own small group. Along with Willie came Louis Bellson to replace Duke's original drummer, Sonny Greer; and Juan Tizol, who returned to the Ellington fold.[52] Since James's band wasn't working on a full time basis, it was ripe for picking.

Asked about the raid, Harry James good-naturedly remarked, "If I were them, I'd have done the same thing," which reflected his own longtime admiration for Ellington. Herb Steward replaced Willie Smith on alto, Jackie Mills took over the drum chair from Louis Bellson, and Ziggy Elmer came back to take over from Tizol. After slightly over two years, Willie, Louis, and Juan all returned to the James band.

But despite all these upheavals, certain things remained constant with

Harry James—his drinking, his sexual appetite, and baseball. Although Buddy Combine spoke of Harry's emptying a pint of bourbon on the bus en route to dates, "Uncle Lew" (as Harry dubbed trombone player Lew McCreary) claims he didn't drink during the day. "He encouraged everybody to get as stoned as they wanted to," he remembered. "He was very tolerant as long as you could play your part. He would have drinks before dinner, but he would always eat well. Between sets, he would maybe have another drink. It got to where he wanted a drink poured for him and left in the piano, which he sipped while on the bandstand."[53]

Harry's close friend, the bandleader and raconteur, Phil Harris, whom many think was the real-life model for Dean Martin's drinking image, once said, "Harry could drink me under the table anytime." According to McCreary, on one occasion he saw Harry outdrink Desi Arnaz, another formidable drinker.[54]

The trombonist swears that before one tour started, "A couple of us on the band decided we were going to count the number of girls Harry had during the tour. We played thirty-six one-nighters; we counted thirty different women we saw with him. I well remember going to his room some mornings, where I saw some of the worst looking dogs you'd ever want to meet getting dressed."

"Red" Brown, a devoted friend of Harry's, drove the James band bus during the 1950s and into the early 1960s. I can still remember how Harry relished telling stories about Brown's exploits. One time, while the band was on a series of one-nighters, Red put his legs around the wheel while driving the bus and began to read a newspaper until somebody yelled out, "Red, put your hands on the wheel!"

Living on a steady diet of amphetamines, Brown could stay up for days and usually got the band to its destination well before its planned time of arrival. He was even more blatant in his approach to women on behalf of Harry than Sam Caplan had been. His frequent introduction involved his asking, "Would you like to go to bed with the guy who goes to bed with Betty Grable?"[55]

While Red Brown was driving the bus pell-mell across the Midwest one day, trombonist Dave Wells made an important discovery while looking out of the bus window. He told Harry James he spotted some marijuana plants growing in a field. Harry ordered Red to stop the bus immediately, and Al Monte was sent out to inspect. Bruce McDonald held one of the plants Al had pulled out of the ground and exclaimed, "Yes, by God, that is hemp." Harry and several musicians filled up pillowcases full of grass. Wells was heartily congratulated for his keen eye as the band bus started up again, its passengers grateful for their newly harvested stash.[56]

Bill Richmond, who was James's drummer for several months, remembers getting on the bus at the Musician's Union on Vine Street in Hollywood for his first road trip with the band. "I couldn't believe it—while Harry was standing up in the front of the bus, he started making remarks about every chick we passed on the street: 'Hey, man, I'd like to ...' or 'Look at that ass,' going on and on like that. And I'm sitting there looking at him thinking, 'This is the husband of Betty Grable?'"[57]

Before going to work for Harry James, Richmond had been a member of Horace Heidt's band for three years. I asked him what was it that made a man endure that kind of a life. "There's only one one reason guys do it. They want to be a jazz musician or a big band musician or whatever. They love the music. When I told my mother I was going to California to be a jazz musician, she said, 'What are we going to tell people you do?' One thing you know when you're a musician. You know how good you are and how bad you are. Musicians have a certain arrogance because they work so hard at it, and they do something that's very specific."

With so many unforeseen changes taking place in the band business during the first half of the 1950s, it wasn't that unusual that Harry James hired an eighteen-year-old accordion prodigy named Tommy Gumina. James quickly recognized the commercial potential in the young musician. Although Lawrence Welk had been an accordionist, the instrument rarely became a staple of big band instrumentation. Gumina joined the band in January 1951 when *The Harry James Show* debuted on KNBH-TV in Los Angeles for twenty-six weeks.[58]

After the show's demise, and the band went back on the road, Gumina was featured nightly on three numbers, including "Flight of the Bumble Bee," on which he and James did a trumpet and accordion duet. The success of their version led Harry James to record the piece for the third time. They also collaborated on "Ruby," which was James's last record to make the *Billboard* chart.

Looking back on this experience, Tommy Gumina remembers Harry James with decided respect as well as perspective: "Just before I joined, he couldn't stand the war that was going on with the swing guys versus the beboppers. He had had enough. He came home and closed down the band—he didn't want to put up with the nonsense.... It's tough, the band-leader can be pretty much alone."[59]

As economic conditions worsened for the band during the 1950s, several times Harry James broke up his big band, and, as purely stopgap measures, put together a quintet, sextet, or octet for various engagements. Harry liked the small group feeling, but it simply couldn't replace the pleasure he got from being in front of a big band.

Tommy Gumina had definite reservations about Pee Wee Monte. "Pee

Wee was cheap and Harry was not cheap. [In his defense, Pee Wee knew the value of money, whereas Harry didn't.] Harry didn't like Pee Wee because he was always kissing up to him. He tolerated it, but he didn't like that weakness. When we went to Vegas with the sextet, Pee Wee said to me, 'You've got to take a cut. We can only afford to put the small band in there. You've got to help us out.' Of course, Vegas was the town that paid big money. I went to Harry, whom I called 'Arch' like a lot of other guys did, and told him what Pee Wee wanted me to do. He said, 'Kid, don't worry, I'll take care of it.' He read Pee Wee the riot act. It was $25, big deal, right? For me, it was the principle."[60]

And if an accordionist wasn't unusual for a dance band, what about a female instrumentalist who doubled as a singer? In 1954, along came Corky Hale (originally Marilyn Hecht), a gifted harpist, pianist, flautist, and singer from Freeport, Illinois. She had originally emigrated to Los Angeles to study music at UCLA. James had seen her playing piano with Freddy Martin's band at the Coconut Grove.[61]

Female musicians weren't entirely unheard of in big bands. Woody Herman had employed Billie Rogers on trumpet and the accomplished Margie Hyams on vibes. But now there were two "Corky's" on the James band, since Corky Corcoran had returned after drying out for a few years.

Although Corky Hale was the first female musician he ever hired, Harry James never showed any sexism toward her. As ever, he was only interested in whether she was a good musician. Hale does, however, recall the sexual harassment she endured from various musicians on the band, but she knew exactly how to combat it. "When I first joined the band," she recalled, "I was faced with remarks like, 'That's a nice pair,' or 'I'd like to get a feel of those.' I just laughed and said, 'Don't you wish you could get a feel.' I would add, 'I'm having lunch with your wife on Thursday.' I became their buddy. I can still remember cooking breakfast several nights after midnight for eighteen musicians and their wives or girlfriends at my apartment down the hill from the Crescendo in Hollywood when we played there."[62]

Throughout the history of the band, Harry James often had great difficulty in finding a drummer who satisfied him, a problem that constantly plagued Benny Goodman as well. Two drummers he particularly admired were Don Lamond and Louis Bellson. But the drummer he always wanted in his band was the young man he first met in Ben Pollack days in Chicago and whom he had tried unsuccessfully to hire for his first band—Bernard "Buddy" Rich. The fire with which Rich played, his ability to whip the brass section and lift the entire band with his powerful drumming were ingredients James looked for, but seldom found, in any one drummer. Lew McCreary offered an interesting insight when he said: "I know why he liked Buddy's playing—he had a heavy foot as a drummer just the way Harry did when he played drums."[63] Finally, Harry James was given the opportunity to have the drummer he always wanted.

At the Bandbox in New York in the late winter of 1953, the Buddy Rich Quartet opened for the James band. Harry James and Buddy Rich's friendship was immediately renewed. Several nights Buddy sat in with the band. Harry then recorded three tracks with Buddy's group on Joyce Records; Buddy, in turn, recorded two numbers with the James band.

March in New York is often a time when the flu is rampant—one day it's cold and damp, and the next it's like spring. When a few of his musicians came down with the flu during the first days of the Bandbox engagement, Harry decided, "That's it! We've got to do something about this." Bill Richmond recalled that a doctor was called to come down to the club to administer shots before the first set. Everyone lined up backstage with his left or right sleeve rolled up. In the midst of this procedure, a door accidentally opened into the club itself. The people in the audience glimpsed each musician getting his shot, rolling down his sleeve, putting on his jacket, and then going up on the bandstand. As one can imagine, the audience jumped to their own conclusions and word quickly spread throughout the club about how the whole band "shot up" before they went on stage.[64]

Next to the Bandbox was Birdland, "the Jazz Corner of the World." Between sets, Harry James frequently went to see Miles Davis play with his group. Davis had just emerged from Charlie Parker's shadow and was beginning to make his own musical statement, taking the jazz trumpet in a more subdued, "cool" direction. Surprisingly, Miles Davis had admired Harry James's sound while he was growing up in East St. Louis, Illinois. "I just loved the way [Harry James] played. I almost broke my teeth trying to get that big vibrato sound that Harry had. You've got to start way back before you can play bop. You've got to have a foundation." From their meeting at Birdland, a lasting friendship was formed between the two trumpet titans.[65]

The day after the conclusion of the Bandbox engagement, Lew McCreary remembers that during that gig Harry James called out a familiar blues chart. "I don't remember the name of it ... we played chorus after chorus. When Harry was ready to go out he always played a lick so we knew that was his last chorus, and we'd be ready to come in on the ensemble. On this particular night, while he was playing this chorus in his usual stance, the horn sticking right up there and playing the way he always did—six feet from the mike, he suddenly walked up close to the mike, lowered his horn down to the Miles Davis position, and played a chorus, just one chorus, exactly the way Miles would do it, before going back into his own style."[66]

By then Harry James had turned decidedly against bebop. The dancing public didn't accept him as a bop trumpeter. As he recalled, "It was a big mistake—and I made it myself for a while—playing music that was not fundamentally dance music in places where people came to dance. Now we know that when we play for a dance, we have to play good music, and that means music with a good, solid dance beat."[67]

Nevertheless, traces of bebop were sometimes evident in his playing from that time on. His outward dislike of bebop led to his once substituting Hoyt Bohanon for Lew McCreary on a record date because Lew had recently been including bop quotes in his trombone solos.[68]

Out of the Bandbox engagement came a contract for Buddy Rich that would guarantee him $35,000 a year and give him featured billing with the James band. He replaced Bill Richmond. Further, Buddy could wear his own clothes on the bandstand—no uniforms for him. Buddy Rich was never a follower by the stretch of anyone's imagination!

Once Buddy Rich joined the band, many of the musicians couldn't handle his often abrasive personality, which had also been the case with every band he had ever played with. Saxophonist Herb Steward referred to him as "Machine Gun" Kelly.[69] In typical fashion, Rich asked for a large advance on his future salary. He was anxious to buy a new XK-120 Jaguar convertible. As soon as he completed the deal with Harry James, he went over to the dealer's showroom and purchased the car. He drove with Marie, his future wife, all the way to Los Angeles for his first engagement with the James band at the Hollywood Palladium.[70]

Shortly afterward on a one-nighter in Yuma, Arizona, Harry James served as best man when Buddy and Marie were married by a justice of the peace. The ceremony almost ended before it began when Harry began giggling over the justice's broad English accent. Buddy proceeded to break up laughing. Pee Wee Monte told them to stop all the commotion. Finally, the minister cleared his throat, Harry and Buddy controlled themselves, and the ceremony was completed.[71]

Harry James went one step further for Buddy and Marie by arranging with the Ritzes to rent the apartment over their garage in Beverly Hills to them. He spent a good deal of time there since, as Betty Baez pointed out, "He was very fond of Buddy." Later, Baez gave a baby shower for Marie Rich, when she was about to give birth to their daughter, Cathy.[72]

Working on the same bandstand with Buddy Rich on a nightly basis was a source of consternation for any bandleader, much less his sidemen. Rich and James, however, maintained a solid mutual respect for each other's musical talents over a period of years. Lew McCreary contended: "They both actually contained themselves when it came near to a confrontation, and there were a lot of close calls. Harry would decide he wanted to have a drink, and he would go in back of the bandstand and turn the band over to Buddy. When he did that, Buddy would pull out a couple of Neal Hefti's bebop charts. While we played them, Buddy would shout, 'OK, Lew, take a couple,' and the same thing to other soloists. I can remember quite a few times when Harry came back on the bandstand that we were right in the middle of a Hefti chart, and he'd cut the band off and start playing 'Sleepy Lagoon,' and we'd have to get the arrangements out."[73] (Years later, Buddy told an English disc jockey that the reason he left the James band was so he wouldn't have to play things like "Sleepy Lagoon" every night.)[74]

Buddy Rich complained to Mel Tormé about how Harry James tried to copy Harry "Sweets" Edison's style of playing, since he (Buddy) admired Edison's style. "He'll play the same phrase, the same licks Sweets plays.... Harry's an original. He shouldn't try playing like anyone else. It's wrong." Since Harry James at one time or another successfully imitated among others Ziggy Elman, Miles Davis, and later Clifford Brown, just to have fun, out of admiration or boredom, it would seem that Buddy Rich completely missed the point.[75]

Betty Grable ended her Fox contract on July 1, 1953, by mutual agreement after fifteen years with the studio.[76] The always fickle moviegoing public had finally grown tired of the standard Grable technicolor musicals that were released three times a year.

Eight years earlier, Darryl Zanuck had wanted Betty Grable to play the part of Sophie, the pathetic young alcoholic who eventually commits suicide, in the black-and-white film adaptation of Somerset Maugham's *The Razor's Edge*. The film starred Gene Tierney and Betty's onetime lover, Tyrone Power. Grable abruptly turned down Zanuck's suggestion claiming, "I know my audience." Anne Baxter assumed the role, and it won her the Oscar for "Best Supporting Actress" in 1946.[77] Whether Betty made a mistake in not taking this role and whether that would have changed the direction of her career is pure speculation.

Marilyn Monroe had emerged as the new blonde on the Fox lot. Monroe learned firsthand from Betty Grable many of her screen mannerisms that she later incorporated when they successfully worked together along with Lauren Bacall in *How to Marry a Millionaire*.

In one scene that took place in Vermont, Nunnally Johnson, the picture's screenwriter, captured Grable's breezy style. She is seen listening to the radio when she hears the unmistakable sound of Harry James's trumpet. She remarks, "From New York, good old Harry James." The radio announcer then gives the name of another bandleader. Betty next says, "Turn that thing off!"

Six months after Betty Grable's association with Fox ended, she and Harry James attempted to alleviate their increasing financial problems by doing a theater tour together. They earned a reported $45,000 for their first of two engagements at the Chicago Theater and the Fox Theatre in Detroit. Their act was staged and choreographed by Billy Daniel, who was also featured in the act with the Music Makers and Buddy Rich, Tommy Gumina, along with Lewis and Van, a dancing group of three boys and a girl.[78]

Sam Lesner of the *Chicago American* wrote: "Mr. and Mrs. James complement each other with such theatrical finesse that a logical sequel to Betty's cinemascope debut could be 'How to Marry a Bandleader and Stay Happy.' In person, James and Betty are offering the smoothest and best balanced one-hour stage show we have seen in many a season." The January 4, 1954, *Down Beat* review said, "Buddy Rich, while working with the band throughout, also gets a chance to work up front with a marathon of skin-pounding that has the young seatholders in a frenzy." The *Detroit Free Press* offered, "There's only one thing wrong—it's too short. From the first note of the famous bandleader's trumpet to the colorful finish, the audience applauded for more."

These theater engagements were never recorded, but two "live" recordings captured the James band in performance. The first of two Columbia albums, *One Night Stand*, was recorded at the Aragon Ballroom in Chicago on October 25, 1952, by the redoubtable George Avakian. *Live at the Palladium* was recorded on January 22 and 23, 1954. The latter album reveals the decided influence Buddy Rich had on the James band on such numbers as "Sugar Foot Stomp," "Flash," and "Bye Bye Blues." These two "live" recordings were made after Columbia had realized substantial sales from the Benny Goodman Carnegie Hall concert album and the follow-up album of broadcasts on the road of the Goodman band from 1937 and 1938.[79]

As Avakian recalled, "We realized that jazz and the LP were made for each other. I just wish the LP had come earlier because Harry was a major star on Columbia, and, when the bands began to drift off, his sales dropped off. Harry was unhappy that he wasn't getting hit singles any more (cover versions of contemporary hit tunes like 'Three Coins in the Fountain' and 'Hernando's Hideaway' were unsuccessful), and, when Mitch Miller came on board, he started to do novelty-type arrangements. That was something Harry wouldn't take part in. If the LP had come along earlier, there's no telling what would have happened with Harry's solos because he had such an enormously great sound."

Along with the popularity of the LP, major musical performers had become important staples of weekly network television programs ever since the *Ed Sullivan Show* debuted on CBS in 1948. Sponsors paid large salaries for stars to headline hour-long musical "specials," which garnered high ratings. At this point, Betty Grable and Harry James continued to need money to take care of their IRS difficulties and began appearing on television.

The Jameses were set to star on three Chrysler-sponsored *Shower of Stars* specials in 1954 and 1955. For the first two shows, they were paid $80,000. On their debut show, Betty Grable was petrified at performing on "live" television. Nonetheless, she was a hit and the show garnered a good rating, party because it also featured Mario Lanza.[80]

On the second *Shower of Stars*, which aired on November 18, Grable and James performed together in a comedy sketch. This show was highlighted by Harry James's familiar "Trumpet Blues." In its review of the show, *Variety* wrote: "She seems a far better singer, dancer, and personality than she ever was in pics, largely because with the spontaneity of it she gets across a vivaciousness she never displayed in motion pictures."

Betty Grable was scheduled for the February 17, 1955, show, but a sprained ankle prevented her appearance; she was replaced by the young dancer, Shirley MacLaine. This last *Shower of Stars* featured a huge cast including Edgar Bergen, Dan Dailey, Tony Martin, Ethel Merman, Red Skelton, and MacLaine. The James band was showcased playing "Jam Session."

A little over two weeks later, on March 7, Everette James died at the age of seventy-one from natural causes. He had lived to witness the spectacular results of his dedicated tutelage that had enabled Harry to become a major jazz and pop music trumpet player as well as a highly successful bandleader. The fact that Harry never became a classical musician, as he had hoped, was of small consequence.

There was still a belief that the band business could be saved if bandleaders worked together. This led to the formation of the D.O.L.A. (Dance Orchestra Leaders of America). Les Brown (the D.O.L.A. President), Ray Anthony, Jerry Gray, Lawrence Welk, Harry James, and others posed in Hollywood for a smiling group photograph that made the cover of *Down Beat.*

Following that, in the fall of 1955, D.O.L.A. held a joint convention with ballroom operators who ran a chain of midwestern ballrooms. Tom Archer, the operators' leader, felt that many of the problems facing the business were caused by bands who ignored the tastes of the dancing public. The seventy-five bandleaders who attended the event took this edict so seriously that they vowed that jazz bands that didn't play dance music would be excluded from membership in the D.O.L.A. All this was actually much ado about nothing and a case of too little too late. If the D.O.L.A. had banded together right after the war and purchased ballrooms and radio stations, perhaps the tide might have been stemmed.

*   *   *

In 1955, Universal had enjoyed great success with *The Glenn Miller Story*, which starred James Stewart. As a result, the studio decided to make a musical film biography of Benny Goodman. Benny got together many of the members of the old band—Gene Krupa, Ziggy Elman, Jess Stacy, Teddy Wilson, Hymie Shertzer, and Lionel Hampton, and also added other high caliber musicians such as Harry's good friend, Buck Clayton (whose playing he admired and enjoyed imitating), Stan Getz, and Urbie Green— to form a new band to play in the picture.

Harry James was obviously of great importance to the film, but, like several others, was not about to sell himself cheaply in a project involving Benny Goodman. The financial shenanigans of 1939 were never far from Harry's thoughts as MCA's contract negotiations pressed on with Universal. James finally reached a compromise with Goodman and Universal. In *The Benny Goodman Story*, Harry wound up being billed as a special guest-star in the Carnegie Hall jazz concert scene, in which he soloed on "Shine" (which was cut from the film) and (naturally) on "Sing, Sing, Sing." His famous solo had evolved over the years, but he nevertheless displayed much of the unconquerable spirit that was so much a part of his original epic performance.

The Benny Goodman Story was a box office failure chiefly because of an inept script full of foolish coincidences. It was further hampered by an unconvincing love story involving Donna Reed, playing the part of John Hammond's sister, Alice, who later became Benny's wife, and a rather wooden Steve Allen playing Goodman.

Meanwhile, the James band had left Columbia Records to re-record some of its biggest hits with Capitol Records on the albums *Harry James in Hi-Fi* and *More Harry James in Hi-Fi*. Among the tunes recorded were: "Ciribiribin," "You Made Me Love You," "I Cried for You," "Sleepy Lagoon," "I've Heard That Song Before," "It's Been a Long, Long Time," and "I'm Beginning to See the Light," plus "Trumpet Blues," "Music Makers," and the "Two O'Clock Jump." All these numbers had, of course, originally been hits for James on Columbia. Out of a total of 70 *Billboard* pop chart hits, he had recorded nine #1 hits and had been awarded five gold single records over a 15-year period. Recording these many hits again in high fidelity brought them to a new audience.

Because Kitty Kallen was under contract to Columbia—and in those years an artist signed to one particular label was prohibited from recording for a rival company—she couldn't perform the two tunes she had made famous with James. Helen Forrest re-created her own hits with the band and wound up doing Kitty Kallen's as well. Forrest encountered difficulty with the then-newfangled recording technique wherein the singer was separated from the band and placed in her own recording booth. She was used to recording in front of Harry James and the band, where she could see and hear Harry at the same time.

During the recording sessions, James had an argument with Forrest over the proper key in the arrangement of "I'm Beginning to See the Light." In his rather inebriated condition—according to the albums' producer, F. M. Scott, he was reportedly drinking a fifth of bourbon at each recording session—he didn't comprehend why she was having such difficulty with the chart, failing to recall that she had never sung the song with him before.[81] Despite of these problems, both albums sold well and suggested a future for the James band with Capitol.

Benny Goodman and Harry James were both now exclusive Capitol artists. It was therefore natural for the Hollywood-based label to reunite the two in a recording session that took place at New York's Riverside Studio on December 7 and 9, 1955. Capitol's version of *The Benny Goodman Story* in brilliant new high fidelity recreated many of the tunes that were highlighted in the movie. An all-star Goodman alumni band featured James, who soloed on the "One O'Clock Jump," "And the Angels Sing," "Shine," and "Sing, Sing, Sing." On this collaboration, Harry James offered some of his most convincing hot trumpet playing since his Fresh Sound recording from the late 1940s.

By now Las Vegas had become the showplace of the nation. It seemed that the natural move for Betty Grable and Harry James was a Las Vegas nightclub act. The frenetic choreographer, Jack Cole, put together an act for them that debuted on February 16, 1956 and ran for four weeks at Beldon Katleman's El Rancho Vegas. The house band was under the direction of Betty's old boss, Ted Fio Rito. The Grable-James show, in addition to the Music Makers, also included the comedian Mr. Ballantine and bongo player Jack Costanzo.[82] The hotel billed Betty Grable with typical Las Vegas hyperbole as "The Most Glamorous Personality the Motion Picture Industry Has Ever Produced."

Although the engagement was a resounding hit, the Jameses intensely disliked Katleman, according to Fred Monte. They refused to set foot in the El Rancho's dining room or lounges between shows and did their gambling in other casinos.[83] On the closing day of the engagement, Katleman filed a lawsuit for $53,000 against Betty and Harry. Katleman claimed $48,000 had been given them in advances (against their $51,000 fee for the entire engagement) plus $5,000 for hotel rent.[84] They had used four bedrooms and five cottages—housing their daughters, Lillian Grable, Sal and Fred Monte, members of the band, plus guests—during the period of the rehearsals and performance.

During this troubled engagement at the El Rancho, Harry James and Pee Wee Monte had a major row over a small bill for expenses that Pee Wee had incurred in driving the new girl singer from Los Angeles to Las Vegas and back.[85] Pee Wee promptly quit, but Harry asked that he wait until the El Rancho engagement was finished before leaving. Pee Wee and Vi Monte subsequently met James at the band's office located at 6130 Selma in Hollywood, gave him the keys, and left abruptly without any further words. Sal Monte assumed control of the band, and Fred Monte joined him to take care of all the secretarial and bookkeeping chores, happy to leave his job at Hughes Aircraft.[86]

The suit against Betty Grable and Harry James was eventually settled when Betty worked two engagements at the El Rancho in 1960. The Vegas buzz was that Katleman's temperamental behavior continually angered various mob figures over the years. Perhaps because of that, the El Rancho Vegas, located next to the Sahara Hotel at the end of the strip, fell victim to a mysterious fire and burned to the ground during Grable's final booking.

Harry James laughingly believed that Steve Preston, one of her dancers, caused it to happen because she and Preston had an argument on that particular night before he went back to his hotel. He said, "I wish this place would burn down." On learning of the fire, Harry immediately took a taxi to the El Rancho, very concerned about Betty's safety. When he heard from her what Preston had said, he and Betty called him at his hotel and told him about the fire. Harry said, "You're a witch. Why did you do it?" Reflecting on the incident, Preston said, "Harry had a great sense of humor—when he showed it."[87]

On April 3, 1956, with Milton Berle as host, NBC aired one of the first variety TV specials in color. Harry James appeared on the program with a septet that featured Buddy Rich. It was broadcast live from the USS *Hancock*, docked in San Diego Harbor. James's group played four tunes, included a trumpet duet on "Tiger Rag" with Harry and Milton Berle(!).

Also appearing as a guest star on the show was a raw young singer who had first created a huge national impact the year before with six appearances on CBS-TV's *Stage Show*, hosted by Tommy and Jimmy Dorsey. He had followed that up with a series of smash records on RCA Victor, which revealed his considerable musical debt to black rhythm 'n' blues performers.

"Uncle Miltie" recalled introducing Harry James to Elvis Presley at the rehearsal for the show. "Harry asked Elvis, 'Where's your arrangements?' Elvis picked out one piece of music, a lead sheet, not an orchestral arrangement, and said, 'Here it is.' The musicians laughed at him. He started to strum on the guitar, and I caught a glimpse of James and Buddy Rich looking at each other. Rich made a square sign with his fingers and pointed at Elvis. I walked over and had a little beef with them. I said, 'That's very rude of you. Wait 'til you see him perform. You're going to be surprised.'"[88]

Harry James watched Elvis Presley intently from the back of the stage as he broke into his fabled bump and grind routine, which caused an absolute sensation. Harry told Vicki afterward that Presley had no discernible musical talent and would never last.

Harry James and Betty Grable again needed money to pay back taxes. In 1956, Harry sold the Baby J Ranch for $750,000. This transaction was completed after he sold the smaller (sixty-plus acres) Baby J Ranch to the former cowboy star "Wild Bill" Elliott, for $120,000 on a $60,000 investment. On hearing Harry's decision to sell the larger property, Sal Monte recalled that he had tears in his eyes when he pleaded with Harry, "You don't get rid of the ranch. You develop it. That's your annuity." When Harry received the check for the property, Sal asked him to give it to his business manager to invest. "That's for squares," Harry replied. The IRS took $387,000; Harry kept $363,000. Of that amount, Betty later told Sal Monte she was given $25,000.[89]

Today, the value of the larger Baby J Ranch would probably be well above twenty million dollars because it was immediately adjacent to the Ventura Freeway in the San Fernando Valley. The Motion Picture Relief Home is now located there.

With these transactions, Harry James and Betty Grable now were left owning only their Beverly Hills home. For years, Grable's mother, Lillian, had advised Betty many times that she and Harry should invest their money. Unfortunately, they never followed her suggestion.

By 1953, the band had grossed more than thirteen million dollars. If Harry James had been able to invest two to three million of that amount, he might have been worth about forty million by the 1970s. As trumpeter Art Depew observed, "He thought the joy ride was never going to end."[90]

During late July and August each year, James gave the band time off so that he and Betty could frequent the Del Mar Race Track. Now that he had a substantial amount of cash, James decided to take out a horse trainer's license. In the fall of 1956 he ventured up to Bay Meadows in Northern California for a few months and, following that, to the Pomona Fair, to train his horses for various races. As a result, the band's bookings were cancelled for the rest of the year. Undoubtedly, the mercurial fortunes of the band business at this time also weighed heavily on Harry's decision.[91]

Toward the end of the year, however, Harry made an abrupt about-face. He called Sal Monte and told him to put the band together and begin booking dates for early 1957.[92]

Even though their ranch and their horses were gone by the early 1960s, the Jameses still regularly attended the Del Mar meeting. Chick Romano was the captain in charge of the box seats and reserved section at Del Mar. As he recalled, "Every morning I was there. Betty would be having breakfast in the clubhouse with the racing form in front of her. I would go down the names of the horses with her. Once she picked her horses, she made sure that I would never tell Harry any of her selections."[93] (There is an unwritten rule that professional gamblers don't want anyone else to know of their selections; one wonders why Betty was so circumspect.)

Romano went on to say, "Betty was only a $20 bettor, but Harry was a big bettor. If she was ahead for the day, she would bet more money on the next race.... Harry could never keep a dime in his pocket."[94]

In the summer of 1955, I was elected to help book bands for major social weekends while I was a senior at the University of Virginia. I had a meeting at the MCA office in New York with the agent, Howard McElroy, who later became a close friend. I wanted to book the James band for the November "Openings" weekend, but it was unavailable. Instead, I booked Count Basie and his Orchestra from the Willard Alexander Agency, and the band was an enormous hit.

The bandleader whose orchestra was later called "the Soul of Jazz" and "the Most Explosive Force in Jazz," Count Basie was making a significant comeback with his newly formed "16 Men Swinging" band. Unlike his late 1930s band, the mid-1950s Basie band had an arguably cleaner and more cohesive ensemble sound and, as ever, could swing the blues like no other.

The 1950s band also had noteworthy soloists such as saxophonists Frank Wess (who still calls me "Harry James") and Frank Foster ("The Two Franks"), as well as Eddie "Lockjaw" Davis; Marshall Royal, its invaluable musical director, on alto saxophone; Al Grey on trombone; Joe Newman and Thad Jones on trumpet; and a solid rhythm section anchored by Basie on piano ("the best drummer any band ever had," as former Basieite Johnny Mandel called him); Eddie Jones on bass; the greatest rhythm guitarist of them all, Freddie Green; and the flashy drummer, Sonny Payne.

Harry James heard about the sensation that Basie was creating back east. He realized that the time was ripe for a new band that could create the right kind of excitement. He had always been personally close to Bill Basie and had relished playing with many of his former sidemen back in the '30s on records and jam sessions. He also treasured the memories of sitting in with Basie at the Famous Door in the 1930s.

James had grown tired of nostalgia—working with Benny Goodman again and re-recording his hits—perhaps he realized, as Artie Shaw once said, "Nostalgia ain't what it used to be." Listening to what Basie was doing on records, he suddenly felt much more at home musically. Johnny Mandel further pointed out: "I think Harry felt that there was a place where he belonged once again."

As a result, Harry James made a complete reevaluation of where he was heading in his own musical career. Count Basie had provided the impetus. Now he saw an opportunity to begin playing more challenging and meaningful music. Indeed it was about time.

9

Back to Basie

Harry James now knew exactly what he was after: he wanted to have a band that had a decided Basie flavor. Larry Kinnamon, the band's pianist, contributed the first Basie-inspired tune, "Countin.'" But in order to put together a total Basie kind of presentation he had to hire Ernie Wilkins.

Ernest Brooks Wilkins, Jr., the bebop alto and tenor saxophonist, had joined Count Basie in 1951. Beginning in 1954, his writing became the centerpiece in the resurgence of the Basie band. Among his various charts was the bluesy arrangement of "Every Day" that featured Joe Williams and became a major hit.

Trombonist Jimmy Wilkins, Ernie's brother, who still leads a band in Las Vegas, firmly believes that Ernie left Basie because he felt he wasn't being properly appreciated. His departure made him much in demand. He was quickly hired by Tommy Dorsey and then Dizzy Gillespie, who was forming a new big band for a state department tour of the Middle East.[1]

Harry James met with Ernie Wilkins in Chicago. In the beginning, he admonished James by saying: "Man, why do you want your band to sound like Basie's band? Let me write something just for you—something in my style that would fit your personality and the band's." Harry thought otherwise. He wanted to be the "ofay" (white) Basie.[2]

James excitedly told him: "I want you to start writing. I don't ever want you to stop. I don't care how many of them you write. You get $100 a chart. Keep writing, keep writing, keep writing."[3]

Jimmy Wilkins added, "Basie's band had a way of [playing with] laid back phrasing. Ernie saw that Harry's band had no problems reading the notes, but the interpretation was lacking. He was pretty disgusted because the only one who could really interpret the music [correctly] was Willie Smith." (Jimmy was essentially describing the difference between black and white jazz orchestras.)[4]

Harry's "Fletcher Henderson," in a four-year period, turned out such original compositions and arrangements as "Kinda Like the Blues," "Blues for Harry's Sake," and "Blues for Sale." (Although Ernie Wilkins was already an established blues writer, he was also bowing to James's long-standing penchant for playing the blues.) These were in addition to "One on the House," "Doodlin'," and "The Jazz Connoisseur" (one of James's particular favorites), as well as newly conceived Basie-ish treatments of jazz standards or perennial jazz vehicles like "Take the A Train," "Undecided," "Lester Leaps in," "Willow Weep for Me," and "King Porter Stomp," the latter successfully recorded by James earlier with Goodman, Basie, and his own band.

As a further example of his resourcefulness, Ernie Wilkins decided to write a tune that would get the James band on stage, one musician at a time, each one starting to play his part, the sections suddenly blending together, and finally the roaring ensemble coming alive. He followed that with the inevitable reverse, "Get Off the Stand," with the piano player and finally the bassist contributing the final four bars.[5]

There were contributions from other arrangers such as James "J." Hill, Bob Florence, Bill Holman ("One on the House"), and, later, Thad Jones. J. Hill as a youngster had first seen Harry James in *Springtime in the Rockies* and decided "that's what I wanted to do. Harry had a sound and a style all his own, but I didn't have the chops so I switched to trombone." While spending four years in the navy, he developed his trombone playing and began arranging. When he was discharged, J. Hill joined Perez Prado's band; that was his solo on Prado's highly successful record of "Cherry Pink and Apple Blossom White."[6]

Harry James heard "Bone Voyage" and "Countin' the Blues," Hill's arrangements for Les Brown's Band of Renown. They further revealed the Basie influence that was so pervasive among big bands at the time. He instructed Pee Wee Monte to call Hill about writing for him.

As Hill recalled, "When Harry wanted something from you, he really romanced you. He took me up to Vegas and paid for my room. I also had a bar tab and all that…. You know, when Harry went to Vegas, all he did was drink and gamble. One night, we were talking between sets when he said to me, 'C'mon with me.' We got a drink and went over to the crap table. He's shooting craps, talking about the album, not paying much attention to what he's doing—just raking in the money or giving it out."[7]

About a dozen arrangements soon resulted from that Las Vegas weekend including "Blues on a Count," "Cotton Pickin'," "J. Walkin'," and "Bangtail," along with new interpretations of "You're My Thrill" and "Do You Know What It Means to Miss New Orleans?"

To play Basie's kind of music, however, required the right kind of drummer. Buddy Rich had long since left James's band. When the band's first neo-Basie album, *Wild About Harry*, was scheduled for recording in May 1957, James, knowing Rich's admiration for Basie's music, asked him to play on the album. He was billed as "Buddy Poor" since he was still under contract to Verve Records. No one was fooled by the billing—the sound of his drumming was unmistakable.

Hill remembered: "I had stayed up all night writing the drum part for 'Blues on a Count' because I knew Buddy was gonna be there. When Harry called it, Buddy threw the drum part on the floor. I didn't realize he couldn't read music. After he heard the band play it once, he had it all in his head, and he played it just great."[8]

Harry James was so pleased by the results from the first day of recording that he wore the same black-and-white striped shirt on the other sessions for the album. He also wore it while recording several other albums. Like other bandleaders, he had his own superstitions.

The James–Hill association came to an end (except for an arrangement for Helen Forrest years later on a *Reader's Digest* album) when Harry asked him to become a member of the trombone section and continue writing for the band. "I told him, 'I just can't do it.' I was getting into movie and TV work, while Harry was on the road for nine months of the year.

"A few years later, I was writing for Ann Margret's act in Vegas, and I went over to the Flamingo to see Harry. We had a drink. He was very cordial, but complained about still having to work on the road."[9]

Bob Florence's arrangements of Duke Ellington's "Satin Doll" and his original composition, "Eyes," were two highlights of the MGM album *Harry James Today*. "I sent the original 'untitled' to Harry," remembers the veteran arranger, "and it came back 'Eyes.' It cracked me up because I'm noted for being so nearsighted. He did it a lot slower than anything I had in mind. When I heard the record, I thought, 'Gee, that feels really good.' There was a nice groove they had." Florence wrote arrangements for vocals on "Sweet and Slow," "That Old Black Magic," as well as many other originals for the James band.[10]

He once substituted for Jack Perciful on a date in San Francisco. "I hadn't yet met Harry. He was very friendly, very pleasant. I noticed he was having the greatest time playing. He started to play a little bebop. His bebop playing was really like picking out the clichés because he'd never lose his swing feel.... The band was real relaxed and easy."[11]

Harry James realized that the new kind of contemporary sound he was featuring definitely appealed to him. He still kept the 1940s hits in the book, but was increasingly featuring the new material. Trumpeter Bob Rolfe referred to the Basie material as "Harry's toy ... the thing presented itself, and he picked it up like a kid picking up a yo-yo."[12]

As for the general public, James was still the one jazz trumpeter whose name they recognized. For example, in the Paramount film *The Five Pennies*, a biography of Red Nichols, there was a party scene with teenagers dancing hosted by Red's daughter (Tuesday Weld). One of her young friends says to Red (Danny Kaye), "I just heard your music. You play like Harry James." Red's rejoinder was, "Harry James plays like me."

Harry James fulfilled a lifelong dream when he starred in the black-and-white western, *Outlaw Queen.* Initially, Ronnie Ashcroft, the film's producer, wired Harry, "I want you to read the story quickly before my writers start making necessary plot changes." In retrospect, James should have demanded a series of sweeping changes in the final script. This inept "B" picture co-starred Andrea King.

King laughed uproariously in describing the film. "Betty originally called me telling me Harry had to get it out of his system—he was such a fan of John Wayne. She talked me into doing the picture."[13]

Harry played the part of the foreman at the cattle ranch owned by the "Queen" (King). He didn't make his entrance until well into the film, but just in time to have a fistfight (and later a gunfight) with the villain, played by Robert Clarke, who had framed her. King continued, "Harry tried his best, but we had only a small budget to work with; the whole thing was shot in about six days." *Outlaw Queen* received limited distribution and has long since disappeared from late night television.

When Harry James accepted an offer for a three-week European tour (his first) in the fall of 1957, he again hired Buddy Rich, who was always eager to play in front of the enthusiastic European fans. Corky Corcoran had returned in 1955 and was once again one of the band's most important soloists. Ray Sims, a superb trombonist, left Les Brown to join James. Harry prominently featured these three key soloists during the tour.

After performing on the *Ed Sullivan Show* that taped that week in Hollywood, James, Rich, and Sal Monte left by train for New York. From there they departed for Europe, traveling first class on the original *Queen Elizabeth*, and then proceeded to Paris by boat-train. (The rest of the band flew to Paris.)

After the requisite press interviews for the tour, the triumvirate left Paris for Munich aboard the Orient Express. Slightly over two weeks of concert dates in Germany, Italy, and Austria followed. The excitement generated by the band can be heard on the CDs—*Harry James in Vienna, Volumes I and II*. The latter contains Buddy's vocal on "Goody Goody," when Harry James takes over on drums. One night on the tour, Ray Sims remembered being completely dumbfounded when Harry played "Flight of the Bumble Bee" with one finger![14]

Part of the tour's success was due to the fact that, while European fans had heard Count Basie's records, his band hadn't yet toured there. The James band represented their first "live" connection with the Basie sound.

The tour was scheduled to end in Paris. While the band flew ahead, the promoter, Hans Schlote, headed for Paris with all the band's music and Buddy's drums. Unfortunately, he was held up by heavy traffic at the French border.

The first concert in Paris was a 2 P.M. matinee performance at the Alhambra Theatre. When the musicians arrived, Schlote was nowhere in sight, nor were any of the band's arrangements or music stands. The musicians had their instruments, but Buddy Rich had to borrow a set of Rogers drums. Sal Monte said, "These guys had been playing this same show for this whole tour. They knew the charts. I said, 'Let's do it, let's wing it.' I was never so proud of a god damn band in my life. They played that concert like the charts were there in front of them."[15]

After the completion of the tour, Harry James reflected on the European audiences: "So intelligent about music, so appreciative. You know, they treat jazz as an art form there ... why, they even applauded good ensemble playing. Can you imagine an American audience doing that?"[16]

In mid-November, he took the band to Texas and Louisiana for a ten-day tour and broke attendance records in Houston (8,700), San Antonio (9,000), and Shreveport (7,300). He joked, "The secret of success with the Texas youngsters was the admission price of 25 cents. You just couldn't keep them away. Once they heard the band, they were amazed that they liked it and could even dance to it ... they've been dancing to rock 'n' roll groups so long, they'd forgotten how much fun a swingin' big band really is."[17]

In a momentary return to their former glory in movie musicals, the Motion Picture Academy booked Harry James and Betty Grable to perform a medley of Oscar-winning songs on the opening number of the 30th Annual Academy Awards show aired on NBC on March 26, 1958. They were joined by Mae West, Rock Hudson, Bob Hope, Tony Martin, Janet Leigh, and other stars. Betty sang and Harry played melodic fills behind her as they delivered lively renditions of "Lullaby of Broadway" and "Baby, It's Cold Outside."

Trombonist Bob Edmondson, a member of the James band from 1957 to 1959 and later an original member of Herb Alpert & The Tijuana Brass, believes that it was Harry Ritz who arranged a booking in the Flamingo showroom over the 1958 July 4th weekend as a favor to Harry. The band played for special 2 A.M. shows that were a big draw.[18]

During the course of that weekend, Al Parvin, who ran the hotel, met with Harry James, Sal Monte, and Chester Sims, who was in charge of the casino. Parvin and Sims suggested putting the band in the hotel's newly built Driftwood Lounge. They were concerned, however, that the open area containing crap tables, "21" tables, and slot machines, which was adjacent to stage-right of the Lounge, might be overpowered by the sound of the band. Nothing, of course, could be permitted to interfere with the gambling. Al Parvin finally concluded, "I know what we can do. There's a Dr. Knudson at UCLA who's an acoustics expert. Let's see what he can do about this problem."[19]

Dr. Knudson immediately ordered construction that entailed covering the ceiling with different sizes and weights of cork to deaden the sound and confine it to an area in front of the circular bar. Plastic discs were placed on the ceiling and throughout the bar area. The musicians complained that this made playing difficult—they were blowing into the cork and couldn't hear themselves because there was a complete lack of reverberation.[20]

Every night, the smoke-filled, gaudily appointed casino in the Flamingo Hotel started to reach its fever-pitch at around 9:30 P.M., and often continued until daybreak. The whirl of the roulette wheel, the ka-chung of the one-armed bandits, the shrieks of ecstasy from winners mingled with cries of "Go seven!" filled the air. The shills, dressed in bright-colored, low-cut, skintight sheaths, leaned over the gambling tables and enticed the spenders to part with their money. At precisely 9:45 P.M., the circular stage atop the bar in the adjacent Driftwood Lounge slowly began to revolve. From the bandstand came the opening bars of "Ciribiribin," the musical signature of Harry James and his Orchestra. This signaled the beginning of the first of five nightly sets, timed to start right after the end of the first show in the main room.

Las Vegas had all the nonstop action that Harry James wanted. After work, he could stay up all night gambling, drinking, or carousing with one or more of the always available women. As part of his deal with the Flamingo, he also had a free room. And by day there was golf, another sport at which he excelled.

At this point in his life, Harry James could look back on a successful show business career—starting out as a child star in the circus as a drummer, contortionist, and trumpeter, the toast of the Swing Era as a sideman, a bandleader at twenty-three, and finally a superstar—on records, in films, on radio and television. Now, at the age of forty-two, he was about to embark on his second career as a bandleader.

To celebrate his renewed career, he had to own the latest and most spectacular car, a 1958 silver Mercedes Benz 300SF roadster convertible with a black leather interior that he purchased from John Stiegler at Mercedes Benz of Hollywood. Stiegler has a photo of himself handing the keys to Harry James that over forty years later is still prominently displayed on the wall of Auto Stiegler Mercedes Benz in Encino, California.[21]

Harry's enjoyment of his Mercedes roadster was short-lived. He lost $8,500 in a crap game in Las Vegas a few months later, which meant that Sal Monte had to drive the car back to Los Angeles to sell it.[22] Harry rationalized the loss by telling saxophonist Sam Firmature that it really didn't matter since he was always getting speeding tickets driving the car.[23]

After a six-week booking at the Flamingo, a contract was signed for another engagement starting in late 1958 that extended into January 1959. Harry James negotiated the agreement himself. As part of the deal, the hotel agreed to give him $3,000 a week under the table for his own gambling purposes. Sal Monte explained, "Harry didn't, like, spend his $3,000 this week, then wait for the next five weeks—he went through it all within the first two or three weeks. It was all the money they gave him for the rest of the year!"[24]

Nonetheless, these engagements were an absolute godsend for James. They came at a time when one-nighters were drying up fast for big bands, and few prime location venues were playing big bands. Within two years, based on the substantial business the James band consistently did, the number of weeks a year for the band at the Driftwood Lounge was increased to twenty-six. However, this entailed one serious problem: with such easy access to the gambling tables, this deal also sowed the seeds of Harry James's financial ruin.

His success caused the Flamingo to want to play more name bands—and who better than Benny Goodman? Harry enjoyed telling the story of how he and Chester Sims called Goodman to explore the possibility of putting a band together to work there. Goodman asked what time the first set began. "9:45," Harry said. "And the second set?" Harry informed him that it was 12:15. "12:15?! I'm asleep by then! What's the one after that?" "1:45," said Harry. "I'm in the middle of my dreams by that time," Benny said, and with that, he abruptly hung up.

After that, several big bands were booked into Las Vegas lounges, among them Ray Anthony, Duke Ellington, Stan Kenton, and Lionel Hampton.

None of them, however, made anything resembling the impact of the James band.

Lionel Hampton and Harry James continued their long friendship, often playing ballgames with their two bands and then hanging out together when they worked in neighboring hotels in Nevada. Hampton told me, "I always caught Harry's band when I had the chance, but it was really Harry I came to see."[25]

Jerry Lewis, then a major film and television star, relished working with big bands and had seen the James band at the Flamingo. It was therefore natural for him to present Harry James and the band on one of his NBC-TV specials in December 1958. On one number, he played in Harry's trumpet section as part of a comedy skit. The moment Harry spots him, he throws him off the bandstand.

The band was later featured in an unusual dance number in Lewis's Paramount comedy, *Ladies Man*, in which the dancers' and musicians' costumes, the instruments, and even the sets were all in white. (Bill Richmond, James's former drummer, now turned writer, suggested to Jerry Lewis that he use the band.) After that, the band's appearance was one of the few highlights on the disastrous debut of Lewis's weekly "live" show on ABC when it contributed a driving rendition of the "Two O'Clock Jump." This rendition was complete with choreographed movements of the horns in the various sections leaning to the left and then to the right in unison, similar to the method of Jimmie Lunceford's band.

The history of the Flamingo Hotel has been well chronicled in films and books because its original owner was none other than the notorious Ben "Bugsy" Siegel. He named the hotel after his girlfriend Virginia Hill's thin legs. It opened with considerable fanfare on December 28, 1946. A contingent of Hollywood stars that included Bugsy's pal George Raft, as well as Vivian Blaine, Charles Coburn, Sonny Tufts, George Sanders, and Georgie Jessel welcomed the hotel's first headliner, Jimmy Durante. The Flamingo quickly became established as the showplace of the Las Vegas Strip.[26]

Unfortunately, the building had incurred large cost overruns and within the first few weeks of the operation its casino losses were staggering. The behind-the-scenes owner, Meyer Lansky, the financial brains of "the Outfit" famous for the statement, "We're bigger than U.S. Steel," had had his fill of Siegel's profligate spending and paranoid behavior. He gave the approval for a mob hit that took place on the night of June 20, 1947.[27]

By the early 1950s, Las Vegas had become synonymous with the now clichéd terms "glitter" and "glitz." Its showrooms boasted topless showgirls and major headliners, its lounges featured brash comedians and boisterous musical groups, and the gambling was twenty-four hours a day. In 1955, the

Riviera Hotel announced it was paying Liberace $50,000 a week. Nobody could believe it, but "the Boys," who controlled almost all the hotels, had no trouble paying such salaries since they were raking in mountains of money in gambling revenue. Besides that, the publicity was good for business. Toward the end of the decade, Frank Sinatra's engagements at the Sands Hotel established it as the home of the high rollers. Why, even Noel Coward was imported from England to perform at the Desert Inn.

Such well-publicized appearances brought in important Hollywood stars, who became regulars. (It was only 285 miles away from Los Angeles and less than an hour by plane.) Las Vegas suddenly was the mecca for those seeking a good time, and middle-class America flocked there to sample the excitement. They returned home and told their friends and relatives of their adventures and described how well they had been treated.

The lounge shows lured the gamblers with inexpensive drinks and no cover or minimum. This was the perfect setting for another swing era bandleader, Louis Prima, and his band vocalist, Keely Smith, whose group performed in the lounge of the Sahara Hotel at the Strip's northern end. Prima's was the only lounge show in Las Vegas that outdrew James's at the Flamingo. Prima, however, was selling suggestive humor mixed with vocals, certainly not big band jazz.

As a result of the Capitol albums *Wild About Harry* and *The New James*, the jazz world became aware that Harry James had returned to the fold. Jimmy Lyons, an important radio personality interested in jazz, had interviewed Harry on the air many times over the years. He admired what James was doing so much that, when he became the promoter of the first Monterey Jazz Festival, he booked the band. On Sunday night, October 5, 1958, the James band appeared at the Monterey Fairgrounds, with comedian Mort Sahl as master of ceremonies. It marked Harry James's first of three appearances there.

Mort Sahl vividly recalled his impressions of that night: "Harry was preceded by a couple of groups made up of guys wearing sportshirts with lots of microphones and exposed wires, debating about what tunes they would play. One guy would walk offstage while somebody else soloed. Here comes Harry—tall and imposing—with fifteen guys wearing dark suits with white shirts and all that gold [the brass] staring right at you. They were like a formal portrait. Harry created his own reality. It was so theatrical. When he got up there and played alongside his trumpet section— it was a powerhouse! His drive led the band and nobody in the audience walked around during that set. They listened."[28]

The September 1965 Monterey Jazz Festival highlighted the jazz trumpet and featured Louis Armstrong, Dizzy Gillespie, Miles Davis, and Harry

James. On James's arrival, he was met by Davis and Gillespie, who threw their arms around him and kissed him. Trumpeter Tommy Porrello recalled, "They both revered him. There had been a false rumor around that Harry wasn't feeling too good. Miles helped him off with his trench-coat and asked, 'Harry, are you OK? You all right?' Harry said, 'What are you talking about? I'm fine.'"[29]

A joyous reunion ensued. Miles Davis grabbed Gillespie's famous tilted trumpet and used it for a short-lived game of touch football before the three trumpet greats headed for the bar at the Festival's Hunt Club. When it came time for Dizzy to play his set, he discovered his horn was missing. That was the cue for Miles and Harry to march onstage together to present the maestro with his trumpet on a pillow, after which they bowed respectfully, turned on their heels, and left the stage.[30]

The James band immediately followed Clark Terry's exciting set. Tommy Porrello continued: "Harry had called the set, but when he saw what had happened, he said, 'Forget it. We've got to start by burning them immediately.' We did just that by playing Ernie Wilkins' composition 'The Jazz Connoisseur' and really got to that audience."[31] Bassist Red Kelly called this "the best set I ever heard that band play." This was indeed quite a statement since Kelly was on the James band for thirteen years![32]

A little over three weeks after the first Monterey Jazz Festival appearance, I saw the James band perform for the first time. It was a dance date at the Boulevard Ballroom in North Philadelphia at the end of October 1958 during my last week in the army at Fort Dix, New Jersey. The dance floor that night was filled with couples. The band played within a section of the circular balcony that overlooked the large dance floor. I watched the proceedings from the other side of the balcony, diagonally across from the band.

From this somewhat distant vantage point, I witnessed "the New James." James naturally offered the dancers a generous sprinkling of his biggest hits. I was immediately taken by how crisp the band sounded and how clean the section work was. The authority with which Harry still played was incredible. I also noticed the playing of Sam Firmature, the Stan Getz-influenced replacement for Corky Corcoran, and the strong drumming of Tony DeNicola.

At the end of the evening, I headed back to downtown Philadelphia to take the last bus back to Fort Dix. The clerk at the station informed me that the departure time for the last bus had been delayed for close to an hour. He suggested I go across the street to a bar and have a drink. I took his advice and, when I pushed open its western-style swinging saloon doors, I was confronted with a surreal scene. There, sitting on a bar stool with a B-girl on his lap, was none other than Harry James, wearing a lascivious grin. I was so taken aback that I quickly turned around and left the bar. I naively thought, "How could that be? He's married to Betty Grable!" My image of the fabled perfect Hollywood marriage was forever shattered.

A few weeks later, Harry James completed his second booking at the Flamingo for the year. It was time to renegotiate his contract. He threatened to go elsewhere, knowing full well his band would be in demand by other hotels. James told Chester Sims that, for the band to remain at the Flamingo, he needed his personal gambling allowance increased. Based on the business he was doing, Sims acquiesced. James got a raise in his gambling allowance, plus a deal for more weeks during 1959.[33] In turn, the Flamingo got exactly what it wanted—a star attraction led by a bandleader who would be financially beholden to the hotel for a long time.

Shortly thereafter, Chester Sims approached Sal Monte and said, "Where's the chemist?" "What d'you mean, the chemist?" Sal asked. "You know, your boss, the chemist. He's the only guy I know who can turn money into shit."[34]

Bob Rolfe recalled: "When he played craps, he had special chips. They were plain white chips, no numbers on them. Each one was $500, and he would bet five and six at a time—$2,500, $3,000 at a time."[35] After playing craps and roulette, he tried baccarat, but he was wiped out in the first game. "That scared him a little bit," recalled pianist Jack Perciful.[36]

Harry James enjoyed keno more than any other game. Later, while playing in the lounge at Harrah's in Lake Tahoe, he relished how, while playing a solo, he could watch the results of keno games that flashed on the board on the casino wall. Art Depew recalled, "He used to play keno at $110 a crack. He was afraid not to play, afraid to go to bed because he might miss something. He served all his appetites and all his desires. He wasn't terribly concerned with other people."[37]

For a time, James constantly played number six in the game over a period of several days and then again years later at the racetrack. This was the baseball uniform number of Stan Musial. Later, James would often bet the numbers seventeen and twenty. He once hit for $25,000 in a keno game at Lake Tahoe and proceeded to blow it all the same night. Another time he hit for $37,000. It didn't much matter—the fever had long since set in and was to remain an integral part of him for the rest of his life.

Red Kelly believes, "Harry felt gambling was the way you got in with 'the in crowd.' He liked the back talking, the hard playing. He liked that lifestyle."[38] As perhaps a way of justifying his gambling habit, he once told his daughter Vicki: "I work very hard for my money. Nobody is going to tell me how I can spend it."[39]

Trumpeter Ollie Mitchell subbed for Don Paladino on lead trumpet one night in 1958 while the band was headlining at the Hollywood Palladium.

After the gig, Harry James was so impressed by his playing that he called him into his dressing room and explained that occasionally a musician came along who fit in so well that the band played better. "Playing with Harry's band that first night was pretty much like putting on a new suit that fit like a friendly old glove," Mitchell recalled.[40]

James offered Mitchell $300 a week—an above-average salary for a big band musician at the time. "I had to cancel my forty students, and I had to try to explain to my wife and kids of my need inside to play with Harry's band. When I was on the bus with Harry, it was one of the highlights of my musical experience. I loved it."

Ollie, who now lives on the Hawaiian island of Maui, was succinct in his appraisal of Harry James: "He was a mature, grown-up trumpet player and master musician and yet remained a perpetual teenager as a man. As a leader he was just and fair. When he got mad at somebody, he always had a reason."[41]

When the Count Basie band's *The Atomic Basie* album was released by Roulette Records that fall, Ollie Mitchell and Bob Edmundson were wildly enthusiastic about it and encouraged Harry James to listen to it. The album consisted of original tunes written and arranged by Neal Hefti.[42] Its cover photo of an atom bomb explosion served as the perfect metaphor for the music.

The Atomic Basie was to big band fans what the Beatles' *Sgt. Pepper's Lonely Hearts Club Band* was to rock devotees nine years later. The album showcased the brilliance as well as the versatility of Hefti's writing. The driving ensembles—"Splanky," "Flight of the Foo Birds," "The Kid from Red Bank"—served as vehicles for Basie's formidable corps of soloists. There were also a few ballads (e.g., the poignant "Li'l Darlin'") that allowed Freddie Green one of his very few recorded guitar solos.

Harry James responded enthusiastically to the album, but ordered more Basie-like charts from Ernie Wilkins, not Neal Hefti. James invited Wilkins to come to Las Vegas to see his current band in action before he began writing. There was another important reason he needed more charts—the Basie band was booked into the Driftwood Lounge and the two bands were about to work in tandem.

It was Harry James's novel idea to present the two bands together, one following the other. He agreed to have his band stay over one night after its engagement was supposed to end to coincide with Basie's opening night. "All I ask is that I get to play my arrangements first," said Basie, with tongue firmly planted in cheek. Over a six-hour period, there were no empty tables, and $100 tips were dispensed to the maitre d'. The tables were so close to one another that the musicians couldn't walk into the audience after a set. Ollie Mitchell called it "the swingingest night Vegas ever witnessed."[43]

The next day, Bob Edmundson stopped by the Flamingo on his way home to Los Angeles. "I saw Basie at the bar. I said to him, 'Man, thank you for a wonderful experience.' I really respected that man. He was so humble. He replied, 'Oh, you guys blew us off the stage.' Of course, we had really played over our heads that night."[44]

The trombonist added, "We closed one of our sets with 'Shiny Stockings.' As I was leaving the stand, one of Basie's guys said to me, 'What was that chart you just played?' Our arrangement was exactly the same as Frank Foster's. (Ernie Wilkins had transcribed it from Basie's original record; he felt guilty about having done so.) However, Harry's tempo was a little more like Benny Goodman than Count Basie—a little more on top. Basie's time was right down the middle, you know. We played 'Shiny Stockings' a little faster."[45]

The Goodman band that had featured Harry James still remained a commercial entity. In the fall of 1957, there was a serious attempt made to produce a twentieth-anniversary commemoration of the famous Carnegie Hall jazz concert the following January and to televise it. Once again, "The King of Swing" needed Harry James. But James had already decided he wasn't ever going to work for Benny Goodman again unless it was financially worth his while.[46]

Berle Adams, James's MCA agent, wanted $10,000 for his services and remained steadfast in his demands. "Why should Harry work for small money?" he insisted. "He went through that when he was an employee. He's no longer an employee; he's a star. You want him to solo, he'll play solos; you want him to play in the band, he'll play in the band, but he's not an employee of anybody." Adams maintained that the only way James would do the show would be for him to be an independent contractor. In other words, it was necessary for Harry James to be booked separately and paid a guest star's fee. The entire deal ultimately fell through.

This negotiating ploy, however, was the basis for Harry James's appearance on the Benny Goodman NBC-TV special, *Swing into Spring*. Sponsored by Texaco and airing on April 9, 1958, the show was justifiably acclaimed as a truly magical hour of jazz on television. Goodman's well-rehearsed orchestra included among others Billy Butterfield, Buck Clayton, Urbie Green, Hymie Schertzer, Zoot Sims, Hank Jones, Kenny Burrell, and George Duvivier. As a member of the band, Harry James played solos on "Ciribiribin," "King Porter Stomp," and "Gotta Be This or That." However, when he joined Goodman, Red Norvo on vibes, Teddy Wilson on piano, Arvell Shaw on bass, and Roy Burns on drums he showed his true virtuosity, playing muted trumpet accompanying Ella Fitzgerald and Jo Stafford. But then, hadn't Harry always been impeccable in embroidering on a melody behind great singers?

*   *   *

In September 1959, I became an MCA agent and the assistant to Frank Modica, Jr., who headed the one-nighter department. I learned more about the business of music then than at any other period of my career. Like so many others (myself included) who worked for Harry James in one capacity or another, he was a teenage hero of Modica's. When Modica started working at MCA, he couldn't understand why Harry James no longer toured in the East. His boss, Howard Mc Elroy, informed him, "Bill Richard (the agent in the Chicago office who booked bands) says, 'James doesn't like New York and doesn't want to work there.'"[47]

A year or so later, Modica took over booking bands in the New York office. He began talking to Richard, who continued affirming Harry's aversion to working in the East and warned him about the futility of discussing the matter with Pee Wee Monte. Bill Richard was being territorial; he didn't want an upstart agent showing Harry James dates on his commission report.

Out of the blue, Monte called Modica, wondering why he never had any work for James in the East. Modica cut to the chase and said, "When does he want to come?" He booked a highly successful tour in the spring of 1959, which started a successful association that lasted for several years.[48]

During the late 1950s, Harry was grossing about $20,000 a week on one-nighters. Of the MCA bands still touring, only Guy Lombardo was more successful. Pee Wee Monte wouldn't entertain any offers of less than $1,500 a night; Lombardo's minimum fee was $2,000.

As Modica recalled, "We weren't playing that many ballrooms. We were playing private parties. Harry had a way that he liked to work. He didn't like to deviate. He liked to travel in a straight line not cutting back and forth if it was [at all] possible. I spent a lot of time convincing Pee Wee that sometimes it's not the guarantee we make, sometimes it's the comfort of getting to the job and what you put in your pocket as a result of playing it. I used to hear the stories of how you could stay in Pennsylvania for weeks with a band. By then, however, the market had radically changed."

Exactly a year after I had first seen the James band at the Boulevard Ballroom in North Philadelphia, Frank Modica and I drove down from New York to see Harry James at the same locale. When we met with James between sets, I mentioned my friendship with Buddy Rich. (I had written a magazine piece on Rich earlier that year and had begun hanging out with him when he was in New York.)

"What's Bernard up to now?" Harry asked. I told him that he was doing his singing act at a small East Side club in New York called the Living Room. I remarked that his voice could barely be heard across the room, adding that his engagement ended the next night.

"I guess you'll be talking to him soon then, won't you?" James asked. I told him that I would be talking to him the next day. Grinning, he said, "Tell Bernard I'm auditioning drummers at Sunnybrook (Ballroom) in Pottstown (Pennsylvania) on Saturday night."

The next afternoon I told Buddy Rich of my conversation with Harry James. He laughed and said, "Oh, yeah? Well, come on over at 5 o'clock on Saturday and we'll drive down to see him."

When I arrived at his apartment, Cathy, Buddy Rich's vivacious five-year-old daughter, came to the door. I could hardly miss the fact that Buddy and his wife, Marie, were having a heated argument. Just as Buddy came to the door, one of Marie's shoes sailed through the air and whammed into the door behind him. He barked out, "Let's get a limousine." "A limousine!" I shouted. "I can't afford a limousine. I'm making $65 a week." "Don't worry about it," Buddy insisted. We settled for a Pontiac sedan.

When we entered the Sunnybrook Ballroom that night, the sea of dancers parted to allow Buddy Rich to walk toward the bandstand. The band had almost completed the first set by the time we arrived. After a short intermission, Harry James announced Rich's presence and asked him to come up and sit in. The crowd loved it and burst into applause. James purposely called a brace of Basie tunes, aware of the response it would engender in his old friend. Rich handled the tunes with such ease it seemed impossible to believe that he hadn't been playing with the band all along.

After the gig was over, we sat and talked with Harry in his dressing room. As the night drew to a close, he said to me: "Pardon me. Bernard and I have to talk some business." Thirty minutes later we got in the car. Buddy Rich asked me to drive.

I asked him what happened with Harry. He replied, "He wants me to join the band in Vegas right after the first of the year." After that, he fell dead asleep while I listened to the Birdland Show on the car radio coming from New York. For the first time, I heard several tracks from Charlie Parker's famous *Bird With Strings* album. This was the cue for Buddy to suddenly awaken and declare, "That's me on drums." He then abruptly burst into, "What do I want to play drums again for—I'm a singer." "You're a drummer who wants to be a singer. Playing drums is what you do best," I said matter-of-factly. He growled some more and went back to sleep.

Right after that, Buddy Rich had a few weeks booked with his small group in New Orleans and Atlanta. He brought along a black musician, which naturally presented problems in these two southern cities where mixed bands were still prohibited. In Atlanta, on December 9, while entering a restaurant, Buddy suffered a major heart attack. Frank Sinatra heard the news and took care of all his medical expenses.

I came to see Buddy Rich a few weeks later in singer Eileen Barton's Central Park South apartment, where he was recuperating. He looked ghastly—tired, listless, and totally forlorn. His doctor had told him he could never play drums again. "Maybe I could start singing again," he offered weakly. There went his plans to rejoin the James band.

Jackie Mills had been Harry's drummer during four different periods in the late 1940s and 1950s. He had followed Buddy Rich after the European tour in the fall of 1957. Fellow drummer Jake Hanna believes that "Jackie sounded better than Buddy Rich with that band. He had very good time and swung." Harry James once told bassist Ira Westley, "I had some wonderful drummers on this band, and they were great soloists, but the one guy that really did the most for the band's performance was Jackie Mills."

Mills thoroughly enjoyed his years with James, but stated: "I don't think anybody really liked him. I got the feeling that everybody was there because it was a good job. It was a good band, and they enjoyed playing in it, but Harry never got close to people. He was closer to the players on the St. Louis Cardinals than he was to the guys in the band. I don't think the Montes knew him. I don't think anybody knew him."49

During Mills's last stint with the James band he played on the MGM album *Harry James and His New Swingin' Band*, which contained more Basie-type instrumentals. At about that same time, he also found singer Ernie Andrews. Actually, it was Betty Grable who had first discovered Andrews on the radio when a Los Angeles disc jockey played his album, *'Round about Midnight*, on which Andrews was backed by a group that included Benny Carter and pianist Gerald Wiggins. Betty called Harry on the road in Boston to tell him of her find, whereupon James mentioned Andrews to Jackie Mills, who had been the drummer with Wiggins's trio. By calling Wiggins in Los Angeles, the search for Ernie Andrews ended.50

"And so I met Harry two weeks later, in 1959, in Chicago at the Blue Note and joined the band," recalled Andrews. Like Mills, his employment with James also lasted a decade, off and on. Andrews left for periodic short-term gigs (although one lasted a full year) that offered better singing opportunities and more money. "I was maneuverable, but I wasn't controllable," he explained.51

Ernie Andrews informed me that by the late 1950s, Clifford Brown had replaced "Fats" Navaro as the trumpeter Harry most admired. On "The Jazz Connoisseur," James's strong feeling for Brown's style is obvious. Andrews said, "I remember when Harry would carry a portable record player with him on the road along with five or six albums of Clifford's. You'd talk with him about Clifford and you'd see tears in his eyes. He said to me once, 'I don't know why the Lord took him' " [referring to Clifford's tragic death in a car crash on the Pennsylvania Turnpike at the age of twenty-five].

With Harry James on the bandstand, Ernie Andrews sang alongside such girl singers as Jilla Webb, Ruth Price, and Judy Branch. On James's suggestion, Ernie Wilkins arranged some traditional blues for Andrews. The singer developed a genuine fondness for Harry James. He called him "Hesh," while Harry called him "Audio" due to his inability to say anything briefly or with subtlety. According to trumpeter Tony Scodwell, "Ernie could talk himself in and out of a deal in the same conversation."[52]

Ernie Andrews had problems traveling with the James band because he was an African American. In one situation, Andrews recalled, "When the bus pulled up, and we went into the hotel, they started passing the rooms out. They called my name, but they told me to wait. Harry asked, 'What's the problem?' He got up and yelled, 'Mr. Monte!' [in that exasperated tone of voice that I well remember] 'Do we have a manifest?' Harry looked at it and saw my name on it and said to the room clerk, 'Now, what is the problem?'

"The clerk said something like, 'Well, we don't have a room for him, but we could put him two blocks down the street, and he'd be close to the band.' Harry said, 'Pee Wee, go down the street and see if they can accommodate us. Take the stuff out of the lobby, put it back on the bus, and let's go.' Then the room clerk said, 'Wait a minute, we might be able to find something here,' and Harry said, 'Well, find Mr. Andrews a corner room.' He said, 'Why a corner room?' and Harry said, 'Because that's the biggest room. It gets plenty of air from three sides, and right now he needs it.'"[53]

Another time, somewhere in the South, Andrews was asked, "Boy, can you sing 'The Yellow Rose of Texas?'" "I told him I didn't know it, and he told me to sing it anyway. Harry stopped the band, and said, 'Just a minute, I don't know how big boys are where you come from, but this is a grown man…. We don't have 'Yellow Rose of Texas,' and if we had it, we wouldn't play it, and furthermore, we're going to pack this band up if they don't put you out of here because you're leaving now.' And the guy was tossed out."[54]

Although Harry James was born in Albany, Georgia, and raised in Beaumont, Texas, he hadn't tolerated racism against Lionel Hampton in the 1930s or against Willie Smith and Juan Tizol in the 1940s and 1950s. He wasn't about to tolerate similar treatment of Ernie Andrews in the 1960s, at a time when America was at last coming to terms with its racial problems. For Harry James, the skin color of any musician was never an issue. The only question was, "Can he play?"

Ernie Andrews should have become a star. There was never any question about his singing ability, and in person he has a warm and likable presence. Unfortunately, he was never recorded properly. The American public made Eddie Fisher a star while genuine talents like David Allyn, Johnny Hartman, and Ernie Andrews never achieved that status.

The late Joe Williams was a close friend of Harry James for many years. "I remember, when I left the Basie band in early 1961, I worked at the Flamingo in the lounge. Harry used to sit in the back with maybe two or three young showgirls from the Stardust and watch me perform. I remember one night in particular. I was doing 'Autumn Leaves' and I would always, like, hum the first sixteen bars. He yelled out, 'Hum it, baby!' That old Texas devil!"[55]

Joe Williams strongly believed that Harry James never provided a showcase for Ernie Andrews. "Anything that Ernie sang with that band was good … the band would come up a notch, actually, when Ernie sang, and he was a valuable asset, but Harry didn't give it time … some people lend themselves to developing artists—like Harry did for Corky Corcoran, for instance—but Harry's band was not [really] a band that developed stars."

The late alto saxophonist Joe Riggs echoed Joe's sentiments: "Harry didn't promote anybody. He just wanted to go out and play. He hired you because he liked the way you did things."[56]

Always an astute observer of the jazz business, Joe Williams saw Harry James in a rather severe light: "He had some good arrangements from Ernie Wilkins, Thad Jones, and Neal Hefti, but most people don't understand the relationship between the heartbeat and the music. The heart goes, if it's healthy, 'lub-dub'. It's only if the heart goes 'dub-lub' that you're in trouble. Harry did a lot of 'dub-lubbing.' He missed the feeling. He did have orchestrations that could jump. He had some that did that on given nights. You could see Harry getting it, but not often. Buddy Rich could swing, however."[57]

Speaking of his years with Count Basie, Joe Williams said, "I was with a group of musicians who every single night took pride in being the best there was anywhere. With Harry James for a long time there were no new challenges, especially to somebody like Willie Smith. No new anything. Therefore, there's no growth. There's stagnation. Suddenly, Harry had a fresh idea and there was a challenge for his musicians even though it was [merely] his version of Basie."

It was Joe Williams's feeling that, even though Harry James had very accomplished soloists in Corky Corcoran, Ray Sims, and Buddy Rich, plus a first-rate rhythm section in Jack Perciful, Red Kelly, and Buddy Rich, he never took the same kind of pride that Count Basie did in *his* band. He further believed that Basie wanted to have the greatest jazz orchestra again and handpicked the musicians who melded together to become that great orchestra. For Harry James, it was just a job. He enjoyed having a wonderful band to lead, but he never really wanted to take his band to the next level.

To maintain the image of a jazz orchestra, Harry James again needed a bona-fide drummer and in the process went through several drummers, one of them Charli Persip. Today, Persip refers to his association with Harry James as "a mistake." He said, "Buddy Rich had recommended me. Harry wanted Buddy Rich. I'm a bebop drummer." However, it wasn't a total loss for the drummer. "I insisted that Harry pay for bringing my sports car out from New York, so my wife and I got to see the Grand Canyon before we returned to New York," he recalled.[58]

For James's new band, the acid test was the February 1960 booking at Basin Street East, then New York's hottest nightclub. It was located off Lexington Avenue on 48th Street. It was a major step up from a Birdland booking for any jazz band.

I don't remember if it was due to Frank Modica's or my enthusiasm (perhaps both), but the former bandleader-turned-MCA agent, Larry Funk, made the deal with Ralph Watkins, the owner of Basin Street East. I set guitarist Kenny Burrell, whom I had recently signed to the agency, as the opening act for the James band.

While playing at the Astor Roof in July 1944, Harry James had been quoted about the necessity of playing New York once a year. "A bandleader has to. Otherwise, people all over the country will forget you. New York is the showcase." Contrary to his own pronouncement, the Basin Street East gig was his first New York engagement since the appearance at the Band Box in 1953.

A guest shot on the *Ed Sullivan Show*, which paid $7,500, took care of the transportation of the band from Las Vegas. I picked up Harry James and Sal Monte the night they flew to New York. They were anxious to see the club before they turned in. That night, I noticed how Harry favored casually draping his overcoat over his shoulders as though it were a cape, leaving his arms free. This was a fashion that was later adopted by European film directors.

James enjoyed reminiscing with Chris Griffin, who was a member of the CBS Orchestra that backed the other acts on the Sullivan show. There he also met up with a tall, shapely young blonde dancer from the cast of Ethel Merman's Broadway hit, *Gypsy*, who was performing in the "Gotta Have a Gimmick" number. Harry and the blonde spent many nights together during the next two weeks in his suite at the Lexington Hotel.

The Basin Street East engagement was a smash. New York studio musicians Doc Severinsen, Bernie Glow, Bennie Leighton, Mel Davis, Sol Gubin, and, of course, Chris Griffin formed a sober jury of his peers.

Several raved to their colleagues at Jim and Andy's Bar (then the official New York jazz watering hole) about what they had witnessed.

Frank Quinn of the *New York Daily Mirror* observed: "James can wail and hit those high notes on the trumpet with ease and true and clear tones…. The reaction of a full house indicates James has lost no ground as a top musician and bandleader."[59] Gene Knight of the *Journal-American* wrote, "I closed my eyes and thought: man, this is music. It's what the jazz lovers call a sound…. An especially nice thing is the way Harry gives the arranger credit…. It's [the band] so well organized, so well disciplined, that Harry can lead with a look or a wave of his hand."[60]

Guitarist Kenny Burrell divides his career between heading the Jazz Department at UCLA and leading his own group. Reminiscing about the Basin Street East gig he said, "I enjoyed the fact that my trio could open for a big band, and the people liked it. I also recall that Willie Smith enjoyed sitting in with us after Harry's set. I'll always remember Harry as a gentleman, but a down-to-earth gentleman. The other thing—I admired the fact that he dressed real sharp. I also don't know many people who could play a melody better than him, and he didn't cheat on the chord changes. He negotiated them. As Dexter Gordon said, 'He did not strong-arm the changes; he played them.'"[61]

On the Sunday between the two weeks of the Basin Street engagement, the James band performed at a Smith College concert in Northampton, Massachusetts. I accompanied the band on the band bus. The female students paid only polite attention—it simply wasn't their music. Afterward, Harry James, Sal Monte, and I were joined by Tino Barzie, Tommy Dorsey's last manager, at Wiggins Tavern for New England pot roast, the house specialty. Before dinner, Harry had a few vodkas on the rocks to unwind after the concert. He soon became very mellow. I listened while the band veterans told road stories that included a generous helping of amusing tales about Tommy Dorsey.

Unbeknownst to me, it was prearranged for Harry James to drive Tino Barzie's white Cadillac convertible back to New York because Tino was going on the road himself. The hour was getting late, and since Harry had tossed back a great deal of vodka, I became the designated driver. Harry sat up front next to me with Sal Monte in the back seat. I tuned the car radio to WNEW in New York. Within minutes, Frank Sinatra was singing the title song of his *Where Are You?* album. Harry remarked, "Frank sure sounds tired," before he himself fell asleep. Driving someone else's Cadillac convertible the 169 miles to New York with Harry James alongside was a heavy responsibility that weighed on me during the drive and certainly helped in keeping me alert.

One afternoon the following week at the Lexington Hotel, while I was talking with Harry James and Sal Monte in their suite, the doorbell rang. I answered it, and a young man with a striking resemblance to Harry James, complete with a thin mustache and dark brown wavy hair, was standing in front of me. Over my left shoulder, Harry barked, "What are you doing here?" It was Harry Jeffrey James, who had come to New York to see his father.

"I guess you think you're good enough to play in my band," James continued. Young Harry was completely taken aback by his father's outburst. He meekly replied, "Well, Dad, I've got some time left before I'm discharged from the air force. I was just beginning to think about what I'm going to do when I'm out." At this point, sensing the beginnings of an unfortunate confrontation between father and son, I excused myself and left the suite.

Young Harry had attended North Texas State on a scholarship, intent on being a classical musician. North Texas State (now the University of North Texas) is perhaps best known as the first college that offered a jazz major, and it continues to develop young jazz musicians.

He had been recruited by the air force to become a member of the prestigious Airmen of Note Band, in which he was billed as "Harry James, Jr." This was likely the main source of young Harry's problem with his father, who believed that his son was using his name to jump-start his career. Besides that, he really wasn't Harry James, "Jr." After being turned down by his father on his release from the service, he played lead trumpet with Les Elgart, Tex Beneke, and other bands for about a year, apparently using an alias. That ended his career as a musician.

Changing careers, he moved to Southern California and started working as a real estate developer. He subsequently returned to Texas after five years there and began working for the celebrated Texas tycoon H. L. Hunt. For several years, he made a very good living as a developer, floundered for a time during a real estate recession, only to rebound and achieve even more success. Currently, he is a consultant to several real estate companies in Texas. Twice divorced and with five grandchildren, he is very involved with the promotion of the American Swing Band in Dallas and part of a well-financed effort to introduce swing into high-definition television (HDTV) on a national basis.[62]

Although Harry James was never close to his sons, he cared that their lives took the right turns. As a prime example of "do what I say, not what I do," Harry Jeffrey recalled one night at the roulette table in the Flamingo during the 1960s when he was on a winning streak. "All of a sudden, this hand comes down on my shoulder and turns me [around]. There's Dad standing there. He looked right at me. All he said was, 'Get up from the table right now, take your chips to the cage, get a cashier's check, and mail it to yourself right now.'"

*   *   *

One day, a month after the Basin Street East engagement, Sal Monte was getting ready to fly to Las Vegas with the weekly payroll. Suddenly, he came to the realization that, because he had been constantly on the road or in Vegas, he really didn't know his daughter, Christene, who was growing up without him. He told Harry of his decision to leave the band. James asked him if he could really afford to do it. Sal told him, "Harry, I'm gonna do it even if I can't afford it. I can't stand this anymore."

Harry James was compelled to call Pee Wee Monte and ask him to return to the band. During their estrangement, Pee Wee had been unsuccessful in launching a new band led by trumpeter Claude Gordon. Harry James and Pee Wee Monte patched up their differences and went back to work.

Pee Wee told Sal that Harry James wanted to write him a check for two weeks' severance pay. Sal told his brother: "I don't even want one week. Tell Harry he can buy some keno tickets with the money." He doesn't remember exactly how much he settled for. After taking a year off, on Bob Edmundson's recommendation, he joined Herb Alpert & The Tijuana Brass when the group first went on the road.[63]

I first met Pee Wee Monte at the Croydon Hotel in Chicago while the James band was at the Blue Note over Memorial Day weekend 1960. I had been fired from MCA with the valid explanation that, while I had done well booking Charlie Barnet and had signed Kenny Burrell, there was simply no other agent who shared my passion for jazz in the company.

I flew to Chicago to plead my case to Harry James, offering to move to Las Vegas and become the band's publicist. I asked for $90 a week. Pee Wee Monte said he and Harry would consider my offer over that weekend. For the first time, I witnessed groupies (then referred to by jazz musicians as "bandaids" and later a mainstay of the rock era that followed) in operation. Five young women from Findlay, Ohio, went through the entire James band, starting, of course, with the leader.

Vince Diaz, then a trombonist in the band, had the most outlandish explanation I ever heard concerning Harry's voracious sexual appetite. "I have learned from reading C. W. Leadbetter that Harry may have been the victim of spinal energies that settled in his groin and made him sexually ravenous and insatiable. Whatever it was that drove Harry, it made him miserable. I could see it in his eyes the last time I saw him at the MGM Grand in Las Vegas in 1975."[64]

On Monday afternoon, Pee Wee Monte informed me, "We can't afford you at the moment." Whether it was my inexperience or the fact that Pee Wee was faced with the insurmountable job of getting Harry out of debt, which precluded hiring me, I have no idea.

I never did get to represent Harry James, but in 1964 I convinced *Newsweek* to run a piece on James in conjunction with the twenty-fifth anniversary of the band. Twenty-five years after that, Pee Wee Monte called offering me the chance to work for the Harry James "ghost" band under the direction of Art Depew in an engagement at Merv Griffin Resorts International in Atlantic City. I turned down the offer since I felt there was little I could do for the band at that point.

One afternoon during the summer of 1961, Pee Wee Monte called Frank Modica about joining him and Harry James in the drive up to Freedomland, a short-lived theme park north of New York, where Modica had booked the James band. In the back seat was an attractive woman named Louise, who was never formally introduced. Once the band started playing, Modica asked Louise to dance. He learned that she was, in fact, Louise Tobin, Harry James's first wife. By now she and Harry were on better terms, and she was also friendly with Pee Wee Monte. She admitted to Modica that she would enjoy working as a singer around New York.

A few weeks later, Modica booked a date for Louise in New England with Peanuts Hucko's group.[65] Louise Tobin and Peanuts Hucko eventually married, a union that has endured to the present. At Hucko's eightieth birthday party, Harry Jeffrey James toasted his stepfather: "I don't mean to be unkind to my Dad. I just didn't know my Dad very well. Peanuts, you've already granted my wish 'cause you're the best father I've ever had."[66]

That Christmas, Frank Modica received an inscribed Omega watch from Harry James. He didn't have Harry's telephone number in Las Vegas so he called Pee Wee Monte to thank him. Pee Wee explained, "You introduced Louise to Peanuts Hucko [although Louise contends George Simon actually introduced them] and, as a result of their meeting, they got married so Harry doesn't have to pay any more alimony. That's the reason why you got the watch, not because it was Christmas. That was just a coincidence."

Jack Perciful described the experience that every new musician faced on joining the Harry James Orchestra: "When you were a newcomer, you didn't get on the bus; you waited outside until everybody else got on the bus first. It took me almost a year to get a permanent seat. For the first six months, I stood in the well of the bus and talked to the bus driver. Everybody'd sit in their seat, and they'd put their horn beside them. That would last for four or five hours until somebody else would want to stand. Then I'd go back and sit in their seat.... And when Red Kelly joined the band, there was no place for him to sit down so I let him sit with me. I sat next to him for the rest of the time I was on the band."[67]

By the early 1960s, James insisted that if a bus trip would take more than six hours Pee Wee Monte had to arrange to fly the band. As Red Kelly, the original inveterate road rat, contended, "It was the easiest band to travel with." However, Kelly pointed out that if Harry James thought a musician was deliberately late in getting on the bus, he would order the bus driver to depart without him.[68] Red Kelly added: "Harry loved it. He often said, 'I want to go back on the bus.'"[69] Jack Perciful said, "He was on the bus almost before anybody every morning. He was always reading a book or a newspaper and always carried a lot of sports books with him."[70]

Harry James insisted that the band members keep up high standards in their playing. For years, musicians spoke about how Benny Goodman was notorious for giving the evil eye, known as "The Ray," to any musician who made mistakes. On the other hand, Harry James would walk up and down in front of the band in order to carefully listen to a newcomer. He could test anybody in the band by calling for certain arrangements that would provide a perfect example of their playing. If he didn't like what he heard, after the set he would make it clear to the errant musician exactly what he didn't like.

Trumpeter Rob Turk remarked, "He could be nasty. I remember one time he noticed a member of the trumpet section lighting up a cigarette while on the bandstand. He didn't say a word. He proceeded to call a tune. He said to me, 'Rob, give him your part.' On the next tune, he said, 'Give him your part.' At the end of four tunes, which were ball-breakers, this kid was wasted. He couldn't play a note. Harry said, 'Don't screw around with me, kid. I know all the answers.' I thought to myself, 'Boy, I'm glad he did-n't call those four tunes in a row for me.'[71]

"On the other hand, Harry was really great in looking out for his guys and standing behind them. On one road trip, after playing a date in Minneapolis, it was over 400 miles to the next job. As we were about to leave, Harry stood up in the front of the bus and said, 'I want to tell you guys something. This date coming up means a lot of money to me. That's why you're doing it. It'll be reflected in your next check.'"

Red Kelly said that, whenever the band was down, perhaps from too much traveling, James would say to Willie Smith when the band got on the bandstand: "Go up and play some time." He would call for something that featured Smith, like "Things Ain't What They Used to Be," which would serve to lift the musicians out of their funk.[72]

With four successful years behind him at the Flamingo Hotel and lucrative bookings on the road, Harry James's fortunes were now at a new high. Things were going so well that James was moved to tell various people facetiously that he had started work on his memoirs, which would be enti-tled *Now Is the Good Old Days*. As a result of his drawing power in Las

Vegas, Harrah's—and later Harold's Club in Reno, and Harrah's in neighboring Lake Tahoe—signed Harry to term contracts. Three-week engagements in both Reno and Tahoe would follow back-to-back.

The musicians made the 450-mile trip to Reno in individual cars. Since there was no bus involved, Harry James should have netted a substantial amount of money from the three steady Nevada engagements that, for several years in the 1960s, totalled close to forty weeks a year. Unfortunately, he merely transferred his gambling habit from southern to northern Nevada, and he suffered because of it.

In between one of the Las Vegas and Reno-Tahoe engagements in the early 1960s, the James band played a one-nighter in Coeur D'Alene, Idaho. Don Sickler, the respected musician, record producer, and educator, was then an up-and-coming bebop trumpeter. He had gained a considerable reputation in the neighboring Spokane, Washington, area, leading his own quintet, which was hired to play during intermission that night.

As Sickler recalls, "I thought of Harry James as somebody who was old hat. I thought of him in terms of 'Ciribiribin' and 'Flight of the Bumble Bee.' Dizzy and Clifford Brown were the main guys for me."

While Sickler's group was playing, a terrible accident took place. The lead man in the James trumpet section slipped and fell off the riser. He cut his lip severely and had to be taken to the hospital. Harry James took his place standing up in the section playing both the lead part and his own solos. Of necessity, he had to switch from one kind of trumpet playing to another.

"I was absolutely amazed," Sickler remembered. "Harry suddenly became another person to me. It was a real awakening. I also discovered that when he was playing those Ernie Wilkins arrangements he could swing like mad. I realized how tremendously talented he was. My mouth was hanging open when I went up to him after the set to congratulate him on what he had done. He admitted, 'I really got a workout!'"[73]

Willie Smith had long had a serious drinking problem. He continued showing up late for the sets at the Driftwood Lounge. James tolerated any musician's drinking until his playing was adversely affected by it. Smith's drinking, however, was out of control. Finally, James had no choice but to send him home, thus ending an association that had lasted almost eighteen years. Joe Riggs moved over from second alto to take his place and became an impressive replacement.

In the winter of 1966, I saw Willie Smith featured with Charlie Barnet's superb band at Basin Street East. The Barnet band's saxophone section was excellent, no doubt due to the way Barnet (himself a rousing tenor saxophone player) had Smith rehearse the section. In his autobiography, he mentioned that this particular band was his all-time favorite.[74]

While Barnet was at Basin Street East, the James band was playing at the Riverboat. One night, Barnet and Willie Smith came over to see Harry James. During intermission, someone asked Barnet who was in his band. He pointed to Willie Smith and said, "That's my band."[75]

The talented arranger Billy May had persuaded Willie Smith to join Alcoholics Anonymous. The intervention was successful, but sadly the many years of abuse had taken a heavy toll. Willie Smith died of cancer in 1967 at the age of 56.

Following Smith's departure from the band, Jimmy Rushing, the rollicking blues singer from the original Basie band, replaced Ernie Andrews for a time. Jimmy proved a great draw, performing ten to twelve tunes a night. Every lounge group in Las Vegas came in to listen to him. Unfortunately, Rushing had signed on only for back to back engagements in Vegas and Tahoe, and his association with Harry James ended too soon.[76]

In addition to Nick Bono, another longtime veteran, Corky Corcoran, remained in the band. Corcoran had returned for yet a fourth time in 1962. James allowed Corcoran to return because by now he was completely sober. This time, except for brief interruptions, Corcoran stayed for fifteen more years.

One night in the winter of 1962, Harry James came into the band room below the stage in the Driftwood Lounge and announced to his musicians, "Buddy Rich, 'the world's greatest drummer,' called about joining the band."[77] Free of the restrictions from his heart attack, Rich had made a strategic career decision: he fully realized his attempt to make it as a singer had failed; he could now play Count Basie's music with James for a salary that Basie simply couldn't afford to match. Buddy Rich's third and last tenure with the James band was the best for all concerned. Harry James reaped the benefit of Rich's playing. It made the band sound hotter, and his presence also helped the attendance on the road. As James told bandleader Ray Anthony, "Buddy takes the work out of playing."[78]

Buddy Rich insisted on being paid $1,500 a week plus expenses so that he could drive his Jaguar to Las Vegas. He refused to open at the Flamingo with the band until his name was given featured billing on the hotel marquee. As he told Red Kelly and Jack Percifial, his cohorts in the rhythm section, "I can't help it. I have to have it that way." He told Harry, "I'll never leave this band again.... I'm very happy to be back, and it's good to be like coming home."[79]

Speaking for himself and Percifial, Red Kelly observed: "We were convinced that the first thing he was going to do was [have Harry] get rid of us. Buddy was on the band about two weeks, and Jack and I completely ignored him. One night he played something that was just fantastic. We got off the stand, and I said to him, 'That's the greatest thing I've ever seen in my life!' He grabbed me and gave me a big hug. He said, 'I didn't think you were ever gonna speak to me.'"[80]

Kelly added, "With every other drummer, Harry would control the tempo. He'd do a thing with his hands while we were playing. It was a signal for the drummer. He never did that with Buddy."

Jack Perciful offered: "I think the rhythm section jelled faster than any rhythm section in the world. Buddy played for the band; he never played for himself except when he took his solos. If anybody in the band was doing something, he would know where he was going, and he would enhance it."[81]

During a particularly dreary one-nighter tour, Kelly asked Rich, "How do you do it?" Rich answered, "You set a certain standard for yourself and you never go below that, no matter what goes on around you." "I found that to be rather inspirational," remarked the bassist.[82]

A significant facet of the Basie band was the firm, yet subtle, understatement of Freddie Green, "Mr. Rhythm Guitar." Green, Basie on piano, Walter Page on bass, and Jo Jones on drums were dubbed "The All American Rhythm Section." In order to attempt to duplicate the strong undercurrent of a rhythm guitar in his Basie presentation, James hired a number of guitarists. After Buddy had settled in with Jack Perciful and Red Kelly, however, the band dispensed with a guitarist—James found it was no longer necessary.

One of the overlooked gems of Harry James's entire recording career is the MGM album *In a Relaxed Mood*, a particular favorite of Buddy Rich's.[83] This small group album featured an intimate brand of jazz; James's playing is what one might describe as "gently swinging," yet he also offered several prime examples of bebop trumpet playing. Valuable contributions were made by the other principal soloists, Ray Sims and Corky Corcoran. Jack Perciful also showed a sensitivity in his playing that was never better displayed on records.

On another well-executed album, *Double Dixie*, the band brilliantly reproduced the spirit of the old Bob Crosby band (and the Ben Pollack Band by association); it featured a frontline of ex-Bob Crosby stalwarts Matty Matlock on clarinet and Eddie Miller on tenor saxophone, along with Harry and Dick Cathcart on trumpets, and Ray Sims. A concerto grosso approach was used with the horns supported by the entire band, followed by interplay between the smaller group and the big band. The James band sounded inspired, partly because of Matty Matlock's arrangements and partly because of the superb contributions of the soloists. Buddy Rich combined two-beat drumming with a solid 4/4 big band swinging beat and kept the music at a high level. For the first time, Harry

James recorded his versions of Louis Armstrong's "Cornet Chop Suey" and "Weather Bird" classics on the album.

There were, of course, moments when Harry James and Buddy Rich were at odds despite their obvious mutual respect. Some nights their finely tuned egos clashed, which was inevitable, but Jack Perciful said, "I never heard any words or anything."[84]

Tino Barzie was at the Flamingo often during the time Buddy Rich was on the band. He knew exactly the way Rich handled himself from when he had played for Tommy and Jimmy Dorsey. He remarked, "As ornery as he could get, the guys appreciated what he could do behind the drums and how he could motivate the whole band, including Tommy. Tommy was tough on him, but I really believe Harry catered to him.

"Sometimes, Buddy would goof around and Harry would moan and groan to Corky or somebody. He wouldn't speak directly to Buddy. The only time he would go after him is if he had enough vodka in him. That gave him a little bit more nerve."[85]

"Off the stand they were great strangers," remarked saxophonist Jay Corre, who recalled the nightly routine that would precede the opening set at the Flamingo. "It was always formal, always with great enthusiasm. Harry would be backstage drinking his vodka … he always had it in a champagne bucket to keep it cold. In his high-pitched voice, with great enthusiasm, Harry would say, 'Hi, Bernard,' and then Buddy 'Fred Astaire'd' in. Buddy would look around to make sure that everyone was looking at him first. That was very important to Buddy—it was sort of like the staging. He would say, 'Whaddaya say, Harry,' in his deep voice. He'd be wearing one of those short, continental jackets with his hands slanted toward the pockets but never in the pockets. He wore boots, and maybe one pant leg was a little up where you could see a little more of the boot. It seemed like it was planned that way."[86]

Red Kelly believed that the trumpeter and the drummer really had much in common. "They both went through that formative period so young that they grew up retaining a lot of teenage traits. Buddy was very petulant at times, but the brilliance was always there, whereas Harry had a hard time throwing humorous adlibs, although he sure tried."[87]

Kelly mused about how Harry James had never really had a normal childhood or the typical teenage years like other adolescents. "At fifteen, at a time when most teenagers are becoming interested in girls and want to learn how to drive so they can take girls out on dates in their dad's car, Harry was sharing pints of whiskey on band buses and learning to smoke grass. He knew nothing about courting a girl. Girls were only there for the taking. Harry always talked about chicks the way a teenager would. He just figured he had to talk like that. It was so sophomoric."

Jazz musicians have rarely been considered important enough for advertising agencies to feature them as the focal point of television commercials. A rare exception occurred in January 1962 when John Mann of Foote, Cone, & Belding realized that Harry James was the best known trumpeter in the public's mind and could be effective in selling a product.[88]

The creative department at Foote, Cone & Belding decided to focus on James for its client, Kimberly-Clark, as the subject of a Kleenex television commercial that would demonstrate the product's great strength. At first, James balked at doing the commercial until Pee Wee Monte convinced him what it could accomplish. A Kleenex was wrapped tightly around the bell of his trumpet as he played the accompanying jingle and hit a high note at the end of the tune. The commercial proved conclusively that even with the air pressure generated by Harry's trumpet the Kleenex was durable. The jingle: "Kleenex has something new to blow its horn about." This commercial was the forerunner of the Memorex spot years later that featured Ella Fitzgerald.[89]

In the second of three commercials that were shot, six trumpeters formed a semicircle behind Harry James in front of the band. Well-established players such as Pete Candoli played trumpet choruses that were blown in pantomime by actors posing as trumpeters. One of the actual trumpeters seen on camera was the then unknown Herb Alpert, who told John Mann what an honor it was to be able to work with his idol Harry James.

The Kleenex commercials became highly popular and brought an awareness of Harry James to a completely new audience. Realizing the impact of this commercial and figuring on Kimberly-Clark's continued interest in Harry as a possible sponsor, I thought about putting together a television special to commemorate Harry's upcoming twenty-fifth anniversary as a bandleader for airing in February 1964. Nick Sevano and I were partners in the venture.

In September 1963, we met with James at the Disneyland Hotel during the band's annual Disneyland gig. He seemed very interested in working with us. We mentioned that we wanted to approach Frank Sinatra as host for the proposed special. Nick and I fully realized that without Sinatra's participation there would be no show.

At that time, Frank Sinatra was involved in a serious dispute with Ed Olsen, the chairman of the Nevada Gaming Commission, over Sam Giancana's presence at Sinatra's Cal Neva Lodge. The Chicago mafia don had been under surveillance by FBI agents over a period of several days.

I can remember Harry James saying, "Nick, this problem with Frank, I read about it in the newspaper. What do you think?" Nick Sevano said, "You mean the thing with Sam Giancana? Yeah, I think he's in a lot of trouble."

The mention of Giancana's name meant nothing to Harry James. However, when I mentioned one of Sam Giancana's aliases, "Sam Mooney," he remarked, "Mooney. Oh sure, I know Sam." Any important entertainer who worked regularly in Las Vegas and other big cities in those years would have been hard pressed not to have at least met Giancana, much less known him.

The aftermath of this incident resulted in Sinatra's losing his Nevada gambling license. He again had a serious image problem, which affected the future of our TV special. A few weeks later, Nick Sevano approached Howard Koch, who ran Essex Productions, Sinatra's production company, and discussed our intentions. Koch said he would consult with Sinatra and get back to him. About ten days later, he called Nick and informed him that Sinatra couldn't commit himself to the project. Indeed, timing was everything.

Coincidentally, in the late 1970s, Harry's son Tim revealed to his father, while visiting with him in Lake Tahoe, that in his work as an assistant attorney general in Texas he was the agent in charge of the Organized Crime Unit. His job involved coordinating with the Justice Department in prosecuting organized crime figures. He mentioned the names of several major gangsters, including Moe Dalitz, whose activities were being closely watched. James said, "They're friends of mine." Tim laughed and said, "You shouldn't have such friends."[90]

Tim James had taken a different route than his older brother. He had graduated from Texas Christian University, majoring in government. He then earned a degree at the University of Houston Law School. He is currently in his second term as District Attorney of Nacogdoches County; Nacogdoches is the oldest town in Texas. Married three times, he is the father of four children, the youngest of whom, Jerin Timothy Roger James, is a member of the Brigade Staff at Annapolis and a member of the class of 1999.

During the prime years of the Harry James Orchestra, from 1962 to 1966—one could refer to them as "the Buddy Rich Years"—the Driftwood Lounge became a haven for major singers to relax after their shows. It was a place to see and be seen. Informality was the rule after midnight.

Working regularly at The Sands, Frank Sinatra often visited with Harry James as well as Buddy Rich; he took equal enjoyment in listening to Harry's band. Personal manager Tom Korman remembered seeing Sinatra sit in on a couple of occasions. "I used to spend some time at the Flamingo in those years. I was friendly with Morris Landsberg, the owner. I remember one time when Frank came up and sang 'Ciribiribin' with Harry. It was about two o'clock in the morning. He sat on a stool. It was like a jam session—very casual. And I remember another time—it was about the same time of night—when he sang 'All or Nothing at All.'"[91]

One night Harry James spotted Vic Damone walking in and asked him to come up to sing. Sinatra and his pals Joe E. Lewis and Leo Durocher, along with Betty Grable, were together in the audience. Vic sang "That Old Black Magic" with a wireless mike. Afterward, Harry said, "I guess if the singers can use that mike like that sitting down I can get up here and play on a stool."

Tony Martin headlined the bill in the main room during those years at the Flamingo and other Las Vegas hotels. Martin said of Harry James's playing: "He played trumpet the way I like to sing. I used to love to play [fills] when I was a musician. I played the [fills] on all the ballads. And when I did "There's No Tomorrow"—that was a big smash for me—on the second chorus, I hummed. That's just what Harry James would have done. That was recorded in 1953 so you could say he was an influence on me.

"I couldn't wait for the second shows to be over. I would have a couple of drinks and listen to him play. He never missed. He reached for the two high notes and always got 'em. He never cracked a note. I once said to him, 'Harry, how do you do it at 2:30 or 3:00 in the morning?' He said, 'I have an inner feeling about it.' I said, 'What is it?' He said, 'If I go for 'em and I think they're not gonna come out, I take 'em an octave lower.' We all do that.

"Harry once called me up to do a song. I sang 'I'm in the Mood for Love,' and he got up and played behind me. It was wonderful. I said, 'Do you know something? I like it out here better than the main room.' I did that a couple of times."[92]

An unusual but talented singer—more of a jazz singer than a band singer—Ruth Price joined the James band in 1963. James had pursued her for two years after he had heard her record of "Run, Little Raindrop, Run," a tune Betty Grable had introduced in *Springtime in the Rockies*. This was only one of several offbeat songs Ruth Price has always favored in her repertoire.

The pert, dark-haired singer sings regularly today at her club, The Jazz Bakery in Los Angeles. Price observed: "Harry was a stoic so you really couldn't see what he was feeling, but my impression was, after spending a year-and-a-half with him, he never for a minute lowered his standards, or altered his criteria about how he should play and how the band should sound. He was always really involved. He cared deeply.... He was really proud of that band."

"He was a lonely man. I think there's a certain amount of loneliness built into being in the music business, but I think this was beyond that. I think he would have been lonely in his own home."[93]

Harry James gave Ruth Price total freedom. "He never said 'Boo!' to me about anything I was singing except to compliment me. In order to keep me, because he really did want to keep me, he sensed my obvious musical restlessness. He had Thad Jones come out and write charts for me. Thad used to write charts in the band room at the Flamingo while the band was playing."

Ruth Price noticed the great respect Buddy Rich had for Harry James. "I think that he, like everybody else who was around him for awhile, was aware of what a high level of performance Harry expected from himself. I also noticed that the musicians who had been touring with Harry for many years had this thing about 'Our Band.' They felt it sounded better than the other bands that were in existence then." As if to support that statement, Ted Gioia, in his *The History of Jazz*, referred to "Harry James's unfairly neglected work from his later years found him fronting a hard-swinging band in a Basie mold."[94]

Unbeknownst to most people, at this period of great prominence for his band, Harry James underwent dental surgery that involved implants, a procedure that was then new and extremely painful. Playing the trumpet under these circumstances was really unbearable, but, with his iron constitution, he kept right on performing.

A few weeks later, one afternoon during the usual August break, he called Red Kelly at home. By this time he had lost all his teeth and was having a terrible time fitting his false teeth in his mouth. He confided to Kelly that he was terrified that he wouldn't be able to play anymore. Fortunately, later that day, he found the proper glue that held his teeth in place. He was so elated at his discovery that he called Red back and played a trumpet solo on the telephone.[95]

As an example of the free-wheeling atmosphere that pervaded the band in those years, bass trombonist Dick McQuary, now Senior Loan Officer at the Pacific Southwest Bank in Las Vegas, recalled a unique ballgame that pitted Harry's band against Lionel Hampton's at Lake Tahoe. "The ground rules for the game were established beforehand at the bar at Harrah's at 6:00 in the morning after the last set. If you called the umpire 'motherfucker' more than twice, you were automatically out of the game."[96]

Joe Riggs laughed as he remembered, "Here we are, both teams are huffing and puffing in that high altitude, juiced out of our gourds at daybreak, trying to play baseball."[97]

McQuary continued, "If you hit a double, you would be awarded with a martini, and if you hit a home run, you would get a case of beer. Buddy

Rich was playing centerfield. He missed a fly ball that beat us. He was so uncoordinated." Tony Scodwell chimed in with, "As anything but a drummer, Buddy couldn't cut it."[98]

In April 1964, the band began a three-week concert tour of Japan that was a complete triumph. The Japanese fans knew every conceivable fact concerning James's career. They treated him and Buddy Rich like deities. Jack Perciful noted, "The fans would clap short and fast so as not to interfere with their listening to Harry's various hits. I remember that they brought flowers for Harry at the conclusion of every concert."[99]

That summer Harry James faced a lawsuit. The suit, filed on behalf of his two sons, was based on the fact that he had only contributed a total of twenty thousand dollars to the trust fund that had originally been set up for them, nor had he paid for their insurance when Harry James and Louise Tobin divorced in July 1943. The terms had been established that James would place 10 percent of his gross yearly income into the trust.

In 1963, the Bank of California was about to make its first disbursement on Tim's twenty-first birthday. However, the bank wanted first to be sure that the taxes had been paid on the trust fund. No one had ever looked into the payment of these taxes. Finally, James agreed to pay and his sons dropped the suit. Theoretically, they were entitled to well over one million dollars from this trust fund, had the payments ever been made. Ultimately, Harry blamed Harry Jeffrey for instigating the lawsuit.[100] In reality, Louise Tobin had suggested it since her two sons had never received the monies due them.[101]

On September 28, 1964, Harry kicked off a concert tour with Nina Simone with an appearance at Carnegie Hall. Jack Perciful recalled, "He never said anything, but everybody in the band knew how important that night was because of where we were playing."[102] Right in the middle of the band's set, Harry announced to the audience that the hallowed hall had great memories for him from a night twenty-six years earlier and remarked how glad he was to have finally returned. Having attended this concert, I well remember the vibrancy of the band's performance on that night. It sounded like a new band proudly making its New York debut.

In the summer of 1960, Harry James moved his family to Las Vegas. Purely and simply, there was no reason for living in Beverly Hills any longer. Betty Grable's film career was over. There were occasional TV guest shots in Los Angeles for her and Harry, but James's career was now centered in Nevada. At first they rented and then they bought a house on Country Club Lane, near the ninth hole of the Desert Inn Golf Club.

Vicki James was then about to become a junior at Beverly Hills High School. She had begun her primary education at the Westlake School. She came home one day and told her parents, "The girls at school are teasing me because we only have one Cadillac." Vicki recalled, "They said to me, 'You are not going to a school where that's important.' My sister and I were both pulled out of there and put into a Beverly Hills Catholic school. Since Daddy had been born a Catholic, he used that to get us into the school."[103]

Asked how it felt to be the daughter of two members of the royalty of American entertainment in the 1940s, Vicki responded: "It felt very normal. There was nothing in our upbringing that caused us to feel anything more than normal kids. It was very underplayed, very low key. We were not given everything that we wanted. There was never any pretentiousness.... I do remember that I kept hearing the expression, 'Daddy's on the road,' when I was a little girl."

Vicki's sister, Jessica, showed musical ability while she was in her last year of grade school and her first year of high school in Las Vegas. Blessed with a beautiful singing voice, she wanted to pursue a career as a singer. As Vicki remembered it, "Daddy said, 'How serious are you?' Her range was unbelievable, absolutely phenomenal—she could hit those high notes." He admitted she had real potential and told her, "If you want to be a singer, you're going to do it right. First of all, you're gonna learn to play the piano, and you're gonna learn notes and chords."[104]

Jessie chose not to. Like many teenagers, she was unwilling to make this kind of a commitment. Her interest in a singing career ended abruptly.

Vicki was given a Chevrolet Impala convertible when she was seventeen. Looking back on it she believes, "I think they had an ulterior motive for getting me that car. I had to take my sister everywhere—and to and from school. When I went off to college (University of Arizona) I couldn't take my car with me."

In describing her teenage years, Vicki is quick to refer to herself as "a little bit of a goody two-shoes. I got through high school and college and didn't drink, never took drugs, was never promiscuous." She also recalls that people sometimes referred to her father's being a perfectionist, "I'm a frustrated perfectionist, so the genes carried through."

Vicki became engaged to Bill Bivens while they were both students at Arizona. Reportedly, when he came to discuss their plans with Harry James, Harry made it very clear that Bill wasn't marrying into a family that was well off, despite their celebrity status.[105] Vicki mentioned that on the night before their wedding on August 18, 1964, Bill and Harry stayed out drinking until 7 A.M.[106]

Jessica, on the other hand, being three years younger, was caught up in the sixties generation. She had a strong will and rebelled at her mother's strictness. Lillian had been equally strict with Betty as a child in her pursuit of stardom.[107]

Betty Grable enrolled both girls in Bishop Gorman Catholic High School in Las Vegas to instill a sense of discipline in them. "Although it was the wish of both Betty and Harry that they were enrolled there," said Air Force Colonel Michael Ritz, Henry and Betty Ritz's son, "it bothered Harry a lot that they weren't going to public school. He was gentler—not that Aunt Betty was brash. But discipline was big with her. A lot of the fighting between them was about that discipline problem. I think Harry thought of them still as his little girls."

Unfortunately, attending Gorman had just the opposite effect on Jessica. She began cutting classes and gravitated toward students who were using drugs. Her mother told her that she would have to leave the house once she reached her eighteenth birthday. Betty and Harry refused to acknowledge her birthday and also failed to attend her graduation from Gorman.[108] In a continuing succession of bizarre events, mother and daughter had a serious physical altercation and Jessica was ordered out of the house. Betty called Harry to inform him of her decision. He agreed that Jessica would have to leave home, but he did pay for her hotel room for three months.

Soon afterward, Jessica became pregnant. The father was Ron Yahner, a classmate. Instead of facing the situation head-on with an attempt at understanding and dealing with it, Harry, in an example of extreme hypocrisy and perhaps guilt, became overly hostile and called her a disgrace to the family.[109]

From the beginning, Harry James had left the raising of the children to Betty. By this time, he wasn't home that much anyway. Vicki was once quoted as saying, "He always came home to change his shoes."

Jessica continued going through a hellish period. For a short time, she lived with Yahner's parents, but then left Las Vegas for Palm Springs to room with a girlfriend. After seven months, Betty allowed her to return home. Jessica reconciled with Ron Yahner and married him in December 1965. They had two children and stayed together for three years.[110]

Harry James and Betty Grable's marriage had been increasingly troubled for some years. From interviewing many people who knew the couple, I discovered that Betty had been the victim of frequent beatings by Harry. It's my feeling Harry's alcoholism was partially responsible for such behavior. Of course, this pattern of abuse had started for her with George Raft.

Betty Baez told me about having to work diligently on Betty's face one night at Lake Tahoe in the early 1960s. Harry had beaten her after accusing the two Bettys of playing around with a man who took them out on his boat. Heavy makeup had to be applied before Betty could perform that night at Harrah's.[111]

Another eyewitness, a saxophone player in the band, related the time when an argument ensued at the Coconut Grove in Los Angeles over a problem with the girls when Betty and the children had come to see the band perform. He saw Harry kick Betty as she bent down to pick up something up. As the saxophonist related, "He lifted Betty almost a foot off the ground. When he got mad, he could get mean."

Harry James was always checking on Betty's whereabouts, perhaps not without reason. She too had had several affairs over the years. One was with Dan Dailey, her co-star in *Mother Wore Tights, When My Baby Smiles at Me, My Blue Heaven,* and *Call Me Mister* and years later on stage in *Guys and Dolls* in Miami and Las Vegas. Dailey's wife named her as corespondent in her divorce suit. Jackie Mills confirmed how jealous Harry was of Dailey.[112]

For years, Betty Grable and Harry James had been living on Betty's savings. Harry's fortune had long since been lost at the gambling tables; he was essentially working for the house. Partly because of that fact, in 1962 Betty Grable returned to the musical stage in *Guys and Dolls,* first with Dan Dailey and then with Hugh O'Brien at Melodyland in Anaheim, California. She then starred in *High Button Shoes* with O'Brien in Melodyland a year later.[113]

With both Vicki and Jessie now grown up, Betty Grable decided it was time to end her untenable marital situation. She waited until she had been signed by Broadway's leading producer, David Merrick, to assume the lead in the touring company of *Hello, Dolly.* Merrick had initially considered Grable for the role before casting Carol Channing.

On October 8, 1965, Betty Grable divorced Harry James in Las Vegas after twenty-two years of marriage on grounds of extreme cruelty. She left the courtroom in tears, wearing a wide-brimmed white hat pulled low over her forehead. The group of photographers clicking away was considerably smaller in number than the pack that was present on their circus-like wedding day in the same city, twenty-two years earlier.[114]

That night at Harrah's in Lake Tahoe, where the band was working, Harry James and Red Kelly drank together between sets at the neighboring Sahara Tahoe. On their way to the other hotel, Harry was accosted by a man who had seen the news of the divorce on television. He yelled out to him sarcastically, "Nice going, Harry." Harry had also seen the news report and told Kelly how upset he was to see Betty crying. He explained to him that they had both agreed to the divorce, but that they still planned to see a great deal of each other, which they did.[115]

Betty Grable was devastated at the breakup. She was still very much in love with Harry and was deeply hurt at having to end their once-happy marriage. However, in light of the way their marriage turned out, her various statements to the press over the years—"I aim to be Mrs. Harry James for the rest of my life," "This is where we hope to spend our golden anniversary," and most recently, "Harry is the breadwinner in the family, and that's how it should be"—sounded hollow.[116]

Within days of the divorce, Betty Grable left for New York to rehearse for the *Hello, Dolly* tour. The six-city tour culminated in a ninety-minute, cut-down version of the show at the Riviera Hotel in Las Vegas, where it ran for nine months. Although her reviews were favorable and business sensational, some critics commented on the raspiness of Betty's singing voice.[117]

There were those who considered Betty Grable the best Dolly of them all—a natural comedienne, not a mugger like Carol Channing. And considering that Mary Martin, Ethel Merman, Ginger Rogers, and Pearl Bailey essayed the role as well, that is a triumph in itself. During the Broadway run, when she descended the flight of stairs for the final reprise of the title song and lifted up her skirt for the first time in the show to reveal the fabled million-dollar gams, the audience at the St. James Theatre roared its approval.

Max Showalter played the part of Horace Vandergelder, and therefore was Betty Grable's leading man on the road, in Las Vegas, and later in the Broadway run. Having been in the James household on many occasions while under contract to Fox and having worked with Betty for over two years, Showalter and Grable were very close friends. He noted: "The whole thing was she idolized Harry. I think he's the only man she really ever loved.... During rehearsals, she said to me, 'You know, all of a sudden the girls were grown up and Harry's gone. I just desperately needed another family. I felt like coming back to the theatre so I could have my family again.' And she certainly did because everyone idolized her.

"She never felt she was really very good. But the audience adored her because of that simplicity about her ... the innocence. I had co-starred in two films with Marilyn [Monroe], and I think it was the innocence of Marilyn that added to her appeal.

"Betty was so effervescent. Harry could never come up to that. He was a much quieter kind of person, but yet he was fun. Sometimes he had to drink to have fun, and I think that was his whole problem, of drinking maybe much too much. I felt that maybe he had to compensate with that. He couldn't let himself really go to come up at least halfway to Betty's effervescence.

"I sensed Harry's insecurity. He felt badly because his success could never measure up to hers. She didn't want it that way because that never meant anything to her. Hollywood didn't accept Harry. There was a stigma because he was a musician. The word got around about his womanizing. Betty didn't want to believe it. She said, 'I just had to discount things that

I heard because I loved him so much. I wouldn't listen to people who were trying to help me.'"[118]

Supposedly, one night when Betty Grable was starring in *Hello, Dolly* on Broadway, and Harry James was playing an engagement at the Riverboat, Frank Sinatra, hoping he could put them back together, took her to see Harry perform. I asked Showalter if he knew about that. He said, "I wouldn't doubt it. She would have certainly gone because wherever we were where Harry was playing, she would go to see him perform, no matter how badly he had treated her."[119]

It was Jackie Mills's opinion that "even when you knew Harry well like I did, the real Harry James was a problem because he was a very private man. He was always proving himself to women just as he was always proving himself to people as a trumpet player. Another thing I noticed, in all the years I knew him, I never heard him talk about anything but music, baseball, or women."

I asked Mills if anybody in the band every questioned Harry about his drinking and carousing. "No," he replied. "[The musicians] were afraid of him. They thought they would lose their job. He didn't put up with any interference in his life, even from Betty. Having a band was very important to him. It was his identification. He had to have that because it bugged him to be thought of as 'Mr. Betty Grable.'"[120]

Steve Preston was one of a party of five people Betty Grable brought to Basin Street East during Harry James's triumphant engagement there. He was still a member of her troupe, which was en route to Puerto Rico for an engagement at the El San Juan Hotel. As Preston recalled, "There was a long line waiting to get in. I walked down to the front of the line but Betty was way in the back. I asked her, 'What are you doing? You're Mrs. Harry James—you don't stand in line!' She said, 'I can't do that.' So I said, 'You stand right there.' I went up to the front of the line and got us in. There wasn't a table [available] in the place. They set up one especially for us."

When a photographer wanted to shoot a photo of Betty Grable and her friends, she suddenly became wary that Steve Preston would be photographed sitting next to her. Even though Harry knew him well, she said, "He thinks we're too close." She indicated he would be very upset. "I thought she was crazy. She wasn't as embarrassed about what was happening to her as she was protective of him." (Or was she afraid of what might happen if Harry ever saw the photograph?)[121]

Ray Sims was probably the quietest man in the James band but also one of the most musically consistent. He recalled Harry's coming in to work one night at the Flamingo looking depressed. Sims asked him what was bothering him. Harry said that he had just had a big fight with Betty over a meal she had cooked for him. "Apparently, it was the maid's night off, and Betty had prepared a southern type meal—pork chops and mashed potatoes with gravy. Harry told me how he sat down to eat and screamed at her, 'I wanted chops, not a chop. Where's the gravy?'" He recalled Harry's telling him that he picked up the end of the table, threw everything on the floor, and walked out. "I asked him, 'What the hell did you do that for?' He said, 'I don't know.'"[122]

When Sims decided to leave the band after eleven years ("Things just got monotonous"), he was offered a job at the Flamingo Hotel with the house band. Although the trombonist was one of his favorite musicians, Harry James, upon hearing from Sims that he was giving notice, merely said, "Okay, Babe," and walked away. As Sims noted, he hated anyone's leaving the band.

With strangers, Harry James could be just as sarcastic as Buddy Rich. Once during intermission at a hotel date in Denver, a proverbial little old lady saw Harry walking by. She asked, "Aren't you Harry James?" "No, I'm his mother," he replied, not breaking stride. Another time a woman told him how much she enjoyed his music, but commented about how loudly the band played. Harry said, "You're the kind of a person who watches a movie from the front row of the theater and says the picture is too big."[123]

Frank Modica, Jr., recalls how one night after a gig at the Bainbridge Naval Training Center Harry asked him to accompany him to a strippers' bar at the notorious "Block" in Baltimore. He welcomed the opportunity to possibly get to know Harry a little better over a few drinks. As he remembered, "It got to be 2:30 in the morning, and I was ready to call it a night, but Harry invited one of the strippers, all of whom he knew by name, to his hotel room and insisted I come along with him. I was sitting in one chair in one corner, and he's sitting in the chair in another corner, and the girl was sitting on the bed. The conversation revolved around music and baseball. By 4 A.M. I left and returned to my hotel."[124]

Trombonist Dave Wells believed: "My impression was that Harry was always on the defensive. Somebody was always trying to get to him—too tightly, too much. You could get stoned with him, screw with him, whatever, the night before, and then you'd meet him in the lobby the next day, and he'd walk by you like he didn't even know you."[125]

After interviewing approximately 200 people for this biography, and after having known him for twenty-four years, I have reached my own conclusions about "the man nobody knew." To me he appeared to be two-dimensional—a man and his music. His inner world was partly composed of abuse and self-abuse. It's my belief that Harry James was often abused physically—and certainly mentally—by his father Everette. In addition to the effect alcohol had on him, his constant physical abuse of Betty Grable is most likely based on what he endured himself. Research has shown that men who physically abuse their wives and girlfriends have usually been battered themselves as children.

On the previously mentioned *Merv Griffin Show* appearance, when Griffin asked him how he got started in music, Harry James replied, "Well, it started when my old man had a switch, and he was the trumpet teacher. He said, 'Kid, here's the horn. Learn it.'" On that same show, he also talked about the time when Everette took a strap to him saying, "Someday you'll thank me." Harry tried to give the impression that he genuinely appreciated his father's constant prodding, but his choice of words proved otherwise.

Everette obviously recognized his son's innate musical talent almost immediately. Practically singlehandedly, he turned Harry into the virtuoso he became, but at a terrible price. Without ever realizing it, Everette became the single most intimidating force in Harry's life. Throughout his childhood, Harry James was constantly seeking his father's approval and firmly believed he never quite measured up to his father's expectations.

He never had a real childhood since he had started working in the strange, isolated world of the circus when he was just a toddler. He often described how Everette would allow him to play baseball with his friends only after Harry had mastered certain trumpet exercises in the Arban Book.[126] For the most part, Harry's entire youth revolved around satisfying Everette's musical demands. Everette didn't respect what Harry wanted. The child in Harry was never nurtured at a time when his only job should have been merely being a little boy.

I strongly believe Everette's physical abuse and constant prodding had a significant adverse effect on Harry's psychological well-being. As a result, he never developed any self-esteem as a child should. He had constant pressure put upon him in the circus to perform and excel in front of a band. That was his skill—the way he would seek approval. He needed an audience to feel alive—special, important, and loved. Without it, he believed he really wasn't worth very much.

His entire existence until the family settled in Beaumont followed this routine. Along with a constant feeling of loneliness and worthlessness as a child, moving from one town to another with the circus, Harry James had few friends of his own age. His only companions were his fellow performers, most of whom were many years his senior. He never went past the eighth grade in school and was ashamed of his lack of education for years to come, although he certainly wasn't devoid of intelligence. Among other things, his success in his early twenties in organizing and putting together a successful orchestra and maintaining its prominence certainly proved that fact.

As the years progressed, however, Harry James believed the only way he could make a real connection with people was through his trumpet. His shyness and lack of education made him reluctant to talk to the audience. Inwardly, without the horn, he felt inferior. He wouldn't allow people to get close to him—they might find out he was a fraud. These insecurities led to his keeping people at arm's length. He was afraid they wouldn't like what they found behind the facade.

He began drinking in his early teenage years and discovered that it made him feel better. Drinking became the defense that enabled him to relate to people a little easier, and it helped him blot out his various problems. It also made dealing with superstardom and being married to a Hollywood icon that much easier. Soon, it became an addiction and ruined his life. Before he was thirty-five years old, Harry had progressed from being a heavy drinker into a functioning alcoholic. This was the principal reason for his aloof behavior and constantly fluctuating moods. Fortunately, he was smart enough to realize that nothing must prevent him from continuing to make a substantial living through his prowess on the trumpet.

Gambling became his other addiction, with one addiction fueling the other. He became dependent on these prime examples of self abuse. He enjoyed the drama involved in gambling—It gave him a rush. Why shouldn't he gamble and lose all his money? When he lost heavily, his feelings of inferiority surfaced all over again.

Harry's pattern of behavior toward women makes one wonder if he was respectful to his mother, Maybelle. In his last years, he confided to Joe Cabot that he should have been kinder to her.[127] It appears as if he grew up not really knowing the meaning of love. More than perhaps anything else, his constant womanizing certainly reflected his deep-set insecurities.

Harry James tried to love his children, but that took too much time and effort. How could he express love for them if he rarely experienced it himself? He thought that taking care of them was Louise's or Betty's job.

As Sal Monte pointed out, the trumpet provided the means for him to attract women and gave him the money for gambling.[128] Women and keno tickets were disposable; they were merely part of a night's play. The passion with which he played the trumpet reflected the warmth and beauty that were an integral part of him, but couldn't be expressed in other ways.

His love of baseball, and later golf, and the fact that he was a celebrity gave him access to Stan Musial, Joe DiMaggio, Ted Williams, Mickey Mantle, Arnold Palmer, Jack Nicklaus, and other sports legends who were his true heroes. He developed a prized collection of their caps as mementos of his friendship with them.[129]

As soon as Harry James was successful, he felt it was time to show his father he could and would do things his own way. It was his method of rebelling—his way of saying, "I am somebody." But instead, like so many others who struggle and achieve success at a young age, excess and self-destruction become the bywords of their existence. When events in his life turned against him, he lashed out at those close to him—Louise Tobin, Betty Grable, the Montes, his musicians. He treated them as though they were singlehandedly to blame for his deep-seated problems.

If an artist has an extraordinary talent, as Harry James surely did, but during the process of growing up had neither his parents nor close friends to serve as role models, that person often has a problem treating other people with respect. In addition, with all the enormous success he achieved, he never developed any true self confidence.

Harry James was not alone in this kind of behavior. Buddy Rich grew up in vaudeville, and his life closely paralleled Harry's childhood. Unlike Harry, however, Buddy never succeeded in leading his own band despite having had several opportunities. He was a star sideman, while Harry was a superstar bandleader. This was a continuing source of great frustration to Rich.

By the winter of 1966, Buddy Rich had at last had his fill of being featured with Harry James and his Orchestra. He wanted to lead his own band once again. When he approached ICM, the talent agency, the agents told him they were certain that the agency could launch a new band that would be based upon playing the latest rock tunes with equally strong dynamics but in a jazz context.

"The Boys of Swing" had been through a lot together; Buddy Rich thought this was the right time for him to try it again with his own band. Unfortunately for Harry James, he never found a drummer he liked playing with quite as much as Buddy Rich.

From the very beginning of his new band, Buddy Rich's brash and irreverent personality grabbed the attention of young people. (Frank Sinatra once said about Buddy, "He thinks he's me.") Johnny Carson became extremely intrigued by both his playing and his cocky attitude and provided him with frequent exposure on the *Tonight Show*.

With two important back-to-back engagements, the first at the Aladdin Hotel in Vegas with Sammy Davis, Jr., which Reprise Records recorded, and an even more startling "live" album on World Pacific, recorded at the Chez in Hollywood, the Buddy Rich band made an immediate impact. Miraculously, the album from the Chez even made the *Billboard* pop chart. Buddy and Harry remained friendly, but inwardly Harry was envious of Buddy's sudden success with young people.

Dot Records had tried hard to come up with hit albums for Harry James when Buddy Rich was with the band by combining contemporary tunes played with a rock beat, as evidenced by the *Ballads and the Beat* album.

Unfortunately, this idea failed to register with record buyers. The record company's thinking was that, if Herb Alpert could come up with hit after hit, why couldn't Harry James? The times, however, were now very different. James's playing was still first rate, but to young record buyers his music represented something from a bygone era.

The arrival of the Beatles in New York to perform on the *Ed Sullivan Show* in February 1964 marked the start of a turbulent era. Disillusioned with the older generation—a distrust of anyone over the age of thirty—the so-called "baby boomer generation" questioned a meaningless war in Vietnam. Their anger at middle-class mores was transmitted by the sound of amplified guitars and thunderous drums. Brass instruments didn't fit into their music. Their songs sometimes discussed sex in songs like "Come Together" and "I Can't Get No Satisfaction," which caused the romanticism of "I Had the Craziest Dream" and "I Don't Want to Walk Without You" to sound pathetically naive. In this atmosphere of political unrest and rebellion, Harry James perpetuated his brand of swing while still trying vainly to keep up with the changing musical scene.

James's second career, starting in the late 1950s, had disproved F. Scott Fitzgerald's well-remembered cynical belief, "There are no second acts in American lives." In fact, there had been a glorious second act during which he led the greatest band he ever had. A fulfilling third act, however, was in question.

10

I Don't Want
to Walk Without You

Harry James knew that there would be life after Buddy Rich's departure. It would be difficult, however. Rich had given the band an
electrifying and unmistakably swinging definition. He appreciated having the kind of a band that jazz musicians like Erroll Garner enjoyed
coming in to catch after their own sets. In a way, the decision Harry James
faced was akin to what Benny Goodman encountered when Gene Krupa
angrily left him in March 1938. Goodman didn't come up with merely
another whirlwind; instead, he hired perhaps a more musical drummer in
the person of Dave Tough.

James did much the same thing when he hired Louis Bellson. From past
experience, he knew exactly what Bellson could do. He could play fast and
with great power, but he also had a delicate touch. Equally important, he
played for the band. Harry once again gave Louis featured numbers such
as his compositions "The Hawk Talks" and "Caxton Hall Swing" to which
he added "Apples."[1]

Ray Sims's apt comparison between the two drummers was, "Buddy was
a hoofer and Louis was a soft shoe dancer."[2] Tommy Porrello, James's lead
trumpeter from 1964 to 1968, noted: "The drummer and the first trumpeter have to lock in or the band ain't going anywhere. That band had
some of the tightest ensemble playing the world has ever seen. The time
was beautiful with both of them so I was very comfortable. Buddy put it a
little on top; Louis put it right where it was."[3]

In May 1966, a month after Buddy Rich left, Louis Bellson helped Harry James enjoy another smash engagement in New York. This time it was at the Riverboat, the nightclub in the basement of the Empire State Building where the old gambling parlor decor was designed by Oliver Smith, who designed the sets for *Hello, Dolly.*

As happened six years before, a booking on the *Ed Sullivan Show* paid for the cost of flying the band from Las Vegas. On the show, after displaying its jazz image playing Neal Hefti's "Sunday Morning," the band was paired with the McGuire Sisters, who performed a medley of eight of the band's hits.

The *Ed Sullivan Show* provided effective promotion for the gig at the Riverboat, but what also greatly contributed to the engagement's success was James's appearance on the *Tonight Show.* He had been asked several times previously to appear on Johnny Carson's show, but remained steadfast in insisting on working with his own band rather than fronting Skitch Henderson's band, despite the fact that he had great respect for the caliber of its musicians.

Doc Severinsen, the highly regarded trumpeter who became an important television personality by being the butt of Carson's jokes over his outlandish wardrobe rather than for his splendid musicianship during the twenty-five years he led the *Tonight Show* band, took over its leadership in 1967. Over the years, there have been few trumpeters who have expressed a keener appreciation for James's trumpet playing.

One night, during one of the James band's engagements at the Riverboat, Severinsen described how he and James "drank dinner." As he recalled, "He was putting away a lot of vodka martinis, and I was thinking, how the hell's this guy going to get up and play a trumpet? He got up on the stand to play his horn, absolutely no warmup ... all of a sudden he came up to a long break, an eight-bar break ... he just took that horn and rotated it like a radar machine around the room until he picked up where I was sitting, and he locked onto me. Then he just started playing the most incredible trumpet. It wasn't jazz, it wasn't swing, it wasn't classical—it was just trumpet. It was one trumpet player to another—his way of saying, 'I've still got it, haven't I!' He was doing it for me. I was honored, and it was electrifying."[4]

Reflecting further on Harry James's artistry, Severinson said, "There literally wasn't anything that he couldn't do on a trumpet. Nothing was hard for Harry. He developed his lazy kind of romantic style. He never played up on the beat. He was always right smack down on the bottom of the beat in that kind of a Texas style, ya know, like the blues. He came by it honestly. He played Texas blues. And don't forget that in the early forties he had a band that sounded more black than it did white. Listen to the bottom of his arrangements. They had a rolling beat that Harry got from listening to

Basie and Lunceford. People also forget that he got a lot of people interested in good music when he played a ballad—and, by God, he played a
ballad. He might have played in a schmaltzy style, but he always played
good and clean trumpet."

In his continuing quest to reinvent Harry James as a top-selling recording
artist, Randy Wood, the president of Dot Records, assigned Jimmy Haskell
to write and conduct the arrangements for *Harry James and His Western
Friends*.[5] Recorded only a few weeks after a "live" date at the Riverboat,
Western Friends was an attempt to cash in on the country and western
craze that really began when Eddy Arnold first took the "Nashville Sound"
to Carnegie Hall and other major city concert halls in 1965. In fact, James
recorded Arnold's hit record of the time, "Make the World Go Away," in
this album. Only the rhythm section from the band—Perciful, Kelly, and
Bellson—was used to go along with three guitarists and a big band of studio musicians (on a few tunes) plus strings. One of the guitarists was the
studio musician Glen Campbell, who would soon become an important
pop country recording star in his own right, beginning with his hit "By the
Time I Get to Phoenix."

Harry James fit in perfectly with Haskell's musical settings, displaying
some of his warmest and most passionate playing, mostly in the lower register. The sentiments he expressed were reminiscent of his ballad renditions from the war years. The entire album was recorded in two days without any overdubbing, which was then becoming de rigeur in recording.
This was despite the fact that Harry had initially been dead-set against
doing a country and western album. ("Jimmy, my mother told me that I'd
have to have one day like this.")[6]

On completing the sessions he realized just how well the music worked.
In reality, it wasn't that much different from what he had listened to while
growing up in the South. A few weeks later, Harry called Haskell to see if
he could use his basic charts on two tunes from *Western Friends* for the
band's forthcoming engagement at the Flamingo. Haskell was terribly
flattered; it was like having Harry James's stamp of approval.

By this time, James was trying hard to incorporate whatever was happening in pop music into the band's repertoire, although the Ernie Wilkins
charts were still being played frequently. For him to feature hit contemporary tunes like "The 'In' Crowd," "Goin' Out of My Head," "A Taste of
Honey," or "A Walk on the Wild Side," worked at a Watusi tempo for dance
dates, but in concert performances these renditions came across as ill-con-
ceived attempts to appear hip.

Harry James was now over fifty years old and beginning to show it. His
once slim waist had long since expanded, and his dark brown hair was

turning white, which caused him to dye his hair reddish brown. Perhaps that's the reason why, for a time, he wore his hair long, slightly over his ears in the fashion of young people. The results of years of heavy drinking had also begun to show on his face.

He still retained his sex appeal, though. He had been involved for a few years in a passionate relationship with Joan Boyd, a tall blonde showgirl from the Flamingo chorus line. On several occasions, he brought Boyd with him to Reno and Lake Tahoe.[7] He also flew her to various cities to join him when the band was on the road, and she would ride on the bus. Trumpeter Tony Scodwell recalled, "I roomed next to them once in Tahoe. All I heard was—scream! Ba-da-boom-scream! Ba-da-boom."[8]

After eight months with the James band, Louis Bellson left to return to work with his wife, Pearl Bailey, in her popular nightclub act. After trying approximately ten drummers, some of whom lasted only one night, James finally made the right choice by hiring "Sonny" Payne, Basie's drummer for most of the previous decade. (In hiring trumpet players, he once told Tommy Porello, "By the time they get here, I want them to know how to play. I'm not running a training camp." Once again baseball was his metaphor.)

Sonny Payne supplied a pronounced snap to the band. Joe Riggs noted, "it was a swing element. When you think of Basie's band, you think of a certain type of feel. The James band had that similar kind of feel when Sonny joined us."

The late bassist Bob Stone, who had been on the band earlier and substituted for years afterward, worked alongside quite a few drummers. Evaluating Payne's playing, Stone remarked, "He grooved with the band, and that would have been my dream when I was with the band. He knew how to get the right sound and played so loose."[9]

Having watched Sonny Payne play with the James band during a gig at Caesar's Palace in late 1968, which was headlined by Frank Sinatra, I noticed how his presence differed from that of Buddy Rich, Louis Bellson, and other drummers I had seen with the band. He was equally strong, but, in addition to his flashiness, there was an undercurrent in his playing.

This engagement at Caesar's Palace was the first time since recording "Castle Rock" and "Deep Night" for Columbia in 1951 that James and Sinatra had worked together. At that time, I flew from New York to Las Vegas ostensibly to meet Peggy Lee, a new client. As a bonus, I was able to see Sinatra and the James band perform twice.

Previously, I had been fortunate to see Frank Sinatra perform many times during the 1960s at recording sessions, nightclubs, and in concert. Sinatra's appearance with Harry James served to underscore how Sinatra was, more than anything else, the definitive swing band singer. His previous excursions with Count Basie and Duke Ellington were calculated attempts to prove his mettle as a jazz singer. But, as Pete Hamill observed, "As an artist, Sinatra had only one subject: loneliness." There was an obvious musical rapport onstage between the two veterans, which was apparent in the way the James band played Sinatra's standard arrangements as well as his more contemporary material such as "Little Green Apples" and "Cycles."

Frank Sinatra introduced "All or Nothing at All" as "the song brought to me by this wonderful man when I was a little boy back when I was his band singer." The arrangement of the tune wasn't the original by Jack Mathias but rather a driving version written by Nelson Riddle that was a study in modern swing.

Frank Sinatra and Harry James didn't perform together again until they appeared on the imaginative John Denver special that was aired on ABC March 29, 1976; there was no dialogue in the entire show as the musical presentation segued from one song to another. They reprised "All or Nothing at All," and Harry James contributed a cutdown version of the "Two O'Clock Jump."

The trumpeter also performed the latter instrumental in the NBC special taped in December 1979 (aired in February 1980) that was a salute to Frank Sinatra on his fortieth anniversary in show business. Leaning into the microphone, James, wearing a garish red-and-black-striped dinner jacket, introduced the number by saying, "Remember this one, Frank, from the Paramount?" As the band broke into the famous rideout chorus, the camera caught Sinatra rocking to the beat of the music. Following this number, Harry James brought on Red Skelton and mentioned their old routine at the Shea Theater in Buffalo. The television camera caught Frank Sinatra wearing a broad grin of recognition.

The musical scene in Las Vegas and in the Reno–Lake Tahoe area was undergoing its own changes. Big bands had definitely become an endangered species. On New Year's Eve 1967, a national radio broadcast from Harrah's in Lake Tahoe marked the end of the James band's term deal. In 1968, the band also left the Flamingo for the Frontier Hotel. For Harry James to have lasted at one hotel for nine years—a lifetime in Las Vegas terms, where talent was so disposable—was an extraordinary feat.

As Joe Riggs pointed out: "I don't think it was a case of the band not drawing. The entertainment directors were starting to change, and they had other ideas. They didn't have any understanding of what the band was about. Also, some of the young people who came into the hotel didn't know who Harry James was."[10]

Within a few years, most, if not all, of the lounges were dismantled. Slot machines, keno parlors, and sports books took their place. This was one of several aftermaths resulting from the corporate takeover of Nevada gaming. With the closing of the lounges, Harry James could no longer delay paying off his gambling debts to the hotels where he had been working. Once again, he approached Betty Grable to help him out of his financial problems. Even though they had been divorced for several years, they had remained close friends. Some said they were better friends than when they were married. Whenever she would come into the Driftwood Lounge to see Harry, he would always introduce her in the audience, and she would beam.

It has been reported that in the late 1960s James wrote Betty I.O.U.s totaling over one million dollars. Their daughter Vicki acknowledged that James did borrow money from her mother during this period to pay off various gambling debts. These loans were never repaid.

Tino Barzie recalled, "Harry was tough on her, there's no question about that. It was always when Harry would get drunk. He was constantly borrowing money, not big money but that was always the basis for their arguments. Then Betty, in return, would go over and gamble herself, shooting craps. She wasn't a good gambler. She was doing it to spite him."[11]

Betty Grable had begun a new and formidable stage career as a result of establishing herself as a box office draw in *Hello, Dolly*. Her manager at the time, Kevin Pines, had the fantasy of re-teaming her with Dan Dailey in the movie version at 20th Century Fox.[12] They were the right age for the roles and had definitely exhibited a chemistry together on-screen, something that the ill-matched combination of Barbra Streisand and Walter Matthau never achieved. The opportunity of casting Barbra Streisand outweighed the idea of bringing back the one-time queen of the lot. The film ultimately wound up a costly failure.

Betty Grable had been living for some time with Bob Remick, a gypsy in the *Dolly* company, who was born two months before she married Harry James. Despite the difference in their ages, Remick was totally devoted to her. What's more, Harry James and Remick even struck up an almost instant rapport.[13]

After *Hello, Dolly*, Betty Grable starred on the road in a production of *Guys and Dolls*, playing Adelaide. Years before, Sam Goldwyn had met with her twice about starring in the screen version, but a sudden injury to her dog had prevented Betty from attending their third meeting. That clinched it. The role instead went to Vivian Blaine, who had originated it on Broadway.[14]

Eight months later, in 1969, Betty Grable went to Europe for the first time to star in the new musical *Belle Starr* (the real *Outlaw Queen*) in

Glasgow and London. The music and lyrics were by Steve Allen. England loved Betty, if not the show.[15]

Michael Leavitt, the Chicago hairdresser Betty referred to as "Mikey," remained her confidante until she died. Michael agrees, "Harry was the only man she ever loved. (After the divorce, Betty Grable told her daughter Jessica, 'There will never be anyone else for me but your father.') I also think she needed a strong man. She had to have someone around her."[16]

Bob Osborne, the host of Turner Classic Movies and the New York-based columnist for the *Hollywood Reporter*, spent time with Betty Grable in Las Vegas after she had divorced Harry James. She freely discussed her movie career with him. "Betty had great energy and was always best on the first take. She told me once her only real regret was that she never got to do a film with a really important leading man. She never worked with Fred Astaire or Gene Kelly.... Dan Dailey was a great talent, but he wasn't the star Betty was.

"There wasn't a photograph in her house depicting anything from her career except one of her with Louis Armstrong that was taken when he came backstage to see her in *Hello, Dolly*. There wasn't a speck of memorabilia." [When I visited Vicki's lovely home in Orange County, strangely enough I noticed only one picture of her parents with her grandparents among the multitude of photographs on display.] "When Betty took me on a tour of the house, I noticed some plastic swans in the pool. She said, 'If I'd been with MGM, of course, there would be real swans!'"[17]

On January 8, 1968, two months short of his fifty-second birthday, Harry married his companion of the last few years, Joan Boyd, who was twenty-seven.[18] The wedding took place at Harold's Club in Reno. The band played for the reception, and several of Duke Ellington's musicians (his band was working in Reno) delightedly sat in. Among them were trumpeters Mercer Ellington and "Cootie" Williams and tenor saxophonist Paul Gonsalves. Harry got so excited seeing "Cootie" again that he got up and played alongside him and Mercer.[19]

A son, Michael Everette Anthony, was born to Joan and Harry on July 18, 1968. Harry was proud to have a new male heir. When I spent a Sunday afternoon with Pee Wee and Vi Monte at Caesar's Palace during the James band's Thanksgiving week engagement with Frank Sinatra, Pee Wee was enthusiastic about how Harry's life had changed. "He has a new family. He goes home every night. He's a much different guy," he related.

Their wedded bliss didn't last, however. A year later, the James-Boyd union was history. Joan tried vainly for a large settlement; instead she wound up getting a trust fund for Michael once he turned twenty-one. To protect his assets, Harry had the First Interstate Bank of Las Vegas act as executor of his will. Today, Michael receives 50 percent of all the royalties from Harry James's estate, with Vicki and Jessica sharing the other half.

With the closing of the Reno and Tahoe lounges (Harold's Club finally terminated Harry James at the end of 1970), the James band suddenly became more visible on one nighters across the country. Bill Richard, who had become one of the partners in APA (Agency for the Performing Arts) on the demise of MCA, booked the band during the 1960s. After that, Willard Alexander, the architect of the big band era, took over as the agency handling the band. It was Willard who, back in 1939, had initially warned Harry against accepting Benny Goodman's one-sided offer of financial assistance when he started his band.

Years ago, I dubbed Richy Barz "The Agent Superior" for precisely that reason. He did much of the booking for Willard Alexander, Inc., in those years. As Barz explained, "The (James) band wasn't that easy a sale, although it was easier than Woody Herman or Buddy Rich because it was a dance band. Pee Wee, however, would always fight you about mileage. My standard line was, 'Pee Wee, we can't build a ballroom every 250 miles.' Ya know, sometimes you gotta go 325 miles. Other days you only go 100 miles. Most of the buyers bought Harry year after year because the band did business for them. At the end, Harry was still grossing about $25,000 a week on the road." Harry was quoted as saying, "Touring is quite easy now compared to what it used to be what with much better highways and flying."[20]

Pee Wee Monte designed a tour that would travel across the South during the winter months to avoid the bad weather, usually winding up in south Florida in mid-March so Harry could spend time with the Cardinals during their annual spring training stint in St. Petersburg. The annual tour through the Midwest and into the East was generally scheduled during the summer months.

Richy Barz dealt almost exclusively with Pee Wee Monte, "But I always felt Harry was on top of things. He was screaming and yelling at Pee Wee, but we knew it was Pee Wee who kept him alive and in business. Of course, Harry was Pee Wee's meal ticket. Harry referred to me as either 'his fucking agent' or 'the good guy from Willard's office,' depending on how the tour was going."

At the end of various dates he serviced, Barz often found Harry James drunk. One of the young trumpeters in the band once told him, "Man, I don't know how this guy plays drinking as much as he does, but he sounds better at the end of the night."

"They couldn't understand it," the agent remembered, "and he might even play 'Trumpet Blues' and 'Cantabile,' which were really hard tunes to play." These quotes echoed Herb Alpert's statement: "Harry was the only musician I ever knew who could play well when he was drunk."[21]

One of the people who always looked forward to seeing Harry James on tour in the Deep South was Harry Walker, the 1947 National League batting champion who also spent nine years as the manager of the St. Louis Cardinals, the Pittsburgh Pirates, and the Houston Expos. Originally, George Simon had introduced him to Harry. During his playing and managerial career, the two Harrys would get together two or three times during the baseball season and years later in Las Vegas and at La Costa, the resort near Del Mar. "Whenever he'd come through the Birmingham (Alabama) area he'd stop here, bring three or four of his boys out; we'd have a barbeque for 'em and then go and watch 'em play. They put on a heck of a show," Walker related.[22]

The National League veteran had a great affection for Harry James but said, "He lived the life a normal man lives in ninety years. That's the fast lane. I didn't know anything except that he drank a little more than he should, but he was never drunk when I was with him. That's a profession I'd never want to be in."

I asked Harry Walker what were the things he liked about Harry. He replied, "I guess we both liked baseball, we both were southerners, and we both liked to play golf. There was nothing else we talked about."

Another southerner Harry James enjoyed spending time with was Phil Harris, who was twelve years his senior. Harris had been Jack Benny's bandleader for many years on his popular radio show. Fortunately for Harris, Benny had encouraged him to buy southern California real estate in the 1940s. By the mid-1950s, after having dispensed with his band, he registered as a radio and television personality (he also starred in eight films including *Wabash Avenue* with Betty Grable) and recording artist, and worked only when he felt like it.

Phil Harris and his wife, the late Alice Faye, also a leading lady in movie musicals, formed a close relationship with the Jameses. Alice Faye remembered, "We were all great friends. Everybody expected Betty and me to have a feud because Betty took over from me as 'The Blonde' at Fox, just as Marilyn Monroe replaced her. The opposite happened. We were very friendly, but, you know, we never were over at each other's house for dinner. It's remarkable."[23]

Harry James and Phil Harris shared many of the same experiences growing up. Harris's father, Harry (whom he called "George"), was a clarinetist and conductor with a tab show. Phil played the drums in the show. The fathers' and sons' paths crossed on tour in the South, and they became friendly.

Harry James admired Phil Harris's warmth and earthiness. Phil was also naturally funny. He was everything Harry James wished he was. Don Cherry, who has been both a professional singer and golf player, and is best remembered for his "Band of Gold" record, believes Phil and Harry's friendship was based on the fact that they were complete opposites. As Cherry observed, "Phil was so outgoing and easy to get to, and Harry was just so closed."[24]

Phil Harris also enjoyed drinking equally as much as Harry did and also loved to play golf and keno. Unlike Harry, however, Phil had a limit; if he lost more than $5,000, he stopped playing for the night. They began working together in the main room at the Frontier Hotel after Phil Harris's long run at the Desert Inn. Harris had already developed a following among high rollers in Las Vegas; therefore, an offer for the two of them was forthcoming from Harrah's in Lake Tahoe. He and Harry played there, but Phil discovered that he much preferred the desert climate in Las Vegas, which was similar to his home in Rancho Mirage, California. In the early 1970s, Frank Sinatra, Jr., who had earlier alternated with Harry James at the Flamingo, joined them for about twenty more engagements at the Frontier.

As personal manager of Frank Sinatra, Jr., Tino Barzie often observed the three headliners on stage. "Most of the time, Phil and Harry had so many inside jokes going that went over the audience's head. They had so much fun doing this that the audience had fun just watching these two guys carry on. Phil and Harry loved Junior because they could make fun of him as they spun off stories about his old man. And, I must say, Junior fell right into it."[25]

The Frontier management quickly became aware that the Harris/James/Sinatra, Jr., combination delivered business and signed them to a term contract for sixteen weeks a year. Phil Harris and Harry James (occasionally working with others) were headliners at the hotel for seven years. In view of their popularity, the Frontier even paid for strings to be added to the James band, and this enhanced its performance of his many hit ballads.

Joe Bushkin, a pianist from the Swing Era, remembers that Phil Harris told him how he had tried in vain to reason with Harry James about his keno playing. "I don't know how he does it," Harris said. "I keep telling him they didn't build these joints with the winners' money."[26]

One night Phil Harris, Alice Faye, and Harry James were gambling at the Desert Inn. Harris had lost his $5,000 and was finished for the night. James had already dropped $20,000. Phil said, "Let's go." Harry said, "No, I've just started. I haven't warmed up yet."[27]

Reprising his hits—"That's What I Like about the South," "Downtown Poker Game," "The Thing," "Old Man Time," and "Smoke, Smoke, Smoke

That Cigarette"—and by merely being himself, Phil Harris charmed his audiences. He and Harry James sang and did comedy bits together. By the time they had completed several engagements together, Harry started to become comfortable on stage as the focal point of Phil's barbs, something he had learned from doing radio shows with Jack Benny, Danny Kaye, and Johnny Mercer.

"Phil was able to bring everything out in Harry on stage," added Don Cherry.[28] Joe Riggs, Jack Perciful, and Red Kelly concurred that Harry was never looser nor more relaxed than when he worked with Phil Harris.[29]

Lionel Hebert, the retired PGA player, first met Harry and Phil at the Tournament of Champions. "We used to spend a lot of time together, and I got to know Harry that way," Hebert recalled. "I would sometimes drive fifty miles to see him perform because I'm also a trumpet player. I was a fairly good local player.

"When he got on the golf course, Harry was a helluva competitor. Anybody that loves our sport, we're gonna love them. I think if Harry had started playing as a younger man, he would've been awesome because he was such a strong guy.

"To have guys like Harry, Phil Harris, and Bing Crosby show up at a tournament to play golf with us—man, let me tell you something—that meant a lot to us. I knew how to handle myself around Harry. He didn't like too much small talk."

Hebert is proud of the fact that James gave him two of his King trumpets and contends: "I might be the only guy to get him to play away from his band. We had jam sessions at the Sky Room of the Desert Inn after the Tournament of Champions and later at the Indian Wells Country Club after the Bob Hope Desert Classic. I played cornet, Harry was on trumpet, Murray Arnold was on piano, and Phil played drums," he remembered.[30]

Oddly enough, Phil Harris preferred living in his own trailer rather than in hotel rooms. He relished cooking dinner in the double-wide trailer that was parked at the rear of the stage, and personally saw to it that the food he cooked was marinated during the day to enhance its flavor. The food was prepared for Harry James, Frank Sinatra, Jr., and all the musicians to eat between and after the shows.[31] Phil's specialties were pork chops, red beans, and rice. Joe Bushkin said, "Phil would eat that jazz up, and it was great."[32]

According to trumpeter Fred Radke, "Phil used to say, 'Ya know something, I was a famous musician, too. The only difference between my band and Harry's band was Harry's band reads music.' Another time, someone was bugging him about upcoming bookings. Phil said, 'Listen, I don't know if I'll be available in six months. I don't even buy green bananas'—one-liners all the time."

Referring to the experience of playing lead trumpet behind Harry James in the trumpet section, Fred Radke said, "I sat there every night and took a lesson." He also stressed that "there was always a lot of jealousy among the trumpet players who had been on the band. Whenever you ask one, 'Were you with Harry?' if he answers, 'Yeah, that asshole,' you know he was fired. Of course, when Harry fired you, he really fired you. He would walk up to a guy and say, 'Go home. Go home to your mother. Grow up and come back when you're grown.' Another line was, 'You don't like how I do it? Get your own band.'"[33]

Bobby Arvon replaced Ernie Andrews as the band's singer in 1969. As a result of his interest in writing contemporary pop music, Harry James assigned him tunes like Blood, Sweat and Tears' "Spinning Wheel" and told him, "You have a job as long as you want it." He showed his gratitude even further that summer by giving him featured billing at the Frontier.

After he became a member of the James band, Sonny Payne remembered Bobby Arvon from a date when he had sung a few tunes with the Count Basie band at the Ritz Ballroom in Bridgeport, Connecticut. Thereafter, Payne and Arvon began spending time off stage with Harry James.

Arvon recalls, "Sometimes, Harry and Sonny began drinking, and they would get into battles over small things that would eventually get to the 'I'm gonna quit' and 'I'm gonna fire you' stage. But they had this real strong bond because I never saw anything serious develop from that."[34]

(Right after Bobby Arvon left the band, however, Sonny Payne and Harry James had a serious confrontation that led to Sonny's joining a small group in Las Vegas; eventually he went back to Basie. In line with Yogi Berra's famous pronouncement, "It ain't over 'til it's over," he later returned to the James band.)

Even though Rob Turk had left the band in 1964, Harry James remained well aware of his talents as an arranger and conductor, as well as his effectiveness as a lead trumpeter. Back in 1959, Turk had even duplicated James's solos on an album of Harry's hits that was recorded by members of the James Orchestra.

In early January 1972, James took Turk to London to conduct an English band made up of several former Ted Heath sidemen, including the trumpeters Stan Roderick and Bobby Pratt, that was playing songs associated with various trumpeters like "And the Angels Sing," "When It's Sleepy Time Down South," "When the Saints Go Marchin' in" and other warhorses. The album was released by Longine watches as a special promotion under the title of *Mr. Trumpet*.

Rob Turk remarked, "I have to tell about the human side of Harry. He found out that the recording scale was only $35 a man for a session. He wanted the guys to make some money so he said, 'Let's stretch it out to three days.' And he did—make a mistake, do the tune over. The guys in the band loved him for it."[35]

After recording one night, Harry went over to see Maynard Ferguson's band at Ronnie Scott's jazz club. "His visit was kind of fleeting," Maynard recalled.[36]

As a fourteen-year-old in Montreal, Ferguson, the son of a school principal, had been billed as "Canada's answer to Harry James." It was with Stan Kenton's band, however, that he first achieved fame for his high note pyrotechnics. He eventually hit with his own band in the early 1980s, beginning with his record of the theme from the motion picture *Rocky*.

"MF," as he is most often called, made an interesting observation about Harry James and "schmaltz": "I don't think the schmaltz that Harry got known for was done because it was commercial. That was really his romanticism coming out. Romanticism is reflected in the way I play 'Maria' [from *West Side Story*] for instance. I tend to play tunes like that the way an opera singer would if you listen to the vibrato. When Harry began playing that way, it became his trademark. Then, of course, they started talking about schmaltz. As new stylistic things came in, for awhile it was very unhip to use a vibrato, and Harry had a very wide one. If you listen to Heifitz and he's playing a gorgeous part of the Beethoven, or it could be Isaac Stern, do we call them schmaltzy? Because, you know, that left hand is really throbbing up and down, and that's called a wide vibrato.

"People loved to say he sold out when he played ballads. Hell, he just loved playing them that way. When you're playing a ballad, sometimes a lot of what you are comes out. I loved the way he played them, too."[37]

While in London, Harry James did an interview with the English jazz critic, Steve Voce. When Voce asked him if the biggest audience was for the commercial numbers he had recorded, he visibly bristled. James answered, "That would depend on for whom you're playing. If you're playing for a jazz audience, I'm pretty sure that some of the jazz things we do would be a lot more popular than 'Sleepy Lagoon,' and if we're playing at a country club or playing in Vegas, in which we have many, many types of people, then I'm sure that 'Sleepy Lagoon' would be more popular at that particular time. But I really get bugged about these people talking about commercial tunes, because to me, if you're gonna be commercial, you're gonna stand on your head and make funny noises and do idiotic things. I don't think we've ever recorded or played one tune that I didn't particularly love to play. Otherwise, I wouldn't play it."[38]

His reaction reminded me of an interview I was doing with him for a magazine piece when I dared ask his comment on why jazz reviewers con-

stantly referred to his playing as schmaltzy. I was the recipient of an equally angry barrage of words. "What are you talking about? They don't know
a god damn thing!" he exclaimed.

Frank Sinatra, Jr., has long held strong feelings about the legacy of the best
of American popular music—something he learned from his father and
that led to his own singing career and later to conducting his father's
music. Appearing on the same bill with Harry James and Phil Harris from
1972 to 1975, he was in a position to make some acute observations about
James.

The younger Sinatra remarked: "Harry had the best taste. He would hire
different orchestrators to write his music, and they changed with the
times, decade by decade. He would allow other people in the band to take
solos, not just every so often but for most of the show. When he would pick
up and play an actual number himself, it was something to look forward
to.... Harry always surrounded himself with some heavyweights: Corky
was there, Willie was there, Ray Sims was there, Buddy Rich was there.

"I have patterned my own show after him, and I've taken a great deal of
criticism because of it. It's all right for a bandleader to do that, but not a
singer. I love singing, but not all the time. I don't think anybody wants to
hear any sound all the time. When you've got a band that's got, like in my
case, twenty-one voicings in it, you've got a lot to choose from."[39]

Sinatra took great pride in relating how he got his friend Vic Foquet to
write an arrangement overnight of "Autumn Serenade" for him to sing
with the James band at the Frontier. (Harry James had recorded the song
in July 1945, but had rarely played it in recent years.) Previous to that, he
had sung duets with Phil Harris but had no songs with Harry James and
felt that this might possibly be the right piece of material for both of them.

According to Sinatra, on the night when they first performed the tune
together, Pee Wee Monte came backstage with tears in his eyes and
exclaimed, "The old man hasn't played like that in twenty-five years." He
countered with, "Of course, Pee Wee! Because all they let him play is the
15,000th [version of] the 'Two O'Clock Jump.'

"For once he had something to play that was lovely. Harry just broke my
heart with it. People stood up that night in the audience. For the rest of the
engagement we did the tune. Harry smiled at me just a little bit paternal-
ly because of the fact that he remembered once before when he had another young singer ... well, actually many young singers."

He went on to emphasize how facilely James played behind him and
other singers. "He knew what to play and what to leave out. The word is
musicianship. I asked [my dad] Sinatra once why Nelson Riddle had such
a profound effect on all his orchestras. He said, 'Nelson is the finest musi-

cian.' I thought that's an interesting comment, and it does cover about everything."

One night during one of their first engagements at the Frontier, Sinatra walked past Harry James's dressing room and heard Harry crying. "I said to him, 'You don't know me that well. You and I aren't close friends, but I wish there was something I could do to tell you how sorry I am.' "

Harry James tearfully related how he and Vi Monte had picked up his young son, Michael, at McCarran Airport and had taken him to get an ice cream cone. As happens with little boys, Michael dropped his cone. Harry scooped it up with a napkin and threw it in a waste receptacle. When Michael saw the napkin, he said, "That looks like the thing mommy uses to roll her joints." Harry was appalled and heartsick that this was the atmosphere Michael was exposed to at home with Joan Boyd. The gravity of the incident stayed with him all day. That night Sinatra saw exactly how much it had affected him. "He wept on my shoulder. I won't forget it."[40]

In 1970, Les DeMerle replaced Sonny Payne. Harry James had met him when his five-piece group played during the cocktail hour at the Riverboat. He asked him for his business card and told him, "Kid, one day I'd like to have you on the band if you're available. Let's keep in touch."[41]

Three years later, DeMerle was working for Wayne Newton in the main room of the Frontier when Pee Wee Monte asked him to join the band for an eastern tour. He replied, "I really felt that musically I should go with Harry's band and get this great experience that I needed at the time.

"There would be nights we'd be on the road, and we'd get tired. We'd be out there doing one nighters night after night on the bus. I'd look over at Harry and think, 'Man, if he can do it every night, and he's like sixty, sixty-five years old, then me in my thirties, I should have no trouble.' In a way, he was a father figure to me."

One night while playing the Peachtree Plaza in Atlanta, DeMerle saw how down he was. Corky Corcoran had left the band for the last time and was dying of cancer. "I just figured I'm going to help him out of this slump so I went up to the microphone and said, 'Ladies and gentlemen, to begin our third set of the evening we'd like to feature our wonderful drummer, Mr. Harry James.' Harry looked at me like 'What the hell are you doing?' He proceeded to sit down behind my drum set and called 'More Splooty' or one of those Ernie Wilkins blues that he loved. All of a sudden he started smiling and the people got into it. It allowed him to release that tension which, of course, playing drums allows you to do. That made him feel really good. He was happy when the band was on and when things were going well on the road, and we had some decent gigs lined up."[42]

The drummer did clinics on his own in high schools and colleges when the band was off the road as well as while it was on tour. On one such occasion in Houston, Harry James watched from the hotel bar as DeMerle worked with some student musicians in the lounge. The young musicians were playing tunes by Freddie Hubbard, Chick Corea, and Hubert Laws. Afterward, as he was packing up, James remarked, "Les, you should maybe think about doubletiming that rhythm section behind the horn passage."

"He gave me really solid criticism about what we had rehearsed, which was a kind of music that had nothing to do with big bands. He was digging it and asking about the writing. Harry let me into that very special place where, instead of that front, he would come over and blow my mind with positive feedback."

Les DeMerle finally left the band for good in 1982 to lead his own contemporary jazz group. "I could see Harry's health disintegrating, and the gigs were getting less and less."[43]

Throughout his entire career Harry James's role model was Louis Armstrong. They shared many good times together over the years and a feeling of deep mutual respect always existed between them. Shortly after Armstrong's death on July 6, 1971, George Avakian, who produced one of Louis's finest latter day recordings, *Louis Armstrong Plays W. C. Handy*, came to the viewing at the Park Avenue Armory. As he was leaving the armory weeping, an intrepid television reporter recognized him and asked him, "Did Louis resent the fact that Harry James made much more money than he did?" Completely taken aback by the inappropriateness of the question, Avakian said, "Well, you know Louis had a heart of gold. He loved Harry, and it didn't bother him at all that anybody made more money than he did. He had his place in history and had everybody's love and respect."

The next day Avakian talked to his brother, Aram, the late film editor and director. Aram had seen the interview on the news. He remarked, "You should have told him that Harry would have loved to have been Louis Armstrong."

A few months later, George Avakian ran into Harry James, who said, "I saw you on TV. What a dumb question that guy asked you. You didn't give him the right answer. You should have said, 'Harry James would have given anything to have had what Louis Armstrong had.'" Avakian related, "I told Harry that my brother had said basically the same thing. Harry said, 'Well, you should have said it. You should have been smart enough to say it.' I answered him, 'Harry, I was so shook up at the time.' Harry added, 'Don't worry about it.'"[44]

Betty Grable had received a deafening standing ovation from the studio audience at the Academy Awards in April 1972 while appearing as a presenter with Dick Haymes for the "Best Original Film Score" Oscar. The next day she was overcome with pain on the flight back to Las Vegas. She was lifted onto a luggage cart when she was unable to walk from the baggage area and then put into a cab for the ride home with Bob Remick.[45]

Three weeks later, before embarking on a tour of Australia in *No, No, Nanette*, her Las Vegas doctor strongly suggested she consult with her former physician in Los Angeles. After reporting to Dr. Robert Kositchek, Chief of Staff at St. John's Hospital in Santa Monica, she was diagnosed with lung cancer. Cyd Charisse was immediately signed to replace her.[46]

In May, Grable had an exploratory operation that indicated that the cancer had spread to her lymph glands. She was given cortisone and radium treatments for three weeks in the hospital in an attempt to halt the cancer from metastasizing.

Returning to Las Vegas, after taking more cobalt treatments, she discovered her hair was coming out and, to hide it, began wearing a wig or a turban. Her features became bloated from the medication and her voice deepened. In September, she returned to St. John's for more surgery. The malignancy had been arrested in her lungs, but had spread to her intestines. Various newspaper columnists began speculating in print about her health. She started to feel stronger shortly after returning to Las Vegas.

When Betty Grable went home, Betty Ritz came up from Acapulco to spend Thanksgiving anxious to see her old friend and stayed for a week. Grable, gesturing with her cigarette holder, spoke ironically about how her mother had suggested she use a cigarette holder when she smoked to avoid getting cancer. They tried to keep things light by remembering the old days with constant laughter.[47]

Betty Baez recalled: "One day the phone rang and Betty sort of figured it was Harry calling. She told me to answer the phone. She was right. He knew my voice. He called me 'Mohawk,' which he had called me for years because I have a high forehead and a widow's peak. That was the last time I ever talked with him."[48]

During the Christmas holidays, Betty Grable spent time gambling and seeing various shows, among them Harry James and Phil Harris's performance at the Frontier. She regretted the fact that her doctor restricted her to one martini a day.

On January 23, 1973, Grable began a lucrative four-week booking in Jacksonville, Florida, at the Alhambra Theater in *Born Yesterday*. She was so popular that the engagement was extended to eight weeks. Harry James was appearing in Jacksonville during the last part of her run. Betty went over to see him during a band rehearsal. When it was over, she informed him that her illness was terminal. He was devastated. His voice broke when he told Pee Wee Monte the news. She threw her remaining energy into the play and managed to complete the engagement.[49]

For the third time within a year, Betty Grable checked into St. John's Hospital. Her sister Marjorie, Alice Faye, Jim Bacon, June Haver, and many old friends from the Hollywood days visited her. Dorothy Lamour and Jackie Coogan were among the many people who telephoned.

The hospital's spokesman sent out a press release stating that Betty was diagnosed with a duodenal ulcer. Her condition was described as serious, and there were indications that further surgery was likely. This was followed by the column item by Joyce Haber, the influential Hollywood gossip columnist of the *Los Angeles Times*, who announced that Betty was being treated for cancer and would never leave the hospital alive.[50]

On reading this item, Charlie Price, Betty's great love from the Ted FioRito Orchestra days, called her. In the intervening years Charlie had worked as a tympanist and contractor for David Rose, the successful composer, who had also been a member of the Fio Rito band with Charlie and Betty. The two had a long conversation, which gave Grable a great lift.[51]

After several weeks of further treatment, the hospital released her. Her doctor realized that medically nothing further could be done. She returned home to Las Vegas, where Bob Remick saw immediately that he wouldn't be able to handle the required nursing care. She had to return to the hospital. Betty refused to fly back to Santa Monica, so he drove them there in a van. She was down to seventy pounds. One of the tabloids offered $5,000 for a photograph of her in the hospital.[52]

Michael Leavitt related: "When she was in the hospital at the end of her life, Harry wouldn't visit her—he had a thing about hospitals—but he talked to her constantly on the phone. He sent her some huge, long-stem roses that looked like trees, not roses. Betty said, 'They're very pretty, but I'd rather have the money he owes me.'"[53]

On July 2, 1973, just before 5:00 P.M. Betty Grable died at St. John's at the age of fifty-six.[54] Vicki, Jessica, Marjorie, Bob Remick, and Michael Leavitt were at her bedside. Harry had opened the night before at Disneyland. Several members of the media approached him for a statement, but he avoided them.

Three days later her funeral was held at All Saints Episcopal Church in Beverly Hills. Among the 600 people who attended were Mitzi Gaynor, Dorothy Lamour, Alice Faye, Dan Dailey, Robert Wagner, Johnny Ray, Caesar Romero, June Haver, and Hugh O'Brien.[55] Bob Osborne noticed that Harry insisted that Bob Remick be seated with the family.[56]

Betty's favorite flower, red carnations, were everywhere in the church. The casket was closed. The organist highlighted Harry and Betty's song, "I Had the Craziest Dream," which had been introduced in *Springtime in the*

Rockies. Harry looked wan as he stared straight ahead during the entire service. Betty's minister from Las Vegas remarked, "Betty Grable was one of the most popular women who ever lived on this earth."[57]

As Harry James was departing from the church to an awaiting car, he remarked to Marjorie, "You know, today is our thirtieth wedding anniversary." A few days later he told the press, "People who had known her and hadn't seen her in over twenty years came to pay their respects. Grooms from the racetracks, little people from the studios—they were all there. It takes a very special person, a lady in the true sense, to inspire that."

Betty was buried in a crypt in the Inglewood Memorial Park in south Los Angeles. It was marked by a simple brass plaque, "Betty Grable 1916–1973."[58]

Her Las Vegas home was sold for $125,000 to the Tropicana Hotel Corporation to pay off her huge medical bills as well as an IRS debt and estate taxes. Other than a brown Mercedes sedan, some costumes, and household possessions, there was reportedly less than $50,000 in cash and stocks.[59] Her own gambling addiction plus Harry James's heavy losses had squandered the millions she had made during her long career.

Betty Grable never considered herself a real talent. When the *Harvard Lampoon* had named her "The Worst Actress of the Year," she had sent a return wire, "You're so right." Nevertheless, she had a lively and appealing screen personality. On film, she possessed a certain wholesomeness, but in addition she was also a very sexy woman. Her wartime poster was an inspiration to millions of GIs as they valiantly fought in World War II.

Just as he changed markedly after marrying Betty Grable, most people believe Harry James was never the same after her death. His reckless gambling and insatiable quest for women remained unabated. He realized he had blown a magnificent career and a wonderful marriage. The band still grossed about a million dollars a year, but it meant nothing.

"Traces" was a ballad Harry James always played with tremendous feeling. Rob Turk wrote the plaintive arrangement. The lyrics reminded him of Betty, and he stopped playing it because it became too painful for him. To compound that, he was still confronted on an almost nightly basis by someone who would yell out, "How's Betty?" Sometimes he would get so infuriated that he would grab the microphone and yell out, "She's dead!"[60]

According to baritone saxophonist Beverly Dahlke, Pee Wee Monte remarked that "between Harry and Betty, they had gambled away twenty-four million dollars."[61] Pee Wee Monte had saved his money and invested wisely; his client was still gambling, seriously in debt, and had to continue working. Several musicians pointed out, however, that, although he was financially independent of him, Pee Wee would jump whenever Harry wanted something.

Harry kept borrowing money from Pee Wee. As Pee Wee confided to both Beverly Dahlke and her husband, baritone saxophonist Greg Smith, "If I don't take the money, he's going to gamble it away." Sometimes he would say to him, "Here's some money from such and such a date that you didn't know about."

The one-nighter tours continued. Tenor saxophonist Ed Easton, who joined the band for the first time in 1972 and was promptly dubbed "Madman" by James because he was a disciple of John Coltrane, remembered doing forty-nine one nighters in a row. He quipped, "When I was off the road, I was walking with my wife downtown in Reno. We passed a Greyhound bus. I almost got on it."[62]

In Harry James's final decade, the band was booked on college and high school dates, at country clubs, on various cruise ships, periodic Nevada gigs, in ballrooms, jazz concerts, at a state dinner at the White House given by President Gerald Ford, at Ronald Reagan's second inaugural, plus concert tours of Brazil and Argentina as well as England. No record company, however, wanted to record Harry James any longer. Why should they? Big band records didn't sell, and Harry James had long since ceased making hit records. He was on a hopeless treadmill toward becoming a nostalgia act— the end of the road for any self-respecting, creative artist.

A perfect example of the direction his career had taken is illustrated by his engagement at the MGM Grand Lounge in Las Vegas beginning on March 22, 1975. As Bill Willard of *Variety* observed in reviewing a bill combining Harry James with Fabian and Kirby Stone (once the leader of the Kirby Stone Four): "Harry James is definitely in tune with his time, pouring out the trumpet solos and having his band supply the heavy sounds prior to Fabian's period. James was, and still is, an authentic purveyor of all these ballads and swing tunes of yore, and quite a draw for middle-aged folk. Corky Corcoran still blows the same old tenor sax choruses."[63]

Another example was the community concert tour he did with Phyllis Diller and the Mills Brothers. It is interesting to note that Phyllis Diller has been a pianist longer than she has been a comedienne and is also a longtime jazz fan. I asked her how it felt to tour with Harry James. "You know me. I like to have happy people around me. It was obvious Harry was very unhappy at the time because he was drinking heavily. He kept the door to his dressing room closed. It seemed like he didn't want to see anybody."[64]

In October 1974, Frank Sinatra, Jr., was a guest with Harry James on *Swing*, a thirty-minute pilot for a syndicated show aired on CBS stations. It was produced by Jerry Frank and executive produced by Pierre Cossette, Harry's former MCA agent.

Jerry Frank remembered, "I went down to Disneyland to see what Harry looked like and to see if he could still play because it had been over ten years since I had seen him in Vegas. I figured he would have a bunch of ninety-year-old musicians, and I thought the band would consist of six or seven pieces. When I got there, the dance floor was crowded. As I got close to the bandstand, out came this moist sound. Harry played a wet trumpet. It was there, and I could hear it. There he is standing there dressed nice, and I'm looking at the band, and they're all kids. This was a band that was choreographed and in motion. That made it even better for me. The charts were great, and so were the musicians.

"I moved around to the back where you could see behind the stage. Harry would disappear. I watched him take a paper bag down from a shelf and drink something. He was only gone for less than a minute, and then he went back on stage to finish the number. I went backstage to talk to him before he reached for the bag again. I introduced myself and explained I was doing this pilot for a big band show. He said, 'Wait a minute, talk to this fellow. He gave me Pee Wee's phone number.'

"When I spoke to Pee Wee, he said, 'Harry wants to bring his band.' I told him I couldn't afford that. Next thing I know Harry is on the phone. One thing led to another, and I agreed to use his band.

"Harry showed up on time. I said, 'Harry, there are three things I want you to do. Number one: the kids, the singers, I want to carve out a segment where they talk to you.' 'That's fine,' he said. I continued, 'I want to do a segment where you pay tribute to the big bands.' 'That's easy,' he said. And number three, I want you to dance with one of the singers. He said, 'I'll never do that.' I figured two out of three wasn't bad, so I let it go.

"I think we made him feel comfortable. He was so easy. When we started to shoot the 'Two O'Clock Jump,' I told one young blonde, 'You grab Harry. He won't refuse you if he sees people dancing.' She yanked him out in the middle of the floor, and he danced with her."[65]

When I watched a tape of this show, I noticed the high energy level with which Harry James conducted himself. In the final jitterbug scene, I immediately remembered a similar scene in which he had equated himself well thirty-one years beforehand dancing with Nancy Walker in *Best Foot Forward*. Despite the passing of the years, he remained a loose and agile dancer.

For many years, the James band hadn't played in the East during the summer jazz festival season. George Wein, long established as the leading producer of jazz festivals, began booking Harry James two years after his Newport Jazz Festival moved to New York. On July 2, 1974, a Carnegie Hall concert was billed as "Lionel Hampton Presents" (Lionel Hampton) Teddy Wilson, Milt Hinton, and Buddy Rich (during an interval when he was between bands) along with the James band. This was followed by a Roseland dance date two days later during which the bands of Sy Oliver and Tito Puente also appeared. "The Trumpet and the Drum" was the title of the concert with the James and Rich bands in Carnegie Hall, preceded by the Ruby Braff/George Barnes Quartet on June 29, 1975; Rich sat in with James and played spectacularly on the last few numbers to close the concert.[66]

At the Roseland date, Harry James approached the critic Dan Morgenstern to inquire about Miles Davis's health. "He seemed very concerned about him," Dan recalled. Miles was then going through a debilitating period of cocaine addiction that preceded his re-emergence a few years later playing contemporary jazz.[67]

For a Newport Jazz Festival date on July 1, 1978, in Saratoga, New York, George Wein booked the James band along with those of Stan Kenton, Count Basie, and Woody Herman. Kenton had been seriously ill as a result of a stroke and had only recently returned to the road. His young men delivered a thrilling set. When the James band came on right after them James remarked candidly to the audience, "The band of the day just played. We can all go home."[68]

Harry James's accolade to Stan Kenton ran contrary to his often expressed opinion that Kenton had helped bring about the demise of dance bands because he played concert music. Audree Coke Kenton, Kenton's widow, who continues to skillfully run his Creative World company, told me, "During his illness, of all the bandleaders, Harry was on the telephone the most. He was concerned about Stanley's health. He'd usually call about three o'clock in the morning, and he often sounded as if he was drunk, but he was simply calling to inquire about him. I thought that was extraordinarily kind." Kenton died on August 25, 1979.[69]

George Wein distinctly recalled that his first real impression of Harry James was not musical but rather something he said. "When I was very young and was just becoming interested in jazz," recalled Wein, "I remember when Harry said he wasn't deserving of winning the *Down Beat* award, but that Louis should have won it. It was only a little thing, about two inches in a column. That stuck with me."

The veteran jazz promoter continued: "I always wanted to play Harry at Newport, but because he had been a more commercial name and had more work available and his price was higher, we couldn't get him. I always thought Harry was totally underrated as a swing band. Also, I always respected him as a jazz trumpet player.... When he went into that Basie groove, his band played the hell out of those arrangements. That was a cooking band.[70]

"You know, some people like to deprecate anything that's pretty and beautiful. Harry played that romantic way, and people remembered it; it was the sound of a whole era. As much as I'm a jazz purist, I also love nice music.... When he played 'Sing, Sing, Sing,' when he played 'Just a Mood,' that was Harry James, too. Harry was a personality. He knew how to be part of showbiz. We don't have any personalities now—I wish we had one."[71]

Harry James's fervent interest in baseball never ceased. In addition to spending time in Florida with the Cardinals during spring training, he still would usually get to St. Louis during the course of the season and also watch the team play on the road. In Las Vegas, he saw former players like Stan Musial, Red Schoendienst, and Harry Walker. He frequently wore the Cardinal jacket Musial had given him.

It was always a pleasure for me to see Harry—not just because I appreciated his music so much, but because we would talk about the Cardinals—my favorite team, too. He usually seemed to have a certain insight into why the team might not be playing up to its potential and would often quote the current manager or a prominent player to explain what was really going on. His daughter Jessica believes his enthusiasm about talking about his favorite team was based on the fact that "it was something that was nonthreatening to him."[72]

One afternoon Marty Marion, formerly known as "Mr. Shortstop" when he played for the Cardinals and who later managed the team, encountered James in the stadium club wearing his Cardinal jacket and looking ragged. At the time, Marion ran the stadium club for the Cardinals. He recalled, "Harry looked like he'd been up all night. I asked him, 'Where have you been? You look tired.' James said, 'Marty, can you cook me a steak right away?' That took care of things. He suddenly started looking a lot better."[73]

Singer Stephenie Caravella spent two periods with the James band, the first from 1974 to 1977. She had sung with Doc Severinson's band and later left James to work in dancer Juliet Prowse's nightclub act. Today, the Glendale "supermom," the mother of three, still fills in on occasion with the Harry James Orchestra under the direction of Art Depew.

Caravella can never forget how she started working for Harry James. "Pee Wee called me and told me he needed to have me come down and see the band that night at Disneyland. I went down there in the car with my best friend, Doc's daughter, Nancy. I went backstage, and Harry said to me, 'Can you sing?' I said to him, 'Can you play?'

"I listened to the band at Carnation Plaza for about an hour. Harry glanced over at me and said, 'C'mon up here and sing!' I told him I wasn't even warmed up. He handed me what he called his menu. It was a list of all the songs the band played. We did 'What Are You Doing the Rest of Your Life?' I was so embarrassed appearing on stage dressed in jeans and a T-shirt. At the end of the song, Harry said, 'You're hired.' " He immediately began calling her "Stevie."

She started with three songs: "I'm Beginning to See the Light," "What Are You Doing the Rest of Your Life?," and "Embraceable You." The lyrics were left on the piano. After three nights, James told her to sing "That Old Black Magic," but he had removed the sheet music from sight. This was the start of an often bantering relationship between them.

"He taught me all about singing with a band. It's a whole different way of phrasing and feeling the songs. He used to tell me that when Frank Sinatra was the band singer he showed Frank how to phrase with the trumpet section.

"He often talked about Betty—the things they did, the places they worked. He told me that singing with a band was no life for me, saying that I should be married and have kids.

"I asked him about why he felt he had messed up his marriage. He said that he never really understood why he played around. 'After you do it, you always hate yourself. But why do I do it—it seems like fun.' He often said, 'Stevie, you make sure you don't make the mistakes I made.'"[74]

When Stephenie left the band, Jeannie Thomas took over as the band vocalist. "Harry drew the best out of me, and he was generous in spirit— very supportive and very caring." She saw how the rapidly changing musical scene and the continuing retreat from elegance affected him. "I remember his saying, 'Whatever happened to pretty?'"[75]

Girl singers had been a staple of dance bands almost from the beginning, but female baritone saxophonists definitely weren't. Beverly Dahlke was perhaps the first one to occupy that chair on a previously all-male band during the six months she spent on the band in 1976. *People* magazine was so taken by the novelty of it that a "Lookout" feature story on her was published that led to a *Johnny Carson Show* appearance on which she played with the Buddy Rich band.[76] (Of course, Beverly Dahlke was not the first female musician Harry had hired; Corky Hale had been a member of the James band over twenty years before that.)

Beverly Dahlke's first night as a member of the James band was difficult. "I thought, what did I get myself into? That probably was the worst night. Harry was so drunk because he had been at Del Mar, and he had lost his butt. He could barely play. I was so young, but I just thought this is ridiculous—I don't want to do this, but as the week went along he got much better. There were shades of what he was really like in his heyday because he really sounded wonderful some nights. His breathing technique was what he taught all the brass players. He said that he had learned it from his mother. He would school a lot of the trumpet players and the trombones, too, because they were young guys.

"But I really didn't feel anything from him as far as sex.... You know, coming on to me. It was more like you were his daughter or something. He had a real control thing, though. While I was playing 'Sweet Georgia Brown,' he would say, 'Sounds like you've got a real buzzy reed on there tonight.' He was trying to get me to react."[77]

In 1977, Pee Wee Monte made a lucrative offer to Sam Firmature to return as the replacement for Corky Corcoran, who had replaced him fifteen years earlier. Corky had been diagnosed with cancer again after previously having left earlier for surgery. He returned to Tacoma, Washington, where he died on October 3, 1979.

Firmature's first date back with the band was at the Playboy Mansion on Hugh Hefner's birthday, where the band plus Mel Tormé entertained. He was surprised at how James had aged and was appalled at his appearance. That day Harry wore a light blue sport jacket with the stitching prominently showing on both the lapels and cuffs. "It had the look of a J. C. Penney jacket," as Firmature recalled. He was also wearing a navy blue necktie that was rolled over the knot without being tied, a fashion he favored for several years hence. (Apparently one reason he did this was to avoid buttoning the top button of his shirt; his neck would bulge while he was playing.) Here was a performer who had always taken great pride in his physical appearance and had once cut a dashing figure in custom-tailored clothes; it was obvious to Sam Firmature that he was working for a fading star.

In the weeks ahead, Sam Firmature and Harry James renewed their old friendship with long intimate talks on the bus. "I remember one conversation in particular. He told me how he still loved Betty, how much he missed her, and how he dreamed of her every night, how proud he was of his children, how lucky he had been in his life, and how he wished the same for all of his children. Harry was having a bout of melancholia. I thought immediately of the German philosopher Arthur Schoepenhauer, who said, 'The more intelligent a man is, the more pain he has. The man gifted with genius suffers most of all.'"[78]

At this time, Benny Goodman solicited Harry James's cooperation in a fortieth anniversary reunion concert at Carnegie Hall, scheduled for January 16, 1978. According to the jazz critic Leonard Feather, when James got the call, he made himself unavailable for the date by saying, "That's a hell of an idea, Benny, if you can bring Ziggy and Krupa [both deceased] back."[79]

The late 1970s saw a constant stream of veterans returning to the James band. In 1978, Jay Corre rejoined the band in Georgia for a southern tour. James seemed to resent that in the intervening years Corre had changed his style of playing and was concentrating on playing in the upper register.

This was during the period when the younger musicians like Ed Easton were increasingly coming under the influence of John Coltrane, the last major innovator in jazz. Corre admired him, too, but James wanted the softer sound of a dance band tenor saxophonist.

As Jay Corre remembered, "He's listening to this new style of jazz tenor, and he doesn't understand it, much less like it. I realized this wasn't the kind of band that I had played in before. I was hurt. Harry had always meant a lot to me because of his musicianship. He started to knock me a little musically, and the guys in the band were thinking, 'Why's he doing that?' I started to doubt myself."

Corre spoke of the spiritual feeling he had enjoyed while working for Harry James in the early 1960s. "When a band's swinging together, you love everybody in the band. It's the greatest feeling in the world. For that moment, in music, you can reach one another. I knew Harry at that level, and I wouldn't want to know him on those other levels—all of that other junk."[80]

It was one of Harry James's mottos that indeed "He didn't need anyone," when the reality was that he did. By now, among other things, he needed a record deal. Except for a brief flurry by Maynard Ferguson, big bands would never become important record sellers ever again. At this opportune moment, Lincoln Mayorga, the highly regarded classical concert pianist, entered his life. He had gone to see the band at the Coconut Grove at the Ambassador Hotel on the suggestion of Fred Hall, the host of the nationally syndicated *Swing Thing* radio show. Lincoln recalled: "I was curious to see whether this swing band still had anything and whether Harry could still play. (As we have seen, this was a feeling shared by producers in various fields at this stage of his career.)

"It was such a good band," Mayorga discovered. "I went right up to Harry and said, 'I'm with Sheffield Lab, a small recording company, and I was just wondering if you had any recording commitment.' He said, 'We can talk, absolutely.' He told me to call Pee Wee Monte."[81]

The album for Sheffield Lab was recorded direct to disc, a major fad of the mid-1970s that had been embraced by Woody Herman, Benny Goodman, and Les Brown. Everything was recorded on a cylinder. Only eighteen minutes maximum could be recorded on either side of an album. Because there was no tape involved, no mistakes were allowed—otherwise the recording process had to start all over again.

There were serious recording problems, however, involved in capturing the brilliance of Harry James's trumpet. Among them was phasing, having to do with the way the left and right recording channels came together. Lincoln Mayorga went down to Disneyland to deliver the bad news that the recording had to be scratched and that new recording sessions were necessary. Surprisingly, Harry was very understanding and merely said, "No problem, we'll find a new date."

During the first session, James said he wanted to record a tune he referred to as "a nice cowboy song." He called his old Texan friend, Dave Matthews, and described it to him so that Dave could write an arrangement of what turned out to be Maurice Jarre's haunting "Lara's Theme" from *Dr. Zhivago*. As Mayorga detailed Matthews's chart, "It was a little two-beat thing that opened with a walking bass figure, some choice paraphrasing of the theme from the trumpets with Basie-like fills from Tommy Todd's piano (Jack Perciful's able replacement). Then James entered, and you forgot all about those snow-covered Russian landscapes. The ending in fact was more down-home piney woods."[82]

Mayorga noticed that the sax section was playing out of tune. He reluctantly approached James and was instructed by him to deal with the musicians directly, which he did. Five minutes later, Harry was asked if he was ready to start recording again. He replied sarcastically, "We can't go, the saxes are out of tune." He waited until James said, "Okay." "As it turned out, the reed section was still out of tune, but we never changed it," Mayorga admitted.

After that the musicians took a break. James told him: "In the future, if you've got a problem with the band, you come and see me about it. Don't go talking to my band." Mayorga noted, "He had completely forgotten about all of that. Obviously, it was the vodka talking."

The three Sheffield Lab CDs were recorded in 1976 and 1979 and were originally available as LPs. The first two were released six months apart. They were a boon to audiophiles and sold over 80,000 copies, more than Harry James had sold in years.[83]

The recording of the last of the three albums came off without any audio—or personality—problems; the intricate process in recording a big band direct to disc was at last easier for all concerned. Mayorga found Harry's trumpet playing throughout the recording sessions "amazingly consistent" despite his continuous drinking. "He had incredible stamina. He could have played it safe, especially toward the end of the record where, if you ruin it, you have to go back to the top. He'd go for a high C with all abandon, he'd just swing out and take all the risks. He never seemed to be phased by it.

"I remember a funny incident at the Palladium just before we were about to record again. There was a platinum blonde type in front of the bandstand who was of another era. She had clearly been a bobbysoxer in 1940, but here we were in 1979. She was starry-eyed; she had that look of the totally transfixed fan. I remember he came down from the bandstand and approached her with a certain kind of swagger. She was on his arm right away. In her mind, she was seventeen, but she must have been sixty."

Sonny Payne had worked New Year's Eve 1978 with the band at the MGM Grand in Las Vegas while suffering from double pneumonia. Two days later, he went to Cedars Sinai Hospital in Los Angeles, but was turned away because he had neither insurance nor credit. His mother called Harry James and explained how ill he was, emphasizing that he needed hospital treatment. The hospital demanded payment of $800 up front. Harry insisted that his medical expenses be taken care of by the band. Vi Monte drove over with a check. Sonny Payne spent just under three weeks in the intensive care unit before he died.[84]

Gregg Field replaced Sonny Payne. Shortly after he joined the band, Harry James asked him to get a larger bass drum. As Field recalled, "I had a 22" bass drum, but he wanted 24". It was like sitting behind a desk. He also wanted me to play four beats on the bass drum." (This was not surprising—it was the way Buddy Rich played.)

Gregg Field eventually left Harry James in 1980 to accept an offer from his idol, Count Basie. He observed: "Basie was 180 degrees personality-wise the opposite of Harry. He was the warmest, most inclusive guy I ever worked for. When you worked for Count Basie, he was my rhythm section mate, he was the piano player. There was never a wall up between Basie and his band. It was family."[85]

Harry James made his last film appearance in 1979, a bit part in *Sting II*, the sequel to Universal's highly successful Paul Newman-Robert Redford movie that starred Jackie Gleason and Karl Malden. Once again, he played a bandleader. Lalo Schifrin wrote the score for the film. By coincidence, Schifrin saw the James band perform at a benefit dinner in Beverly Hills around the same time: "I told Harry how much I enjoyed hearing his Ernie Wilkins arrangements," Schifrin recalled. "What's remarkable about Harry James is that he always wanted to renew himself and was curious about the new styles. He was always playing his own personality, but it was surrounded by different textures and harmonies which enlarged his vision. When he played more modern, it made me think he'd been listening to Chet Baker because of the harmonies. He'd also listened to Dizzy and Clifford Brown."[86]

All through the years, Harry James had kept in constant touch with Chris Griffin. They had recorded with Benny Goodman in 1955 and met several times during various appearances Harry made on the *Ed Sullivan Show*.

On a weekend in the late 1970s, Griffin and his wife drove to Atlantic City to take care of some personal business. The trumpeter noticed an advertisement in the *Atlantic City Press* that indicated the James band was playing nearby in Somers Point at the Mediterranean Lounge. He and his wife spent the evening watching the band and talking with James between sets. As the last set approached, Chris Griffin noticed that Harry seemed reluctant to return to the bandstand. He sat out the last set at the table and said, "This is the way to run a band." It seems obvious that seeing Chris again meant a lot to him, and he didn't want the moment to end.[87]

Another important person from the past, Larry Barnett, who for many years ran the variety department at MCA, was in Detroit on business for Chris Craft where he was then CEO. He was staying at the same hotel where the James band was playing at a dance. After dinner, he wandered into the hotel ballroom and stood near the bandstand. Harry noticed him and gestured for him to join him backstage afterward. The distinguished now-retired executive said, "He seemed very happy to see me. We hadn't seen each other in probably twenty years. I couldn't get over how much he was drinking. He didn't want me to leave. I felt very sorry for him."[88]

Sal Monte returned to work with Pee Wee after the Tijuana Brass had disbanded. He remembered meeting with Harry and Pee Wee soon after. Harry told him, "I've lost my enjoyment of blowing." Speaking of Pee Wee he said, "If it wasn't for that dude to keep me comfortable, I wouldn't be out there." Sal asked him, "What in the world would you do?" "Screw it! I'll drive a cab in Vegas," he said.[89]

In the midst of Harry's funk, Lee Guber, then the co-owner with Shelley Gross of the Valley Forge Music Fair on Long Island and the Valley Forge Musical Theatre outside Philadelphia, had come up with a novel concert package concept that appealed to James. It was called "The Big Broadcast of 1944" and was conceived in the format of an old radio show, complete with Don Wilson as the announcer. The entire show was scripted. Harry James played his hits, and Helen Forrest and Dick Haymes were brought back to perform theirs as well. (Helen left the show after an argument with Harry because once again she wanted to do her arrangement of "I Had the Craziest Dream" rather than the original version she had done with Harry. Dick departed when he was diagnosed with cancer, which later claimed his life.)[90] Several other musical participants in the show over the period of its three-year run included Hildegarde, Dennis Day, Gordon MacRae, Fran Warren, the Pied Pipers, the Mills Brothers, and the Ink Spots—all of whom had recorded hits that dated back to the mid-part of World War II.

"The Big Broadcast of 1944" did remarkable business when it debuted in Detroit at the Fisher Theatre in October 1979. It next played at the Shubert in Philadelphia in January 1980. From there, over the next year and a half, it played at several major theaters across the country. Lee Guber discussed bringing the show to Broadway, but James was dead set against it because of an aversion he had lately developed to playing New York and Los Angeles. "If you go to Broadway, it will be without the Harry James band," he said.[91]

During its second engagement at the Westbury Music Fair, my office began handling public relations for the theater. I hadn't seen Harry James in almost seven years and was delighted to be able to spend time with him again. I noticed that the years in between hadn't been kind to him. He looked worn, and he no longer had a distinguished air; his face was heavily lined and there was a gray pallor to his complexion.

I asked him to do a few interviews in New York to publicize the engagement and assured him that he would have a car at his disposal to take him to and from the city. He begged off saying, "Pedro, you know I don't want to do any interviews. Get somebody else to do them." Instead, Don Wilson and Dennis Day gladly complied.

Appearing as part of the Pied Pipers was a tall, stately blonde singer named Lynn Roberts who sang with real conviction. Harry James convinced her to join the band. She had learned a considerable amount about band singing from working with Charlie Spivak and Tommy Dorsey when she was quite young. Trombonist Mike Millar described her well when he declared: "She had the whole package. She always looked great, and she sang wonderfully. She had the look, the body language, the voice—she commanded your attention."[92] In any other era, Lynn Roberts would have been a major star.

She remembered James telling her, "Don't ever sing anything that you don't love." He was, of course, restating his own quote from years earlier when he had said, "I only play things I believe in." As she related it, the fact that Harry James played with so much soul helped alleviate the inevitable boredom of having to sing more or less the same fifteen to twenty songs every night on dance dates over the three year period she sang with the band.

Having been on the road with other name bands, working for Harry James never intimidated her. "I felt more comfortable with myself by then," Roberts explained. "And besides, he was more of a showman than a bandleader. He could put a show together. His timing was impeccable, and he knew exactly what the audience wanted."

She added, "You know, I believe his spirit is still around. Whenever I sing 'You Made Me Love You' at the very end of my performances, I look up into that light and think of Harry. He's right there."[93]

In 1976, when Dave Stone left, Ira Westley replaced him on bass. Westley had enjoyed extensive experience with the big bands of Orrin Tucker and Alvino Rey and had worked with the original Herb Alpert & the Tijuana Brass (on tuba) and before that with Jack Teagarden's group. Harry James perhaps never employed a more dedicated musician than Ira Westley. As a result, he also became the band's road manager in 1979.[94]

In effect, Westley had to satisfy Harry James musically, get the band set up and torn down after each gig, and take care of Harry's trumpets and various personal chores for him, which often meant dealing with his changeable moods. Today, he handles the same duties for the Harry James "ghost" band and also works frequently as a freelance musician in Los Angeles.

"I had such tremendous respect for him," said Westley, "but when he got drunk, he would abuse people, and he could get really vicious with some of his remarks. I have been around many musicians that have died of alcoholism, however. I know the kind of thing they're going through, and I know how to handle them. In his last years, Harry drank Grand Marnier with hot tea which I put on the piano. In order to prepare his drink, I brought an immersion heater as part of the equipment we took on the road."

Ira Westley gave aloe vera juice to Harry James, which temporarily alleviated his serious problem with gingivitis. "I used to carry an aloe plant that I got from a health food store. He would ask for one of the aloe leaves which he would put on the sores he had in his mouth. He knew that I had his best interests in mind, I have to say. He would come up with some good bread every time I would do something special for him."

While in Boston, during the "Big Broadcast" engagement, the cast members decided to throw a surprise party for James's sixty-fourth birthday. The Penn Hotel was selected specifically because Harry had visited it several times to see Teddy Wilson perform after the nightly concert, and therefore it was easy to lure him there. Everyone yelled out, "Surprise! Surprise!" When two cakes were wheeled out, Ira Westley noticed how unhappy James looked. He remembered: "Harry hated surprises. The expression on his face registered how uneasy he was at being given a party in his honor. After a short time he said to me, 'Let's get out of here.'"

Rarely would Harry James allow himself to dwell on his past. One night, however, while Westley was driving him to the Pantages during the "Big Broadcast" engagement, he confessed, "I've been sued so many times, and I've never won a case yet, even against my own sons." This was at the time he had to sell his condominium at La Costa to Pee Wee Monte so that he could once again pay off an IRS debt.

Ira Westley saw James "close to tears a couple of times. I attributed it at the time to his pain since his liver was hurting from all those years of heavy drinking. On the bandstand, he would turn around and give this grimace and hold his gut."

On one of the several occasions that the bassist flew to Las Vegas to get James's car and drive it down to Del Mar, he noticed a book on the bedside table of Harry's townhouse. It was a volume of philosophy with quotations from many important philosophers. Harry had underlined many of the quotations. One of them was by Nietzsche. Westley related, "I remember it kind of blew my mind that he was so interested in philosophy."

Westley was a frequent witness to the love/hate aspect of the relationship between Harry James and Pee Wee Monte in these final years. "Pee Wee would read the stock reports in the newspaper on the bus. He'd turn to Harry and say, 'Disney is up' and 'Disney just did a double split.' Harry would get so mad. Pee Wee had talked him into buying some Disney stock, but then it got to the point where he needed tax money so he had to sell it. Every time Pee Wee would bring this up, it was like he was rubbing his nose in it. One time, Harry got so mad he said to him, "For Christ sake, Pee Wee, why don't you spend some of *your* money."

Ira Westley was with the band during a B'nai B'rith dinner at the Beverly Hilton in Beverly Hills to honor Danny Kaye. The fact that James had appeared with Kaye on his radio show more than forty years earlier entered into the organization's decision to have the James band play for dancing. Kris Kristofferson also entertained at the dinner on a stage specially built for him.

The James band was given short shrift, however. It was set up in a corner of the ballroom on the floor without any risers. This angered James and made him drink even more. While Danny Kaye was on the dais telling a few jokes, Harry grabbed the microphone in front of the band and challenged Kaye to come over and perform in the corner where the band was. It seemed as if part of Harry's wrath was a residual from years ago. Westley said, "Harry included some kind of anti-Semitic remark." The comedian chose to ignore Harry's comments.

In 1982, Louise Baranger joined the band playing split trumpet lead. The band immediately embarked on a twelve-week eastern road tour with only one night off—a severe test for a twenty-three-year-old on her first major tour.[95]

By this time, Harry James, justifiably, had grown weary of playing "You Made Me Love You" and his other big hits. They were consolidated into a medley. As Baranger explained it, "If you didn't hear the medley, you weren't going to hear them. I think one of Harry's frustrations was that people came to see him almost as a dinosaur to be viewed in a museum of swing music rather than as the great musician he was. They wanted to look at him, and they didn't care if he played that much. Toward the end, he played less and less because he knew it didn't matter."

On the second night of the tour, after the gig, James said, "Let me buy you a drink, little gal." "We talked about the trumpet. I felt accepted. He would buy dinner for Jeannie Thomas and me. He talked about Bunny Berigan, whom he really appreciated. He remarked how funny Bunny was when he got drunk, and how sad he was. He also liked to talk about his years on the road and baseball. I must say he was always a gentleman to me."

Another night Baranger was on the bus eating chocolate-covered donuts. Harry said, "I've got some chocolate-covered Graham crackers. Come to my room after the gig and I'll trade you." She figured she knew how to handle herself. She put her donuts in a small bag and knocked on the door of his room. He opened the door slightly and had this mischievous look on his face as he said, "Here's your Graham crackers." He held them out, and they traded.

As she looks back on the incident, she recalls, "It was cute. He was childlike in a lot of ways. I think Harry was a guy who never had to grow up. Most musicians are like that because we start young. We go from high school band to college band to professional band, and it's all the same, everybody's sort of like kids. Harry was a very smart guy, but he never learned to manage his own affairs, and that's a very childlike thing—to be really brilliant and never learn to do anything at all.... He didn't have any business sense so he just said, 'Okay, Pee Wee, you take care of it.' They fulfilled each other's needs, and they resented each other because of it.

"He talked to me quite a bit and gave me a couple of trumpet lessons. I wish I had written down everything he said, but I thought he'd be around forever. Once, when we were talking about breathing, he said, 'Punch me in the stomach, hard.' It was like hitting a wall. He had this incredible breath support."

At this juncture, Joe Cabot (né Caputo) suddenly came to play a supremely important role in Harry James's life: He had been part of the James trumpet section during the 1952 summer engagement at the Astor Roof. At that time, Harry complimented him by saying, "You're a soloist."[96]

As the musical director for Fran Warren on the "Big Broadcast" tour, Joe Cabot conducted the James band during her segment of the concert. After several weeks on tour, at James's request, he began conducting the band for the other singers as well.

More important than anything else, Joe Cabot became Harry James's close friend and confidante at a time when Harry desperately needed one.

He was aware of the anguish under which James was living. Cabot devised a routine whereby he would knock on Harry's dressing room door after they had finished performing. He would ask, "Dr. Jekyll or Mr. Hyde?" "If he said 'Dr. Jekyll' I'd come in. If he said, 'Mr. Hyde,' I'd keep going, but five minutes later I'd often hear him open the door and yell out my name, or Pee Wee would come get me because Harry wanted to talk. That's the reason we became close in his last three years. I was probably closer to him than anyone," a fact other James musicians confirmed. As Joe Cabot described it, "I was there at the coda."

Naturally, Harry James had to have a nickname for Cabot. Joe Cabot became "Joe Conforti," named for the proprietor of the Chicken Ranch, the celebrated Nevada brothel. "I asked him, 'Why Conforti?' Harry answered, 'Well, it sounds Italian.' I later found out that Harry and Joe Conforti were good friends."

During the "Big Broadcast" tour, Harry James opened the second half by playing "Corner Pocket," followed by "Cherry." Fran Warren would then come on stage, and Joe would conduct the James band while it accompanied the singer. He would always play the trumpet solo behind her on her hit version of "A Sunday Kind of Love."

One night at the Shubert Theatre in Boston, Joe Cabot failed to play the solo on the tune. Harry was listening to the show through the speaker in his dressing room. Backstage, he asked Joe what happened. "Chief ("I never called him Harry in my life"), to tell you the truth, I forgot my horn." Harry said, "My horn was there in the crook of the piano, why didn't you use it?" At the end of the performance, Harry called Joe out to join the cast for bows. He gave him a package with a note that said, "From now on I'll have to ask you when I want to play the horn. Enjoy it. From your friend, Harry James."

After the completion of the "Big Broadcast" tour, Harry James arranged for Cabot to conduct for the Mills Brothers in a tour that included the James band, Hildegarde, and Johnny Desmond. His initial respect for Joe Cabot as a conductor stemmed from a rehearsal he watched him conduct at the Sahara in Las Vegas. Cabot was rehearsing the house band for Fran Warren, going over her material. When it ended, James approached him and said, "I've never seen anybody rehearse a band like you."

Over time, Harry James trusted him so much that he started revealing his innermost thoughts to him. "There was something I did, unknowingly, that struck a chord in him," Cabot remarked. "He had a way of controlling his outer feelings but not his inner feelings. He'd be on stage stoned and still able to do things, but he had very little control over his inner thoughts. He really couldn't relate to many people."

At that time Vicki and Bill Bivens were living in Grosse Point outside

Detroit while Bivens was working for Chrysler. Cabot recalled, "I remember that he hadn't seen his grandkids for three years and admitted to me that he was nervous about seeing them. I couldn't believe it when he came back and said, 'I had one of the greatest days of my life.' Then he said, 'I'd better start getting things together.' I knew right then that it was the beginning of the end for him. I say that because it was the first time in my association with him that I ever heard him say anything like that. He knew something was wrong."

On a nightly basis, Joe Cabot watched the physical and emotional disintegration of a great artist. "In 1980, I was in charge of the peanut butter run. His mouth was gone, his teeth were gone, and he could only eat soft foods. He couldn't even play a middle C because he couldn't find the pocket in his mouthpiece. His false teeth were shifting all over his mouth. He had started to get heavy jowls. He was dying his hair with the dumbest kind of dye I ever saw in my life. Don't forget, he had lived a tough life, and time had started to catch up with him. When he went out to perform, there weren't any screaming throngs any longer. To a guy like Harry, that's the start of a death march.

"Harry was a deep, deep, deep man; he may not have been an academically educated guy, he was street educated. He was as perceptive as anybody I've ever known. His first exposure to life was to circus people. If you want to learn about life, those are the people you want to talk to.

"It takes a lot of strength to go through your life and come out with all the things you screwed up on. He acknowledged what he had done in his life that was wrong, and he was coming to terms with it ... He couldn't go to the people he had wronged and say, 'Gee, I'm sorry.' He knew that he had blown it with Betty and his kids. Some people aren't supposed to be parents; he was one of them. He had come to the realization that he had a lot of guilt. The sadness wasn't anger. He had to go to confession, and I happened to be in the confession box."

His devoted friend described the many late nights after the "Big Broadcast" gig when they would sit and talk for hours in Harry's hotel room. Harry James would drink his Grand Marnier in scalding hot tea, get drunk, take out his false teeth, and then dejectedly say, "Look at that." Sometimes he would ask Joe if he could get him some "gage" (the 1930s term used by musicians for marijuana). What followed were torrents of tears interspersed with the dire confessions of a desperate man, reminiscing about his youth in the circus and often remarking how badly he had treated Betty and his mother. As Cabot related, "For a man to cry in front of another man who isn't his brother is really opening himself up. He was never honest with himself until the end."

Not everything that Harry James and Joe Cabot discussed was as deeply profound. There were also many light moments. He once asked Harry why Louis Armstrong and many of the older trumpet players always wore white socks on stage. Harry smiled and replied, "Conforti, don't you know anything? The reason that you wear white socks is that you stand up all night and your feet sweat. If you wear socks with dye on, the dye gets into your feet, and it can make your feet swell up."

Cabot also noticed that, when horse people came around, Harry's personality completely changed. "He was at home with them. He used to even dress differently on those days. He would wear those western shirts with snap buttons and his suede jacket."

Frank Capp, for many years the leader of the Juggernaut Band in Los Angeles, worked for Harry James during a southern tour just before Buddy Rich returned in 1962 and filled in for short periods during the 1970s. While Les DeMerle was on one of his hiatuses, he took over the drum chair for a short tour.

Frank Capp recalled: "One morning I got up around 8 o'clock and walked through the courtyard of the motel in Phoenix where we were staying. Harry was sitting there with a pitcher of vodka martinis. He asked me if I wanted one. I said, 'No, Harry, it's too early for me to drink.' That was my first indication of where he was going. I noticed that Pee Wee kept a fifth of vodka in his trumpet case. He'd have a vodka on stage all night long and would drink it from a paper cup."[97]

A video from a date in West Virginia in the fall of 1982 revealed just how much Harry James was slipping. The fast trumpet runs that were once commonplace for him now included many missed notes and shortened phrases. Despite that, various members of the audience were thrilled to see him perform for the first time and expressed their great enthusiasm. Several remarked to Sal Monte how they couldn't wait until the band returned.[98]

On that same tour, Bill Pruyn, a former circus trumpeter who had first known Harry in the 1940s and hadn't seen him in some time after he retired to Sarasota from leading the Ringling Brothers band, saw the James band play a dance date in Venice, Florida. Harry spotted him from the bandstand and sat down with him afterward to discuss circus days. He requested that Bill have his wife drive the car home so that the two could continue to reminisce together on the bus. James then had the bus driver drop Pruyn off at his home.[99]

Later that fall, the band played in Oklahoma City at a huge celebration before 20,000 people commemorating the seventy-fifth anniversary of the State of Oklahoma. Native Oklahoman jazz guitarist Barney Kessel jammed with Harry James and the Band. Offstage, James spent considerable time drinking with another honored guest, the film and television star James Garner, as the time for the band to perform kept getting delayed. At one point he got so drunk that he grabbed the microphone and requested that some woman would come up and perform oral sex on him. The band screamed with equal parts laughter and embarrassment.[100]

Stephenie Caravella returned as band vocalist after Lynn Roberts departed. She remembered an incredibly bad date in Pennsylvania at a skating rink. "There was sawdust on the floor. There was no sound system set up. When we arrived, the piano was being painted blue, and when Tommy Todd sat down to play it was completely out of tune."

The vivacious singer recalled that night: "You had to have a sense of humor. There was no dressing room for me so I had to change in this smelly room where people put their skates on. There was only one thing left to do. Toward the end of the date—I put on a pair of roller skates and skated across the floor when the band started playing the intro to 'Proud Mary.' Harry was going through a bad night. When I whizzed by, he and the band absolutely cracked up laughing. That gave him something to laugh at for the next two days."

There were unfortunately more such dates in the last years. The sameness of the routine of one-nighters was getting to Harry James. It's no wonder that one night he called up Jimmy Wilkins in the middle of the night and asked him for Ernie Wilkins's telephone number in Copenhagen. "Jimmy, I'm sorry to wake you, but I've got to reach Ernie. I need some new charts," he said.[101]

Stephenie Caravella would often give Harry James a neck and shoulder massage just before the band went on the bandstand. "One night I felt this growth," she recalled. "I asked him, 'What the hell is this?' He said, 'I must have a knot in my neck.' I started rubbing his neck. I said, 'Harry, that's not a knot; something's wrong with your neck.' I begged him day after day to do something about it, but he kept ignoring me. I talked to Gregg Field [who had rejoined the band] about it and some of the other guys. I said, 'Harry's hurting. There's something growing.' I knew he was in pain when he was yelling at us, or at Sal, or at a promoter. When he yelled at us it was done out of love, not out of dislike. He was trying to teach us.

"Then the guys started going up to him and saying, 'Hey, Harry, how are you doing?' He started getting upset with us because he didn't want us worrying about him. He was the head guy, and he was supposed to worry about us. The tables were turning."[102]

James looked haggard at a sellout date with Helen Forrest sponsored by radio station KMPC at the Hollywood Palladium in early March. This was the first time they had appeared together since their row during the "Big Broadcast" tour. Kitty Kallen was in the audience that night. She hadn't seen Harry since leaving the band nearly forty years before. After the gig, the band leader and his two leading female singers got together and reminisced about the old days.[103]

In working as many years as he had in Las Vegas, Harry had come to know a multitude of people in and around the hotels. One of these was an ex-bebop drummer named Maynard Sloate, who carved out a second and considerably more substantial career as an entertainment director and producer for several Las Vegas and Atlantic City hotels for over three decades. But, as Sloate described it, "Harry was more of a racetrack friend than a musician friend. We always think of Harry at Del Mar."

On March 17, 1983, Maynard Sloate booked Harry James for a date on St. Patrick's Day in downtown Las Vegas (then referred to as "Glitter Gulch") at the Union Plaza Hotel. They arranged to have dinner before the gig.

When James arrived, Sloate looked at him in disbelief. Sal Monte, who joined them, remarked, "Jesus, Harry, I don't know if you can play tonight." Sloate and Monte called Dr. Arthur Rando, a Las Vegas doctor, who, using his full name, Arthur (Rando) Grillot, had once been a part of the reed section of the Tommy Dorsey, Jimmy Dorsey, Glenn Miller, and Bob Crosby bands and had also played clarinet with Phil Harris in Las Vegas. He had known Harry since 1936 when he met him in New Orleans at the time James was with Ben Pollack.[104]

Dr. Rando came down to the Union Plaza immediately. When he arrived, according to Sal Monte, Harry James was in a salty mood. Dr. Rando gave him a basic examination with a stethoscope and also checked his blood pressure. He then called Dr. Ellerton, an oncologist, to come over to the Union Plaza. As the musician-turned-doctor remembered, "Harry presented symptoms that I became suspicious of. I could see by his habits and knowing his physical appearance that he was beginning to lose weight. Maynard and I spoke about his condition, and I gave him my opinion."[105]

In examining his neck, Dr. Ellerton thought he might have discovered a tumor. He was strict with James, telling him he had to stop drinking immediately. He wrote a prescription, which, when it arrived later, the bandleader refused to take. He only had the strength to play two tunes on the gig.

The next day, radio personality Jerry Roy saw Harry James at McCarren Field at 10 o'clock in the morning waiting to get on a plane to Phoenix, where the band was about to play two dates. He said, "Hi,

Harry. How you doin'?" "He didn't know who I was. I figured, 'Have I changed that much?' I had done all those radio shows with him, and I had always gotten along with him. I had even filled in singing and playing with the band at one time. I got on my plane feeling awful. It wasn't just his not remembering me; what hit me was that he was so old looking and so obviously ill."[106]

After the Phoenix dates, the band played the Crazy Horse in Santa Ana, California. It was here that a magnanimous patron was so taken by the band that he gave Harry James and all the musicians, plus Sal Monte, $100 each. Other gigs were played in San Diego and, for the second time in a month, at the Hollywood Palladium.

A few days later, James called Dr. Rando, who was then chief of the trauma unit at the Southern Nevada Memorial Hospital, and asked him, "Why can't I have a little to drink?" He rationalized that he had been drinking Bailey's Irish Cream and said, "I need the calories in that." As Rando saw it, "He was getting the wrong kind of nutrients. I told him that, if he stuck to the diet that had been prescribed for him, a glass of brandy wouldn't hurt him, but that I didn't want him drinking a pint of it a day. He could be a great con artist when he wanted to. He called me day and night, but I liked the guy. I welcomed his call."[107]

Harry James also went to see Dr. Angela Clark, a general practitioner, who had been treating him for some time. She told Harry, "You're killing yourself. I can't fool you. You've got a chance … but a chance of living a hell of a lot longer if you stop and do the right thing now." Harry said, "Well, okay," but what he wanted to hear, according to Dr. Rando, was "Keep on doing whatever you want to do."[108]

On April 4, Dr. Kirk V. Cammack, a surgeon, removed the growth from James's neck at Sunrise Hospital in Las Vegas. Dr. Peter R. Graze, another oncologist, discovered that the tumor was cancerous. Further tests indicated that the cancer had spread to his gall bladder. It later moved to his lungs.[109]

Harry James asked Pee Wee to have Sal fly to Las Vegas and proceed directly to Sunrise Hospital. Shortly after Sal Monte arrived, James was advised by Dr. Graze that he could live possibly two years more. He was furious, saying, "Did he have to tell me that?!"

Sal followed Dr. Graze to the nurses' station and told him privately, "Doctor, we have a tour coming up this month. Harry's going to be away for six weeks." He looked at Sal and said, "Cancel it." Sal said, "Really? Well, what are you saying? Two years…? What are you saying now?" The doctor replied, "He has three months." He also advised him that James should immediately begin chemotherapy. In the meantime, Harry was given four units of blood because of his low blood count.

Two days later, Harry James was released from the hospital, and Sal

Monte drove him home. He had arranged for James to be photographed at his home with Nelson Riddle and singer Kei Miramura for the back cover of a forthcoming album for Discomate Records, a Japanese record company. Harry wore a scarf to hide the large incision on his neck. His cheeks resembled caves, and his deep-set blue eyes were now those of a weary and beaten man.

Harry James began to realize fully what loomed ahead for him and started scrambling around looking for things to leave to his daughters. He discussed with Sal the possibility of republishing the *Harry James Trumpet Method* that he had written with Everette's assistance back in 1941. Sal tried to explain to him that trumpet teaching had changed considerably in forty years and that it would be of little relevance now.

Harry James's will had already been changed so that Harry Jeffrey and Tim were excluded. His reasoning was that they had already been recipients of a trust fund, although he had contributed very little to it. The fact that they had earlier sued him for failure to adhere to the divorce agreement regarding the trust fund may have entered into this decision.

As part of these preparations, James had to look to the immediate future regarding various dates that had already been booked. It was then that Ray Anthony, who had long been anything but a friend of Harry's (James referred to him as "Ray Agony"), received a call from him. He told Anthony that he was ill and wanted him to take over some of his scheduled dates.[110]

Ray Anthony candidly discussed with me the problems they had with one another. He said, "We never had much of a relationship so that was a downer, but it rekindled a bit toward the end."

Ray Anthony grew up admiring Louis Armstrong and Roy Eldridge and appreciating Harry James. As he described it: "Then Harry became my all time favorite because he could do everything. He could play fast, slow, blues and great jazz as well. What he did was he put emotion into it ... he played from the heart. If you're going to put passion into playing trumpet, you're gonna sound like Harry James."

Anthony admitted that the conflict between them was caused by a remark he had made in the early 1960s to Forrest Duke on Duke's television show. James was scheduled to join Anthony as a guest on the show but failed to appear. Anthony said to Duke, "He's probably out drinking somewhere." Harry James heard about the remark and came over to the Desert Inn looking for Anthony, who was having a drink in the lounge. He finally simmered down, but the incident caused a rift that lingered until Harry's last months.

On the bus shortly thereafter, while en route to a date in Bakersfield, California, and with only one week's notice, Sal Monte informed the musicians that the six-week eastern tour had to be canceled. They were told of the seriousness of James's illness; they weren't the least bit surprised. Ray Anthony fronted the band on the Bakersfield date. Gregg Field said: "Ray sounded like a young, healthy Harry James that night."[111]

Ira Westley remembers that, while at Harry James's townhouse one afternoon, he picked up a message from Frank Sinatra on Harry's answering machine. Sinatra had learned the grave news concerning James's condition. He wanted to fly him to Switzerland to be treated by a cancer specialist he had heard was getting miraculous results. James turned him down, believing that no miracles were in store for him at this point.[112]

On April 12, after having recuperated from his surgery for only eight days, Harry James flew to Los Angeles to overdub three tunes for the Discomate album. Richy Barz had arranged for him to get $15,000 for the recording session. The arrangements, written by Nelson Riddle, were not up to Riddle's usual high standard and were probably ghost written.

At the beginning of the recording session, due to the severity of his illness, Harry James was having great difficulty figuring out exactly where his solos fit in. He asked Sal Monte to have Nelson Riddle come down from the recording booth to conduct for him. Despite the genius Riddle brought to arranging, he was never much of a conductor. He stood a few feet away from James and gave him his cues.

For Harry James, his performance on these tracks proved the nadir of his long recording career. He sounded tentative at best on "I Had the Craziest Dream," and his playing on all the tunes was completely devoid of any verve. Sadly, he sounded like a novice trumpet player.

While in Los Angeles, Harry James and the Montes had a meeting with Bob Morgan, then of Morgan and Martindale, the business management firm that represented him. They went over his assets, which were few, in great detail. Bob Morgan said to him, "Well, we both know where the money went," whereupon Harry said, "I don't regret a thing."[113]

The next day, Harry James spent the afternoon at Santa Anita, where he met up with Chick Romano, then in charge of the reserved and box seat section for VIPs, just as he had been at Del Mar years before. Romano remembered: "We talked about the days years ago when I saw Harry's band in New York. He told me that he hadn't been feeling well lately.

"A few minutes later, he slipped on the steps and fell down. His eyes were bulging out of his head. I could tell he was very sick, but I didn't know just how sick he was. He wouldn't let me call anybody to assist him. He had an oxygen contraption in his pocket, which he quickly made use of."[114]

Harry James had his first chemotherapy treatment on May 9. After that treatment, he told Vi Monte that he didn't mind the chemotherapy, but he soon stopped showing up for his appointments.[115] He had seen Betty Grable lose her hair and probably had reservations about how it would affect his vanity as well as his potency.

Connie Haines learned about Harry James's condition and encouraged him to continue the treatments. "Harry, I had a breast removed ten years ago. I took my chemo treatments faithfully, and I'm still here. You've got to keep taking them," she scolded him.[116]

Dr. Rando saw him frequently. Phil Harris came up to Las Vegas to visit him with Rando. "When we arrived the first thing he said was, 'Let's have a taste.'" At that time, Dr. Rando told Phil, "When you die, we'll have to get a big stick and beat that liver of yours to death because it will never die." (Harris died on August 11, 1995, shortly before his ninety-second birthday!)[117]

The trumpeter Pete Candoli sent Harry James a huge get-well card after he heard the news of his condition. It was also signed by other trumpeters, including his brother Conte, Conrad Gozzo, Uan Rasey, Johnny Audino, Manny Klein, and several other musicians.

Shortly after, Candoli was back home in Hammond, Indiana. He walked past a pawn shop and saw a magnificent silver cigarette case in the window. He remembered: "I went in the shop and asked to see the case. The guy in the shop said, 'It's engraved, too.' I opened up the case and it said, 'To Harry James, from the gals at the so-and-so.' It was from the showgirls or the dancing girls at some showplace in Denver from the early 1900s." He bought it as a gift for Harry. Unfortunately, he delayed sending it to him until it was too late. Candoli still has it in his possession.[118]

With it all, the veritable lion in winter imposed his strong will and insisted on playing two good money dates in Denver, June 10 and 11. The discipline that Everette had instilled in him as a boy had never left—he was a professional musician. It was his job to play the gig, no matter what. As Louise Baranger said, "He felt obligated to the music."[119]

Dr. Graze said he would allow him to perform on these dates, but only on the condition that he undergo a massive dose of cobalt before he left for Denver. At both the Denver dates, Sal set up an oxygen tank as a precaution. With the help of the oxygen, James withstood the mile-high altitude and completed both gigs.[120]

At the first date, which was presented by KEZW, the *Music of Your Life* (the syndicated radio format that plays adult pop standards) station in Denver, word had circulated about the seriousness of James's illness. A gigantic card was presented to him with the signatures of all the people attending, which moved him to tears.[121]

In talking with a friend of Pee Wee Monte's, Tim James learned about his father's illness. He called Jack Kent, a friend who lived in Denver and asked him to attend the concert and let him know how his father looked. The next day Kent called and said, "Your dad is in terrible shape." Tim and the other children talked with him over the phone over the next several days.[122]

Joe Cabot continued calling Harry frequently and urged him to continue his chemotherapy treatments. Harry said, "What does it matter? It means replacing one chemical with another chemical. You can't fight poison with poison." He added, "Joe, I've been on the road for sixty years." Referring to death, he said, "It's just another road trip."[123]

He had often told Red Kelly over the years, "I'm not afraid of death. I figure I've lived five lifetimes already."[124]

A few weeks later, on Sunday, June 26, James was booked to play a private party for the International Association of Building Owners and Managers Convention at the Century Plaza Hotel in Los Angeles. Harry called Sal Monte and asked him to pick him up the day before at LAX and bring him to the Airport Park Hotel on the grounds of Hollywood Park. He was accompanied by Anita Bradshaw, a divorcée from Newport Beach, California, whom he had been living with and was planning to marry. When they arrived at the suite, James asked, "Anita, what did you do with the package?" In Denver, when Harry was signing the payroll at the Cherry Hills Country Club (the second of the two dates), Sal Monte had given him his Mark Cross pen with his name on it to sign the payroll checks.

As Sal recalled, "I had forgotten about it, but he didn't forget. As sick as he was, he went down to a jeweler in Vegas and bought another Mark Cross pen. He had my name inscribed on it and gave it to me at the hotel. He said, 'Here, kid, I don't have anything to tie it with except what you see there.' It was a shoelace." Sal still has the pen. "I don't take it anywhere with me except on the road. I take it with me because when I use it I see Harry."

Harry, Sal, and Anita Bradshaw took the shuttle over to the Turf Club at Hollywood Park and went to see Frank Panza, an old friend of Harry's, who was the bartender there. Panza admired his tie. Harry took it off and gave it to him. He was so weak that he couldn't sit on a barstool or even in a booth.[125]

The next night, Frank Panza drove Harry James to and from an appearance at the Los Angeles Ballroom of the Century Plaza. (This was the same showroom where Count Basie would give his last performance a year later.) Before the band went on stage, Harry told Stephenie Caravella that he wasn't going to be able to give her away at her wedding three months later as he had promised. She understood why. "You take care of yourself, Stevie," he said. After the gig, she drove home in tears.[126]

Harry James spent most of the evening leaning against the piano for support, yet somehow managed to play. Between sets he went to his dressing room, leaned his arms on the table, dropped his head down in intense pain, and then went back on the bandstand to begin playing again. In Gregg Field's opinion, "He sounded better than I had heard him in close to a year. I also noticed he had put on some weight since the Denver dates. I think that was because his body was bloated from the cancer."[127]

Pee Wee Monte noticed that a video camera had been set up and was taping Harry James on the bandstand, which the dancers could see on screens set up around the ballroom. He demanded and got custody of the videotape, explaining to the videographer that he would have to pay James and all the musicians for shooting and distributing such a video; this was true, but he also didn't want anyone to have footage showing Harry's debilitated condition.[128]

John and Virginia Greenman, who hailed from Minnesota, were at the date. Virginia had danced to his music on records, but had never seen him play in person; John had once seen him play with Benny Goodman in the Twin Cities. Virginia remembered, "He looked terrible, just awful. I could tell it was a tremendous effort for him to even play, and yet his music was wonderful to dance to."[129]

Toward the end of the evening, Gregg Field was playing with brushes on a ballad. He looked over to the right and saw Pee Wee put Harry's trench-coat over his shoulders as the two of them went out the door. "It hit me like a laser. I thought to myself, 'That's the last time I'm ever going to see him.'"[130]

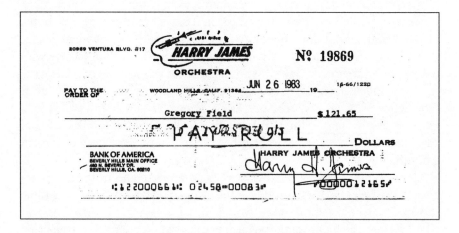

On his return to the hotel, Harry James was restless. In the middle of the night he told Anita Bradshaw that they should fly back to Las Vegas as soon as possible. They took an early morning flight. Anita checked him into Valley Hospital on July 1 and, against Harry's wishes, called his daughters to inform them of his rapidly deteriorating condition.[131]

Tim heard the news that his father was in the hospital from David Goldwater, James's lawyer, who suggested he fly up right away. He quickly left for Las Vegas. Harry Jeffrey joined him two days later.

As Tim James recalled, "Dad was very heavily medicated, but he was conscious. I walked in, and he said, 'Hi, Babe, how ya' doing?' His stomach and his cavities were filling with fluid, and he wouldn't let the doctors draw the fluid. It would have made him more comfortable, but he didn't want it."

All the children met in the hallway before they went in as a group to see him. Knowing Harry's withdrawn nature, they weren't sure how he would react to their coming to see him en masse. However, he was visibly moved by their arrival and had tears in his eyes.[132]

For the last few days, he was mostly in a coma. On July 2, he was given communion by Father William Kenny, pastor of Christ the King Catholic Church. In one of his more lucid moments, he said, "If I can only get past the fifth."[133] Jessica told me, "I think he kept himself alive because he realized that was the date of my mother's funeral."[134] Ironically, on that same day, July 5, 1983, the fortieth anniversary of his marriage to Betty Grable in Las Vegas, Harry James died at 5:30 A.M. while all his children, except Michael, were gathered outside his room.[135]

On hearing the news, Frank Modica called Howard McElroy in Los Angles and arranged to meet in Las Vegas to attend the funeral.[136] Joe Cabot left Bardonia, New York, for Las Vegas.[137] Lionel Hebert left Syracuse, New York, in the middle of a tournament and flew there as well.[138] Red Kelly and Jack Perciful came down from Tacoma, Washington.[139] Louise Tobin flew up from Palm Desert, California.[140] Michael James flew over from northern California.[141] Dick Maher, Harry's #1 fan, came up with the Montes.[142]

When word of Harry's death reached Frank Sinatra, he immediately called Pee Wee Monte and told him he wanted to deliver the eulogy.[143] Sinatra, Frank, Jr., and Jilly Rizzo flew to Las Vegas from Palm Springs. On their arrival, Steve Wynn, owner of the Golden Nugget, where Sinatra was then under contract, accompanied them to Bunker Chapel, where the service took place. It was located diagonally across from the Edendale Memorial Park where Harry was to be buried. The two Sinatras, dressed appropriately in dark suits, were appalled to see some of the early arrivals attired in T-shirts and shorts.[144]

The funeral was attended by approximately 200 people, including many performers such as Joe Williams, members of the band, and, as Frank Sinatra, Jr., noted, "every trumpet player in Las Vegas." Several of Harry's recordings were played before and again during the latter part of the fifty-five-minute service on Thursday, July 7, 1983. Father Kenny said that during his last days Harry had written his own epitaph. It read, "May it simply be said and written of me, 'He's gone on the road to do one-nighters with Gabriel.'"[145]

Phil Harris spoke lovingly of the long and close relationship they had shared. He referred to Harry as "the lovable loner who loved to play the trumpet" and added, "He played all those one-nighters because he loved to make music. That's when he was happiest. He kept the whole world dancing for years. I'm going to miss him. He was my unique friend." He had trouble finishing and frequently broke into tears.[146]

Frank Sinatra's voice faltered slightly as he looked down at Harry James's closed coffin, the trumpeter's horn glistening atop the flower-covered beige casket. He began by saying, "I loved Harry James. I loved him for a long time. He was one of the finest musicians I have ever known. He was a dear friend and a great teacher."[147]

He went on to reminisce about the night at the Rustic Cabin back in 1939. He said, "Harry asked me when I could leave, and I said, 'Right now.'" He recalled the camaraderie of the band during the difficult weeks on the road when Harry couldn't meet the payroll.

He ended his close to ten-minute talk by turning toward the casket and saying, "Thanks for everything. So long, ole buddy. Take care of yourself."

Chapter 1

1   Telephone conversation with representative of Albany, Georgia, Chamber of Commerce, 1996.
2   *Billboard*, April 1, 1916.
3   *Circus Report*, September 22, 1997, p. 17.
4   *Circus Report*, October 6, 1997, p. 11.
5   *Circus Report*, September 22, 1997, p. 3.
6   Author's interview with James T. Maher, 1997.
7   *Billboard*, May 26, 1906.
8   *Billboard*, June 14, 1913.
9   *Beaumont* (Texas) *Journal*, September 30, 1933.
10 Author's interview with Joe Cabot, 1998.
11 *Merv Griffin Show*, November 15, 1977.
12 Joe Cabot interview.
13 *Billboard*, December 18, 1920.
14 *Music Today*, March–April, 1945.
15 Ibid.
16 Ibid.
17 Author's interview with Jimmy Ille, 1997.
18 Robert M. Yoder, "High Note Harry," *Saturday Evening Post*, July 24, 1943.
19 Jimmy Ille interview.
20 *Music Today*, March–April, 1945.
21 Jimmy Ille interview.
22 Author's interview with Uan Rasey, 1996.
23 Jimmy Ille interview.
24 *Merv Griffin Show*, November 15, 1977.
25 *Beaumont* (Texas) *Journal*, September 30, 1933.
26 Author's interview with Bill Abel, 1998.
27 Author's interview with Tom Jenkins, 1998.
28 Ibid.
29 Author's interview with Jack McGee, 1998.

Chapter 2

1   Frank Driggs and Harris Lewine, *Black Beauty, White Heat: A Pictorial History* (New York: William Morrow, 1982), p. 165.
2   Author's interview with Spud Murphy, 1996.
3   Author's interview with James T. Maher, 1997.

4   John Phillips, *Running with Bonnie and Clyde—The Ten Fast Years of Ralph Fults* (Norman: University of Oklahoma Press, 1996), p. 197.

5   *Merv Griffin Show*, November 15, 1977.

6   Author's interview with Louise Tobin, 1997.

7   Ibid.

8   Ibid.

9   Ibid.

10   Ibid.

11   Ibid.

12   Charlie Barnet with Stanley Dance, *Those Swinging Years* (Baton Rouge: Louisiana State University Press, 1984), p. 14.

13   Author's interview with Alex Beller, 1997.

14   Louise Tobin interview.

15   Ibid.

16   Drew Page, *Drew's Blues: A Sideman's Life with the Big Bands* (Baton Rouge: Louisiana State University Press, 1985), p. 98.

17   Author's interview with Jerry Jerome, 1997.

18   Louise Tobin interview.

19   Albert McCarthy, *Big Band Jazz* (New York: Exeter Books, 1974), p. 240.

Chapter 3

1   Author's interview with Jimmy Ille, 1997.

2   Ibid.

3   Kevin Starr, *The Dream Endures: California Enters the 1940s* (New York: Oxford University Press, 1997), pp. 5, 8, 16, 19.

4   Author's interview with Bill Savory, 1996.

5   *Beaumont Enterprise*, January 10, 1937.

6   Author's interview with Chris Griffin, 1997.

7   Arthur Rollini, *Thirty Years with the Big Bands* (Urbana and Chicago: University of Illinois Press, 1987), pp. 54 and 55.

8   Author's interview with Jess Stacy, 1994.

9   D. Russell Connor, *The Record of a Legend* (New York: Let's Dance Corporation, 1984), p. 76.

10   Author's interview with Loren Schoenberg, 1997.

11   Jess Stacy interview.

12   Author's interview with Jimmy Maxwell, 1997.

13   Author's interview with Buddy Childers, 1998.

14   Author's interview with Lionel Hampton, 1997.

15   Author's interview with Kenny Washington, 1998.

16   Chris Griffin interview.

17   Rollini, *Thirty Years with the Big Bands*, p. 54.

18   Bill Savory interview.

19   George Avakian liner notes for Columbia album *Benny Goodman 1937–1938. Jazz Concert No. 2.*

20   Chris Griffin interview.

21   Author's interview with James T. Maher, 1997.

22   Author's interview with George T. Simon, 1998.

23   Chris Griffin interview.

24   Ibid.

25   Jess Stacy interview.

26   Author's interview with Van Alexander, 1998.

27   PBS television show on Benny Goodman, *Adventures in the Kingdom of Swing*, 1994.

28   Author's interview with Martha Tilton, 1996.

29   *Dallas Morning News*, "Goodman Band Makes Debut to a Sellout," September 12, 1937.

30   John Hammond, "Predicted Race Riot Fades As Dallas Applauds Quartet!", *Down Beat*, October 1937, pp. 1 and 4.

31   Lionel Hampton interview.

32   Billie Holiday with William Dufty, *Lady Sings the Blues* (New York: Doubleday, 1955), pp. 55 and 56.

33   Ibid.

34   Loren Schoenberg interview.

35   Albert McCarthy, *Big Band Jazz City* (New York: Exeter Books, 1974), p. 241.

36   Author's interview with Bill Willard, 1998.

37   Author's interview with Red Norvo, 1997.

38   Lionel Hampton interview.

39   Ibid.

40   Jimmy Maxwell interview.

41   *Down Beat*, H.E.P., "Goodman Came, Saw, And Laid A Golden Egg!", February 1938.

42   *Metronome*, "Hall of Fame," May 1938, p. 37.

43   Author's interview with Jerry Jerome, 1997.

44   Author's interview with Noni Bernardi, 1996.

45   Author's interview with Louise Tobin, 1997.

46   Author's interview with Vi Monte, 1997.

47   Loren Schoenberg interview.

48   Rollini, *Thirty Years with the Big Bands*, p. 66.

Chapter 4

1   Author's interview with Bill Finnegan, 1996.

2   Author's interview with Jerry Jerome, 1997.

3   Author's interview with Jess Stacy, 1994.

4   Author's interview with Jack Palmer, 1998.

5   Author's interview with Artie Shaw, 1996.

6   Author's interview with Joe Pardee, 1997.

7   Author's interview with Louise Tobin, 1997.

8   Ibid.

9   Author's interview with Connie Haines, 1997.

10   Louise Tobin interview.

11   Pete Hamill, *Why Sinatra Matters* (Boston, New York, Toronto, London: Little, Brown, 1998), p. 71.

12   Kitty Kelly, *His Way* (New York: Bantam Books, 1986), p. 48.

13   Connie Haines interview.

14   Jack Palmer interview.

15   Connie Haines interview.

16   Drew Page, *Drew's Blues: A Sideman's Life with the Big Bands* (Baton Rouge: Louisiana State University Press, 1985) p. 118.

17   Author's interview with Jack Lawrence, 1997.

18   Author's interview with Van Alexander, 1997.

19   *Down Beat*, October 15, 1939, p. 1.

20   Ibid.

21   Author's interview with Dr. Billy Taylor, 1996.

22   Author's interview with Jimmy Maxwell, 1997.

23   Louise Tobin interview.

24   Larry Billman, *Betty Grable—A Bio-Bibliography* (Westport, CT: Greenwood Press, 1993), p. 178.

25   Author's interview with Jim Bacon, 1997.

26   Author's interview with Mickey Scrima, 1996.
27   Jimmie Fidler's syndicated column, October 30, 1941.
28   Author's interview with Nick Sevano, 1998.
29   Fred Hall, *More Dialogues In Swing* (Ventura: Pathfinder Publishing of California, 1991), p. 184.
30   Mickey Scrima interview.
31   Will Friedwald, *Sinatra, The Song Is You* (New York: Scribners, 1996), p. 69.

Chapter 5

1   Joe Klein, *Woody Guthrie: A Life* (New York: Ballantine Books, 1980), p. 141.
2   Author's interview with Louise Tobin, 1997.
3   *Down Beat*, "Hines With WKBW," October 1940.
4   Walter Winchell, "On Broadway," *New York Daily Mirror*, October 6, 1940.
5   Author's interview with Al Lerner, 1997.
6   Author's interview with Jimmy Maxwell, 1997.
7   Author's interview with Mickey Scrima, 1997.
8   Author's interview with Joe Cabot, 1998.
9   Al Lerner interview.
10   Author's interview with Nick Sevano, 1998.
11   Mickey Scrima interview.
12   Author's interview with Mel Powell, 1997.
13   Author's interview with Elizabeth Teachout, 1998.
14   Author's interview with James T. Maher, 1997.
15   Al Lerner interview.
16   Ibid.
17   Ibid.
18   Ibid.
19   Author's interview with George T. Simon, 1998.
20   Al Lerner interview.
21   Mel Tormé, *It Wasn't All Velvet* (New York: Zebra Books, 1988), pp. 40–42, 45–57.
22   Ibid.
23   Ibid.
24   Ibid.
25   Ibid.
26   Doug Warren, *Betty Grable, The Reluctant Movie Queen* (New York: St. Martin's Press, 1981), p. 61.
27   Ibid.
28   *Metronome*, "All-Stars Spotted Goodman, Dorsey Men," January 1941.
29   John Ross, *Brooklyn Eagle*, "Harry James Band Leader Tries His Newest Ditty on Theatre Audience in Brooklyn," January 30, 1941.
30   Louise Tobin interview.
31   Ibid.
32   Author's interview with Dan Morgenstern, 1997.
33   Author's interview with George Avakian, 1997.
34   Author's interview with Chris Griffin, 1997.
35   Ibid.
36   Author's interview with Jess Stacy, 1994.
37   Author's interview with Pat Stacy, 1994.
38   Author's interview with Mort Sahl, 1997.
39   Al Lerner interview.
40   Ibid.
41   Author's interview with Johnny Fresco, 1997.

42   Al Lerner interview.

43   Author's interview with Sam Firmature, 1997.

44   Johnny Fresco interview.

45   Ibid.

46   Art Sekro, "He Manages a $1,000,000 a Year Band," *The Orchestra World*, June 1943, p. 7.

47   Ibid.

48   "'I'm Kicking My Soul'—Harry James," *Metronome*, May 1939, p. 10.

49   Author's interview with Helen Forrest, 1996.

50   Ibid.

51   Ibid.

52   Ibid.

53   Ibid.

54   Mel Tormé, *My Singing Teachers* (New York: Oxford University Press, 1995), p. 32.

55   *Metronome*, November 1941.

56   Sol Levy, "The Sportsman's Low-Down" column, *The Coney Island Times*, November 1, 1941.

57   Author's interview with E. D. Holland, 1997.

58   Author's interview with Herbie Mann, 1997.

Chapter 6

1   Joe Fisher's "Reviews," Topics, Santa Monica, California, May 22, 1942.

2   David Meeker, *Jazz In The Movies* (New York: DaCapo, 1981), p. 5.

3   *Los Angeles Times*, June 25, 1942.

4   *Time*, September 18, 1942.

5   Author's interview with Mel Powell, 1997.

6   *Los Angeles Times*, June 19, 1942.

7   Author's interview with Helen Forrest, 1996.

8   Author's interview with Mickey Scrima, 1997.

9   Author's interview with Louise Tobin, 1997.

10   Ibid.

11   Ibid.

12   Author's interview with Col. Michael Ritz, 1998.

13   Louella Parsons, "Paging the Stars," *New York Daily News*, May 1, 1942.

14   Columbia Records Memo, CRC Sales Dept. from Paul Southard, Sales Manager, March 4, 1942.

15   Author's interview with Al Lerner, 1997.

16   Ibid.

17   Ray Peacock, *Wide World Features*, May 28, 1942.

18   Louise Tobin interview.

19   Author's interview with Sal Monte, 1997.

20   Author's interview with Helen Forrest, 1996.

21   Walter Winchell, "On Broadway," *New York Daily Mirror*, May 14, 1942.

22   Helen Forrest interview.

23   Author's interview with Eddie Bracken, 1997.

24   Author's interview with Jerry Roy, 1997.

25   Robert Dupuis, *Bunny Berigan: Elusive Genius of Jazz* (Baton Rouge: Louisiana State University Press, 1993), p. 267.

26   Helen Forrest interview.

27   Helen Forrest, *I Had the Craziest Dream* (New York: Coward McCann & Geoghegan, 1982), pp. 27–29.

28   Roy Hoopes, *When the Stars Went to War* (New York: Random House, 1994), page unknown.

29   Tom McGee, *The Girl with the Million Dollar Legs* (London: Vestal Press, 1995), p. viii.

30   *Time*, "Music—Horn of Plenty," September 28, 1942.

31   Ibid.
32   Author's interview with Enos Slaughter, 1996.
33   Al Lerner interview.
34   Author's interview with Artie Shaw, 1997.
35   Doug Warren, *Betty Grable: The Reluctant Movie Queen* (New York: St. Martin's Press, 1981), pp. 75–76.
36   *New Yorker*, September 27, 1995.
37   *Time*, July 19, 1943.
38   *Variety*, movie review, "Best Foot Forward," March 20, 1943.
39   Spero Pastos, *Pinup—The Tragedy of Betty Grable* (New York: G. P. Putnam's Sons, 1986), p. 48.
40   Author's interview with Betty Baez, 1997
41   Pastos, *Pinup—The Tragedy of Betty Grable*, p. 53.
42   McGee, *The Girl With the Million Dollar Legs*, p. 102.
43   Ibid.
44   Ibid.
45   Author's interview with Betty Rose, 1999.
46   Ibid.
47   Ibid.
48   Pastos, *Pinup—The Tragedy of Betty Grable*, p. 42.
49   Artie Shaw interview.
50   Pastos, *Pinup—The Tragedy of Betty Grable*, p. 55.
51   Ibid.
52   Ibid.
53   *Hollywood Reporter*, May 30, 1997.
54   McGee, *The Girl with the Million Dollar Legs*, p. 107.
55   Author's interview with Arnold Eidus, 1997.
56   Earl Wilson, "Gabriel In Jive," *Liberty Magazine*, July 3, 1943, pp. 52–54.
57   Author's interview with Pete Candoli, 1998.
58   "Jitterbugs Jam James's Jive Jag," *Life*, May 4, 1943, p. 34.
59   Ibid.
60   *Harper's Bazaar*, June 1943.
61   Author's interview with Al Lerner, 1997.
62   Ibid.
63   *Life*, May 4, 1943, p. 34.
64   Author's interview with Buddy Moreno, 1996.
65   Louise Tobin interview.
66   McGee, *The Girl with the Million Dollar Legs*, p. 104.
67   Ibid.
68   Doug Warren, *The Reluctant Movie Queen* (New York: St. Martin's Press, 1981), p. 86.
69   Helen Forrest interview.
70   Author's interview with Jim Bacon, 1997.
71   Louise Tobin interview.
72   McGee, *The Girl with the Million Dollar Legs*, p. 111.

Chapter 7

1   Doug Warren, *Betty Grable: The Reluctant Movie Queen* (New York: St. Martin's Press, 1981), p. 92.
2   Ibid., p. 88.
3   *New York Times*, July 14, 1943.
4   Author's interview with Helen Forrest, 1996.
5   *Time*, September 28, 1942.

6 Helen Forrest interview.
7 *New York Times*, June 28, 1944, p. 20.
8 *New York Herald Tribune*, July 21, 1944.
9 Author's interview with Viola Monte, 1996.
10 Author's interview with Fred Monte, 1997.
11 Spero Pastos, *Pinup—The Tragedy of Betty Grable* (New York: G. P. Putnam's Sons, 1986), p. 86–87.
12 Author's interview with Col. Michael Ritz, 1998.
13 Author's interview with Betty Baez, 1997.
14 Ibid.
15 Doug Warren, *Betty Grable, The Reluctant Movie Queen* (New York: St. Martin's Press, 1981), p. 111.
16 Fred Monte interview.
17 Ibid.
18 Ibid.
19 *The Blood-Horse*, "Harry James Obituary," July 10, 1983, p. 4840.
20 Fred Monte interview.
21 Warren, *Betty Grable, The Reluctant Movie Queen*, p. 104.
22 Ibid., p. 91.
23 *Time*, "Fine Shapes," August 28, 1944.
24 Author's interview with Hugh Hefner, 1997.
25 Author's interview with Dean Pratt, 1996.
26 Helen Forrest interview.
27 Ibid.
28 Ibid.
29 Author's interview with Richard Dondiego, 1997.
30 Helen Forrest interview.
31 Author's interview with Helen Ward, 1996.
32 Tom McGee, *The Girl with the Million Dollar Legs* (London: Vestal Press, 1995), p. 120.
33 Author's interview with Vicki Bivens, 1997.
34 McGee, *The Girl with the Million Dollar Legs*, pp. 121–122.
35 Associated Press, " 'Gambling Game' Holdup in Hollywood Reported," January 2, 1946.
36 Warren, *Betty Grable: The Reluctant Movie Queen*, p. 95.
37 Author's interview with Ann Miller, 1997.
38 Fred Monte interview.
39 Author's interview with Kitty Kallen, 1996.
40 Ibid.
41 Author's interview with Jimmy Maxwell, 1996.
42 Kitty Kallen interview.
43 Ibid.
44 Ibid.
45 Author's interview with Buddy DiVito, 1997.
46 *Merv Griffin Show*, November 15, 1977.
47 Author's interview with Buddy DiVito, 1997.
48 Ibid.
49 Ibid.
50 Author's interview with Al Lerner, 1997.
51 Author's interview with Mickey Scrima, 1997.
52 Author's interview with Red Kelly, 1997.
53 Author's interview with Lew McCreary, 1997.
54 Author's interview with Jackie Mills, 1996.
55 Ibid.
56 Author's interview with Buddy Combine, 1997.
57 Ibid.

58   Red Kelly interview.
59   Author's interview with Arnold Ross, 1997.
60   Ibid.
61   Ibid.
62   Ibid.
63   Al Lerner interview.
64   Arnold Ross interview.
65   Author's interview with Ray Conniff, 1997.
66   Ibid.
67   Author's interview with Billy May, 1996.
68   Ibid.
69   Author's interview with Bea Wain, 1998.
70   *Time*, June 10, 1945.
71   Bosley Crowther, *New York Times*, September 20, 1946.
72   *Time*, Music Section, December 23, 1946.

Chapter 8

1   Author's interview with Eames Bishop, 1997.
2   Author's interview with Larry Barnett, 1996.
3   Author's interview with Joe Garagiola, 1997.
4   Author's interview with Red Schoendienst, 1996.
5   Author's interview with Buddy DiVito, 1997.
6   Author's interview with Buddy Combine, 1997.
7   Author's interview with Jack Rael, 1997.
8   Author's interview with Marion Morgan, 1998.
9   Buddy Combine interview.
10   Ibid.
11   Marion Morgan interview.
12   Buddy Combine interview.
13   Marion Morgan interview.
14   Buddy Combine interview.
15   Marion Morgan interview.
16   Ibid.
17   Ibid.
18   David Meeker, *Jazz in the Movies* (New York: Da Capo Press, 1981), p. 17.
19   Buddy Combine interview.
20   Gene Lees, *Leader of the Band* (New York: Oxford University Press, 1995), pp. 151–55.
21   Author's interview with Don Lamond, 1997.
22   George T. Simon, *Metronome*, November 1947.
23   Author's interview with Johnny Mandel, 1997.
24   Author's interview with Neal Hefti, 1997.
25   Ibid.
26   Author's interview with Louise Baranger, 1997.
27   Author's interview with Kenny Washington, 1998.
28   Author's interview with Jimmy Ille, 1996.
29   Author's interview with George Hamid, Jr., 1995
30   Author's interview with Jay Livingston, 1996.
31   Author's interview with Louis Bellson, 1997.
32   Author's interview with Buddy Baker, 1998.
33   Louis Bellson interview.
34   Author's interview with Lalo Schifrin, 1998.
35   Meeker, *Jazz in the Movies*, p. 19.

36 *New York Times*, February 10, 1950.
37 *Time*, February 27, 1950.
38 Author's interview with Les Brown, 1995.
39 Johnny Mandel interview.
40 Author's interview with Sal Monte, 1997.
41 Author's interview with Louise Tobin, 1996.
42 Ibid.
43 Ibid.
44 Author's interview with Viola Monte, 1996.
45 Ibid.
46 Author's interview with Nick Sevano, 1998.
47 Author's interview with Chuck Panama, 1996.
48 Author's interview with Fred Monte, 1997.
49 Ibid.
50 Author's interview with Mitch Miller, 1997.
51 Author's interview with Rosemary Clooney, 1997.
52 *Down Beat*, May 18, 1951.
53 Author's interview with Lew McCreary, 1997.
54 Ibid.
55 Ibid.
56 Author's interview with Dave Wells, 1997.
57 Author's interview with Bill Richmond, 1997.
58 Author's interview with Tommy Gumina, 1997.
59 Ibid.
60 Ibid.
61 Author's interview with Corky Hale, 1997.
62 Ibid.
63 Lew McCreary interview.
64 Bill Richmond interview.
65 Miles Davis with Quincy Troupe, *Miles* (New York: Simon & Schuster, 1989), p. 32.
66 Lew McCreary interview.
67 Charles Emge, *Down Beat*, February 23, 1951, p. 3.
68 Lew McCreary interview.
69 Author's interview with Herb Steward, 1997.
70 Mel Tormé, *Traps, the Drum Wonder* (New York: Oxford University Press, 1991), pp. 111–112.
71 Sal Monte interview.
72 Author's interview with Betty Baez, 1996.
73 Lew McCreary interview.
74 Author's interview with Joe Pardee, 1997.
75 Tormé, *Traps, the Drum Wonder*, p. 114.
76 Ibid.
77 Tom McGee, *The Girl with the Million Dollar Legs* (London: Vestal Press, 1995), p. 229.
78 Author's interview with George Avakian, 1996.
79 Doug Warren, *Betty Grable: The Reluctant Movie Queen* (New York: St. Martin's Press, 1981), p. 138.
80 Author's interview with Helen Forrest, 1996.
81 Author's interview with Fred Monte, 1997.
82 Ibid.
83 "Las Vegas Hotel Sues Jameses," *New York Herald-Tribune*, March 15, 1958.
84 Sal Monte interview.
85 Ibid.
86 Author's interview with Steve Preston, 1998.
87 *TV Guide*, April 6, 1956.
88 Sal Monte interview.

89   Author's interview with Art Depew, 1996.
90   Sal Monte interview.
91   Ibid.
92   Author's interview with Chick Romano, 1997.
93   Ibid.

Chapter 9

1   Author's interview with Jimmy Wilkins, 1997.
2   Ibid.
3   Author's interview with Sal Monte, 1997.
4   Author's interview with Jimmy Wilkins, 1997.
5   Sal Monte interview.
6   Author's interview with J. Hill, 1998.
7   Ibid.
8   Ibid.
9   Ibid.
10   Author's interview with Bob Florence, 1996.
11   Ibid.
12   Author's interview with Bob Rolfe, 1996.
13   Author's interview with Andrea King, 1997.
14   Author's interview with Ray Sims, 1997.
15   Sal Monte interview.
16   John Tynan, "The Horn Still Blows," *Down Beat*, January 23, 1958, p. 34.
17   Ibid.
18   Author's interview with Bob Edmondson, 1997.
19   Sal Monte interview.
20   Bob Edmondson interview.
21   Author's interview with John Stiegler, 1996.
22   Sal Monte interview.
23   Author's interview with Sam Firmature, 1997.
24   Sal Monte interview.
25   Author's interview with Lionel Hampton, 1997.
26   Andy Edmonds, *Bugsy's Baby—the Secret Life of Mob Queen, Virginia Hill* (New York: Birch Lane Press, 1993), p. 131.
27   Ibid.
28   Author's interview with Mort Sahl, 1997.
29   Author's interview with Tommy Porrello, 1997.
30   Ibid.
31   Ibid.
32   Author's interview with Red Kelly, 1996.
33   Author's interview with Sal Monte, 1997.
34   Ibid.
35   Bob Rolfe interview.
36   Author's interview with Jack Perciful, 1996.
37   Author's interview with Art Depew, 1996.
38   Red Kelly interview.
39   Author's interview with Vicki Bivens, 1997.
40   Author's interview with Ollie Mitchell, 1996.
41   Ibid.
42   Bob Edmondson interview.
43   Ollie Mitchell interview.
44   Bob Edmondson interview.

45   Ibid.
46   Author's interview with Berle Adams, 1998.
47   Author's interview with Frank Modica, Jr., 1997.
48   Ibid.
49   Author's interview with Jackie Mills, 1997.
50   Ibid.
51   Author's interview with Ernie Andrews, 1996.
52   Author's interview with Tony Scodwell, 1997.
53   Ernie Andrews interview.
54   Ibid.
55   Author's interview with Joe Williams, 1996.
56   Author's interview with Joe Riggs, 1996.
57   Joe Williams interview.
58   Author's interview with Charli Persip, 1997.
59   Frank Quinn's "Nitelife," *New York Daily Mirror*, February 10, 1960, p. 34.
60   Gene Knight, "Harry James Clicks," *New York Journal-American*, February 10, 1960.
61   Author's interview with Kenny Burrell, 1998.
62   Author's interview with Harry Jeffrey James, 1998.
63   Sal Monte interview.
64   Vince Diaz, "Close Encounters 7," *LA Jazz Scene*, November 1996, p. 4.
65   Frank Modica interview.
66   Harry Jeffrey James interview.
67   Jack Perciful interview.
68   Red Kelly interview.
69   Ibid.
70   Jack Perciful interview.
71   Author's interview with Rob Turk, 1996.
72   Red Kelly interview.
73   Author's interview with Don Sickler, 1997.
74   Red Kelly interview.
75   Ibid.
76   Jack Perciful interview.
77   Red Kelly interview.
78   Author's interview with Ray Anthony, 1997.
79   Jack Perciful interview.
80   Red Kelly interview.
81   Jack Perciful interview.
82   Red Kelly interview.
83   Jack Perciful interview.
84   Ibid.
85   Author's interview with Tino Barzie, 1996.
86   Author's interview with Jay Corre, 1998.
87   Red Kelly interview.
88   Author's interview with John Mann, 1997.
89   Ibid.
90   Author's interview with Tim James, 1998.
91   Author's interview with Tom Korman, 1998.
92   Author's interview with Tony Martin, 1997.
93   Author's interview with Ruth Price, 1997.
94   Ted Gioia, *History of Jazz* (New York: Oxford University Press, 1998), p. 271.
95   Red Kelly interview.
96   Author's interview with Dick McQuary, 1996.
97   Author's interview with Joe Riggs, 1996.
98   Author's interview with Tony Scodwell, 1997.

99   Jack Perciful interview.
100   Tim James interview.
101   Author's interview with Louise Tobin, 1997.
102   Jack Perciful interview.
103   Vicki Bivens interview.
104   Ibid.
105   Sal Monte interview.
106   Vicki Bivens interview.
107   Ibid.
108   Jack Perciful interview.
109   Author's interview with Jessica Trotter, 1998.
110   Author's interview with Betty Baez, 1997.
111   Jackie Mills interview.
112   Doug Warren, *Betty Grable: The Reluctant Movie Queen* (New York: St. Martin's Press, 1981), p. 156.
113   Ibid.
114   Red Kelly interview.
115   Tom McGee, *The Girl with the Million Dollar Legs* (London: Vestal Press, 1995), p. 165.
116   Warren, *Betty Grable: The Reluctant Movie Queen*, p. 161.
117   Author's interview with Max Showalter, 1997.
118   Ibid.
119   Jackie Mills interview.
120   Steve Preston interview.
121   Author's interview with Ray Sims, 1997.
122   Red Kelly interview.
123   Frank Modica, Jr. interview.
124   Author's interview with Dave Wells, 1997.
125   *Merv Griffin Show*, November 15, 1977.
126   Author's interview with Joe Cabot, 1998.
127   Sal Monte interview.
128   Joe Cabot interview.

Chapter 10

1   Author's interview with Louis Bellson, 1997.
2   Author's interview with Ray Sims, 1997.
3   Author's interview with Tommy Porrello, 1998.
4   Author's interview with Doc Severinsen, 1998.
5   Author's interview with Jimmy Haskell, 1998.
6   Ibid.
7   Author's interview with Red Kelly, 1996.
8   Author's interview with Tony Scodwell, 1997.
9   Author's interview with Bob Stone, 1997.
10   Author's interview with Joe Riggs, 1996.
11   Author's interview with Tino Barzie, 1996.
12   Doug Warren, *Betty Grable: The Reluctant Movie Queen* (New York: St. Martin's Press, 1981), p. 179.
13   Ibid.
14   Tom McGee, *The Girl with the Million Dollar Legs* (London: Vestal Press, 1995), p. 244.
15   Warren, *Betty Grable: The Reluctant Movie Queen*, p. 180.
16   Author's interview with Michael Leavitt, 1997.
17   Author's interview with Bob Osborne, 1996.
18   Spero Pastos, *Pinup—The Tragedy Of Betty Grable* (New York: G.P. Putnam's Sons, 1986), p.

128.

19   Author's interview with Jack Perciful, 1996.

20   Author's interview with Richy Barz, 1996.

21   Author's interview with Herb Alpert, 1997.

22   Author's interview with Harry Walker, 1997.

23   Author's interview with Alice Faye, 1996.

24   Author's interview with Don Cherry, 1997.

25   Tino Barzie interview.

26   Author's interview with Joe Bushkin, 1997.

27   Ibid.

28   Don Cherry interview.

29   Joe Riggs, Jack Perciful, Red Kelly interviews, 1996.

30   Author's interview with Lionel Hebert, 1997.

31   Joe Riggs interview.

32   Joe Bushkin interview.

33   Author's interview with Fred Radke, 1997.

34   Author's interview with Bobby Arvon, 1997.

35   Author's interview with Rob Turk, 1996.

36   Author's interview with Maynard Ferguson, 1997.

37   Ibid.

38   Author's interview with Roland Smith, 1996.

39   Author's interview with Frank Sinatra, Jr., 1998.

40   Ibid.

41   Author's interview with Les DeMerle, 1995.

42   Ibid.

43   Ibid.

44   Author's interview with George Avakian, 1996.

45   Pastos, *Pinup—The Tragedy of Betty Grable*, p. 12.

46   Ibid., p. 159

47   Ibid., p. 164.

48   Betty Baez interview.

49   McGee, *The Girl with the Million Dollar Legs*, p. 337.

50   Pastos, *Pinup—The Tragedy of Betty Grable*, p. 165.

51   Author's interview with Betty Rose, 1999.

52   Author's interview with Steve Preston, 1998.

53   Author's interview with Michael Leavitt, 1997.

54   Pastos, *Pinup—The Tragedy of Betty Grable*, p. 167.

55   Ibid., 168.

56   Bob Osborne interview.

57   Pastos, *Pinup—The Tragedy of Betty Grable*, p. 167.

58   Ibid., 169.

59   Warren, *Betty Grable: The Reluctant Movie Queen*, pp. 215–216.

60   Les DeMerle interview.

61   Author's interview with Beverly Dahlke, 1996.

62   Author's interview with Ed Easton, 1998.

63   *Variety*, April 4, 1975.

64   Author's interview with Phyllis Diller, 1996.

65   Author's interview with Jerry Frank, 1998.

66   Author's interview with George Wein, 1997.

67   Author's interview with Dan Morgenstern, 1996.

68   Author's interview with Audree Kenton, 1998.

69   Ibid.

70   George Wein interview.

71   Ibid.

72   Author's interview with Jessica Trotter, 1998.
73   Author's interview with Marty Marion, 1996.
74   Author's interview with Stephenie Caravella, 1998.
75   Author's interview with Jeannie Thomas, 1998.
76   "Lookout—A Guide To The Up and Coming," *People*, January 9, 1978.
77   Beverly Dahlke interview.
77   Author's interview with Sam Firmature, 1997.
78   Leonard Feather, "Calendar," *Los Angeles Times*, April 6, 1980.
80   Author's interview with Jay Corre, 1997.
81   Author's interview with Lincoln Mayorga, 1997.
82   Ibid.
83   Ibid.
84   Author's interview with Viola Monte, 1997.
85   Author's interview with Gregg Field, 1998.
86   Author's interview with Lalo Schifrin, 1998.
87   Author's interview with Chris Griffin, 1997.
88   Author's interview with Larry Barnett, 1996.
89   Author's interview with Sal Monte, 1997.
90   Author's interview with Helen Forrest, 1996.
91   Author's interview with Joe Cabot, 1998.
92   Author's interview with Mike Millar, 1998.
93   Author's interview with Lynn Roberts, 1996.
94   Author's interview with Ira Westley, 1998.
95   Author's interview with Louise Baranger, 1998.
96   Joe Cabot interview.
97   Author's interview with Frank Capp, 1998.
98   Sal Monte interview.
99   Author's interview with Bill Pruyn, 1998.
100   Louise Baranger interview.
101   Author's interview with Jimmy Wilkins, 1997.
102   Author's interview with Stephenie Caravella, 1998.
103   Author's interview with Kitty Kallen, 1996.
104   Author's interview with Maynard Sloate, 1998.
105   Author's interview with Dr. Arthur Rando, 1998.
106   Author's interview with Jerry Roy, 1997.
107   Dr. Arthur Rando interview.
108   Ibid.
109   Viola Monte interview.
110   Author's interview with Ray Anthony, 1997.
111   Gregg Field interview.
112   Ira Westley interview.
113   Sal Monte interview.
114   Author's interview with Chick Romano, 1998.
115   Viola Monte interview.
116   Author's interview with Connie Haines, 1996.
117   Dr. Arthur Rando interview.
118   Author's interview with Pete Candoli, 1998.
119   Louise Baranger interview.
120   Sal Monte interview.
121   Ibid.
122   Author's interview with Tim James, 1998.
123   Joe Cabot interview.
124   Red Kelly interview.
125   Sal Monte interview.

126   Stephenie Caravella interview.
127   Gregg Field interview.
128   Ibid.
129   Author's interview with Virginia and John Greenman, 1998.
130   Gregg Field interview.
131   Tim James interview.
132   Ibid.
133   Sal Monte interview.
134   Author's interview with Jessica Trotter, 1998.
135   Tim James interview.
136   Author's interview with Frank Modica, Jr., 1997.
137   Joe Cabot interview.
138   Lionel Hebert interview.
139   Red Kelly interview.
140   Author's interview with Louise Tobin, 1998.
141   Ibid.
142   Author's interview with Dick Maher, 1998.
143   Vi Monte interview.
144   Frank Sinatra, Jr. interview.
145   Author's interview with Pete Mikla, 1997.
146   *New York Times*, July 8, 1983.
147   Ibid.

∽ BIBLIOGRAPHY

Collier, James Lincoln. *Benny Goodman and the Swing Era: The Life and Times of Benny Goodman.* New York: Oxford University Press, 1989.

Delaunay, Charles. *New Hot Discography.* New York: Criterion, 1948.

Erlewine, Michael, Vladimir Bogdanov, Chris Woodstra, and Scott Yanow. *All Music Guide to Jazz.* San Francisco: Miller Freeman Books, 1998.

Firestone, Ross. *Swing, Swing, Swing.* New York: W. W. Norton, 1993.

Goodman, Benny, and Irving Kolodin. *The Kingdom of Swing.* New York: Stackpole, 1939.

Johnson, Peter. *The Complete List of All Harry James Recordings.* Hudson, Quebec: self-published, 1995.

Lees, Gene. *Singers and the Song.* New York: Oxford University Press, 1987.

Oliphant, Dave. *Texan Jazz.* Austin: University of Texas Press, 1996.

Schuller, Gunther. *The Swing Era.* New York: Oxford University Press, 1989.

Simon, George T. *The Big Bands.* New York: Macmillan, 1967.

Stacy, Frank. *Harry James.* New York: Avco Publishing, 1944.

Walker, Leo. *The Wonderful Era of the Great Dance Bands.* Berkeley, Calif.: Howell North, 1964.

Whitburn, Joel. *Pop Memories.* Menomonee Falls, Wisc.: Record Research, 1985.

JUNE 1944

James Opens At Astor Roof

Los Angeles—The re-organized Harry James band, as it lined up when the unit left here for the series of one-nighters that were to precede the Astor Roof opening, had a total of 12 new men, a smaller number of replacements than was expected when the Horn temporarily disbanded recently.

The personnel of band, as it left here included: strings: John de Voodgt, Al Saparoff, Hal Korn, Bill Speer, Jack Gootkin, Alex Neiman, Ernest Karpati, Sam Kaplan, Al Freed; saxes: Corky Corcoran, Mack Sterling, Cliff Jackson, Claude Lakey, Mario Babidillo; brass: Claude Bowen, Buzz King, Mario Serritello, Verne Rowe, trumpets; Ray Heath, Charlie Small, Juan Tizol, Russ Brown, trombones; rhythm: Jerry Simonin, piano; Ed Mihelich, bass; Carl Maus, drums; Allan Reuss, guitar.

Johnny Thompson is still doing the scoring chores but the arranging department, in which Johnny carried almost entire burden for a time after departure of Calvin Jackson, has a newcomer in Herschel Gilbert.

Kitty Kallen and Buddy De Vito hold the vocal spots.

Harry James

HARRY JAMES

and his Chesterfield Music Makers